Network Basics Lab Manual

Cisco Networking Academy

Cisco Press

800 East 96th Street

Indianapolis, Indiana 46240

Network Basics Lab Manual

Cisco Networking Academy

Copyright © 2014 Cisco Systems, Inc.

Published by:
Cisco Press
800 East 96th Street
Indianapolis, IN 46240 USA

Library of Congress Control Number: 2013944490

Printed in the United States of America

First Printing July 2013

ISBN-13: 978-1-58713-313-8

ISBN-10: 1-587-13313-X

Warning and Disclaimer

This book is designed to provide information about Network Basics. Every effort has been made to make this book as complete and as accurate as possible, but no warranty or fitness is implied.

The information is provided on an "as is" basis. The authors, Cisco Press, and Cisco Systems, Inc. shall have neither liability nor responsibility to any person or entity with respect to any loss or damages arising from the information contained in this book or from the use of the discs or programs that may accompany it.

The opinions expressed in this book belong to the author and are not necessarily those of Cisco Systems, Inc.

Trademark Acknowledgments

All terms mentioned in this book that are known to be trademarks or service marks have been appropriately capitalized. Cisco Press or Cisco Systems, Inc., cannot attest to the accuracy of this information. Use of a term in this book should not be regarded as affecting the validity of any trademark or service mark.

This book is part of the Cisco Networking Academy® series from Cisco Press. The products in this series support and complement the Cisco Networking Academy curriculum. If you are using this book outside the Networking Academy, then you are not preparing with a Cisco trained and authorized Networking Academy provider.

For more information on the Cisco Networking Academy or to locate a Networking Academy, please visit www.cisco.com/edu.

CISCO.

Feedback Information

At Cisco Press, our goal is to create in-depth technical books of the highest quality and value. Each book is crafted with care and precision, undergoing rigorous development that involves the unique expertise of members from the professional technical community.

Readers' feedback is a natural continuation of this process. If you have any comments regarding how we could improve the quality of this book, or otherwise alter it to better suit your needs, you can contact us through email at feedback@ciscopress.com. Please make sure to include the book title and ISBN in your message.

We greatly appreciate your assistance.

Publisher	**Paul Boger**
Associate Publisher	**Dave Dusthimer**
Business Operations Manager, Cisco Press	**Jan Cornelssen**
Executive Editor	**Mary Beth Ray**
Managing Editor	**Sandra Schroeder**
Project Editor	**Seth Kerney**
Editorial Assistant	**Vanessa Evans**
Cover Designer	**Mark Shirar**
Compositor	**TnT Design, Inc.**

ıllıılıı
CISCO

Americas Headquarters
Cisco Systems, Inc.
San Jose, CA

Asia Pacific Headquarters
Cisco Systems (USA) Pte. Ltd.
Singapore

Europe Headquarters
Cisco Systems International BV
Amsterdam, The Netherlands

Cisco has more than 200 offices worldwide. Addresses, phone numbers, and fax numbers are listed on the Cisco Website at **www.cisco.com/go/offices.**

CCDE, CCENT, Cisco Eos, Cisco HealthPresence, the Cisco logo, Cisco Lumin, Cisco Nexus, Cisco StadiumVision, Cisco TelePresence, Cisco WebEx, DCE, and Welcome to the Human Network are trademarks; Changing the Way We Work, Live, Play, and Learn and Cisco Store are service marks; and Access Registrar, Aironet, AsyncOS, Bringing the Meeting To You, Catalyst, CCDA, CCDP, CCIE, CCIP, CCNA, CCNP, CCSP, CCVP, Cisco, the Cisco Certified Internetwork Expert logo, Cisco IOS, Cisco Press, Cisco Systems, Cisco Systems Capital, the Cisco Systems logo, Cisco Unity, Collaboration Without Limitation, EtherFast, EtherSwitch, Event Center, Fast Step, Follow Me Browsing, FormShare, GigaDrive, HomeLink, Internet Quotient, IOS, iPhone, iQuick Study, IronPort, the IronPort logo, LightStream, Linksys, MediaTone, MeetingPlace, MeetingPlace Chime Sound, MGX, Networkers, Networking Academy, Network Registrar, PCNow, PIX, PowerPanels, ProConnect, ScriptShare, SenderBase, SMARTnet, Spectrum Expert, StackWise, The Fastest Way to Increase Your Internet Quotient, TransPath, WebEx, and the WebEx logo are registered trademarks of Cisco Systems, Inc. and/or its affiliates in the United States and certain other countries.

All other trademarks mentioned in this document or website are the property of their respective owners. The use of the word partner does not imply a partnership relationship between Cisco and any other company. (0812R)

Contents

About This Lab Manual

Network Basics Lab Manual contains all the labs and class activities from the Cisco Networking Academy course of the same name. It is meant to be used within this program of study.

This course introduces the architecture, structure, functions, components, and models of the Internet and other computer networks. The hands-on labs and class activities help you to practice performing tasks that will help you to learn how to build simple LANs, perform basic configurations for routers and switches, and implement IP addressing schemes.

More Practice

If you would like more practice activities, combine your Lab Manual with the new *CCENT Practice and Study Guide* ISBN: 9781587133459

Other Related Titles

CCNA Routing and Switching Portable Command Guide ISBN: 9781587204302 (or eBook ISBN: 9780133381368)

Network Basics Companion Guide ISBN: 9781587133176 (or ebook ISBN: 9780133475494

Network Basics Course Booklet ISBN: 9781587133145

Command Syntax Conventions

The conventions used to present command syntax in this book are the same conventions used in the IOS Command Reference. The Command Reference describes these conventions as follows:

- **Boldface** indicates commands and keywords that are entered literally as shown. In actual configuration examples and output (not general command syntax), boldface indicates commands that are manually input by the user (such as a **show** command).

- *Italic* indicates arguments for which you supply actual values.

- Vertical bars (|) separate alternative, mutually exclusive elements.

- Square brackets ([ ]) indicate an optional element.

- Braces ({ }) indicate a required choice.

- Braces within brackets ([{ }]) indicate a required choice within an optional element.

Chapter 1 — Exploring the Network

1.0.1.2 Class Activity — Draw Your Concept of the Internet

Objectives

Networks are made of many different components

In this activity, you will visualize how you are connected, through the Internet, to those places, people, or businesses with whom (or which) you interact on a daily basis. After reflection and sketching your home's or school's topology, you can draw conclusions about the Internet that you may not have thought of prior to this activity.

Background / Scenario

Draw and label a map of the Internet as you interpret it now. Include your home or school/university location and its respective cabling, equipment, devices, etc. Some items you may want to include:

- Devices or equipment

- Media (cabling)

- Link addresses or names

- Sources and destinations

- Internet service providers

Upon completion, save your work in a hard-copy format, it will be used for future reference at the end of this chapter. If it is an electronic document, save it to a server location provided by your instructor. Be prepared to share and explain your work in class.

For an example to get you started, please visit: http://www.kk.org/internet-mapping

Required Resources

- Internet access
- Paper and pencils or pens (if students are creating a hard copy)

Reflection

1. After reviewing your classmates drawings, were there computer devices that you could have included on your diagram? If so, which ones and why?

2. After reviewing your classmates' drawings, how were some of the model designs the same or different? What modifications would you make to your drawing after reviewing the other drawings?

    _____

3. In what way could icons on a network drawing provide a streamlined thought process and facilitate your learning? Explain your answer.

    _____

1.1.1.8 Lab — Researching Network Collaboration Tools

Objectives

Part 1: Use Collaboration Tools

- Identify current awareness of collaboration tools.
- Identify key reasons for using collaboration tools.

Part 2: Share Documents with Google Drive

Part 3: Explore Conferencing and Web Meetings

Part 4: Create Wiki Pages

Background / Scenario

Network collaboration tools give people the opportunity to work together efficiently and productively without the constraints of location or time zone. Collaborative tool types include document sharing, web meetings, and wikis.

In Part 1, you will identify collaboration tools that you currently use. You will also research some popular collaborative tools used today. In Part 2, you will work with Google Drive. In Part 3, you will investigate Conferencing and Web meeting tools and, in Part 4, you will work with wikis.

Required Resources

Device with Internet access

Part 1: Use Collaboration Tools

Step 1: List some collaboration tools that you currently use today.

_____

_____

Step 2: List some reasons for using collaboration tools.

_____

_____

Part 2:   **Share Documents with Google Drive**

In Part 2, you will explore the document sharing functions by using Google Drive to set up document sharing. Google Drive, formally Google Docs, is a web-based office suite and data storage service that allows users to create and edit documents online while collaborating in real-time with other users. Google Drive provides 5 GB of storage with every free Google account. You can purchase additional storage, if needed.

Step 1:   **Create a Google account.**

To use any of Google's services, you must first create a Google account. This account can be used with any of Google's services, including Gmail.

a.   Browse to www.google.com and click **Sign in** (located at the top-right corner of the web page).

b.   On the Google Accounts web page, if you already have a Google account, you can sign in now; otherwise, click **SIGN UP**.

c.   On the Create a new Google Account web page, fill out the form to the right. The name you enter in the **Choose your username** field becomes the account name. It is not necessary to supply your mobile phone or current email address. You must agree to the Google Terms of Service and Privacy Policy before clicking **Next step**.

d. The next web page allows you to add a profile photo if you would like. Click **Next Step** to complete the account creation process.

Step 2:   **Create a new document.**

a. Sign in to Google using the access credentials you created in Step 1. Type **http://drive.google.com** in your browser and press Enter. This navigates you to Google Drive.

b. Click the **CREATE** button to display a drop-down menu that allows you to select the type of document to create. Choose **Document**.

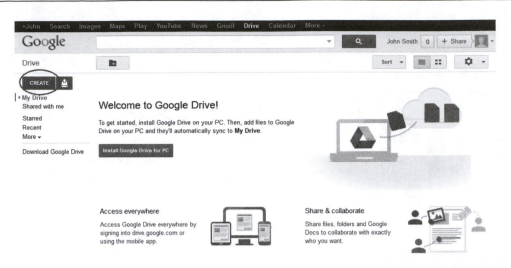

The new document displays. Many of the functions of the Google editor work similarly to Microsoft Word.

Step 3: **Share a Google document.**

a. After the blank Google document opens, you can share it with others by clicking the **Share** button (at the top-right corner of the web page).

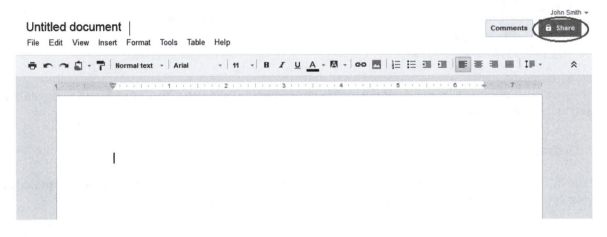

b. Name your new document, then click the **Save** button.

Name before sharing

Let collaborators know what this document is about

Untitled document

Save   Skip

c. Here on the Sharing settings web page, in the **Add people** text field, you can enter Google email names, email addresses, or groups with whom to share this document.

d. As soon as you start entering information into the **Add people** box, the box provides more options. The **Can edit** drop-down menu allows you to choose the document privileges (Can edit, Can comment, Can view) for the people you add. You can also specify how to notify these people of this document (**Send a copy to myself** or **Paste the item itself into the email**). Click **Share & save**.

e. Click the **Done** button. This will navigate you back to the open document.

f. All users with share privileges can view this document at the same time. Users with edit privileges can edit this document while others view it.

g. If the document is being viewed by someone while you are in it, you can see who they are by clicking the **other viewer(s)** drop-down menu (in the upper-right corner of the document).

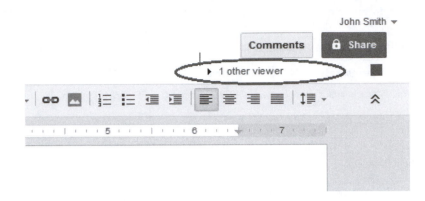

Step 4:   **Close a Google document.**

To close a Google document, move your cursor to the document name at the top of the screen and a left arrow will appear to the left of the name. Click that arrow to return to your Google Drive home page. The document is automatically saved.

The new document will appear at the top of your documents list under My Drive.

Step 5:   **Additional Information**

Google has developed apps for PCs and Smart phones. For more information about Google Drive, go to http://drive.google.com. YouTube is also a viable source of Google Drive tutorials.

Part 3:   **Explore Conferencing and Web Meetings**

Web meetings combine file and presentation sharing with voice, video, and desktop sharing. Cisco WebEx Meeting Center is one of the leading web meeting products available today.

In Part 3 of this lab, you will watch a video produced by Cisco that reviews the features contained within WebEx Meeting Center. The video is located on YouTube at the following link: http://www.youtube.com/watch?v=fyaWHEF_aWg

Part 4:   Create Wiki Pages

"Wiki" is a Hawaiian-language word that means fast. In networking terms, a wiki is a web-based collaboration tool that permits almost anyone to immediately post information, files, or graphics to a common site for other users to read and modify. A wiki provides access to a home page that has a search tool to assist you in locating the articles that interest you. A wiki can be installed for the Internet community or behind a corporate firewall for employee use. The user not only reads wiki contents, but also participates by creating content within a web browser.

Although many different wiki servers are available, the following common features have been formalized into every wiki:

- Any web browser can be used to view or edit pages or create new content.

- Edit and auto links are available to edit a page and automatically link pages. Text formatting is similar to creating an email.

- A search engine is used for quick content location.

- Access control can be set by the topic creator, defining who is permitted to edit content.

- A wiki is a grouping of web pages with different collaboration groups.

In this part of the lab, you will use the Google account that you created in Part 2 and create a wiki page in Google Sites.

Step 1:   Sign in to Google Sites.

Go to http://sites.google.com and sign in using the Google account that you created in Part 2 of this lab.

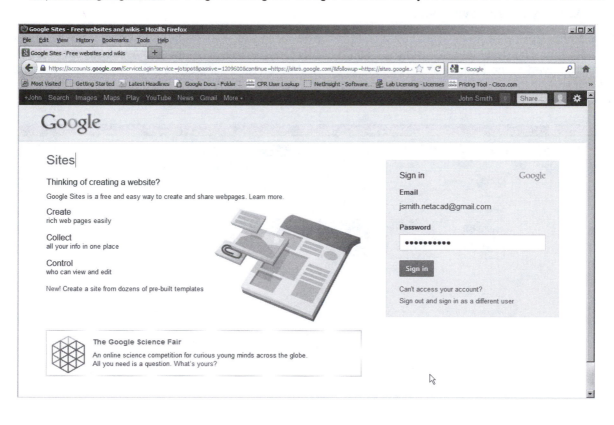

Step 2:   **Click CREATE.**

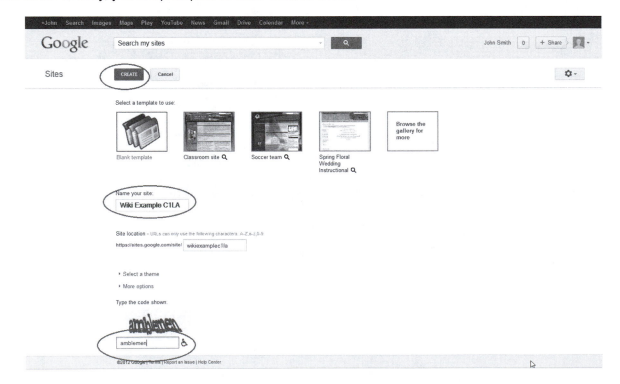

Step 3:   **Name your new wiki site.**

In the **Name your site** field, type in a name for your new wiki site. You will need to come up with a unique name for your site that has not been used by any other Google user. Google also requires that you enter the code (displayed at the bottom of the screen) to prevent automated scripts, called web robots, from creating multiple sites. After you have entered your site name, click the **CREATE** button. If someone has used your site name already, you are prompted to enter another name.

Step 4:   **Edit the look of your new wiki site.**

a. Google has provided templates for you to change the look of your new wiki site. Click the **More** drop-down menu, and then click **Manage site**.

b. Click **Themes** at the bottom of the left sidebar.

Manage Site

‹ **Wiki Example C1LA**

Recent site activity

Pages

Attachments

Page templates

Apps Scripts

Deleted items

General

Sharing and
Permissions

AdSense

Web Address

Site layout

Colors and Fonts

Themes

c. Select a theme that appeals to you and click **SAVE**.

+John   Search   Images   Maps   Play   YouTube   News   Gmail   Drive   Calendar   More ▾

Google   Search my sites   🔍

Manage Site   SAVE   Preview   Cancel

‹ **Wiki Example C1LA**   Select a theme to use or build your own custom theme

Recent site activity

Pages

Attachments

Page templates   Iceberg 🔍   Open Sky 🔍   Rounders 🔍   Slate 🔍   Simple 🔍

Apps Scripts

Deleted items

General

Sharing and
Permissions   Legal Pad 🔍   Blank Slate 🔍   Micro Blueprint 🔍   Micro Lite 🔍   Micro Sport 🔍

d. After you have saved your theme selection, click your site name under **Manage Site**.

Step 5:   Update the Home page.

a. The Home page is the first page that everyone sees when they come to your wiki site. You can edit the content of this page by clicking the edit button. From here, you can add text, pictures, or anything else to show on this page.

b. Click **Save** after you make your changes. This takes you out of page edit mode.

Step 6:   Create a wiki page.

a. To create a new page that you and your visitors can use to make posts, click the new page icon.

b. In the **Name your page** field, enter a page name. In the example below, the name Routers is used as the topic for this page.

c. Click the **Web Page** drop-down menu and select **Announcements**. Google uses this term to indicate a wiki page.

d. Click **CREATE** to create your new wiki page.

Sites   CREATE   Cancel

Create a page in Site: Wiki Example C1LA

Name your page:

Routers

Your page URL: /site/wikiexamplec1la/routers change URL

Select a template to use (Learn more)

Announcements ⬍

Select a location:

e. Your new wiki page, called Routers, displays and has a **New post** menu option that allows information to be added to the page. (Notice that the left sidebar has a new link to allow your site visitors access to this page.)

Step 7:   **Share your web site.**

A wiki site is not really a wiki site unless other people can contribute. There are a number of ways to share your new site. In this example, we will show you how to share your site to designated people who have Gmail accounts.

a. On your wiki site, click **Share**.

b. Add a name, email address, or group who you grant access to this site.

Who has access

Public on the web - Anyone on the Internet   Change...
can find and **view**

John Smith (you) jsmith.netacad@gmail.com   Is owner

Add people:

Enter names, email addresses, or groups...

Only the owner can change the permissions.

c. As soon as you start entering information into the **Add people** box, the box provides more options. The **Can edit** drop-down menu allows you to choose the document privileges (Can edit, Can comment, Can view) for the people you add. You can also specify how to notify these people of this document (**Send a copy to myself** or **Paste the item itself into the email**). Click **Share & save**.

Add people: Choose from contacts

janedoe@gmail.com   Can edit ▾

☑ Notify people via email - Add message

Share & save   Cancel   ☐ Send a copy to myself

d. Click **Share & save** to save **your sharing settings**.

Add people: Choose from contacts

janedoe@gmail.com   Can edit ▾

☑ Notify people via email - Add message

Share & save   Cancel   ☐ Send a copy to myself

e. The **Manage Site** page displays the people who have access to your site. Click your site name to return to your home page.

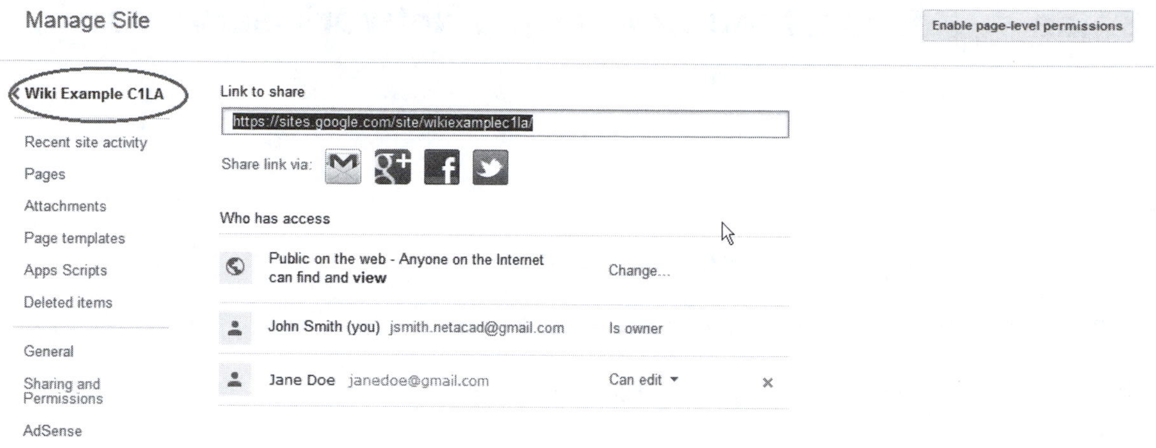

Manage Site   Enable page-level permissions

Wiki Example C1LA   Link to share

Recent site activity   https://sites.google.com/site/wikiexamplec1la/

Pages   Share link via: M g+ f

Attachments

Page templates   Who has access

Apps Scripts   🌐   Public on the web - Anyone on the Internet   Change...
                                  can find and **view**
Deleted items

                             👤   John Smith (you) jsmith.netacad@gmail.com   Is owner
General

Sharing and   👤   Jane Doe janedoe@gmail.com   Can edit ▾   ✕
Permissions

AdSense

Step 8: **Provide the URL of your site.**

You can provide your URL to your new site by adding your site name to the end of the Google site URL, as shown here: http://sites.google.com/site/(sitename).

Step 9: **Find additional information.**

You can find a quick overview of how a wiki works at http://www.youtube.com/watch?v=-dnL00TdmLY.

Other examples of wikis and their web sites include:

- Wikipedia — http://www.wikipedia.org/
- Atlassian Confluence (a popular business wiki) — http://www.atlassian.com/software/confluence/
- Wikispaces (another free wiki) — http://www.wikispaces.com/

Reflection

1. Can you think of other collaboration tools used in the business world today?

_____

2. What collaboration tools do you see as useful to a network administrator?

_____

1.2.1.3 Lab — Researching Converged Network Services

Objectives

Part 1: Survey Your Understanding of Convergence

Part 2: Research ISPs Offering Converged Services

Part 3: Research Local ISPs Offering Converged Services

Part 4: Select Best Local ISP Converged Service

Part 5: Research Local Company or Public Institution Using Convergence Technologies

Background / Scenario

Convergence in the context of networking is a term used to describe the process of combining voice, video, and data communications over a common network infrastructure. Converged networks have existed for some time, but were only feasible in large enterprise organizations because of the network infrastructure requirements and complex management required to make them work seamlessly. Technology advances have made convergence readily available to large, medium, and small businesses, as well as for the home consumer.

In Part 1, you will describe your current understanding of convergence and any experience you have with it.

In Part 2, you will research which providers have this service, regardless of geographical location, using the predefined form included in the lab.

In Part 3, you will research which local ISPs in your area offer converged services for end-user consumers, using the predefined form included in the lab.

In Part 4, you will select the ISP you like best for home use and list the reasons why.

In Part 5, you will find a local company or public institution using convergence technologies in their business, using the predefined form included in the lab.

Required Resources

Device with Internet access

Part 1:   Survey Your Understanding on Convergence

Step 1: **Describe convergence as you understand it and give examples of its use in the home.**

Write a definition of convergence and list some examples.

_____

_____

_____

_____

_____

_____

_____

Part 2: **Research ISPs Offering Converged Services**

In Part 2, you research and find two or three ISPs who offer converged services for the home, regardless of geographical location.

Step 1: **Research various ISPs that offer converged services.**

List some of the ISPs that you found in your search.

_____

Step 2: **Fill in the following form for the ISPs selected.**

Internet Service Provider	Product Name of Converged Service

Part 3: **Researching Local ISPs Offering Converged Services**

In Part 3, you research and find two or three local ISPs who offer converged services for the home in your geographic area.

Step 1: **Research various ISPs that offer converged services.**

List some of the ISPs that you found in your search.

_____

Answers will vary based on geographic location.

Step 2: **Fill in the following form for the ISPs selected.**

Internet Service Provider	Product Name of Converged Service	Cost per Month	Download Speed

Part 4:   **Select Best Local ISP Converged Service Offering**

Select your top choice from the list of local ISPs that you selected and give reasons why you chose that particular one.

_____

_____

_____

_____

_____

_____

Part 5:   **Research Local Company or Public Institution Using Convergence Technologies**

In Part 5, you research and locate a company in your area that currently uses convergence technologies in their business.

Step 1: **Research and find a local company using convergence.**

In the following table, list the company, industry, and convergence technologies used.

Name of Company	Industry	Convergence Technologies

Reflection

1. What are some of the advantages of using convergence technologies?

   _____

   _____

   _____

2. What are some of the disadvantages of using convergence technologies?

   _____

   _____

   _____

1.3.3.3 Lab — Mapping the Internet

Objectives

Part 1: Test Network Connectivity Using Ping

Part 2: Trace a Route to a Remote Server Using Windows Tracert

Part 3: Trace a Route to a Remote Server Using Web-Based and Software Tools

Part 4: Compare Traceroute Results

Background

Route tracing computer software is a utility that lists the networks data has to traverse from the user's originating end device to a distant destination network.

This network tool is typically executed at the command line as:

> `tracert <destination network name or end device address>`

> (Microsoft Windows systems)

or

> `traceroute <destination network name or end device address>`

> (Unix and similar systems)

Route tracing utilities allow a user to determine the path or routes as well as the delay across an IP network. Several tools exist to perform this function.

The **traceroute** (or **tracert**) tool is often used for network troubleshooting. By showing a list of routers traversed, it allows the user to identify the path taken to reach a particular destination on the network or across internetworks. Each router represents a point where one network connects to another network and through which the data packet was forwarded. The number of routers is known as the number of "hops" the data traveled from source to destination.

The displayed list can help identify data flow problems when trying to access a service such as a website. It can also be useful when performing tasks such as downloading data. If there are multiple websites (mirrors) available for the same data file, one can trace each mirror to get a good idea of which mirror would be the fastest to use.

Two trace routes between the same source and destination conducted some time apart may produce different results. This is due to the "meshed" nature of the interconnected networks that comprise the Internet and the Internet Protocols ability to select different pathways over which to send packets.

Command-line-based route tracing tools are usually embedded with the operating system of the end device.

Other tools, such as VisualRoute™, are proprietary programs that provide extra information. VisualRoute uses available online information to graphically display the route.

This lab assumes the installation of VisualRoute. If the computer you are using does not have VisualRoute installed, you can download the program using the following link:

http://www.visualroute.com/download.html

If you have any trouble downloading or installing VisualRoute, ask your instructor for assistance. Ensure that you download the Lite Edition.

VisualRoute Lite Edition	Windows XP\2003\Vista\7	4.0Mb	**Download**
	Mac OS X (dmg) 10.3+, universal binary	2.0Mb	**Download**

Scenario

Using an Internet connection, you will use three route tracing utilities to examine the Internet pathway to destination networks. This activity should be performed on a computer that has Internet access and access to the command line. First, you will use the Windows embedded tracert utility. Second, you will use a web-based traceroute tool (http://www.subnetonline.com/pages/network-tools/online-traceroute.php). Finally, you will use the VisualRoute traceroute program.

Required Resources

1 PC (Windows 7, Vista, or XP with Internet access)

Part 1: Test Network Connectivity Using Ping

Step 1: Determine whether the remote server is reachable.

To trace the route to a distant network, the PC used must have a working connection to the Internet.

a. The first tool we will use is ping. Ping is a tool used to test whether a host is reachable. Packets of information are sent to the remote host with instructions to reply. Your local PC measures whether a response is received to each packet, and how long it takes for those packets to cross the network. The name ping comes from active sonar technology in which a pulse of sound is sent underwater and bounced off of terrain or other ships.

b. From your PC, click the **Windows Start** icon, type **cmd** in the **Search programs and files** box, and then press Enter.

c. At the command-line prompt, type **ping www.cisco.com**.

```
C:\>ping www.cisco.com

Pinging e144.dscb.akamaiedge.net [23.1.48.170] with 32 bytes of data:
Reply from 23.1.48.170: bytes=32 time=56ms TTL=57
Reply from 23.1.48.170: bytes=32 time=55ms TTL=57
Reply from 23.1.48.170: bytes=32 time=54ms TTL=57
Reply from 23.1.48.170: bytes=32 time=54ms TTL=57

Ping statistics for 23.1.48.170:
    Packets: Sent = 4, Received = 4, Lost = 0 (0% loss),
Approximate round trip times in milli-seconds:
    Minimum = 54ms, Maximum = 56ms, Average = 54ms
```

d.   The first output line displays the Fully Qualified Domain Name (FQDN) e144.dscb.akamaiedge.net. This is followed by the IP address 23.1.48.170. Cisco hosts the same web content on different servers throughout the world (known as mirrors). Therefore, depending upon where you are geographically, the FQDN and the IP address will be different.

e.   From this portion of the output:

```
Ping statistics for 23.1.48.170:
    Packets: Sent = 4, Received = 4, Lost = 0 (0% loss),
Approximate round trip times in milli-seconds:
    Minimum = 54ms, Maximum = 56ms, Average = 54ms
```

Four pings were sent and a reply was received from each ping. Because each ping was responded to, there was 0% packet loss. On average, it took 54 ms (54 milliseconds) for the packets to cross the network. A millisecond is 1/1,000th of a second.

Streaming video and online games are two applications that suffer when there is packet loss, or a slow network connection. A more accurate determination of an Internet connection speed can be determined by sending 100 pings, instead of the default 4. Here is how to do that:

```
C:\>ping -n 100 www.cisco.com
```

And here is what the output from that looks like:

```
Ping statistics for 23.45.0.170:
    Packets: Sent = 100, Received = 100, Lost = 0 (0% loss),
Approximate round trip times in milli-seconds:
    Minimum = 46ms, Maximum = 53ms, Average = 49ms
```

f.   Now ping Regional Internet Registry (RIR) websites located in different parts of the world:

For Africa:

```
C:\> ping www.afrinic.net
```

```
C:\>ping www.afrinic.net

Pinging www.afrinic.net [196.216.2.136] with 32 bytes of data:
Reply from 196.216.2.136: bytes=32 time=314ms TTL=111
Reply from 196.216.2.136: bytes=32 time=312ms TTL=111
Reply from 196.216.2.136: bytes=32 time=313ms TTL=111
Reply from 196.216.2.136: bytes=32 time=313ms TTL=111

Ping statistics for 196.216.2.136:
    Packets: Sent = 4, Received = 4, Lost = 0 (0% loss),
Approximate round trip times in milli-seconds:
    Minimum = 312ms, Maximum = 314ms, Average = 313ms
```

For Australia:

```
C:\> ping www.apnic.net
```

```
C:\>ping www.apnic.net

Pinging www.apnic.net [202.12.29.194] with 32 bytes of data:
Reply from 202.12.29.194: bytes=32 time=286ms TTL=49
Reply from 202.12.29.194: bytes=32 time=287ms TTL=49
Reply from 202.12.29.194: bytes=32 time=286ms TTL=49
Reply from 202.12.29.194: bytes=32 time=286ms TTL=49

Ping statistics for 202.12.29.194:
    Packets: Sent = 4, Received = 4, Lost = 0 (0% loss),
Approximate round trip times in milli-seconds:
    Minimum = 286ms, Maximum = 287ms, Average = 286ms
```

For Europe:

```
C:\> ping www.ripe.net
```

```
C:\>ping www.ripe.net

Pinging www.ripe.net [193.0.6.139] with 32 bytes of data:
Request timed out.
Request timed out.
Request timed out.
Request timed out.

Ping statistics for 193.0.6.139:
    Packets: Sent = 4, Received = 0, Lost = 4 (100% loss),
```

For South America:

```
C:\> ping lacnic.net
```

```
C:\>ping www.lacnic.net

Pinging www.lacnic.net [200.3.14.147] with 32 bytes of data:
Reply from 200.3.14.147: bytes=32 time=158ms TTL=51
Reply from 200.3.14.147: bytes=32 time=158ms TTL=51
Reply from 200.3.14.147: bytes=32 time=158ms TTL=51
Reply from 200.3.14.147: bytes=32 time=157ms TTL=51

Ping statistics for 200.3.14.147:
    Packets: Sent = 4, Received = 4, Lost = 0 (0% loss),
Approximate round trip times in milli-seconds:
    Minimum = 157ms, Maximum = 158ms, Average = 157ms
```

All these pings were run from a computer located in the U.S. What happens to the average ping time in milliseconds when data is traveling within the same continent (North America) as compared to data from North America traveling to different continents?

_____

What is interesting about the pings that were sent to the European website?

_____

Part 2:   Trace a Route to a Remote Server Using Tracert

Step 1:   Determine what route across the Internet traffic takes to the remote server.

Now that basic reachability has been verified by using the ping tool, it is helpful to look more closely at each network segment that is crossed. To do this, the **tracert** tool will be used.

a.   At the command-line prompt, type **tracert www.cisco.com**.

```
C:\>tracert www.cisco.com

Tracing route to e144.dscb.akamaiedge.net [23.1.144.170]
over a maximum of 30 hops:

  1     <1 ms    <1 ms    <1 ms   dslrouter.westell.com [192.168.1.1]
  2     38 ms    38 ms    37 ms   10.18.20.1
  3     37 ms    37 ms    37 ms   G3-0-9-2204.ALBYNY-LCR-02.verizon-gni.net [130.8
1.196.190]
  4     43 ms    43 ms    42 ms   so-5-1-1-0.NY325-BB-RTR2.verizon-gni.net [130.81
.22.46]
  5     43 ms    43 ms    65 ms   0.so-4-0-2.XT2.NYC4.ALTER.NET [152.63.1.57]
  6     45 ms    45 ms    45 ms   0.so-3-2-0.XL4.EWR6.ALTER.NET [152.63.17.109]
  7     46 ms    48 ms    46 ms   TenGigE0-5-0-0.GW8.EWR6.ALTER.NET [152.63.21.14]

  8     45 ms    45 ms    45 ms   a23-1-144-170.deploy.akamaitechnologies.com [23.
1.144.170]

Trace complete.
```

b.   Save the tracert output in a text file as follows:

Right-click the title bar of the Command Prompt window and choose **Edit** > **Select All**.

Right-click the title bar of the Command Prompt window again and choose **Edit** > **Copy**.

Open the **Windows Notepad** program: **Windows Start** icon > **All Programs** > **Accessories** > **Notepad**.

To paste the output into Notepad, choose **Edit** > **Paste**.

Choose **File** > **Save As** and save the Notepad file to your desktop as **tracert1.txt**.

c. Run **tracert** for each destination website and save the output in sequentially numbered files.

```
C:\> tracert www.afrinic.net

C:\> tracert www.lacnic.net
```

d. Interpreting **tracert** outputs.

Routes traced can go through many hops and a number of different Internet Service Providers (ISPs), depending on the size of your ISP and the location of the source and destination hosts. Each "hop" represents a router. A router is a specialized type of computer used to direct traffic across the Internet. Imagine taking an automobile trip across several countries using many highways. At different points in the trip you come to a fork in the road in which you have the option to select from several different highways. Now further imagine that there is a device at each fork in the road that directs you to take the correct highway to your final destination. That is what a router does for packets on a network.

Because computers talk in numbers, rather than words, routers are uniquely identified using IP addresses (numbers with the format x.x.x.x). The **tracert** tool shows you what path through the network a packet of information takes to reach its final destination. The **tracert** tool also gives you an idea of how fast traffic is going on each segment of the network. Three packets are sent to each router in the path, and the return time is measured in milliseconds. Now use this information to analyze the **tracert** results to www.cisco.com. Below is the entire traceroute:

```
C:\>tracert www.cisco.com

Tracing route to e144.dscb.akamaiedge.net [23.1.144.170]
over a maximum of 30 hops:

  1    <1 ms    <1 ms    <1 ms   dslrouter.westell.com [192.168.1.1]
  2    38 ms    38 ms    37 ms   10.18.20.1
  3    37 ms    37 ms    37 ms   G3-0-9-2204.ALBYNY-LCR-02.verizon-gni.net [130.8
1.196.190]
  4    43 ms    43 ms    42 ms   so-5-1-1-0.NY325-BB-RTR2.verizon-gni.net [130.81
.22.46]
  5    43 ms    43 ms    65 ms   0.so-4-0-2.XT2.NYC4.ALTER.NET [152.63.1.57]
  6    45 ms    45 ms    45 ms   0.so-3-2-0.XL4.EWR6.ALTER.NET [152.63.17.109]
  7    46 ms    48 ms    46 ms   TenGigE0-5-0-0.GW8.EWR6.ALTER.NET [152.63.21.14]

  8    45 ms    45 ms    45 ms   a23-1-144-170.deploy.akamaitechnologies.com [23.
1.144.170]

Trace complete.
```

Below is the breakdown:

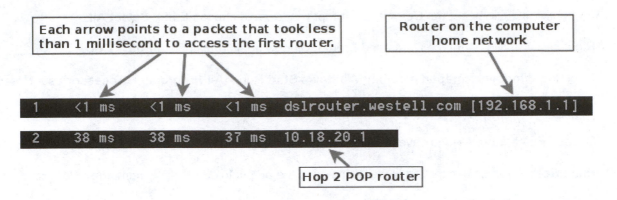

In the example output shown above, the tracert packets travel from the source PC to the local router default gateway (hop 1: 192.168.1.1) to the ISPs Point of Presence (POP) router (hop 2: 10.18.20.1). Every ISP has numerous POP routers. These POP routers are at the edge of the ISP's network and are the means by which customers connect to the Internet. The packets travel along the Verizon network for two hops and then jump to a router that belongs to alter.net. This could mean that the packets have traveled to another ISP. This is significant because sometimes there is packet loss in the transition between ISPs, or sometimes one ISP is slower than another. How could we determine if alter.net is another ISP or the same ISP?

e.   There is an Internet tool known as whois. The whois tool allows us to determine who owns a domain name. A web-based whois tool is found at http://whois.domaintools.com/. This domain is also owned by Verizon according to the web-based whois tool.

```
Registrant:
       Verizon Business Global LLC
       Verizon Business Global LLC
       One Verizon Way
        Basking Ridge NJ 07920
       US
       domainlegalcontact@verizon.com  +1.7033513164 Fax: +1.7033513669


   Domain Name: alter.net
```

To summarize, Internet traffic starts at a home PC and travels through the home router (hop 1). It then connects to the ISP and travels through its network (hops 2-7) until it arrives at the remote server (hop 8). This is a relatively unusual example in which there is only one ISP involved from start to finish. It is typical to have two or more ISP involved as displayed in the following examples.

f.   Now examine an example that involves Internet traffic crossing multiple ISPs. Below is the tracert for www.afrinic.net:

```
C:\>tracert www.afrinic.net

Tracing route to www.afrinic.net [196.216.2.136]
over a maximum of 30 hops:

  1      1 ms    <1 ms    <1 ms  dslrouter.westell.com [192.168.1.1]
  2     39 ms    38 ms     37 ms  10.18.20.1
  3     40 ms    38 ms     39 ms  G4-0-0-2204.ALBYNY-LCR-02.verizon-gni.net [130.8
1.197.182]
  4     44 ms    43 ms     43 ms  so-5-1-1-0.NY325-BB-RTR2.verizon-gni.net [130.81
.22.46]
  5     43 ms    43 ms     42 ms  0.so-4-0-0.XT2.NYC4.ALTER.NET [152.63.9.249]
  6     43 ms    71 ms     43 ms  0.ae4.BR3.NYC4.ALTER.NET [152.63.16.185]
  7     47 ms    47 ms     47 ms  te-7-3-0.edge2.NewYork2.level3.net [4.68.111.137
]
  8     43 ms    55 ms     43 ms  vlan51.ebr1.NewYork2.Level3.net [4.69.138.222]
  9     52 ms    51 ms     51 ms  ae-3-3.ebr2.Washington1.Level3.net [4.69.132.89]

 10    130 ms   132 ms    132 ms  ae-42-42.ebr2.Paris1.Level3.net [4.69.137.53]
 11    139 ms   145 ms    140 ms  ae-46-46.ebr1.Frankfurt1.Level3.net [4.69.143.13
7]
 12    148 ms   140 ms    152 ms  ae-91-91.csw4.Frankfurt1.Level3.net [4.69.140.14
]
 13    144 ms   144 ms    146 ms  ae-92-92.ebr2.Frankfurt1.Level3.net [4.69.140.29
]
 14    151 ms   150 ms    150 ms  ae-23-23.ebr2.London1.Level3.net [4.69.148.193]

 15    150 ms   150 ms    150 ms  ae-58-223.csw2.London1.Level3.net [4.69.153.138]

 16    156 ms   156 ms    156 ms  ae-227-3603.edge3.London1.Level3.net [4.69.166.1
54]
 17    157 ms   159 ms    160 ms  195.50.124.34
 18    353 ms   340 ms    341 ms  168.209.201.74
 19    333 ms   333 ms    332 ms  csw4-pkl-gi1-1.ip.isnet.net [196.26.0.101]
 20    331 ms   331 ms    331 ms  196.37.155.180
 21    318 ms   316 ms    318 ms  fa1-0-1.ar02.jnb.afrinic.net [196.216.3.132]
 22    332 ms   334 ms    332 ms  196.216.2.136

Trace complete.
```

What happens at hop 7? Is level3.net the same ISP as hops 2-6, or a different ISP? Use the whois tool to answer this question.

_____

What happens in hop 10 to the amount of time it takes for a packet to travel between Washington D.C. and Paris, as compared with the earlier hops 1-9?

_____

What happens in hop 18? Do a whois lookup on 168.209.201.74 using the whois tool. Who owns this network?

_____

g.   Type **tracert www.lacnic.net**.

```
C:\>tracert www.lacnic.net

Tracing route to www.lacnic.net [200.3.14.147]
over a maximum of 30 hops:

  1    <1 ms    <1 ms    <1 ms  dslrouter.westell.com [192.168.1.1]
  2    38 ms    38 ms    37 ms  10.18.20.1
  3    38 ms    38 ms    39 ms  G3-0-9-2204.ALBYNY-LCR-02.verizon-gni.net [130.8
1.196.190]
  4    42 ms    43 ms    42 ms  so-5-1-1-0.NY325-BB-RTR2.verizon-gni.net [130.81
.22.46]
  5    82 ms    47 ms    47 ms  0.ae2.BR3.NYC4.ALTER.NET [152.63.16.49]
  6    46 ms    47 ms    56 ms  204.255.168.194
  7   157 ms   158 ms   157 ms  ge-1-1-0.100.gw1.gc.registro.br [159.63.48.38]
  8   156 ms   157 ms   157 ms  xe-5-0-1-0.core1.gc.registro.br [200.160.0.174]

  9   161 ms   161 ms   161 ms  xe-4-0-0-0.core2.nu.registro.br [200.160.0.164]

 10   158 ms   157 ms   157 ms  ae0-0.ar3.nu.registro.br [200.160.0.249]
 11   176 ms   176 ms   170 ms  gw02.lacnic.registro.br [200.160.0.213]
 12   158 ms   158 ms   158 ms  200.3.12.36
 13   157 ms   158 ms   157 ms  200.3.14.147

Trace complete.
```

What happens in hop 7?

Part 3:   Trace a Route to a Remote Server Using Web-Based and Software-Tools

Step 1:   **Use a web-based traceroute tool.**

a.   Using http://www.subnetonline.com/pages/network-tools/online-tracepath.php to trace the route to the following websites:

www.cisco.com

www.afrinic.net

Capture and save the output in Notepad.

How is the traceroute different when going to www.cisco.com from the command prompt (see Part 1) rather than from the online website? (Your results may vary depending upon where you are located geographically, and which ISP is providing connectivity to your school.)

_____

_____

Compare the tracert from Part 1 that goes to Africa with the tracert that goes to Africa from the web interface. What difference do you notice?

_____

_____

Some of the traceroutes have the abbreviation asymm in them. Any guesses as to what this means? What is its significance?

_____

_____

Step 2: Use VisualRoute Lite Edition

VisualRoute is a proprietary traceroute program that can display the tracing path results graphically.

a. Please download the VisualRoute Lite Edition from the following link if it is not already installed:

http://www.visualroute.com/download.html

If you have any trouble downloading or installing VisualRoute, ask your instructor for assistance. Ensure that you download the Lite Edition.

b. Using VisualRoute 2010 Lite Edition, trace the routes to www.cisco.com.

c. Record the IP addresses in the path in Notepad.

Part 4:   Compare Traceroute Results

Compare the traceroute results to www.cisco.com from Parts 2 and 3.

Step 1:   List the path to www.cisco.com using tracert.

Step 2:   List the path to www.cisco.com using the web-based tool on subnetonline.com.

Step 3:   List the path to www.cisco.com using VisualRoute Lite edition.

Did all the traceroute utilities use the same paths to www.cisco.com? Why or Why not?

_____

_____

_____

Reflection

Having now viewed traceroute through three different tools (tracert, web interface, and VisualRoute), are there any insights that using VisualRoute provided that the other two tools did not?

_____

_____

_____

1.4.3.6 Lab — Researching IT and Networking Job Opportunities

Objectives

Part 1: Research Job Opportunities

- Identify the current networking jobs that are in demand.
- Explain the value of Cisco certifications in the job market.

Part 2: Reflect on Research

- Identify current hiring trends in IT/networking.
- Identify future networking career certifications and skills.
- Identify additional networking career paths.

Background / Scenario

Jobs in Information Technology (IT) and computer networking continue to grow. Most employers require some form of industry standard certification, degree, or other qualifications from their potential employees, especially those with limited experience. The Cisco CCNA certification is a known and established entry level networking certification that is respected in the industry. There are additional levels and kinds of Cisco certifications that one can attain, and each certification may enhance employment opportunities as well as salary range.

In this lab, you will do some targeted job searching on the web, to find what types of IT and computer networking jobs are available; what kinds of skills and certifications you will need; and the salary ranges associated with the various job titles.

Required Resources

- Device with Internet access

Part 1:   Research Job Opportunities

In Part 1, you will use a web browser to visit the popular job listing web sites monster.com and salary.com.

Step 1:   Open a web browser and go to a job listing website.

In the URL address bar type in http://monster.com and press Enter.

Note: For job listings outside of the US, use the following link to search for your country:

http://www.monster.com/geo/siteselection/

Step 2:   Search for networking related jobs.

a.   Type the word *Network* in the Job title box. Notice that the website offers context sensitive suggestions based on the keywords provided. Either click on, or finish typing the words, *Network Administrator* and click the **SEARCH** button (see image below).

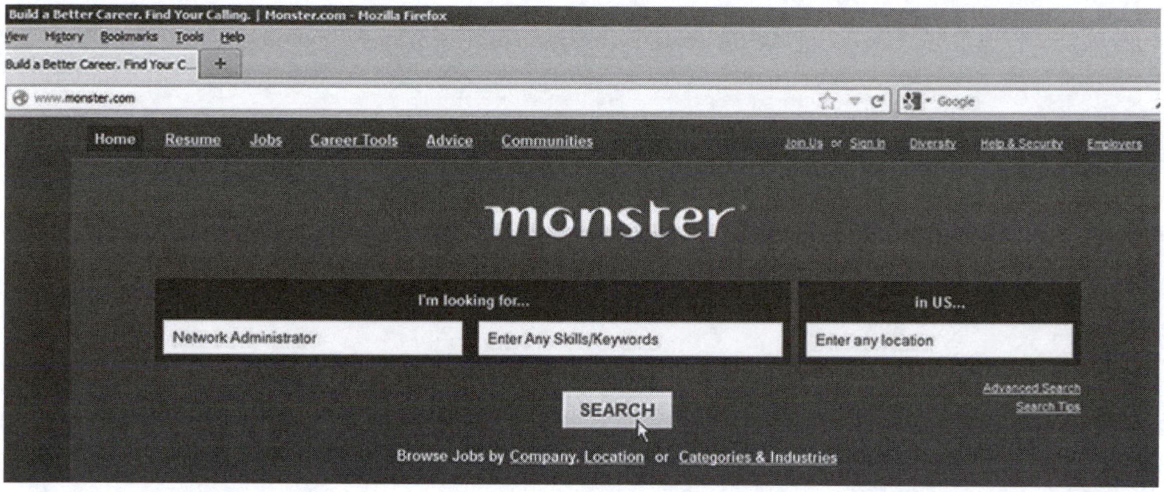

b. Notice the search results:

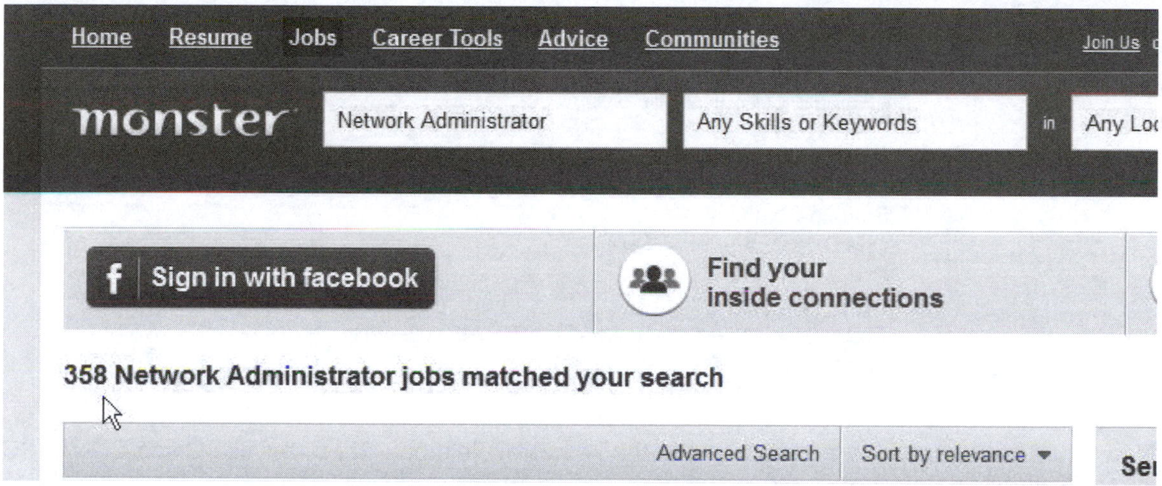

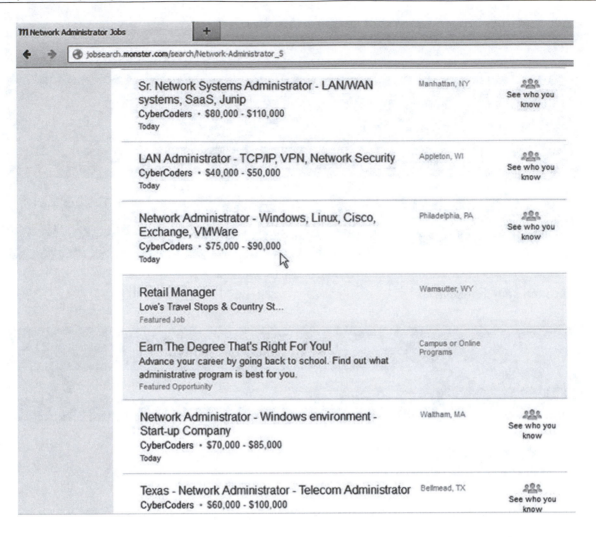

c.   Now focus your search by adding terms to the keywords field box. Try terms like Cisco CCNA, CCNP, CCNA Security, CCNA Voice, etc.

d.   Now try refining your search by adding in different geographical locations. Did you find jobs in the locations you entered?

_____

e.   Try searching a different website. Go to http://salary.com and click the **Job Search** menu bar button.

Note: For salary listings outside of the US, use the following link to search for your country:

http://www.payscale.com/rccountries.aspx

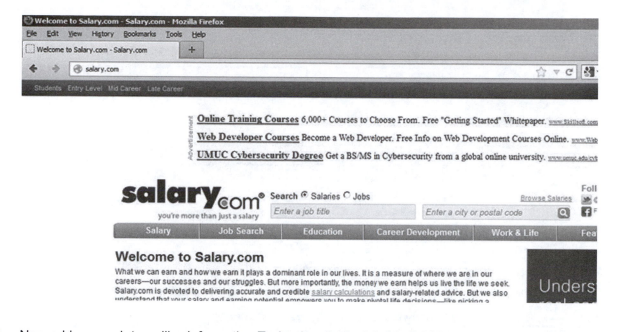

f. Now add a search term like *Information Technology* to the job title field box and click **Submit**.

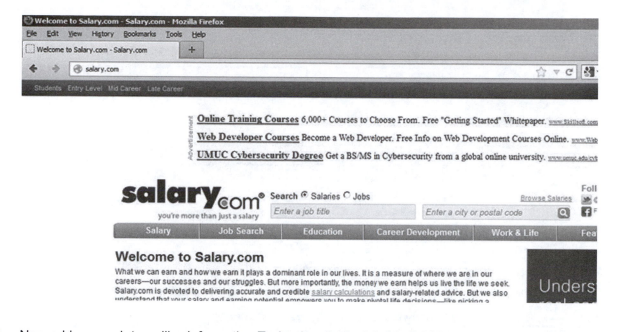

g. In the image below, note the large number of matching search results. There are also easy to use tools for refining your search, in the column to the left.

Job Search Wizard

Save this search

FIND A JOB | Information Technology | IN | city, state or zip | SEARCH

REFINE <<

Information Technology

Minimum Salary

- $0
- $30,000
- $50,000
- $75,000
- $100,000
- $150,000
- $200,000

Job Type

- Full Time
- Part Time
- Contract
- Temporary
- Internship
- All job types

Jobs Published

- AnyTime
- Within 15 days
- Within 7 days
- Within 3 days

Ads by Google

IT Consulting Services
.NET & SQL-Microsoft Certified 100s Of Successful Client Projects
www.amadeusconsulting.com/

Infrastructure Monitoring
System Health, Log Files & Uptime Free trial with excellent support
www.eventsentry.com/FreeEval

Server Health   Event Log
Compliance   Downloads
Log Files   Network Monitoring

1 | 2 | 3 | 4 | 5 | 6 | 7 | 8 | >   Jobs 1 to 10 of 200678 matches

IT Infrastructure and Operations Specialist
Ghirardelli Chocolate - San Leandro, CA

of the following technologies: MS Operating Systems... and interest to learn new IT
skills and new technologies Teamwork (within IT and outside the IT team...
Ghirardelli Chocolate - 88 Days ago   save

Technical Program/Delivery Manager
Garrigan Lyman Group - Seattle, WA

client and the GLG user experience, creative, and technology roles. Working
collaboratively with the user... sensitive information tactfully ▪ Understands how to...
Indeed - 21 Days ago   save

h. Spend some time searching for jobs and looking through the search results. Take note of what skills are required for different job titles and the range of starting salaries.

Part 2: **Reflect on Research**

In Part 2, you answer questions based on your research findings.

a. What job titles did you search for?

_____

_____

b. What skills or certifications were required?

_____

_____

c. Did you find any jobs that you previously did not know existed? If so, what were they?

_____

_____

d. Did you find any jobs that you are interested in? If so, which ones and what skills or certifications do they require?

_____

_____

1.5.1.1 Class Activity — Draw Your Concept of the Internet Now

Objectives

Identify the common components of a network.

In this activity, you will illustrate how concepts from Chapter 1 are applied to show how network devices connect to and throughout the Internet. After reflecting on your home or small-business topology, you will become familiar with using the device icons and knowledge needed to visualize network connectivity through the remaining network courses.

Background / Scenario

In this activity, you will use the knowledge you have acquired throughout Chapter 1, and the modeling activity document that you prepared at the beginning of this chapter. You may also refer to the other activities completed in this chapter, including Packet Tracer activities.

Draw a map of the Internet as you see it now. Use the icons presented in the chapter for media, end devices, and intermediary devices.

In your revised drawing, you may want to include some of the following:

- WANs

- LANs

- Cloud computing

- Internet Service Providers (tiers)

Save your drawing in hard-copy format. If it is an electronic document, save it to a server location provided by your instructor. Be prepared to share and explain your revised work in class.

Required Resources

- Beginning of chapter modeling activity drawing
- Packet Tracer (<u>may be optional</u> if students sketch their own drawing)
- Paper and pencils or pens

Reflection

1. After completing Chapter 1, are you more aware of the devices, cabling, and physical components of a small-to-medium size network? Explain your answer.

Modeling Activity Graphic Representation

Chapter 2 — Configuring a Network Operating System

2.0.1.2 Class Activity — It Is Just an Operating System!

Objectives

Describe the command structure of Cisco IOS software

In this activity, you will recognize that text commands used in command-line interfaces are intentionally chosen from spoken language. Text commands are often abbreviated, or otherwise simplified in their syntax, to keep the resulting command set concise. They may be grouped into context modes that simplify their usage. Configuring a device using written commands is similar to giving out short orders verbally. The commands are executed by the operating system and the actual process is performed by the device.

Background/Scenario

Imagine that you are employed as an engineer for a car manufacturing company. The company is currently working on a new car model. This model will have selected functions that can be controlled by the driver giving specific voice commands.

You must design the set of commands used by this voice-activated control system.

The functions of the car that can be controlled by voice commands are:

- Lights
- Wipers
- Radio
- Telephone set
- Air conditioning
- Ignition

Your task is to devise a simple set of spoken commands that will be used to control these systems and identify how they are going to be executed.

Required Resources

Paper and pencils or pens, or computer

Reflection

1. How can devising a set of voice commands assist in operating a vehicle? How could these same commands be used on a computer or network operating system?

2.1.4.9 Lab — Establishing a Console Session with Tera Term

Topology

Objectives

Part 1: Access a Cisco Switch through the Serial Console Port

- Connect to a Cisco switch using a serial console cable.
- Establish a console session using a terminal emulator, such as Tera Term.

Part 2: Display and Configure Basic Device Settings

- Use **show** commands to display device settings.
- Configure the clock on the switch.

Part 3: (Optional) Access a Cisco Router Using a Mini-USB Console Cable

Note: Users on Netlab or other remote access equipment should complete only Part 2.

Background / Scenario

Various models of Cisco routers and switches are used in networks of all types. These devices are managed using a local console connection or a remote connection. Nearly all Cisco devices have a serial console port to which you can connect. Some newer models, such as the 1941 Integrated Services Router (ISR) G2 used in this lab, also have a USB console port.

In this lab, you will learn how to access a Cisco device via a direct local connection to the console port, using a terminal emulation program, Tera Term. You will also learn how to configure the serial port settings for the Tera Term console connection. After you have established a console connection with the Cisco device, you can display or configure device settings. You will only display settings and configure the clock with this lab.

Note: The routers used with CCNA hands-on labs are Cisco 1941 ISRs with Cisco IOS Release 15.2(4)M3 (universalk9 image). The switches used are Cisco Catalyst 2960s with Cisco IOS Release 15.0(2) (lanbasek9 image). Other routers, switches, and Cisco IOS versions can be used. Depending on the model and Cisco IOS version, the commands available and output produced might vary from what is shown in the labs. Refer to the Router Interface Summary Table at the end of the lab for the correct interface identifiers.

Note: Make sure that the switch and router have been erased and have no startup configuration. If you are unsure, contact your instructor.

Required Resources

- 1 Router (Cisco 1941 with Cisco IOS software, release 15.2(4)M3 universal image or comparable)
- 1 Switch (Cisco 2960 with Cisco IOS Release 15.0(2) lanbasek9 image or comparable)
- 1 PC (Windows 7, Vista, or XP with terminal emulation program, such as Tera Term)
- Rollover (DB-9 to RJ-45) console cable to configure the switch or router via the RJ-45 console port
- Mini-USB cable to configure the router via the USB console port

Part 1: Access a Cisco Switch through the Serial Console Port

You will connect a PC to a Cisco switch using a rollover console cable. This connection will allow you to access the command line interface (CLI) and display settings or configure the switch.

Step 1: Connect a Cisco switch and computer using a rollover console cable.

a. Connect the rollover console cable to the RJ-45 console port of the switch.

b. Connect the other cable end to the serial COM port on the computer.

Note: Serial COM ports are no longer available on most computers today. A USB-to-DB9 adapter can be used with the rollover console cable for console connection between the computer and a Cisco device. These USB-to-DB9 adapters can be purchased at any computer electronics store.

Note: If using a USB-to-DB9 adapter to connect to the COM port, you may be required to install a driver for the adapter provided by the manufacturer on your computer. To determine the COM port used by the adapter, please see Part 3 Step 4. The correct COM port number is required to connect to the Cisco IOS device using a terminal emulator in Step 2.

c. Power up the Cisco switch and computer if these devices are not already on.

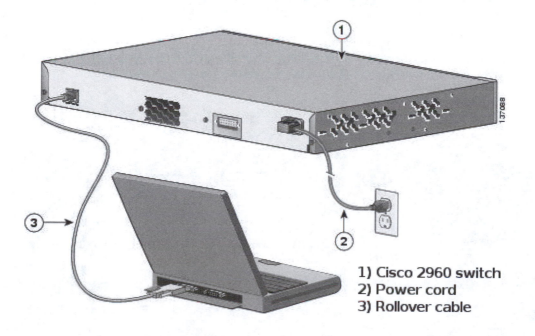

1) Cisco 2960 switch
2) Power cord
3) Rollover cable

Step 2: **Configure Tera Term to establish a console session with the switch.**

Tera Term is a terminal emulation program. This program allows you to access the terminal output of the switch. It also allows you to configure the switch.

a.   Start Tera Term by clicking the **Windows Start** button located in the task bar. Locate **Tera Term** under **All Programs**.

Note: If the program is not installed on the system, Tera Term can be downloaded from the following link by selecting **Tera Term**:

http://logmett.com/index.php?/download/free-downloads.html

b.   In the New Connection dialog box, click the **Serial** radio button. Verify that the correct COM port is selected and click **OK** to continue.

c.   From the Tera Term **Setup** menu, choose the **Serial port...** to verify the serial settings. The default parameters for the console port are 9600 baud, 8 data bits, no parity, 1 stop bit, and no flow control. The Tera Term default settings match the console port settings for communications with the Cisco IOS switch.

d. When you can see the terminal output, you are ready to configure a Cisco switch. The following console
    example displays the terminal output of the switch while it is loading.

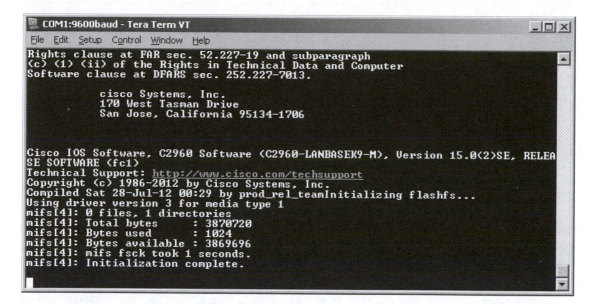

Part 2:   Display and Configure Basic Device Settings

In this section, you are introduced to the user and privileged executive modes. You will determine the Internetwork Operating System (IOS) version, display the clock settings, and configure the clock on the switch.

Step 1:   Display the switch IOS image version.

a. After the switch has completed its startup process, the following message displays. Enter **n** to continue.

    Would you like to enter the initial configuration dialog? [yes/no]: **n**

    Note: If you do not see the above message, please contact your instructor to reset your switch to the
    initial configuration.

b. While you are in the user EXEC mode, display the IOS version for your switch.

    Switch> **show version**

    Cisco IOS Software, C2960 Software (C2960-LANBASEK9-M), Version 15.0(2)SE, RELEASE
    SOFTWARE (fc1)

    Technical Support: http://www.cisco.com/techsupport

    Copyright (c) 1986-2012 by Cisco Systems, Inc.

    Compiled Sat 28-Jul-12 00:29 by prod_rel_team

    ROM: Bootstrap program is C2960 boot loader

    BOOTLDR: C2960 Boot Loader (C2960-HBOOT-M) Version 12.2(53r)SEY3, RELEASE SOFTWARE
    (fc1)

    Switch uptime is 2 minutes

    System returned to ROM by power-on

    System image file is "flash://c2960-lanbasek9-mz.150-2.SE.bin"

    <output omitted>

Which IOS image version is currently in use by your switch?

_____

Step 2: **Configure the clock.**

As you learn more about networking, you will see that configuring the correct time on a Cisco switch can be helpful when you are troubleshooting problems. The following steps manually configure the internal clock of the switch.

a. Display the current clock settings.

```
Switch> show clock
*00:30:05.261 UTC Mon Mar 1 1993
```

b. The clock setting is changed in the privileged EXEC mode. Enter the privileged EXEC mode by typing **enable** at the user EXEC mode prompt.

```
Switch> enable
```

c. Configure the clock setting. The question mark (?) provides help and allows you to determine the expected input for configuring the current time, date, and year. Press Enter to complete the clock configuration.

```
Switch# clock set ?
  hh:mm:ss  Current Time


Switch# clock set 15:08:00 ?
  <1-31>   Day of the month
  MONTH    Month of the year


Switch# clock set 15:08:00 Oct 26 ?
  <1993-2035>  Year


Switch# clock set 15:08:00 Oct 26 2012
Switch#
*Oct 26 15:08:00.000: %SYS-6-CLOCKUPDATE: System clock has been updated from 00:31:43
UTC Mon Mar 1 1993 to 15:08:00 UTC Fri Oct 26 2012, configured from console by console.
```

d. Enter the **show clock** command to verify that the clock setting was updated.

```
Switch# show clock
15:08:07.205 UTC Fri Oct 26 2012
```

Part 3: (Optional) Access a Cisco Router Using a Mini-USB Console Cable

If you are using a Cisco 1941 router or other Cisco IOS devices with a mini-USB console port, you can access the device console port using a mini-USB cable connected to the USB port on your computer.

Note: The mini-USB console cable is the same type of mini-USB cables that are used with other electronics devices, such as USB hard drives, USB printers, or USB hubs. These mini-USB cables can be purchased through Cisco Systems, Inc. or other third-party vendors. Please verify that you are using a mini-USB cable, not a micro-USB cable, to connect to the mini-USB console port on a Cisco IOS device.

Note: You must use either the USB port or the RJ-45 port, and not both simultaneously. When the USB port is used, it takes priority over the RJ-45 console port used in Part 1.

Step 1: Set up the physical connection with a mini-USB cable.

a.   Connect the mini-USB cable to the mini-USB console port of the router.

b.   Connect the other cable end to a USB port on the computer.

c.   Power up the Cisco router and computer, if these devices are not already on.

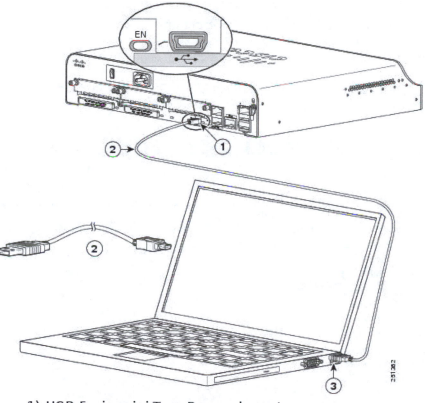

1) USB 5-pin mini Type-B console port
2) USB 5-pin mini Type-B to USB Type-A Console Cable
3) USB Type-A connector

Step 2: Verify that the USB console is ready.

If you are using a Microsoft Windows-based PC and the USB console port LED indicator (labeled EN) does not turn green, please install the Cisco USB console driver.

For a Microsoft Windows-based PC connecting to a Cisco IOS device with a USB cable, a USB driver must be installed prior to use. The driver can be found on www.cisco.com with the related Cisco IOS device. The USB driver can be downloaded from the following link:

http://www.cisco.com/cisco/software/release.html?mdfid=282774238&flowid=714&softwareid=282855122&release=3.1&relind=AVAILABLE&rellifecycle=&reltype=latest

Note: You must have a valid Cisco Connection Online (CCO) account to download this file.

Note: This link is related to the Cisco 1941 router; however, the USB console driver is not Cisco IOS device-model specific. This USB console driver only works with Cisco routers and switches. The computer requires a reboot after finishing the installation of the USB driver.

Note: After the files are extracted, the folder contains instructions for installation and removal and necessary drivers for different operating systems and architectures. Please choose the appropriate version for your system.

When the LED indicator for the USB console port has turned green, the USB console port is ready for access.

Step 3: **(Optional) Enable the COM port for the Windows 7 PC.**

If you are using a Microsoft Windows 7 PC, you may need to perform the following steps to enable the COM port:

a. Click the **Windows Start** icon to access the **Control Panel**.

b. Open the **Device Manager**.

c. Click the **Ports (COM & LPT)** tree link to expand it. The **Cisco Virtual Comm Port00** icon displays with a yellow exclamation point attached.

d. To resolve the issue, right-click the **Cisco Virtual Comm Port00** icon and choose **Update Driver Software**.

e. Choose **Browse my computer for driver software**.

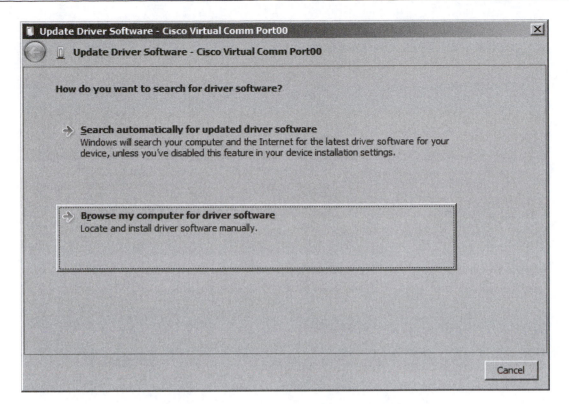

f.   Choose **Let me pick from a list of device drivers on my computer** and click **Next**.

g.   Choose the **Cisco Serial** driver and click **Next**.

h. The device driver is installed successfully. Take note of the port number assigned at the top of the window. In this sample, COM 6 is used for communication with the router. Click **Close**.

Step 4: (Optional) Determine the COM port number.

a. If you need to determine the COM port number, open the **Control Panel** and select the **Device Manager**. Search for the **Ports (COM & LPT)** heading, expand it, and determine the COM port number currently in use. In this example, **Cisco Serial (COM 6)** was selected for connection to the router because a Cisco USB console driver is in use. If you use a rollover console cable, or an adapter from a different manufacturer, the naming convention reflects this information.

b. Open Tera Term. Click the **Serial** radio button and choose **Port COM6: Cisco Serial (COM 6)**. This port should now be available for communication with the router. Click **OK**.

Reflection

1. How do you prevent unauthorized personnel from accessing your Cisco device through the console port?

2. What are the advantages and disadvantages of using the serial console connection as compared to the USB console connection to a Cisco router or switch?

_____

_____

Router Interface Summary Table

Router Interface Summary				
Router Model	**Ethernet Interface #1**	**Ethernet Interface #2**	**Serial Interface #1**	**Serial Interface #2**
1800	Fast Ethernet 0/0 (F0/0)	Fast Ethernet 0/1 (F0/1)	Serial 0/0/0 (S0/0/0)	Serial 0/0/1 (S0/0/1)
1900	Gigabit Ethernet 0/0 (G0/0)	Gigabit Ethernet 0/1 (G0/1)	Serial 0/0/0 (S0/0/0)	Serial 0/0/1 (S0/0/1)
2801	Fast Ethernet 0/0 (F0/0)	Fast Ethernet 0/1 (F0/1)	Serial 0/1/0 (S0/1/0)	Serial 0/1/1 (S0/1/1)
2811	Fast Ethernet 0/0 (F0/0)	Fast Ethernet 0/1 (F0/1)	Serial 0/0/0 (S0/0/0)	Serial 0/0/1 (S0/0/1)
2900	Gigabit Ethernet 0/0 (G0/0)	Gigabit Ethernet 0/1 (G0/1)	Serial 0/0/0 (S0/0/0)	Serial 0/0/1 (S0/0/1)

Note: To find out how the router is configured, look at the interfaces to identify the type of router and how many interfaces the router has. There is no way to effectively list all the combinations of configurations for each router class. This table includes identifiers for the possible combinations of Ethernet and Serial interfaces in the device. The table does not include any other type of interface, even though a specific router may contain one. An example of this might be an ISDN BRI interface. The string in parenthesis is the legal abbreviation that can be used in Cisco IOS commands to represent the interface.

2.3.3.4 Lab — Building a Simple Network

Topology

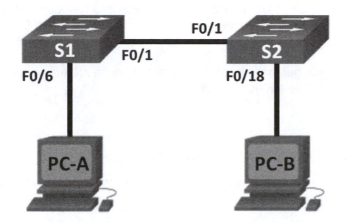

Addressing Table

Device	Interface	IP Address	Subnet Mask	Default Gateway
S1	VLAN 1	N/A	N/A	N/A
S2	VLAN 1	N/A	N/A	N/A
PC-A	NIC	192.168.1.10	255.255.255.0	N/A
PC-B	NIC	192.168.1.11	255.255.255.0	N/A

Objectives

Part 1: Set Up the Network Topology (Ethernet only)

- Identify cables and ports for use in the network.
- Cable a physical lab topology.

Part 2: Configure PC Hosts

- Enter static IP address information on the LAN interface of the hosts.
- Verify that PCs can communicate using the **ping** utility.

Part 3: Configure and Verify Basic Switch Settings

- Configure each switch with hostname, local passwords, and login banner.
- Save the running configurations.
- Display the running switch configuration.
- Display the IOS version for the running switch.
- Display the status of the interfaces.

Background / Scenario

Networks are constructed of three major components: hosts, switches, and routers. In this lab, you will build a simple network with two hosts and two switches. You will also configure basic settings including hostname, local passwords, and login banner. Use **show** commands to display the running configuration, IOS version, and interface status. Use the **copy** command to save device configurations.

You will apply IP addressing for this lab to the PCs to enable communication between these two devices. Use the **ping** utility to verify connectivity.

Note: The switches used are Cisco Catalyst 2960s with Cisco IOS Release 15.0(2) (lanbasek9 image). Other switches and Cisco IOS versions can be used. Depending on the model and Cisco IOS version, the commands available and output produced might vary from what is shown in the labs.

Note: Make sure that the switches have been erased and have no startup configurations. Refer to Appendix A for the procedure to initialize and reload a switch.

Required Resources

- 2 Switches (Cisco 2960 with Cisco IOS Release 15.0(2) lanbasek9 image or comparable)
- 2 PCs (Windows 7, Vista, or XP with terminal emulation program, such as Tera Term)
- Console cables to configure the Cisco IOS devices via the console ports
- Ethernet cables as shown in the topology

Part 1: Set Up the Network Topology (Ethernet only)

In Part 1, you will cable the devices together according to the network topology.

Step 1: Power on the devices.

Power on all devices in the topology. The switches do not have a power switch; they will power on as soon as you plug in the power cord.

Step 2: Connect the two switches.

Connect one end of an Ethernet cable to F0/1 on S1 and the other end of the cable to F0/1 on S2. You should see the lights for F0/1 on both switches turn amber and then green. This indicates that the switches have been connected correctly.

Step 3: Connect the PCs to their respective switches.

a.   Connect one end of the second Ethernet cable to the NIC port on PC-A. Connect the other end of the cable to F0/6 on S1. After connecting the PC to the switch, you should see the light for F0/6 turn amber and then green, indicating that PC-A has been connected correctly.

b.   Connect one end of the last Ethernet cable to the NIC port on PC-B. Connect the other end of the cable to F0/18 on S2. After connecting the PC to the switch, you should see the light for F0/18 turn amber and then green, indicating that the PC-B has been connected correctly.

Step 4: Visually inspect network connections.

After cabling the network devices, take a moment to carefully verify the connections to minimize the time required to troubleshoot network connectivity issues later.

Part 2:   **Configure PC Hosts**

Step 1:   **Configure static IP address information on the PCs.**

a.   Click the **Windows Start** icon and then select **Control Panel**.

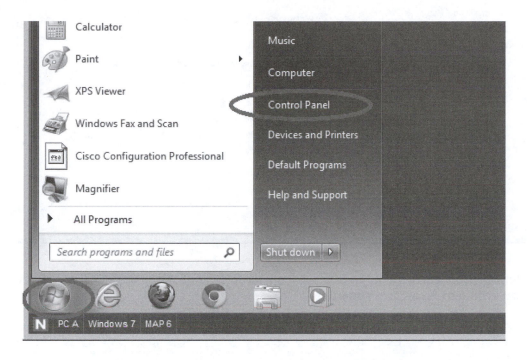

b.   In the Network and Internet section, click the **View network status and tasks** link.

Note: If the Control Panel displays a list of icons, click the drop-down option next to the **View by**: and change this option to display by **Category**.

c. In the left pane of the Network and Sharing Center window, click the **Change adapter settings** link.

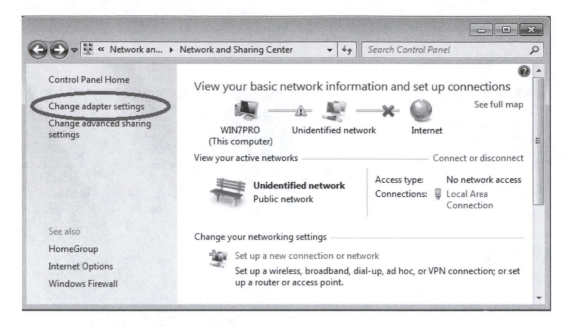

d. The Network Connections window displays the available interfaces on the PC. Right-click the **Local Area Connection** interface and select **Properties**.

e. Select the **Internet Protocol Version 4 (TCP/IPv4)** option and then click **Properties**.

Note: You can also double-click **Internet Protocol Version 4 (TCP/IPv4)** to display the Properties window.

f.   Click the **Use the following IP address** radio button to manually enter an IP address, subnet mask, and default gateway.

Note: In the above example, the IP address and subnet mask have been entered for PC-A. The default gateway has not been entered, because there is no router attached to the network. Refer to the Addressing Table on page 1 for PC-B's IP address information.

g. After all the IP information has been entered, click **OK**. Click **OK** on the Local Area Connection Properties window to assign the IP address to the LAN adapter.

h. Repeat the previous steps to enter the IP address information for PC-B.

Step 2: **Verify PC settings and connectivity.**

Use the command prompt (**cmd.exe**) window to verify the PC settings and connectivity.

a. From PC-A, click the **Windows Start** icon, type **cmd** in the **Search programs and files** box, and then press Enter.

b. The cmd.exe window is where you can enter commands directly to the PC and view the results of those commands. Verify your PC settings by using the **ipconfig /all** command. This command displays the PC hostname and the IPv4 address information.

```
C:\Windows\system32\cmd.exe

C:\Users\NetAcad>ipconfig /all

Windows IP Configuration

    Host Name . . . . . . . . . . . . : PC-A
    Primary Dns Suffix  . . . . . . . :
    Node Type . . . . . . . . . . . . : Hybrid
    IP Routing Enabled. . . . . . . . : No
    WINS Proxy Enabled. . . . . . . . : No

Ethernet adapter Local Area Connection:

    Connection-specific DNS Suffix  . :
    Description . . . . . . . . . . . : Intel(R) PRO/1000 MT Network Connection
    Physical Address. . . . . . . . . : 00-50-56-BE-6C-89
    DHCP Enabled. . . . . . . . . . . : No
    Autoconfiguration Enabled . . . . : Yes
    Link-local IPv6 Address . . . . . : fe80::d428:7de2:997c:b05a%11(Preferred)
    IPv4 Address. . . . . . . . . . . : 192.168.1.10(Preferred)
    Subnet Mask . . . . . . . . . . . : 255.255.255.0
    Default Gateway . . . . . . . . . :
    DHCPv6 IAID . . . . . . . . . . . : 234884137
    DHCPv6 Client DUID. . . . . . . . : 00-01-00-01-17-F6-72-3D-00-0C-29-8D-54-44
```

c. Type **ping 192.168.1.11** and press Enter.

Were the ping results successful? _____

If not, troubleshoot as necessary.

Note: If you did not get a reply from PC-B, try to ping PC-B again. If you still do not get a reply from PC-B, try to ping PC-A from PC-B. If you are unable to get a reply from the remote PC, then have your instructor help you troubleshoot the problem.

Part 3:   Configure and Verify Basic Switch Settings

Step 1:   Console into the switch.

Using Tera Term, establish a console connection to the switch from PC-A.

Step 2:   Enter privileged EXEC mode.

You can access all switch commands in privileged EXEC mode. The privileged EXEC command set includes those commands contained in user EXEC mode, as well as the **configure** command through which access to the remaining command modes are gained. Enter privileged EXEC mode by entering the **enable** command.

```
Switch> enable
Switch#
```

The prompt changed from **Switch>** to **Switch#** which indicates privileged EXEC mode.

Step 3:   Enter configuration mode.

Use the **configuration terminal** command to enter configuration mode.

```
Switch# configure terminal
Enter configuration commands, one per line. End with CNTL/Z.
Switch(config)#
```

The prompt changed to reflect global configuration mode.

Step 4:   **Give the switch a name.**

Use the **hostname** command to change the switch name to **S1**.

```
Switch(config)# hostname S1
S1(config)#
```

Step 5:   **Prevent unwanted DNS lookups.**

To prevent the switch from attempting to translate incorrectly entered commands as though they were host-names, disable the Domain Name System (DNS) lookup.

```
S1(config)# no ip domain-lookup
S1(config)#
```

Step 6:   **Enter local passwords.**

To prevent unauthorized access to the switch, passwords must be configured.

```
S1(config)# enable secret class
S1(config)# line con 0
S1(config-line)# password cisco
S1(config-line)# login
S1(config-line)# exit
S1(config)#
```

Step 7:   **Enter a login MOTD banner.**

A login banner, known as the message of the day (MOTD) banner, should be configured to warn anyone accessing the switch that unauthorized access will not be tolerated.

The **banner motd** command requires the use of delimiters to identify the content of the banner message. The delimiting character can be any character as long as it does not occur in the message. For this reason, symbols, such as the **#**, are often used.

```
S1(config)# banner motd #
Enter TEXT message. End with the character '#'.
Unauthorized access is strictly prohibited and prosecuted to the full extent
of the law. #
S1(config)# exit
S1#
```

Step 8:   **Save the configuration.**

Use the **copy** command to save the running configuration to the startup file on non-volatile random access memory (NVRAM).

```
S1# copy running-config startup-config
Destination filename [startup-config]? [Enter]
Building configuration...
[OK]
S1#
```

Step 9:   **Display the current configuration.**

The **show running-config** command displays the entire running configuration, one page at a time. Use the spacebar to advance paging. The commands configured in Steps 1 – 8 are highlighted below.

```
S1# show running-config
Building configuration...

Current configuration : 1409 bytes
!
! Last configuration change at 03:49:17 UTC Mon Mar 1 1993
!
version 15.0
no service pad
service timestamps debug datetime msec
service timestamps log datetime msec
no service password-encryption
!
hostname S1
!
boot-start-marker
boot-end-marker
!
enable secret 4 06YFDUHH61wAE/kLkDq9BGho1QM5EnRtoyr8cHAUg.2
!
no aaa new-model
system mtu routing 1500
!
!
no ip domain-lookup
!

<output omitted>

!
banner motd ^C
Unauthorized access is strictly prohibited and prosecuted to the full extent of the
law. ^C
!
line con 0
  password cisco
```

```
 login

line vty 0 4

 login

line vty 5 15

 login

!

end


S1#
```

Step 10: **Display the IOS version and other useful switch information.**

Use the **show version** command to display the IOS version that the switch is running, along with other useful information. Again, you will need to use the spacebar to advance through the displayed information.

```
S1# show version

Cisco IOS Software, C2960 Software (C2960-LANBASEK9-M), Version 15.0(2)SE, RELEASE
SOFTWARE (fc1)

Technical Support: http://www.cisco.com/techsupport

Copyright (c) 1986-2012 by Cisco Systems, Inc.

Compiled Sat 28-Jul-12 00:29 by prod_rel_team


ROM: Bootstrap program is C2960 boot loader

BOOTLDR: C2960 Boot Loader (C2960-HBOOT-M) Version 12.2(53r)SEY3, RELEASE SOFTWARE
(fc1)


S1 uptime is 1 hour, 38 minutes

System returned to ROM by power-on

System image file is "flash:/c2960-lanbasek9-mz.150-2.SE.bin"



This product contains cryptographic features and is subject to United

States and local country laws governing import, export, transfer and

use. Delivery of Cisco cryptographic products does not imply

third-party authority to import, export, distribute or use encryption.

Importers, exporters, distributors and users are responsible for

compliance with U.S. and local country laws. By using this product you

agree to comply with applicable laws and regulations. If you are unable

to comply with U.S. and local laws, return this product immediately.


A summary of U.S. laws governing Cisco cryptographic products may be found at:

http://www.cisco.com/wwl/export/crypto/tool/stqrg.html


If you require further assistance please contact us by sending email to
```

```
export@cisco.com.

cisco WS-C2960-24TT-L (PowerPC405) processor (revision R0) with 65536K bytes of memo-
ry.
Processor board ID FCQ1628Y5LE
Last reset from power-on
1 Virtual Ethernet interface
24 FastEthernet interfaces
2 Gigabit Ethernet interfaces
The password-recovery mechanism is enabled.


64K bytes of flash-simulated non-volatile configuration memory.
Base ethernet MAC Address       : 0C:D9:96:E2:3D:00
Motherboard assembly number     : 73-12600-06
Power supply part number        : 341-0097-03
Motherboard serial number       : FCQ16270N5G
Power supply serial number      : DCA1616884D
Model revision number           : R0
Motherboard revision number     : A0
Model number                    : WS-C2960-24TT-L
System serial number            : FCQ1628Y5LE
Top Assembly Part Number        : 800-32797-02
Top Assembly Revision Number    : A0
Version ID                      : V11
CLEI Code Number                : COM3L00BRF
Hardware Board Revision Number  : 0x0A



Switch Ports Model              SW Version          SW Image
------ ----- -----              ----------          ----------
*    1 26    WS-C2960-24TT-L     15.0(2)SE           C2960-LANBASEK9-M



Configuration register is 0xF
S1#
```

Step 11: **Display the status of the connected interfaces on the switch.**

To check the status of the connected interfaces, use the **show ip interface brief** command. Press the space-bar to advance to the end of the list.

```
S1# show ip interface brief
Interface            IP-Address      OK? Method Status            Protocol
Vlan1                unassigned      YES unset  up                up
```

```
FastEthernet0/1      unassigned    YES unset   up                     up
FastEthernet0/2      unassigned    YES unset   down                   down
FastEthernet0/3      unassigned    YES unset   down                   down
FastEthernet0/4      unassigned    YES unset   down                   down
FastEthernet0/5      unassigned    YES unset   down                   down
FastEthernet0/6      unassigned    YES unset   up                     up
FastEthernet0/7      unassigned    YES unset   down                   down
FastEthernet0/8      unassigned    YES unset   down                   down
FastEthernet0/9      unassigned    YES unset   down                   down
FastEthernet0/10     unassigned    YES unset   down                   down
FastEthernet0/11     unassigned    YES unset   down                   down
FastEthernet0/12     unassigned    YES unset   down                   down
FastEthernet0/13     unassigned    YES unset   down                   down
FastEthernet0/14     unassigned    YES unset   down                   down
FastEthernet0/15     unassigned    YES unset   down                   down
FastEthernet0/16     unassigned    YES unset   down                   down
FastEthernet0/17     unassigned    YES unset   down                   down
FastEthernet0/18     unassigned    YES unset   down                   down
FastEthernet0/19     unassigned    YES unset   down                   down
FastEthernet0/20     unassigned    YES unset   down                   down
FastEthernet0/21     unassigned    YES unset   down                   down
FastEthernet0/22     unassigned    YES unset   down                   down
FastEthernet0/23     unassigned    YES unset   down                   down
FastEthernet0/24     unassigned    YES unset   down                   down
GigabitEthernet0/1   unassigned    YES unset   down                   down
GigabitEthernet0/2   unassigned    YES unset   down                   down
S1#
```

Step 12: **Repeat Steps 1 to 12 to configure switch S2.**

The only difference for this step is to change the hostname to S2.

Step 13: **Record the interface status for the following interfaces.**

Interface	S1		S2	
	Status	Protocol	Status	Protocol
F0/1				
F0/6				
F0/18				
VLAN 1				

Why are some FastEthernet ports on the switches are up and others are down?

_____

_____

Reflection

What could prevent a ping from being sent between the PCs?

_____

Note: It may be necessary to disable the PC firewall to ping between PCs.

Appendix A: Initializing and Reloading a Switch

Step 1: Connect to the switch.

Console into the switch and enter privileged EXEC mode.

```
Switch> enable
Switch#
```

Step 2: Determine if there have been any virtual local-area networks (VLANs) created.

Use the **show flash** command to determine if any VLANs have been created on the switch.

```
Switch# show flash


Directory of flash:/


    2  -rwx        1919   Mar 1 1993 00:06:33 +00:00  private-config.text
    3  -rwx        1632   Mar 1 1993 00:06:33 +00:00  config.text
    4  -rwx       13336   Mar 1 1993 00:06:33 +00:00  multiple-fs
    5  -rwx    11607161   Mar 1 1993 02:37:06 +00:00  c2960-lanbasek9-mz.150-2.SE.bin
    6  -rwx         616   Mar 1 1993 00:07:13 +00:00  vlan.dat


32514048 bytes total (20886528 bytes free)
Switch#
```

Step 3: Delete the VLAN file.

a. If the **vlan.dat** file was found in flash, then delete this file.

```
Switch# delete vlan.dat
Delete filename [vlan.dat]?
```

You will be prompted to verify the file name. At this point, you can change the file name or just press Enter if you have entered the name correctly.

a.   When you are prompted to delete this file, press Enter to confirm the deletion. (Pressing any other key will abort the deletion.)

```
Delete flash:/vlan.dat? [confirm]
Switch#
```

Step 4:   **Erase the startup configuration file.**

Use the **erase startup-config** command to erase the startup configuration file from NVRAM. When you are prompted to remove the configuration file, press Enter to confirm the erase. (Pressing any other key will abort the operation.)

```
Switch# erase startup-config
Erasing the nvram filesystem will remove all configuration files! Continue? [confirm]
[OK]
Erase of nvram: complete
Switch#
```

Step 5:   **Reload the switch.**

Reload the switch to remove any old configuration information from memory. When you are prompted to reload the switch, press Enter to proceed with the reload. (Pressing any other key will abort the reload.)

```
Switch# reload
Proceed with reload? [confirm]
```

Note: You may receive a prompt to save the running configuration prior to reloading the switch. Type **no** and press Enter.

```
System configuration has been modified. Save? [yes/no]: no
```

Step 6:   **Bypass the initial configuration dialog.**

After the switch reloads, you should see a prompt to enter the initial configuration dialog. Type **no** at the prompt and press Enter.

```
Would you like to enter the initial configuration dialog? [yes/no]: no
Switch>
```

2.3.3.5 Lab — Configuring a Switch Management Address

Topology

Addressing Table

Device	Interface	IP Address	Subnet Mask	Default Gateway
S1	VLAN 1	192.168.1.2	255.255.255.0	N/A
PC-A	NIC	192.168.1.10	255.255.255.0	N/A

Objectives

Part 1: Configure a Basic Network Device

- Cable the network as shown in the topology.
- Configure basic switch settings including hostname, management address, and Telnet access.
- Configure an IP address on the PC.

Part 2: Verify and Test Network Connectivity

- Display device configuration.
- Test end-to-end connectivity with ping.
- Test remote management capability with Telnet.
- Save the switch running configuration file.

Background / Scenario

Cisco switches have a special interface, known as a switch virtual interface (SVI). The SVI can be configured with an IP address, commonly referred to as the management address that is used for remote access to the switch to display or configure settings.

In this lab, you will build a simple network using Ethernet LAN cabling and access a Cisco switch using the console and remote access methods. You will configure basic switch settings and IP addressing, and demonstrate the use of a management IP address for remote switch management. The topology consists of one switch and one host using only Ethernet and console ports.

Note: The switches used are Cisco Catalyst 2960s with Cisco IOS Release 15.0(2) (lanbasek9 image). Other switches and Cisco IOS versions can be used. Depending on the model and Cisco IOS version, the available commands and output produced might vary from what is shown in the labs.

Note: Make sure that the switch has been erased and has no startup configuration. If you are unsure, contact your instructor.

Required Resources

- 1 Switch (Cisco 2960 with Cisco IOS Release 15.0(2) lanbasek9 image or comparable)
- 1 PC (Windows 7, Vista, or XP with terminal emulation program, such as Tera Term)
- Console cables to configure the Cisco IOS devices via the console ports
- Ethernet cables as shown in the topology

Part 1:   Configure a Basic Network Device

In Part 1, you will set up the network and configure basic settings, such as hostnames, interface IP address-es, and passwords.

Step 1:   Cable the network.

a.   Cable the network as shown in the topology.

b.   Establish a console connection to the switch from PC-A.

Step 2:   Configure basic switch settings.

In this step, you will configure basic switch settings, such as hostname and configuring an IP address for the SVI. Assigning an IP address on the switch is only the first step. As the network administrator, you must spec-ify how the switch will be managed. Telnet and Secure Shell (SSH) are two of the most common management methods; however, Telnet is a very insecure protocol. All information flowing between the two devices is sent in plain text. Passwords and other sensitive information can be easily looked at if captured by a packet sniffer.

a.   Assuming the switch had no configuration file stored in nonvolatile random-access memory (NVRAM), you will be at the user EXEC mode prompt on the switch with a prompt of `Switch>`. Enter privileged EXEC mode.

```
Switch> enable
Switch#
```

b.   Verify a clean configuration file with the `show running-config` privileged EXEC command. If a con-figuration file was previously saved, it will have to be removed. Depending on the switch model and IOS version, your configuration may look slightly different. However, there should be no configured passwords or IP address set. If your switch does not have a default configuration, ask your instructor for help.

c.   Enter global configuration mode and assign the switch hostname.

```
Switch# configure terminal
Switch(config)# hostname S1
S1(config)#
```

d.   Configure the switch password access.

```
S1(config)# enable secret class
S1(config)#
```

e.   Prevent unwanted Domain Name System (DNS) lookups.

```
S1(config)# no ip domain-lookup
S1(config)#
```

f.   Configure a login message-of-the-day (MOTD) banner.

```
S1(config)# banner motd #
Enter Text message.  End with the character '#'.
Unauthorized access is strictly prohibited. #
```

g.   Verify your access setting by moving between modes.

```
S1(config)# exit
S1#
S1# exit
Unauthorized access is strictly prohibited.
S1>
```

What shortcut keys are used to go directly from global configuration mode to privileged EXEC mode?

_____

h.   Return to privileged EXEC mode from user EXEC mode.

```
S1> enable
Password: class
S1#
```

Note: Password will not show up on screen when entering.

i.   Enter global configuration mode to set the SVI IP address to allow remote switch management.

```
S1# config t
S1#(config)# interface vlan 1
S1(config-if)# ip address 192.168.1.2 255.255.255.0
S1(config-if)# no shut
S1(config-if)# exit
S1(config)#
```

j.   Restrict console port access. The default configuration is to allow all console connections with no password needed.

```
S1(config)# line con 0
S1(config-line)# password cisco
S1(config-line)# login
S1(config-line)# exit
S1(config)#
```

k.   Configure the virtual terminal (VTY) line for the switch to allow Telnet access. If you do not configure a VTY password, you will not be able to Telnet to the switch.

```
S1(config)# line vty 0 4
S1(config-line)# password cisco
S1(config-line)# login
```

```
S1(config-line)# end

S1#

*Mar  1 00:06:11.590: %SYS-5-CONFIG_I: Configured from console by console
```

Step 3: **Configure an IP address on PC-A.**

a. Assign the IP address and subnet mask to the PC, as shown in the Addressing Table on page 1. The procedure for assigning an IP address on a PC running Windows 7 is described below:

Click the **Windows Start** icon > **Control Panel**.

Click **View By:** > **Category**.

Choose **View network status and tasks** > **Change adapter settings**.

Right-click **Local Area Network Connection** and select **Properties**.

Choose **Internet Protocol Version 4 (TCP/IPv4)**, click **Properties** > **OK**.

Click the **Use the following IP address** radio button and enter the IP address and subnet mask.

Part 2: **Verify and Test Network Connectivity**

You will now verify and document the switch configuration, test end-to-end connectivity between PC-A and S1, and test the remote management capability of the switch.

Step 1: **Display the S1 device configuration.**

a. Return to your console connection using Tera Term on PC-A to display and verify your switch configuration by issuing the **show run** command. A sample configuration is shown below. The settings you configured are highlighted in yellow. The other configuration settings are IOS defaults.

```
S1# show run

Building configuration...


Current configuration : 1508 bytes

!

! Last configuration change at 00:06:11 UTC Mon Mar 1 1993

!

version 15.0

no service pad

service timestamps debug datetime msec

service timestamps log datetime msec

no service password-encryption

!

hostname S1

!

boot-start-marker

boot-end-marker
```

```
!
enable secret 4 06YFDUHH61wAE/kLkDq9BGho1QM5EnRtoyr8cHAUg.2
!
no aaa new-model
system mtu routing 1500
!
!
no ip domain-lookup
!
spanning-tree mode pvst
spanning-tree extend system-id
!
vlan internal allocation policy ascending
!
!
interface FastEthernet0/1
!
interface FastEthernet0/2

<output omitted>

interface FastEthernet0/24
!
interface GigabitEthernet0/1
!
interface GigabitEthernet0/2
!
interface Vlan1
 ip address 192.168.1.2 255.255.255.0
!
ip http server
ip http secure-server
!
banner motd ^C
Unauthorized access is strictly prohibited. ^C
!
line con 0
 password cisco
 login
line vty 0 4
 password cisco
```

```
  login
line vty 5 15
  login
!
end
```

b. Verify the status of your SVI management interface. Your VLAN 1 interface should be up/up and have an IP address assigned. Notice that switch port F0/6 is also up because PC-A is connected to it. Because all switch ports are initially in VLAN 1, by default, you can communicate with the switch using the IP address you configured for VLAN 1.

```
S1# show ip interface brief
```

Interface	IP-Address	OK?	Method	Status	Protocol
Vlan1	192.168.1.2	YES	manual	up	up
FastEthernet0/1	unassigned	YES	unset	down	down
FastEthernet0/2	unassigned	YES	unset	down	down
FastEthernet0/3	unassigned	YES	unset	down	down
FastEthernet0/4	unassigned	YES	unset	down	down
FastEthernet0/5	unassigned	YES	unset	down	down
FastEthernet0/6	unassigned	YES	unset	up	up
FastEthernet0/7	unassigned	YES	unset	down	down
FastEthernet0/8	unassigned	YES	unset	down	down
FastEthernet0/9	unassigned	YES	unset	down	down
FastEthernet0/10	unassigned	YES	unset	down	down
FastEthernet0/11	unassigned	YES	unset	down	down
FastEthernet0/12	unassigned	YES	unset	down	down
FastEthernet0/13	unassigned	YES	unset	down	down
FastEthernet0/14	unassigned	YES	unset	down	down
FastEthernet0/15	unassigned	YES	unset	down	down
FastEthernet0/16	unassigned	YES	unset	down	down
FastEthernet0/17	unassigned	YES	unset	down	down
FastEthernet0/18	unassigned	YES	unset	down	down
FastEthernet0/19	unassigned	YES	unset	down	down
FastEthernet0/20	unassigned	YES	unset	down	down
FastEthernet0/21	unassigned	YES	unset	down	down
FastEthernet0/22	unassigned	YES	unset	down	down
FastEthernet0/23	unassigned	YES	unset	down	down
FastEthernet0/24	unassigned	YES	unset	down	down
GigabitEthernet0/1	unassigned	YES	unset	down	down
GigabitEthernet0/2	unassigned	YES	unset	down	down

Step 2: Test end-to-end connectivity.

Open a command prompt window (cmd.exe) on PC-A by clicking the **Windows Start** icon and enter **cmd** into the **Search for programs and files** field. Verify the IP address of PC-A by using the **ipconfig /all** command.

This command displays the PC hostname and the IPv4 address information. Ping PC-A's own address and the management address of S1.

a. Ping your own PC-A address first.

    C:\Users\NetAcad> **ping 192.168.1.10**

Your output should be similar to the following screen:

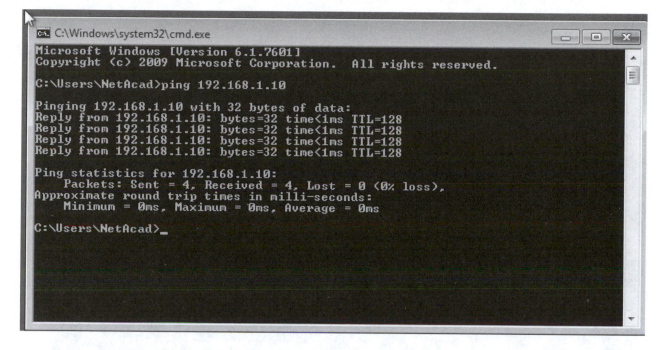

b. Ping the SVI management address of S1.

    C:\Users\NetAcad> **ping 192.168.1.2**

Your output should be similar to the following screen. If ping results are not successful, troubleshoot the basic device configurations. You should check both the physical cabling and IP addressing, if necessary.

```
C:\Users\NetAcad>
C:\Users\NetAcad>ping 192.168.1.2

Pinging 192.168.1.2 with 32 bytes of data:
Request timed out.
Reply from 192.168.1.2: bytes=32 time=2ms TTL=255
Reply from 192.168.1.2: bytes=32 time=2ms TTL=255
Reply from 192.168.1.2: bytes=32 time<1ms TTL=255

Ping statistics for 192.168.1.2:
    Packets: Sent = 4, Received = 3, Lost = 1 (25% loss),
Approximate round trip times in milli-seconds:
    Minimum = 0ms, Maximum = 2ms, Average = 1ms

C:\Users\NetAcad>
```

Step 3: Test and verify remote management of S1.

You will now use Telnet to remotely access the switch S1 using the SVI management address. In this lab, PC-A and S1 reside side by side. In a production network, the switch could be in a wiring closet on the top floor while your management PC is located on the ground floor. Telnet is not a secure protocol. However, you will use it in this lab to test remote access. All information sent by Telnet, including passwords and commands, is sent across the session in plain text. In subsequent labs, you will use Secure Shell (SSH) to remotely access network devices.

Note: Windows 7 does not natively support Telnet. The administrator must enable this protocol. To install the Telnet client, open a command prompt window and type **pkgmgr /iu:"TelnetClient"**.

```
C:\Users\NetAcad> pkgmgr /iu:"TelnetClient"
```

a. With the command prompt window still open on PC-A, issue a Telnet command to connect to S1 via the SVI management address. The password is **cisco**.

```
C:\Users\NetAcad> telnet 192.168.1.2
```

Your output should be similar to the following screen:

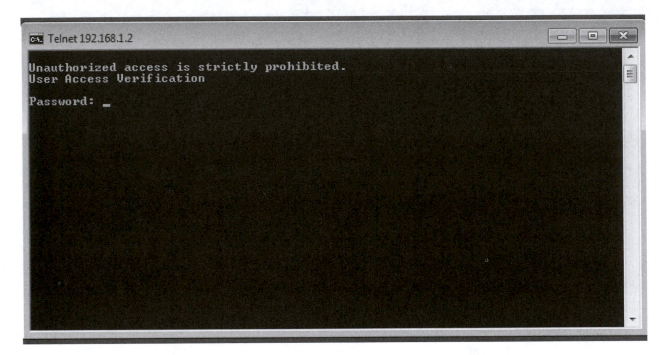

b. After entering the **cisco** password, you will be at the user EXEC mode prompt. Type **enable** at the prompt. Enter the **class** password to enter privileged EXEC mode and issue a **show run** command.

Step 4: Save the configuration file.

a. From your Telnet session, issue the **copy run start** command at the prompt.

```
S1# copy run start
Destination filename [startup-config]? [Enter]
Building configuration ..
S1#
```

b. Exit the Telnet session by typing **quit**. You will be returned to the Windows 7 command prompt.

Reflection

Why must you use a console connection to initially configure the switch? Why not connect to the switch via Telnet or SSH?

2.4.1.1 Class Activity — Tutor me!

Objectives

Configure initial settings on a network device using the Cisco IOS software.

In this activity, you will use and reinforce your knowledge of the Cisco Internetwork Operating System (IOS) command-line interface (CLI) by explaining it to other students. You will look for different ways to explain the meaning of individual commands. You will also find the optimal grouping of commands to be used when configuring a device to minimize the necessary count of mode changes.

Background/Scenario

(Students will work in pairs. Packet Tracer is required to be used with this activity.)

Assume that a new colleague has asked you for an orientation to the Cisco IOS CLI. This colleague has never worked with Cisco devices before.

You explain the basic CLI commands and structure, because you want your colleague to understand that the CLI is a simple, yet powerful, command language that can be easily understood and navigated.

Use Packet Tracer and one of the activities available in this chapter as a simple network model (for example, Lab Activity 2.3.3.5 LAB – Configuring a Switch Management Address). Focus on these areas:

- While the commands are technical, do they resemble any statements from plain English?

- How is the set of commands organized into subgroups or modes? How does an administrator know which mode he or she is currently using?

- What are the individual commands to configure the basic settings of a Cisco device? How would you explain this command in laymen's terms? Use parallels to real life whenever appropriate.

Suggest how to group different commands together according to their modes so that a minimum number of moves between modes will be needed.

Required Resources

- Packet Tracer
- Any simple network model activity available from Chapter 2

Reflection

1. After completing Chapter 2, do you feel as though you have a concrete understanding of what the Cisco IOS does and how it operates? What were some of the difficulties you encountered when explaining the basic CLI commands and structure to your colleague? If you were the "new colleague," what would be some of the difficulties that you would have learning the basic CLI commands and structure?

_____

_____

_____

2. Answer the following questions, and discuss your answers with the entire class:

    a) While the commands are technical, do they resemble any statements from plain English?

    b) How is the set of commands organized into subgroups or modes? How does an administrator know which mode he or she is currently using?

    c) What are the individual commands to configure the basic settings of a Cisco device? How would you explain this command in laymen's terms? Use parallels to real life whenever appropriate.

    d) With the help of your colleague, try to suggest how to group different commands together according to their modes so that a minimum number of moves between modes will be needed.

Chapter 3 — Network Protocols and Communications

3.0.1.2 Class Activity — Let's just talk about this...

Objectives

Explain the role of protocols and standards organizations in facilitating interoperability in network communications.

In this activity, you will determine ways to communicate when standards are not present or agreed upon. You will also resolve a communication issue by establishing standards for communication.

Background/Scenario

You have just purchased a new automobile for your personal use. After driving the car for a week or so, you find that it is not properly functioning.

After discussing the problem with several of your peers, you decide to take it to a highly recommended automotive repair facility. It is the only repair facility located in close proximity to you.

When you arrive at the repair facility, you find that all of the mechanics speak another language. You are having difficulty explaining the automobile's performance problems, but the repairs really need to be done. You are not sure you can drive it back home to research other options.

You must find a way to work with the repair facility to ensure your automobile is properly repaired.

How will you communicate with the mechanics in this firm? Design a communications model to ensure that the car is properly repaired.

Reflection

1. What steps did you identify as important to communicating your repair request? Justify your answer.

3.1.3.6 Lab — Researching Networking Standards

Objectives

Part 1: Research Networking Standards Organizations

- Gather information about the major networking standards organizations by going on a web surfing treasure hunt.

- Identify important characteristics of some of the organizations.

Part 2: Reflect on Internet and Computer Networking Experiences

- Reflect on how the various networking standards organizations enhance our experience of the Internet and computer networking.

Background / Scenario

Using web search engines like Google, research the non-profit organizations that are responsible for establishing international standards for the Internet and the development of Internet technologies.

Required Resources

Device with Internet access

Part 1:   Research Networking Standards Organizations

In Part 1, you will identify some of the major standards organizations and important characteristics, such as the number of years in existence, the size of their membership, the important historical figures, some of the responsibilities and duties, organizational oversight role, and the location of the organization's headquarters.

Use a web browser or websites for various organizations to research information about the following organizations and the people who have been instrumental in maintaining them.

You can find answers to the questions below by searching the following organizational acronyms and terms: ISO, ITU, ICANN, IANA, IEEE, EIA, TIA, ISOC, IAB, IETF, W3C, RFC, and Wi-Fi Alliance.

1. Who is Jonathan B. Postel and what is he known for?

    _____

    _____

    _____

2. Which two related organizations are responsible for managing the top-level domain name space and the root Domain Name System (DNS) name servers on the Internet?

    _____

    _____

3. Vinton Cerf has been called one of main fathers of the Internet. What Internet organizations did he chair or help found? What Internet technologies did he help to develop?

_____

_____

4. What organization is responsible for publishing Request for Comments (RFC)?

_____

5. What do RFC 349 and RFC 1700 have in common?

_____

_____

6. What RFC number is the ARPAWOCKY? What is it?

_____

7. Who founded the World Wide Web Consortium (W3C)?

_____

8. Name 10 World Wide Web (WWW) standards that the W3C develops and maintains?

_____

_____

9. Where is the Institute of Electrical and Electronics Engineers (IEEE) headquarters located and what is the significance of its logo?

_____

_____

_____

10. What is the IEEE standard for the Wi-Fi Protected Access 2 (WPA2) security protocol?

_____

_____

11. Is the Wi-Fi Alliance a non-profit standards organization? What is their goal?

_____

_____

12. Who is Hamadoun Touré?

_____

13. What is the International Telecommunication Union (ITU) and where is it headquartered?

_____

_____

14. Name the three ITU sectors?

_____

15. What does the RS in RS-232 stand for and which organization introduced it?

_____

16. What is SpaceWire?

_____

_____

17. What is the mission of the ISOC and where are its headquarters located?

_____

_____

_____

18. What organizations does the IAB oversee?

_____

_____

19. What organization oversees the IAB?

_____

20. When was the ISO founded and where are its headquarters located?

_____

_____

Part 2:   **Reflect on Internet and Computer Networking Experiences**

Take a moment to think about the Internet today in relation to the organizations and technologies you have just researched. Then answer the following questions.

1. How do the Internet standards allow for greater commerce? What potential problems could we have if we did not have the IEEE?

_____

_____

2. What potential problems could we have if we did not have the W3C?

_____

_____

3. What can we learn from the example of the Wi-Fi Alliance with regard to the necessity of networking standards?

_____

_____

_____

3.2.2.3 Lab — Researching RFCs

Objectives

Part 1: RFC Editor

- Navigate to the RFC Editor.
- Search for RFCs using keywords.
- Find RFCs by status.
- Search for humorous RFCs.

Part 2: Publishing RFCs

Background / Scenario

Request for Comments (RFCs) were created by Steve Crocker to help record notes on development of Advanced Research Projects Agency Network (ARPANET) in 1969 and eventually evolved into an official collection of memorandum that describes topics that are mainly related to the Internet and the TCP/IP protocol suite. Today the RFCs are managed by the IETF. There are currently over 6,000 RFCs, and the complete list is available at http://www.ietf.org/download/rfc-index.txt.

In this lab, you will learn how an RFC is published today by IETF. Additionally, you will also identify a few well-known RFCs that are used in your network. You can also find a few non-technical RFCs that can provide information or engineering humor.

Required Resources

Device with Internet access

Part 1: RFC Editor

RFCs started as a collection of memorandum on the development of the first Internet (ARPANET). In this collection, only a few RFCs are considered as Internet standards. Most of the RFCs describe experimental protocols. Some of the RFCs are only informational. The main purpose of RFCs is to stimulate comment and discussion.

Step 1: Navigate to the RFC Editor.

All the published RFCs are available for access at http://www.rfc-editor.org. The RFC Editor is an RFC repository maintained by the IETF.

At the top banner of this page, you can click any of the links, and these links direct you to the different searches, databases, and information. A link to **IETF HOME** is also included within this blue banner.

After an RFC is located, you have access to the full text of the document.

Step 2: Search for RFCs using keywords.

a. Open a browser and navigate to http://www.rfc-editor.org. On the RFC Editor Homepage, you can search and retrieve RFCs and other information related to the Internet.

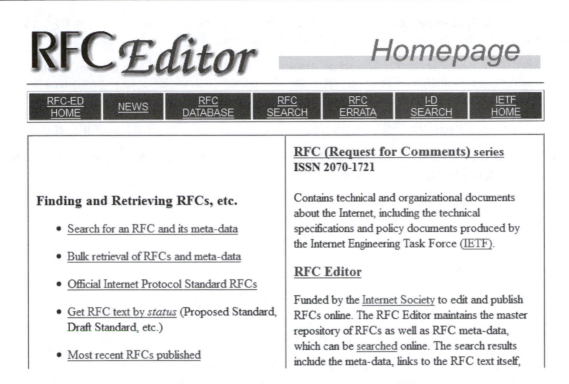

b. In the **Finding and Retrieving RFCs, etc.** pane, these links can help you search for RFCs using different methods. The **Search for an RFC and its meta-data** link displays a list of RFCs after inputting your search parameters, such as number, author, title, or keyword. The word, **pop**, is used in the following example.

o Based on your search of [*pop*] in the *All Fields* field 31 matches were found
  - Below you will find matching items *1 through 25*

Number	Title	Author or Ed.	Date	Format	More Info (Obs&Upd)	Status
STD0053 RFC1939	Post Office Protocol - Version 3	J. Myers, M. Rose	May 1996	ASCII	Obsoletes RFC1725, Updated by RFC1957, RFC2449, RFC6186	STD
RFC6511	Non-Penultimate Hop Popping Behavior and Out-of-Band Mapping for RSVP-TE Label Switched Paths	Z. Ali, G. Swallow, R. Aggarwal	February 2012	ASCII		PROPOSED STANDARD
RFC6186	Use of SRV Records for Locating Email Submission/Access Services	C. Daboo	March 2011	ASCII	Updates RFC1939, RFC3501	PROPOSED STANDARD
RFC6105	IPv6 Router Advertisement Guard	E. Levy-Abegnoli, G. Van de Velde, C. Popoviciu, J. Mohacsi	February 2011	ASCII		INFORMATIONAL

Look for **Post Office Protocol – Version 3** in the list. The associated RFC number is **RFC 1939**. This RFC is also an Internet standard, as indicated by the STD number in the **Number** column.

After an RFC is published and assigned a number, it cannot be changed and the RFC number is never used again for a newer RFC. For example, in the **More Info** column, RFC 1939 has made the previous RFC 1725 obsolete. The information in RFC 1725 has not been modified, but it has been replaced with the information from RFC 1939. RFC 1939 has been updated by RFC 1957, RFC 2449, and RFC 6186, as indicated in the **More Info** column. If you click any of these links, the full text of the RFC displays.

Refer to the **Status** column and locate the **Proposed Standard** status. They may be technically sound, but require further testing and validation.

Refer to the **Status** column and locate the **Informational** status. Informational RFCs can be anything from technical to humorous. For example, RFC 0035 (Network Meeting) provides an insight into the development of a network protocol in the early days of the Internet.

Step 3:   **Find RFCs by status.**

To find a list of RFCs that are either Internet Standards (STD) or by their status, perform the following tasks:

a.   Navigate back to the RFC Editor Homepage.

b.   Click the **Official Internet Protocol Standard RFCs** link in the left column. You will find a list of official standard RFCs followed by other RFC status lists. Each RFC link leads to the full RFC text.

Official Internet Protocol Standards

This page shows the current definitions of STD and BCP numbers. It also lists those standards-track and BEST CURRENT PRACTICE RFCs that have not been obsoleted, as well as current EXPERIMENTAL and HISTORIC RFCs.

RFC numbers more recent than Nov 2007 are starred.

Results are as of Nov-15-2012

Standards Ordered by STD #	Standards Ordered by RFC #
Draft Standards	
Proposed Standards	
Best Current Practice by BCP #	Best Current Practice by RFC #
Experimental RFCs	
Historic RFCs	

🔼 Return to Finding&Retrieving Page   📖 Go to RFC Editor home page

< STANDARDS Ordered by STD > Back to Top			
Mnemonic	Title	RFC#	STD#
--------	[Reserved for Assigned Numbers. See RFC 1700 and RFC 3232.]	xxx	2
--------	Requirements for Internet Hosts - Communication Layers	1122	3
--------	Requirements for Internet Hosts - Application and Support	1123	3

Step 4:   **Search for humorous RFCs.**

Engineering humor can also be found in the RFCs, such as RFC 1300 (Remembrances of Things Past). An Internet search engine can be used to find information on RFCs.

a. Search the Internet for "engineering humor rfc" to see more examples of whimsical RFCs. What did you find?

_____

b. Search for RFC 2795. What is the subject of this RFC? _____

What company does the author of this RFC work for? _____

Part 2: **Publishing RFCs**

The late Dr. Jonathan Postel maintained and managed the archiving of RFCs for 28 years (RFC 2468). Today, RFCs are a collection of documents published and managed by IETF. IETF is a large, open, international community of network designers, operators, vendors, and researchers related to the Internet and the Internet protocol suite.

Anyone can submit a proposal to the RFC Editor for possible publication. The proposal is initially published as an Internet-Draft (I-D). After review by the community and if it is approved by an RFC Editor, it will enter the same publishing process as IETF submission. For more details regarding independent submission, see http://www.rfc-editor.org/indsubs.html.

For proposals that may become Internet Standard or Best Current Practice and some Experimental or Informational RFCs, these submissions are published as Internet-Drafts. The Internet-Drafts are made available for informal review and comments. The Internet-Drafts have no formal status, and they are subject to change or removal at any time. They can be found at http://www.rfc-editor.org/.

a. Navigate to http://www.rfc-editor.org.

b. Click **I-D SEARCH** at the top of the Homepage, and then click **SEARCH**. This will display a list of the current Internet-Drafts.

o Based on your search of [] in the *All Fields* field 2149 matches were found
  - Below you will find matching items *1 through 25*

Name	Title	Author	Source	Date
draft-ietf-6lowpan-btle-11	Transmission of IPv6 Packets over BLUETOOTH Low Energy	Johanna Nieminen, Teemu Savolainen, Markus Isomaki, Basavaraj Patil, Zach Shelby, Carles Gomez	6lowpan	12-Oct-12
draft-ietf-6man-udpzero-07	Applicability Statement for the use of IPv6 UDP Datagrams with Zero Checksums	Gorry Fairhurst, Magnus Westerlund	6man	22-Oct-12

The list of results provides links to the full text of the I-Ds and other useful information. The **Source** column lists the Working Group with IETF that is responsible for the draft. As an example, **6man** is a Working Group that submitted multiple drafts. To find out more information about this Working Group, click **IETF HOME** at the top of the results page.

c.   After arriving at the IETF Homepage, click **WG Charters** in the left column, listed under Working Groups.

The Active IETF Working Groups page displays. The IETF Working Group's (WG) primary function is to develop IETF specifications and guidelines. Many of these specifications and guidelines are intended to become standards or recommendations. By scrolling the page, you see a list of Active Working Groups in different development areas for technology related to networking. The **6man** Working Group can be found listed in the Internet Area. This working group is responsible for maintenance and advancement of the IPv6 protocol specifications and addressing architecture.

d.   Click **6man** to view the complete list of current proposals and other information for this Working Group.

After the I-D has received significant community review and is considered useful, stable, and well-understood by the community, it should become a Proposed Standard. The full text of the Proposed Standard can be found by searching in the RFC-Editor. The Proposed Standard may become an Internet Standard after significant implementation and successful operational experience.

Note: Only a few RFCs published by IETF will become Internet standards.

Reflection

1.   Why are RFCs important for Internet standards and history?

_____

2.   What are the advantages of RFCs as a collaborative effort?

_____

3.3.3.4 Lab — Using Wireshark to View Network Traffic

Topology

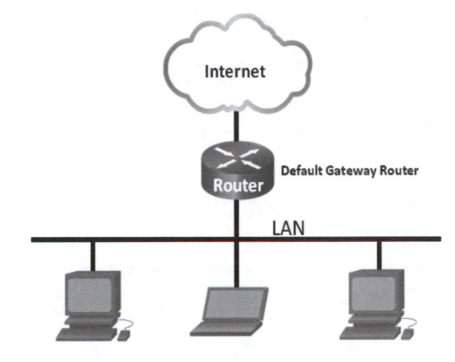

Objectives

Part 1: (Optional) Download and Install Wireshark

Part 2: Capture and Analyze Local ICMP Data in Wireshark

*   Start and stop data capture of ping traffic to local hosts.

*   Locate the IP and MAC address information in captured PDUs.

Part 3: Capture and Analyze Remote ICMP Data in Wireshark

*   Start and stop data capture of ping traffic to remote hosts.

*   Locate the IP and MAC address information in captured PDUs.

*   Explain why MAC addresses for remote hosts are different than the MAC addresses of local hosts.

Background / Scenario

Wireshark is a software protocol analyzer, or "packet sniffer" application, used for network troubleshooting, analysis, software and protocol development, and education. As data streams travel back and forth over the network, the sniffer "captures" each protocol data unit (PDU) and can decode and analyze its content according to the appropriate RFC or other specifications.

Wireshark is a useful tool for anyone working with networks and can be used with most labs in the CCNA courses for data analysis and troubleshooting. This lab provides instructions for downloading and installing Wireshark, although it may already be installed. In this lab, you will use Wireshark to capture ICMP data packet IP addresses and Ethernet frame MAC addresses.

Required Resources

- 1 PC (Windows 7, Vista, or XP with Internet access)
- Additional PC(s) on a local-area network (LAN) will be used to reply to ping requests.

Part 1: **(Optional) Download and Install Wireshark**

Wireshark has become the industry standard packet-sniffer program used by network engineers. This open source software is available for many different operating systems, including Windows, Mac, and Linux. In Part 1 of this lab, you will download and install the Wireshark software program on your PC.

Note: If Wireshark is already installed on your PC, you can skip Part 1 and go directly to Part 2. If Wireshark is not installed on your PC, check with your instructor about your academy's software download policy.

Step 1: **Download Wireshark.**

a. Wireshark can be downloaded from www.wireshark.org.

b. Click **Download Wireshark**.

c. Choose the software version you need based on your PC's architecture and operating system. For instance, if you have a 64-bit PC running Windows, choose **Windows Installer (64-bit)**.

Download Wireshark

Get Wireshark

The current stable release of Wireshark is 1.8.3. It supersedes all previous releases, including all releases of Ethereal. You can also download the latest development release (1.8.0rc2) and documentation.

▾ Stable Release (1.8.3)

   Windows Installer (64-bit)

   Windows Installer (32-bit)

   Windows U3 (32-bit)

   Windows PortableApps (32-bit)

   OS X 10.6 and later Intel 64-bit .dmg

   OS X 10.5 and later Intel 32-bit .dmg

   OS X 10.5 and later PPC 32-bit .dmg

   Source Code

▸ Old Stable Release (1.6.11)

▸ Development Release (1.8.0rc2)

▸ Documentation

Having problems? Explore our download area or look in our third party package list below.

After making a selection, the download should start. The location of the downloaded file depends on the browser and operating system that you use. For Windows users, the default location is the **Downloads** folder.

Step 2: **Install Wireshark.**

a. The downloaded file is named **Wireshark-win64-x.x.x.exe**, where **x** represents the version number. Double-click the file to start the installation process.

b. Respond to any security messages that may display on your screen. If you already have a copy of Wireshark on your PC, you will be prompted to uninstall the old version before installing the new version. It is recommended that you remove the old version of Wireshark prior to installing another version. Click **Yes** to uninstall the previous version of Wireshark.

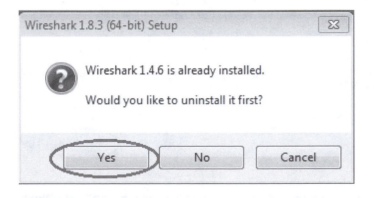

c. If this is the first time to install Wireshark, or after you have completed the uninstall process, you will navigate to the Wireshark Setup wizard. Click **Next**.

d. Continue advancing through the installation process. Click **I Agree** when the License Agreement window displays.

e. Keep the default settings on the Choose Components window and click **Next**.

f. Choose your desired shortcut options and click **Next**.

g. You can change the installation location of Wireshark, but unless you have limited disk space, it is recommended that you keep the default location.

h. To capture live network data, WinPcap must be installed on your PC. If WinPcap is already installed on your PC, the Install check box will be unchecked. If your installed version of WinPcap is older than the version that comes with Wireshark, it is recommend that you allow the newer version to be installed by clicking the **Install WinPcap x.x.x** (version number) check box.

i. Finish the WinPcap Setup Wizard if installing WinPcap.

j. Wireshark starts installing its files and a separate window displays with the status of the installation. Click **Next** when the installation is complete.

k. Click **Finish** to complete the Wireshark install process.

Part 2:   Capture and Analyze Local ICMP Data in Wireshark

In Part 2 of this lab, you will ping another PC on the LAN and capture ICMP requests and replies in Wireshark. You will also look inside the frames captured for specific information. This analysis should help to clarify how packet headers are used to transport data to their destination.

Step 1: Retrieve your PC's interface addresses.

For this lab, you will need to retrieve your PC's IP address and its network interface card (NIC) physical address, also called the MAC address.

a. Open a command window, type **ipconfig /all**, and then press Enter.

b. Note your PC interface's IP address and MAC (physical) address.

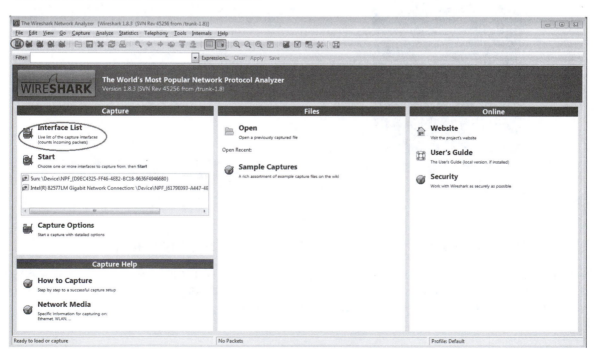

c. Ask a team member for their PC's IP address and provide your PC's IP address to them. Do not provide them with your MAC address at this time.

Step 2: Start Wireshark and begin capturing data.

a. On your PC, click the Windows **Start** button to see Wireshark listed as one of the programs on the pop-up menu. Double-click **Wireshark**.

b. After Wireshark starts, click **Interface List**.

Note: Clicking the first interface icon in the row of icons also opens the Interface List.

c. On the Wireshark: Capture Interfaces window, click the check box next to the interface connected to your LAN.

Note: If multiple interfaces are listed and you are unsure which interface to check, click the **Details** button, and then click the **802.3 (Ethernet)** tab. Verify that the MAC address matches what you noted in Step 1b. Close the Interface Details window after verifying the correct interface.

d. After you have checked the correct interface, click **Start** to start the data capture.

Information will start scrolling down the top section in Wireshark. The data lines will appear in different colors based on protocol.

e. This information can scroll by very quickly depending on what communication is taking place between your PC and the LAN. We can apply a filter to make it easier to view and work with the data that is being captured by Wireshark. For this lab, we are only interested in displaying ICMP (ping) PDUs. Type **icmp** in the Filter box at the top of Wireshark and press Enter or click on the **Apply** button to view only ICMP (ping) PDUs.

f. This filter causes all data in the top window to disappear, but you are still capturing the traffic on the interface. Bring up the command prompt window that you opened earlier and ping the IP address that you received from your team member. Notice that you start seeing data appear in the top window of Wireshark again.

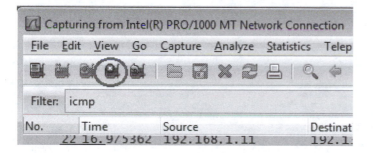

Note: If your team member's PC does not reply to your pings, this may be because their PC firewall is blocking these requests. Please see Appendix A: Allowing ICMP Traffic Through a Firewall for information on how to allow ICMP traffic through the firewall using Windows 7.

g. Stop capturing data by clicking the **Stop Capture** icon.

Step 3: **Examine the captured data.**

In Step 3, examine the data that was generated by the ping requests of your team member's PC. Wireshark data is displayed in three sections: 1) The top section displays the list of PDU frames captured with a summary of the IP packet information listed, 2) the middle section lists PDU information for the frame selected in the top part of the screen and separates a captured PDU frame by its protocol layers, and 3) the bottom section displays the raw data of each layer. The raw data is displayed in both hexadecimal and decimal form.

a. Click the first ICMP request PDU frames in the top section of Wireshark. Notice that the Source column has your PC's IP address, and the Destination contains the IP address of the teammate's PC you pinged.

b. With this PDU frame still selected in the top section, navigate to the middle section. Click the plus sign to the left of the Ethernet II row to view the Destination and Source MAC addresses.

Does the Source MAC address match your PC's interface? _____

Does the Destination MAC address in Wireshark match the MAC address that of your team member's?

_____

How is the MAC address of the pinged PC obtained by your PC?

_____

Note: In the preceding example of a captured ICMP request, ICMP data is encapsulated inside an IPv4 packet PDU (IPv4 header) which is then encapsulated in an Ethernet II frame PDU (Ethernet II header) for transmission on the LAN.

Part 3:   Capture and Analyze Remote ICMP Data in Wireshark

In Part 3, you will ping remote hosts (hosts not on the LAN) and examine the generated data from those pings. You will then determine what is different about this data from the data examined in Part 2.

Step 1:   Start capturing data on interface.

a.   Click the **Interface List** icon to bring up the list PC interfaces again.

b.   Make sure the check box next to the LAN interface is checked, and then click **Start**.

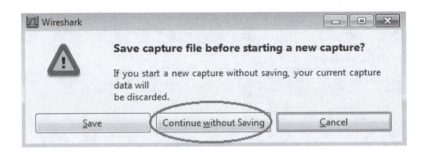

c. A window prompts to save the previously captured data before starting another capture. It is not necessary to save this data. Click **Continue without Saving**.

d. With the capture active, ping the following three website URLs:

www.yahoo.com

www.cisco.com

www.google.com

Note: When you ping the URLs listed, notice that the Domain Name Server (DNS) translates the URL to an IP address. Note the IP address received for each URL.

e. You can stop capturing data by clicking the **Stop Capture** icon.

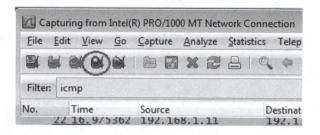

Step 2:   **Examining and analyzing the data from the remote hosts.**

a. Review the captured data in Wireshark, examine the IP and MAC addresses of the three locations that you pinged. List the destination IP and MAC addresses for all three locations in the space provided.

1st Location: IP: _____._____._____._____ MAC: ____:____:____:____:____:____

2nd Location: IP: _____._____._____._____ MAC: ____:____:____:____:____:____

3rd Location: IP: _____._____._____._____ MAC: ____:____:____:____:____:____

b. What is significant about this information?

_____

c. How does this information differ from the local ping information you received in Part 2?

_____

_____

Reflection

Why does Wireshark show the actual MAC address of the local hosts, but not the actual MAC address for the remote hosts?

_____

_____

Appendix A: Allowing ICMP Traffic Through a Firewall

If the members of your team are unable to ping your PC, the firewall may be blocking those requests. This appendix describes how to create a rule in the firewall to allow ping requests. It also describes how to disable the new ICMP rule after you have completed the lab.

Step 1: **Create a new inbound rule allowing ICMP traffic through the firewall.**

d. From the Control Panel, click the **System and Security** option.

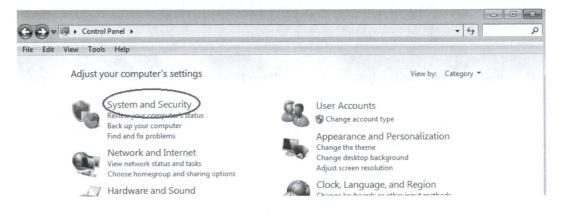

e. From the System and Security window, click **Windows Firewall**.

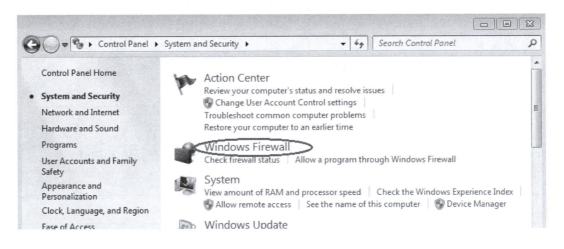

f. In the left pane of the Windows Firewall window, click **Advanced settings**.

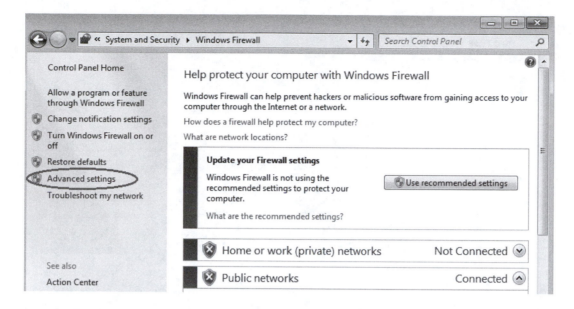

g. On the Advanced Security window, choose the **Inbound Rules** option on the left sidebar and then click **New Rule…** on the right sidebar.

h. This launches the New Inbound Rule wizard. On the Rule Type screen, click the **Custom** radio button and click **Next**

i. In the left pane, click the **Protocol and Ports** option and using the Protocol type drop-down menu, select **ICMPv4**, and then click **Next**.

j. In the left pane, click the **Name** option and in the Name field, type **Allow ICMP Requests**. Click **Finish**.

This new rule should allow your team members to receive ping replies from your PC.

Step 3:   **Disabling or deleting the new ICMP rule.**

After the lab is complete, you may want to disable or even delete the new rule you created in Step 1. Using the **Disable Rule** option allows you to enable the rule again at a later date. Deleting the rule permanently deletes it from the list of Inbound Rules.

a.   On the Advanced Security window, in the left pane, click **Inbound Rules** and then locate the rule you created in Step 1.

b.   To disable the rule, click the **Disable Rule** option. When you choose this option, you will see this option change to **Enable Rule**. You can toggle back and forth between Disable Rule and Enable Rule; the status of the rule also shows in the Enabled column of the Inbound Rules list.

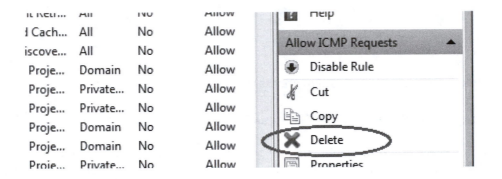

c.   To permanently delete the ICMP rule, click **Delete**. If you choose this option, you must re-create the rule again to allow ICMP replies.

3.4.1.1 Class Activity — Guaranteed to work!

Objectives

Explain the role of protocols and standards organizations in facilitating interoperability in network communications.

In this activity, you will demonstrate how network communications can be compared to everyday activities using established procedures and standards.

Background/Scenario

You have just completed the Chapter 3 content regarding network protocols and standards.

Assuming you resolved the beginning of this chapter's modeling activity, how would you compare the following steps taken to design a communications system to the networking models used for communications?

Steps to Communicate	Possible Answers	Associated TCP/IP Model Layer
Establish a language to communicate		
Divide the message into small steps, delivered a little at a time, to facilitate understanding of the problem		
Verify that the message has been delivered correctly to the mechanic who will perform the repairs		
Deliver the automobile and identify wait time for repairs		

Required Resources

Blank "Steps to Communicate" table (above) for students to record their answers based upon their Chapter 3 content knowledge.

Reflection

1. How does your network model in developing an automotive repair communications plan compare to a network communications interoperability plan?

Steps to Communicate	Possible Answers	Associated TCP/IP Model Layer

Chapter 4 — Application Layer

4.0.1.2 Class Activity — What would happen if…

Objectives

Explain the operation of the application layer in providing support to end-user applications.

In this activity, you will envision what it would be like not to have network applications available to use in the workplace. You may also estimate what it would cost to not be able to use networked applications for a short period of time.

Background/Scenario

It is the beginning of your work week. Your employer has decided to have IP telephones installed in your workplace resulting in the network being inoperable until next week. Your work, however, must continue. You have emails to send and quotes to write for your manager's approval. Because of possible security issues, you are not allowed to use personal or external computer systems, equipment, or offsite equipment and systems, to complete your corporate workload.

Your instructor may ask you to complete the questions from both scenarios below, or to choose one scenario (A. Emails or B. Quote for Manager's Approval). Answer the questions fully for the scenarios. Be prepared to discuss your answers in class.

A. **Emails**

- What methods can you use to send email communication?

- How could you send the same email to multiple recipients?

- How would you get a large attachment to multiple recipients, if necessary?

- Are these methods cost effective to your corporation?

- Do they violate any security policies of your corporation?

B. **Quote for Manager's Approval**

- You have a desktop application software package installed on your computer. Will it be relatively easy to produce the quote your manager needs for the new contract due by the end of the week? What limitations will be experienced while trying to complete the quote?

- How will you present the quote to your manager for approval? How do you think your manager will send the quote to the client for approval?

- Are these methods cost effective to your corporation? Justify your answer.

Reflection

1. What steps did you identify as important to communicating without network applications available to you for a week in your workplace? Which steps were not important? Justify your answer.

4.1.2.4 Lab — Researching Peer-to-Peer File Sharing

Objectives

Part 1: Identify P2P Networks, File Sharing Protocols, and Applications

Part 2: Research P2P File Sharing Issues

Part 3: Research P2P Copyright Litigations

Background / Scenario

Peer-to-peer (P2P) computing is a powerful technology that has many uses. P2P networks can be used to share and exchange music, movies, software, and other electronic materials.

The use of P2P networks to upload, download, or share copyrighted material, such as movies, music, and software, can violate the rights of copyright owners. In the P2P file-sharing context, infringement may occur, for example, when one person purchases an authorized copy and then uploads it to a P2P network to share with others. Both the individual who makes the file available and those making copies may be found to have infringed the rights of the copyright owners and may be violating copyright law.

Another problem with P2P file sharing is that very little protection is in place to ensure that the files exchanged in these networks are not malicious. P2P networks are an ideal medium for spreading malware (computer viruses, worms, Trojan horses, spyware, adware, and other malicious programs). In 2010, Cisco reported increases in P2P activity, coupled with recent P2P malware developments, suggesting that P2P file shares are becoming increasingly favored by users and malware attackers alike.

In this lab, you will research available P2P file sharing software and identify some issues that can arise from the use of this technology.

Required Resources

Device with Internet access

Part 1:   Identify P2P Networks, File Sharing Protocols, and Applications

In Part 1, you will research P2P networks and identify some popular P2P protocols and applications.

Step 1:   Define P2P networking.

a.   What is a P2P network?

_____

_____

b.   What are some advantages that P2P provides over client-server architecture?

_____

_____

_____

_____

_____

_____

c. What are some disadvantages of P2P networks?

_____

_____

Step 2:   Identify P2P file sharing protocols and applications.

a. Identify some P2P file sharing protocols used today.

_____

_____

_____

b. What are some popular P2P file sharing applications available today?

_____

_____

_____

c. What P2P file sharing protocol is attributed to producing the most P2P traffic on the Internet today?

_____

Part 2: Research P2P File Sharing Issues

In Part 2, you will research P2P copyright infringement and identify other issues that can occur with P2P file sharing.

Step 1: Research P2P copyright infringement.

a. What does the acronym DMCA stand for and what is it?

_____

_____

_____

b. Name two associations that actively pursue P2P copyright infringement?

_____

_____

c. What are the penalties for copyright infringement?

_____

_____

_____

d. What are the file sharing copyright laws in your area? Are they more strict or less strict than those in other areas of the world? How aggressively do enforcement agencies in your area pursue those who share copyrighted material?

_____

_____

Step 2: Research other P2P issues.

a. What types of malware can be transported through P2P file sharing?

_____

_____

b. What is Torrent Poisoning?

_____

_____

c. How could identity theft occur through the use of P2P file sharing?

_____

_____

Part 3:   **Research P2P Copyright Litigations**

In Part 3, you will research and identify some historical legal actions that have occurred, as a result of P2P copyright infringement.

a. What was the first well-known P2P application that specialized in MP3 file sharing and was shut down by court order?

_____

b. What was one of the largest P2P file sharing lawsuits ever?

_____

_____

Reflection

1. How can you be sure that the files you are downloading from P2P networks are not copyrighted and are safe from malware?

_____

4.2.2.9 Lab — Observing DNS Resolution

Objectives

Part 1: Observe the DNS Conversion of a URL to an IP Address

Part 2: Observe DNS Lookup Using the Nslookup Command on a Web Site

Part 3: Observe DNS Lookup Using the Nslookup Command on Mail Servers

Background / Scenario

The Domain Name System (DNS) is invoked when you type a Uniform Resource Locator (URL), such as http://www.cisco.com, into a web browser. The first part of the URL describes which protocol is used. Common protocols are Hypertext Transfer Protocol (HTTP), Hypertext Transfer Protocol over Secure Socket Layer (HTTPS), and File Transfer Protocol (FTP).

DNS uses the second part of the URL, which in this example is www.cisco.com. DNS translates the domain name (www.cisco.com) to an IP address to allow the source host to reach the destination host. In this lab, you will observe DNS in action and use the **nslookup** (name server lookup) command to obtain additional DNS information. Work with a partner to complete this lab.

Required Resources

1 PC (Windows 7, Vista, or XP with Internet and command prompt access)

Part 1: Observe the DNS Conversion of a URL to an IP Address

a. Click the **Windows Start** button, type **cmd** into the search field, and press Enter. The command prompt window appears.

b. At the command prompt, ping the URL for the Internet Corporation for Assigned Names and Numbers (ICANN) at **www.icann.net**. ICANN coordinates the DNS, IP addresses, top-level domain name system management, and root server system management functions. The computer must translate www.icann.net into an IP address to know where to send the Internet Control Message Protocol (ICMP) packets.

c. The first line of the output displays www.icann.net converted to an IP address by DNS. You should be able to see the effect of DNS, even if your institution has a firewall that prevents pinging, or if the destination server has prevented you from pinging its web server.

```
C:\>ping www.icann.net

Pinging www.icann.net [192.0.43.22] with 32 bytes of data:
Reply from 192.0.43.22: bytes=32 time=112ms TTL=241
Reply from 192.0.43.22: bytes=32 time=119ms TTL=241
Reply from 192.0.43.22: bytes=32 time=113ms TTL=241
Reply from 192.0.43.22: bytes=32 time=115ms TTL=241

Ping statistics for 192.0.43.22:
    Packets: Sent = 4, Received = 4, Lost = 0 (0% loss),
Approximate round trip times in milli-seconds:
    Minimum = 112ms, Maximum = 119ms, Average = 114ms
```

Record the IP address of www.icann.net. _____

d. Type IP address from **step c** into a web browser, instead of the URL. Notice that the ICANN home web page is displayed.

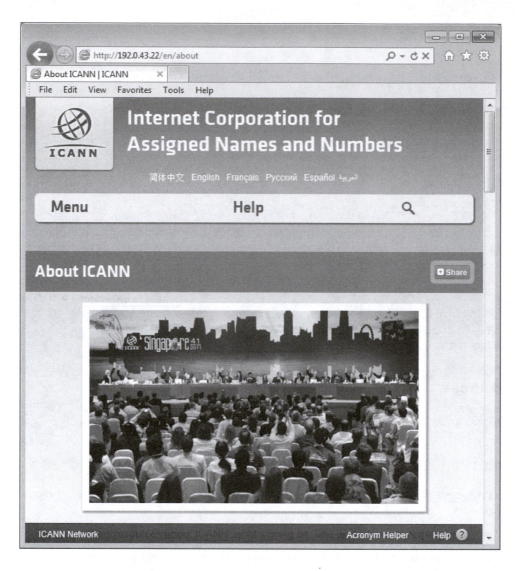

Most humans find it easier to remember words, rather than numbers. If you tell someone to go to **www.icann. net**, they can probably remember that. If you told them to go to 192.0.43.22, they would have a difficult time remembering an IP address. Computers process in numbers. DNS is the process of translating words into numbers. There is a second translation that takes place. Humans think in Base 10 numbers. Computers process in Base 2 numbers. The Base 10 IP address 192.0.43.22 in Base 2 numbers is 11000000.00000000.00101011.00010110. What happens if you cut and paste these Base 2 numbers into a browser?

_____

_____

_____

e. Now type **ping www.cisco.com**.

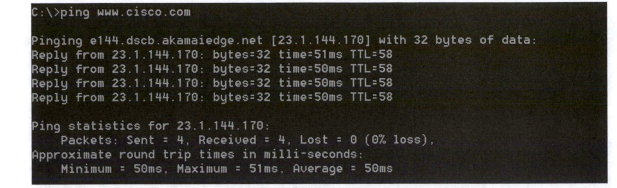

```
C:\>ping www.cisco.com

Pinging e144.dscb.akamaiedge.net [23.1.144.170] with 32 bytes of data:
Reply from 23.1.144.170: bytes=32 time=51ms TTL=58
Reply from 23.1.144.170: bytes=32 time=50ms TTL=58
Reply from 23.1.144.170: bytes=32 time=50ms TTL=58
Reply from 23.1.144.170: bytes=32 time=50ms TTL=58

Ping statistics for 23.1.144.170:
    Packets: Sent = 4, Received = 4, Lost = 0 (0% loss),
Approximate round trip times in milli-seconds:
    Minimum = 50ms, Maximum = 51ms, Average = 50ms
```

f. When you ping www.cisco.com, do you get the same IP address as the example, or a different IP ad-
    dress, and why?

    _____

    _____

    _____

g. Type the IP address that you obtained when you pinged www.cisco.com into a browser. Does the web site
    dlsplay? Why or why not?

    _____

    _____

    _____

Part 2: Observe DNS Lookup Using the Nslookup Command on a Web Site

h. At the command prompt, type the **nslookup** command.

```
C:\>nslookup
Default Server:  dslrouter.westell.com
Address:  192.168.1.1

>
```

What is the default DNS server used? _____

Notice how the command prompt changed to a greater than (>) symbol. This is the **nslookup** prompt.
From this prompt, you can enter commands related to DNS.

At the prompt, type **?** to see a list of all the available commands that you can use in **nslookup** mode.

i.   At the **nslookup** prompt, type **www.cisco.com**.

```
> www.cisco.com
Server:   dslrouter.westell.com
Address:  192.168.1.1

Non-authoritative answer:
Name:     e144.dscb.akamaiedge.net
Addresses:  2600:1408:7:1:9300::90
            2600:1408:7:1:8000::90
            2600:1408:7:1:9800::90
            23.1.144.170
Aliases:  www.cisco.com
          www.cisco.com.akadns.net
          wwwds.cisco.com.edgekey.net
          wwwds.cisco.com.edgekey.net.globalredir.akadns.net
```

What is the translated IP address? _____

Is it the same as the IP address shown with the **ping** command? _____

Under addresses, in addition to the 23.1.144.170 IP address, there are the following numbers:
2600:1408:7:1:9300::90, 2600:1408:7:1:8000::90, 2600:1408:7:1:9800::90. What are these?

_____

j.   At the prompt, type the IP address of the Cisco web server that you just found. You can use **nslookup** to get the domain name of an IP address if you do not know the URL.

```
> 23.1.144.170                              '
Server:   dslrouter.westell.com
Address:  192.168.1.1

Name:     a23-1-144-170.deploy.akamaitechnologies.com
Address:  23.1.144.170
```

You can use the **nslookup** tool to translate domain names into IP addresses. You can also use it to translate IP addresses into domain names.

Using the **nslookup** tool, record the IP addresses associated with www.google.com.

_____

```
> www.google.com
Server:  dslrouter.westell.com
Address:  192.168.1.1

Non-authoritative answer:
Name:    www.google.com
Addresses:  2607:f8b0:400c:c01::93
            173.194.75.147
            173.194.75.105
            173.194.75.99
            173.194.75.103
            173.194.75.106
            173.194.75.104
```

Part 3: Observe DNS Lookup Using the Nslookup Command on Mail Servers

k. At the prompt, type **set type=mx** to use **nslookup** to identify mail servers.

```
> set type=mx
```

l. At the prompt, type **cisco.com**.

```
> cisco.com
Server:  dslrouter.westell.com
Address:  192.168.1.1

Non-authoritative answer:
cisco.com        MX preference = 10, mail exchanger = rcdn-mx-01.cisco.com
cisco.com        MX preference = 15, mail exchanger = alln-mx-01.cisco.com
cisco.com        MX preference = 15, mail exchanger = ams-mx-01.cisco.com
cisco.com        MX preference = 15, mail exchanger = rtp-mx-01.cisco.com

ams-mx-01.cisco.com     internet address = 64.103.36.169
rcdn-mx-01.cisco.com .  internet address = 72.163.7.166
```

A fundamental principle of network design is redundancy (more than one mail server is configured). In this way, if one of the mail servers is unreachable, then the computer making the query tries the second mail server. Email administrators determine which mail server is contacted first using **MX preference** (see above image). The mail server with the lowest **MX preference** is contacted first. Based upon the output above, which mail server will be contacted first when email is being sent to cisco.com?

_____

m. At the nslookup prompt, type **exit** to return to the regular PC command prompt.

n. At the PC command prompt, type **ipconfig /all**.

o. Write the IP addresses of all the DNS servers that your school uses.

_____

Reflection

What is the fundamental purpose of DNS?

_____

4.2.3.3 Lab — Exploring FTP

Objectives

Part 1: Use FTP from a Command Prompt

Part 2: Download an FTP File Using WS_FTP LE

Part 3: Use FTP in a Browser

Background / Scenario

The File Transfer Protocol (FTP) is part of the TCP/IP suite. FTP is used to transfer files from one network device to another network device. Windows includes an FTP client application that you can execute from the command prompt. There are also free graphical user interface (GUI) versions of FTP that you can download. The GUI versions are easier to use than typing from a command prompt. FTP is frequently used for the transfer of files that may be too large for attachment with an email.

When using FTP, one computer is normally the server and the other computer is the client. When accessing the server from the client, you need to provide a username and password. Some FTP servers have a user named **anonymous**. You can access these types of sites by simply typing "anonymous" for the user, without a password. Usually, the site administrator has files that can be copied but does not allow files to be posted with the anonymous user.

In this lab, you will learn how to use anonymous FTP from the Windows command-line C:\> prompt. You will also use the GUI-based FTP program, WS_FTP LE. Finally, you will use an anonymous FTP in a browser.

Required Resources

1 PC (Windows 7, Vista, or XP with access to the command prompt and Internet access and WS_FTP LE installed)

Part 1:   Use FTP from a Command Prompt

a.   Click the **Windows Start** button, type **cmd** in the search field, and press Enter to open a command window.

b.   At the C:\> prompt type **ftp ftp.cdc.gov**. At the prompt that says **User (ftp.cdc.gov:(none)):** type **anonymous**. For the password, do not type anything. Press Enter to be logged in as an anonymous user.

```
Microsoft Windows [Version 6.1.7600]
Copyright (c) 2009 Microsoft Corporation.  All rights reserved.

C:\Users\User1>ftp ftp.cdc.gov
Connected to ftp.cdc.gov.
220 Microsoft FTP Service
User (ftp.cdc.gov:(none)): anonymous
331 Anonymous access allowed, send identity (e-mail name) as password.
Password:
230 Anonymous user logged in.
ftp>
```

Notice that the C:\> prompt has been replaced with the ftp> prompt. Type **ls** to list the files and directories. At the time that this lab was authored, there was a Readme file.

```
ftp> ls
200 PORT command successful.
150 Opening ASCII mode data connection for file list.
aspnet_client
pub
Readme
```

c. At the prompt, type **get Readme**. This downloads the file to your local computer from the anonymous FTP server that the Center for Disease Control has setup. The file will be copied into the directory shown in the C:\> prompt (C:\Users\User1 in this case).

```
ftp> get Readme
200 PORT command successful.
150 Opening ASCII mode data connection for Readme(1428 bytes).
226 Transfer complete.
ftp: 1428 bytes received in 0.00Seconds 1428000.00Kbytes/sec.
ftp>
```

d. Type **quit** to leave FTP and return to the C:\> prompt. Type **more Readme** to see the contents of the document.

```
ftp> quit
221

C:\Users\User1>more Readme

Welcome to the Centers for Disease Control and Prevention and Agency for
Toxic Substances and Disease Registry FTP server.  Information maintained on
this server is in the public domain and is available at anytime for your use.
CDC/ATSDR requests that you provide a valid e-mail address when responding to
the FTP server's password prompt.

FTP POLICY

CDC/ATSDR's file structure is designed to make information easily accessible
for faster response.  All FTP directories and sub-directories should contain
the following files:

        README.TXT        Contains general information and Disclaimer text.
                          (ASCII)
```

e. What is a drawback of using the FTP from the command line?

_____

Part 2:   Download an FTP File Using WS_FTP LE

In Part 2, you will download a file using WS_FTP LE (a free FTP transfer tool).

a. Start **WS_FTP LE**. If the Ipswitch WS_FTP LE window displays, click **Next** to continue and skip to step c. Otherwise, click the **Open a Remote Connection** link.

b. Click **Create Site…**.

c. In the **Site Name** field, type **Center for Disease Control** and click **Next** to continue.

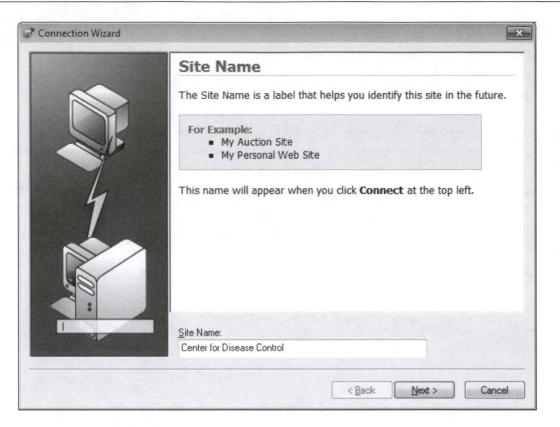

d. Click the **Connection Type** drop-down list, select **FTP** (the default connection type), and click **Next**.

e. In the **Server Address** field, type **ftp.cdc.gov**, and click **Next**.

f.   In the **User Name** field, type **anonymous**, and leave the password field blank. Click **Next**.

g.   Click **Finish**.

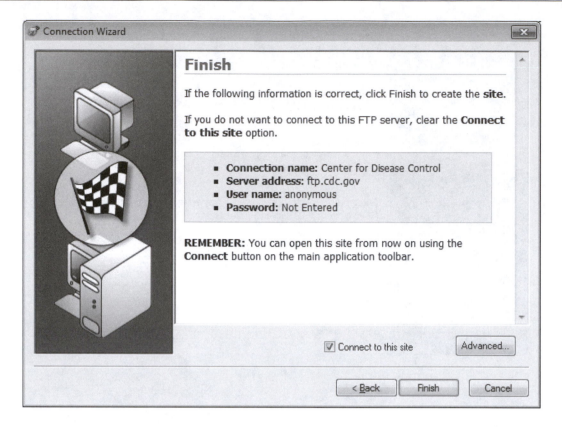

h. When the Login Information Missing dialog box displays, click **OK**. Do not type a password in the **Password** field.

i. You are now anonymously connected to the Center for Disease Control FTP site.

j. On the WS_FTP LE toolbar menu under My Computer, click **New Folder** to create a folder on your local **C:** drive.

k. In the Make Directory dialog box name the folder as **CDC** and click **OK**.

   Note: If the folder already exists, you can use the same folder or create another folder with a different name. If using the same CDC folder, you can replace the existing Readme file with the downloaded Readme file.

l. After the directory is created, in the **My Computer** tab page, double-click the directory to open it.

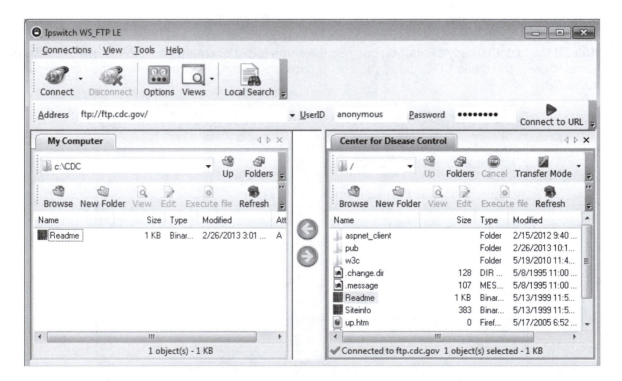

m. Drag the file **Readme** from the right side of the application (the remote CDC FTP server) into the CDC folder on to the local **C:** drive.

n. Double-click the **Readme** file in the **C:\CDC** folder on your local **C:** drive. If prompted for an application to open the document, choose any word processing software. You should see a message that looks something like this:

```
Welcome to the Centers for Disease Control and Prevention and
Agency for Toxic Substances and Disease Registry FTP server.
Information maintained on this server is in the public domain
and is available at anytime for your use.
```

o. Which was easier, using FTP from the **cmd** prompt, or using WS_FTP LE? _____

p. Click **Disconnect** to disconnect from the ftp.cdc.gov site when finished.

q. The remote site will be removed from the saved list of FTP sites. In the Ipswitch WS_FTP LE window, click the **Open a Remote Connection** link. Select the **Center for Disease Control** site, and click **Delete** to remove the FTP site. Click **Yes** to confirm the deletion. Click **Close** to exit the Site Manager.

r. Remove the **C:\CDC** folder.

Part 3:   **Use FTP in a Browser**

It is possible to use a browser as an anonymous FTP client.

a. In a browser, type **ftp://ftp.cdc.gov/**.

FTP root at ftp.cdc.gov

To view this FTP site in Windows Explorer: press Alt, click **View**, and then click **Open FTP Site in Windows Explorer**.

```
05/08/1995 11:00PM             128  .change.dir
05/08/1995 11:00PM             107  .message
02/15/2012 09:40PM       Directory  aspnet_client
11/16/2012 10:01AM       Directory  pub
05/13/1999 11:54AM           1,428  Readme
05/13/1999 11:54AM             383  Siteinfo
05/17/2005 06:52AM               0  up.htm
05/19/2010 11:47PM       Directory  w3c
05/20/2010 06:25AM             218  web.config
09/22/1998 07:25AM             202  welcome.msg
```

b. Click the **Readme** file.

Welcome to the Centers for Disease Control and Prevention and Agency for
Toxic Substances and Disease Registry FTP server. Information maintained on
this server is in the public domain and is available at anytime for your use.
CDC/ATSDR requests that you provide a valid e-mail address when responding to
the FTP server's password prompt.

Reflection

1. Which FTP method was easiest to use?

_____

2. Was there any advantage to using FTP from the command prompt or using WS_FTP LE?

_____

4.3.1.1 Class Activity — Make it happen!

Objectives

Explain the operation of the application layer in providing support to end-user applications.

In this activity, you will apply new knowledge of application layer protocols and methods of the TCP/IP layer in streamlining data/network communication.

Background/Scenario

Refer to the modeling activity from the beginning of this chapter as the basis for this activity.

Your IP telephones were installed in a half day vs. the full week originally anticipated. Your network has been restored to full capacity and network applications are available for your use. You have the same emails to answer and quotes to write for your manager's approval.

Use the same scenario you completed in the introduction modeling activity to answer the following questions:

A. **Emails**

- What methods can you use to send email correspondence now that the network is working?

- What format will your emails be sent over the network?

- How can you now send the same message to multiple recipients?

- How can you send the large attachments to multiple recipients using network applications?

- Would using network applications prove to be a cost-effective communication method for your corporation?

B. **Quote for Manager's Approval**

- Because you have desktop application programs installed on your computer, will it be relatively easy to produce the quote your manager needs for the new contract due by the end of the week? Explain your answer.

- When you finish writing the quote, how will you present it to your manager for approval? How will your manager send the quote to the client for approval?

- Is using network applications a cost-effective way to complete business transactions? Justify your answer.

- Save a hard copy or an electronic copy of your answers. Be prepared to discuss your answers in class.

Reflection

1. Having network applications and services available to you may increase production, decrease costs, and save time. Would this be true with the scenario you chose? Justify your answer. _____

Chapter 5 — Transport Layer

5.0.1.2 Class Activity — We Need to Talk

Objectives

Explain how transport layer protocols and services support communications across data networks.

In this activity, you will determine whether high or low data communication delivery methods should be utilized in a situational context.

Background/Scenario

Note: This activity works best with medium-sized groups of 6 to 8 students per group.

This chapter helps you understand how transport layer protocols and services support network data communications.

Your instructor will whisper a complex message to the first student in a group. An example of the message might be "Our final exam will be given next Tuesday, February 5th, at 2:00 p.m. in Room 1151."

That student whispers the message to the next student in the group. Each group follows this process until all members of each group have heard the whispered message.

Here are the rules to follow:

- You can whisper the message only once to your neighbor.

- The message must keep moving from one person to the other with no skipping of participants. The instructor should ask a student to keep time of the full message activity from first participant to last participant stating the messages. The first or last person would mostly likely be the best one to keep this time.

- The last student will say aloud exactly what he or she heard.

Your instructor will repeat the original message so that the group can compare it to the message that was delivered by the last student in the group.

Required Resources

- Timer for the student who is keeping a record of the conversation's duration.

Reflection

1. Would the contents of this message need to be fully correct when you received them if you were depending on this message to drive your personal/business calendar, studying schedule, etc.?

2. Would the length of time taken to deliver the message be an important factor to the sender and recipient?

5.2.1.8 Lab — Using Wireshark to Observe the TCP 3-Way Handshake

Topology

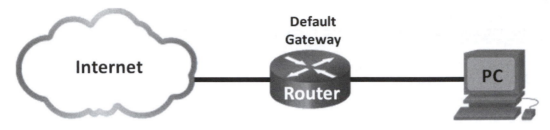

Objectives

Part 1: Prepare Wireshark to Capture Packets

- Select an appropriate NIC interface to capture packets.

Part 2: Capture, Locate, and Examine Packets

- Capture a web session to www.google.com.
- Locate appropriate packets for a web session.
- Examine information within packets, including IP addresses, TCP port numbers, and TCP control flags.

Background / Scenario

In this lab, you will use Wireshark to capture and examine packets generated between the PC browser using the HyperText Transfer Protocol (HTTP) and a web server, such as www.google.com. When an application, such as HTTP or File Transfer Protocol (FTP) first starts on a host, TCP uses the three-way handshake to establish a reliable TCP session between the two hosts. For example, when a PC uses a web browser to surf the Internet, a three-way handshake is initiated and a session is established between the PC host and web server. A PC can have multiple, simultaneous, active TCP sessions with various web sites.

Note: This lab cannot be completed using Netlab. This lab assumes that you have Internet access.

Required Resources

1 PC (Windows 7, Vista, or XP with a command prompt access, Internet access, and Wireshark installed)

Part 1:   Prepare Wireshark to Capture Packets

In Part 1, you start the Wireshark program and select the appropriate interface to begin capturing packets.

Step 1:   Retrieve the PC interface addresses.

For this lab, you need to retrieve your PC's IP address and its network interface card (NIC) physical address, also called the MAC address.

a. Open a command prompt window, type **ipconfig /all** and then press Enter.

```
Physical Address. . . . . . . . . : C8-0A-A9-FA-DE-0D
DHCP Enabled. . . . . . . . . . . : Yes
Autoconfiguration Enabled . . . . : Yes
IPv4 Address. . . . . . . . . . . : 192.168.1.130(Preferred)
Subnet Mask . . . . . . . . . . . : 255.255.255.0
Lease Obtained. . . . . . . . . . : Saturday, December 01, 2012 1:43:35 PM
Lease Expires . . . . . . . . . . : Sunday, December 02, 2012 1:43:35 PM
Default Gateway . . . . . . . . . : 192.168.1.1
DHCP Server . . . . . . . . . . . : 192.168.1.1
DNS Servers . . . . . . . . . . . : 192.168.1.1
NetBIOS over Tcpip. . . . . . . . : Enabled
```

b. Write down the IP and MAC addresses associated with the selected Ethernet adapter, because that is the source address to look for when examining captured packets.

The PC host IP address: _____

The PC host MAC address: _____

Step 2: **Start Wireshark and select the appropriate interface.**

a. Click the Windows **Start** button and on the pop-up menu, double-click **Wireshark**.

b. After Wireshark starts, click **Interface List**.

c. In the **Wireshark: Capture Interfaces** window, click the check the box next to the interface connected to your LAN.

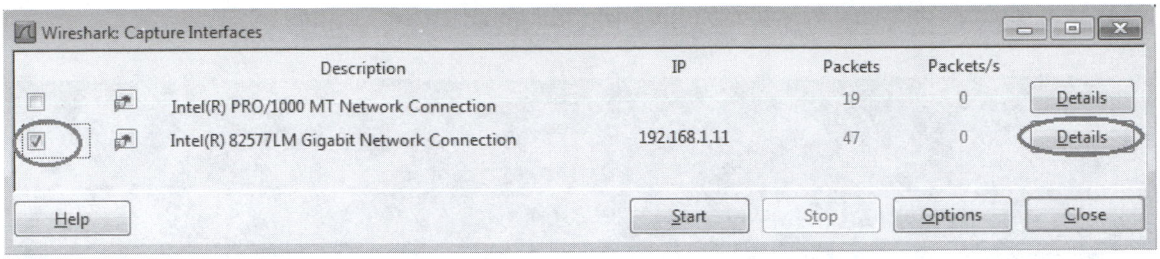

Note: If multiple interfaces are listed and you are unsure which interface to check, click **Details**. Click the **802.3 (Ethernet)** tab, and verify that the MAC address matches what you wrote down in Step 1b. Close the Interface Details window after verification.

Part 2:   Capture, Locate, and Examine Packets

Step 1:   Click the Start button to start the data capture.

a. Go to www.google.com. Minimize the Google window, and return to Wireshark. Stop the data capture. You should see captured traffic similar to that shown below in step b.

Note: Your instructor may provide you with a different website. If so, enter the website name or address here:

_____

b. The capture window is now active. Locate the **Source**, **Destination**, and **Protocol** columns.

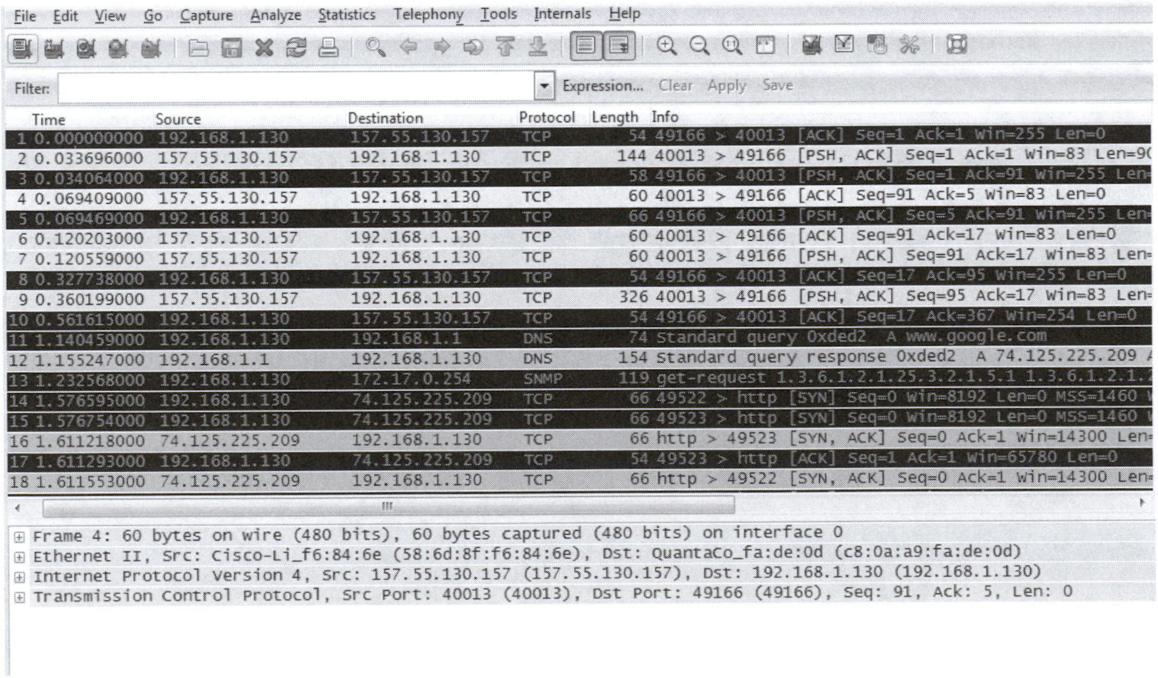

Step 2:   Locate appropriate packets for the web session.

If the computer was recently started and there has been no activity in accessing the Internet, you can see the entire process in the captured output, including the Address Resolution Protocol (ARP), Domain Name System (DNS), and the TCP three-way handshake. The capture screen in Part 2, Step 1 shows all the packets the computer must get to www.google.com. In this case, the PC already had an ARP entry for the default gateway; therefore, it started with the DNS query to resolve www.google.com.

a. Frame 11 shows the DNS query from the PC to the DNS server, attempting to resolve the domain name, www.google.com to the IP address of the web server. The PC must have the IP address before it can send the first packet to the web server.

What is the IP address of the DNS server that the computer queried? _____

b. Frame 12 is the response from the DNS server with the IP address of www.google.com.

c. Find the appropriate packet for the start of your three-way handshake. In this example, frame 15 is the start of the TCP three-way handshake.

What is the IP address of the Google web server? _____

d. If you have many packets that are unrelated to the TCP connection, it may be necessary to use the Wireshark filter capability. Enter **tcp** in the filter entry area within Wireshark and press Enter.

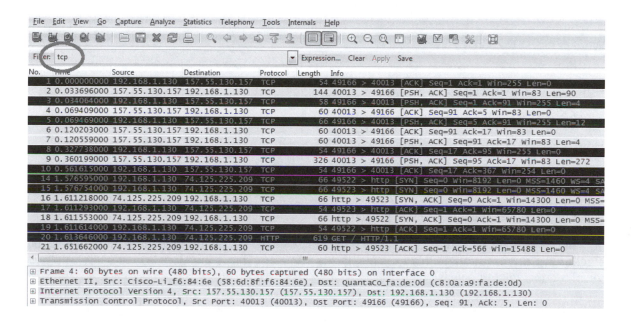

Step 3:   **Examine information within packets including IP addresses, TCP port numbers, and TCP control flags.**

a. In our example, frame 15 is the start of the three-way handshake between the PC and the Google web server. In the packet list pane (top section of the main window), select the frame. This highlights the line and displays the decoded information from that packet in the two lower panes. Examine the TCP information in the packet details pane (middle section of the main window).

b. Click the **+** icon to the left of the Transmission Control Protocol in the packet details pane to expand the view of the TCP information.

c. Click the **+** icon to the left of the Flags. Look at the source and destination ports and the flags that are set.

Note: You may have to adjust the top and middle windows sizes within Wireshark to display the necessary information.

What is the TCP source port number? _____

How would you classify the source port? _____

What is the TCP destination port number? _____

How would you classify the destination port? _____

Which flag (or flags) is set? _____

What is the relative sequence number set to? _____

d.   To select the next frame in the three-way handshake, select **Go** on the Wireshark menu and select **Next Packet In Conversation**. In this example, this is frame 16. This is the Google web server reply to the initial request to start a session.

What are the values of the source and destination ports? _____

Which flags are set? _____

What are the relative sequence and acknowledgement numbers set to?

_____

e. Finally, examine the third packet of the three-way handshake in the example. Clicking frame 17 in the top window displays the following information in this example:

Examine the third and final packet of the handshake.

Which flag (or flags) is set? _____

The relative sequence and acknowledgement numbers are set to 1 as a starting point. The TCP connection is now established, and communication between the source computer and the web server can begin.

f. Close the Wireshark program.

Reflection

1. There are hundreds of filters available in Wireshark. A large network could have numerous filters and many different types of traffic. Which three filters in the list might be the most useful to a network administrator?

_____

2. What other ways could Wireshark be used in a production network?

_____

5.2.3.5 Lab — Using Wireshark to Examine a UDP DNS Capture

Topology

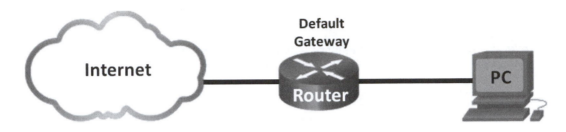

Objectives

Part 1: Record a PC's IP Configuration Information

Part 2: Use Wireshark to Capture DNS Queries and Responses

Part 3: Analyze Captured DNS or UDP Packets

Background / Scenario

If you have ever used the Internet, you have used the Domain Name System (DNS). DNS is a distributed network of servers that translates user-friendly domain names like www.google.com to an IP address. When you type a website URL into your browser, your PC performs a DNS query to the DNS server's IP address. Your PC's DNS server query and the DNS server's response make use of the User Datagram Protocol (UDP) as the transport layer protocol. UDP is connectionless and does not require a session setup as does TCP. DNS queries and responses are very small and do not require the overhead of TCP.

In this lab, you will communicate with a DNS server by sending a DNS query using the UDP transport protocol. You will use Wireshark to examine the DNS query and response exchanges with the name server.

Note: This lab cannot be completed using Netlab. This lab assumes that you have Internet access.

Required Resources

1 PC (Windows 7, Vista, or XP with a command prompt access, Internet access, and Wireshark installed)

Part 1: Record a PC's IP Configuration Information

In Part 1, you will use the **ipconfig /all** command on your local PC to find and record the MAC and IP addresses of your PC's network interface card (NIC), the IP address of the specified default gateway, and the DNS server IP address specified for the PC. Record this information in the table provided. The information will be used in the following parts of this lab with packet analysis.

IP address	
MAC address	
Default gateway IP address	
DNS server IP address	

Part 2: Use Wireshark to Capture DNS Queries and Responses

In Part 2, you will set up Wireshark to capture DNS query and response packets to demonstrate the use of UDP transport protocol while communicating with a DNS server.

a. Click the Windows **Start** button and navigate to the Wireshark program.

   Note: If Wireshark is not yet installed, it can be downloaded at http://www.wireshark.org/download.html.

b. Select an interface for Wireshark for capturing packets. Use the **Interface List** to choose the interface that is associated with the recorded PC's IP and Media Access Control (MAC) addresses in Part 1.

c. After selecting the desired interface, click **Start** to capture the packets.

d. Open a web browser and type **www.google.com**. Press Enter to continue.

e. Click **Stop** to stop the Wireshark capture when you see Google's home page.

Part 3: Analyze Captured DNS or UDP Packets

In Part 3, you will examine the UDP packets that were generated when communicating with a DNS server for the IP addresses for www.google.com.

Step 1: Filter DNS packets.

a. In the Wireshark main window, type **dns** in the entry area of the **Filter** toolbar. Click **Apply** or press Enter.

   Note: If you do not see any results after the DNS filter was applied, close the web browser and in the command prompt window, type **ipconfig /flushdns** to remove all previous DNS results. Restart the Wireshark capture and repeat the instructions in Part 2b –2e. If this does not resolve the issue, in the command prompt window, you can type **nslookup www.google.com** as an alternative to the web browser.

b. In the packet list pane (top section) of the main window, locate the packet that includes "standard query" and "A www.google.com". See frame 4 as an example.

Step 2:   Examine UDP segment using DNS query.

Examine UDP by using a DNS query for www.google.com as captured by Wireshark. In this example, Wireshark capture frame 4 in the packet list pane is selected for analysis. The protocols in this query are displayed in the packet details pane (middle section) of the main window. The protocol entries are highlighted in gray.

a. In the packet details pane, frame 4 had 74 bytes of data on the wire as displayed on the first line. This is the number of bytes to send a DNS query to a name server requesting the IP addresses of www.google. com.

b. The Ethernet II line displays the source and destination MAC addresses. The source MAC address is from your local PC because your local PC originated the DNS query. The destination MAC address is from the default gateway, because this is the last stop before this query exits the local network.

Is the source MAC address the same as recorded from Part 1 for the local PC? _____

c.   In the Internet Protocol Version 4 line, the IP packet Wireshark capture indicates that the source IP address of this DNS query is 192.168.1.11, and the destination IP address is 192.168.1.1. In this example, the destination address is the default gateway. The router is the default gateway in this network.

Can you pair up the IP and MAC addresses for the source and destination devices?

Device	IP Address	MAC Address
Local PC		
Default Gateway		

The IP packet and header encapsulates the UDP segment. The UDP segment contains the DNS query as the data.

d.   A UDP header only has four fields: source port, destination port, length, and checksum. Each field in UDP header is only 16 bits as depicted below.

UDP SEGMENT

0	16	31
UDP SOURCE PORT		UDP DESTINATION PORT
UDP MESSAGE LENGTH		UDP CHECKSUM
DATA		
DATA ...		

Expand the User Datagram Protocol in the packet details pane by clicking the plus (+) sign. Notice that there are only four fields. The source port number in this example is 52110. The source port was randomly generated by the local PC using port numbers that are not reserved. The destination port is 53. Port 53 is a well-known port reserved for use with DNS. DNS servers listen on port 53 for DNS queries from clients.

```
⊟ User Datagram Protocol, Src Port: 52110 (52110), Dst Port: domain (53)
     Source port: 52110 (52110)
     Destination port: domain (53)
     Length: 40
  ⊟ Checksum: 0xe25f [validation disabled]
       [Good Checksum: False]
       [Bad Checksum: False]
```

In this example, the length of this UDP segment is 40 bytes. Out of 40 bytes, 8 bytes are used as header. The other 32 bytes are used by DNS query data. The 32 bytes of DNS query data is highlighted in the following illustration in the packet bytes pane (lower section) of the Wireshark main window.

```
⊟ Domain Name System (query)
     [Response In: 5]
     Transaction ID: 0x3f76
  ⊞ Flags: 0x0100 Standard query
     Questions: 1
     Answer RRs: 0
     Authority RRs: 0
     Additional RRs: 0
  ⊟ Queries
     ⊟ www.google.com: type A, class IN
          Name: www.google.com
          Type: A (Host address)
          Class: IN (0x0001)
```

```
0000   30 46 9a 99 c5 72 90 4c   e5 be 15 63 08 00 45 00    0F...r.L ...C..E.
0010   00 3c 40 9f 00 00 80 11   76 b5 c0 a8 01 0b c0 a8    .<@..... v.......
0020   01 01 cb 8e 00 35 00 28   e2 5f 3f 76 01 00 00 01    .....5.( ._?v....
0030   00 00 00 00 00 00 03 77   77 77 06 67 6f 6f 67 6c    .......w ww.googl
0040   65 03 63 6f 6d 00 00 01   00 01                      e.com.....
```

The checksum is used to determine the integrity of the packet after it has traversed the Internet.

The UDP header has low overhead because UDP does not have fields that are associated with three-way handshake in TCP. Any data transfer reliability issues that occur must be handled by the application layer.

Record your Wireshark results in the table below:

Frame Size	
Source MAC address	
Destination MAC address	
Source IP address	
Destination IP address	
Source Port	
Destination Port	

Is the source IP address the same as the local PC's IP address recorded in Part 1? _____

Is the destination IP address the same as the default gateway noted in Part 1? _____

Step 3:   Examine UDP using DNS response.

In this step, you will examine the DNS response packet and verify that DNS response packet also uses UDP.

a.   In this example, frame 5 is the corresponding DNS response packet. Notice the number of bytes on the wire is 290 bytes. It is a larger packet as compared to the DNS query packet.

```
Filter: dns                                          ▼  Expression... Clear Apply Save

No.      Time           Source          Destination     Protocol  Length  Info
       4 1.613556000 192.168.1.11    192.168.1.1      DNS        74 Standard query 0x3f76  A www.google.com
       5 1.624376000 192.168.1.1     192.168.1.11     DNS       290 Standard query response 0x3f76  A 74.125
      47 2.180985000 192.168.1.11    192.168.1.1      DNS        75 Standard query 0x6bdc  A plus.google.com
      48 2.181866000 192.168.1.11    192.168.1.1      DNS        75 Standard query 0x318f  A maps.google.com
      49 2.182440000 192.168.1.11    192.168.1.1      DNS        75 Standard query 0x5d4f  A play.google.com

⊞ Frame 5: 290 bytes on wire (2320 bits), 290 bytes captured (2320 bits) on interface 0
⊞ Ethernet II, Src: Netgear_99:c5:72 (30:46:9a:99:c5:72), Dst: HonHaiPr_be:15:63 (90:4c:e5:be:15:63)
⊞ Internet Protocol Version 4, Src: 192.168.1.1 (192.168.1.1), Dst: 192.168.1.11 (192.168.1.11)
⊟ User Datagram Protocol, Src Port: domain (53), Dst Port: 52110 (52110)
     Source port: domain (53)
     Destination port: 52110 (52110)
     Length: 256
   ⊟ Checksum: 0xc4ca [validation disabled]
       [Good Checksum: False]
       [Bad Checksum: False]
⊞ Domain Name System (response)
```

b.   In the Ethernet II frame for the DNS response, from what device is the source MAC address and what device is the destination MAC address?

c.   Notice the source and destination IP addresses in the IP packet. What is the destination IP address? What is the source IP address?

Destination IP address: _____ Source IP address: _____

What happened to the roles of source and destination for the local host and default gateway?

d. In the UDP segment, the role of the port numbers has also reversed. The destination port number is 52110. Port number 52110 is the same port that was generated by the local PC when the DNS query was sent to the DNS server. Your local PC listens for a DNS response on this port.

The source port number is 53. The DNS server listens for a DNS query on port 53 and then sends a DNS response with a source port number of 53 back to originator of the DNS query.

When the DNS response is expanded, notice the resolved IP addresses for www.google.com in the **Answers** section.

```
⊟ User Datagram Protocol, Src Port: domain (53), Dst Port: 52110 (52110)
     Source port: domain (53)
     Destination port: 52110 (52110)
     Length: 256
  ⊟ Checksum: 0xc4ca [validation disabled]
       [Good Checksum: False]
       [Bad Checksum: False]
■ Domain Name System (response)
     [Request In: 4]
     [Time: 0.010820000 seconds]
     Transaction ID: 0x3f76
  ⊞ Flags: 0x8180 Standard query response, No error
     Questions: 1
     Answer RRs: 5
     Authority RRs: 4
     Additional RRs: 4
  ⊞ Queries
  ⊟ Answers
     ⊞ www.google.com: type A, class IN, addr 74.125.227.84
     ⊞ www.google.com: type A, class IN, addr 74.125.227.80
     ⊞ www.google.com: type A, class IN, addr 74.125.227.81
     ⊞ www.google.com: type A, class IN, addr 74.125.227.82
     ⊞ www.google.com: type A, class IN, addr 74.125.227.83
  ⊟ Authoritative nameservers
     ⊞ google.com: type NS, class IN, ns ns1.google.com
     ⊞ google.com: type NS, class IN, ns ns2.google.com
     ⊞ google.com: type NS, class IN, ns ns3.google.com
     ⊞ google.com: type NS, class IN, ns ns4.google.com
  ⊟ Additional records
     ⊞ ns1.google.com: type A, class IN, addr 216.239.32.10
     ⊞ ns2.google.com: type A, class IN, addr 216.239.34.10
     ⊞ ns3.google.com: type A, class IN, addr 216.239.36.10
     ⊞ ns4.google.com: type A, class IN, addr 216.239.38.10
```

Reflection

What are the benefits of using UDP instead of TCP as a transport protocol for DNS?

5.2.4.3 Lab — Using Wireshark to Examine FTP and TFTP Captures

Topology – Part 1 (FTP)

Part 1 will highlight a TCP capture of an FTP session. This topology consists of a PC with Internet access.

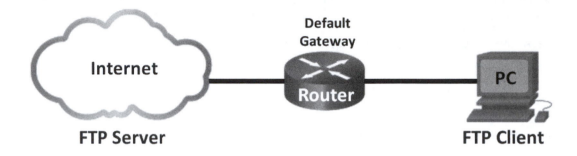

Topology – Part 2 (TFTP)

Part 2 will highlight a UDP capture of a TFTP session. The PC must have both an Ethernet connection and a console connection to Switch S1.

Addressing Table (Part 2)

Device	Interface	IP Address	Subnet Mask	Default Gateway
S1	VLAN 1	192.168.1.1	255.255.255.0	N/A
PC-A	NIC	192.168.1.3	255.255.255.0	192.168.1.1

Objectives

Part 1: Identify TCP Header Fields and Operation Using a Wireshark FTP Session Capture

Part 2: Identify UDP Header Fields and Operation Using a Wireshark TFTP Session Capture

Background / Scenario

The two protocols in the TCP/IP transport layer are the TCP, defined in RFC 761, and UDP, defined in RFC 768. Both protocols support upper-layer protocol communication. For example, TCP is used to provide transport layer support for the HyperText Transfer Protocol (HTTP) and FTP protocols, among others. UDP provides transport layer support for the Domain Name System (DNS) and TFTP among others.

Note: Understanding the parts of the TCP and UDP headers and operation are a critical skill for network engineers.

In Part 1 of this lab, you will use Wireshark open source tool to capture and analyze TCP protocol header fields for FTP file transfers between the host computer and an anonymous FTP server. The Windows command line utility is used to connect to an anonymous FTP server and download a file. In Part 2 of this lab, you will use Wireshark to capture and analyze UDP protocol header fields for TFTP file transfers between the host computer and Switch S1.

Note: The switch used is a Cisco Catalyst 2960s with Cisco IOS Release 15.0(2) (lanbasek9 image). Other switches and Cisco IOS versions can be used. Depending on the model and Cisco IOS version, the available commands and output produced might vary from what displays in the labs.

Note: Make sure that the switch has been erased and has no startup configurations. If you are unsure, contact your instructor.

Note: Part 1 assumes the PC has Internet access and cannot be performed using Netlab. Part 2 is Netlab compatible.

Required Resources – Part 1 (FTP)

1 PC (Windows 7, Vista, or XP with command prompt access, Internet access, and Wireshark installed)

Required Resources – Part 2 (TFTP)

- 1 Switch (Cisco 2960 with Cisco IOS Release 15.0(2) lanbasek9 image or comparable)
- 1 PC (Windows 7, Vista, or XP with Wireshark and a TFTP server, such as tftpd32 installed)
- Console cable to configure the Cisco IOS devices via the console port
- Ethernet cable as shown in the topology

Part 1: Identify TCP Header Fields and Operation Using a Wireshark FTP Session Capture

In Part 1, you use Wireshark to capture an FTP session and inspect TCP header fields.

Step 1: Start a Wireshark capture.

a. Close all unnecessary network traffic, such as the web browser, to limit the amount traffic during the Wireshark capture.

b. Start the Wireshark capture.

Step 2: Download the Readme file.

a. From the command prompt, enter **ftp ftp.cdc.gov**.

b. Log into the FTP site for Centers for Disease Control and Prevention (CDC) with user **anonymous** and no password.

c. Locate and download the Readme file.

```
C:\Users\user1>ftp ftp.cdc.gov
Connected to ftp.cdc.gov.
220 Microsoft FTP Service
User (ftp.cdc.gov:(none)): anonymous
331 Anonymous access allowed, send identity (e-mail name) as password.
Password:
230 Anonymous user logged in.
ftp> ls
200 PORT command successful.
150 Opening ASCII mode data connection for file list.
aspnet_client
pub
Readme
Siteinfo
up.htm
w3c
web.config
welcome.msg
226 Transfer complete.
ftp: 76 bytes received in 0.00Seconds 19.00Kbytes/sec.
ftp> get Readme
200 PORT command successful.
150 Opening ASCII mode data connection for Readme(1428 bytes).
226 Transfer complete.
ftp: 1428 bytes received in 0.01Seconds 204.00Kbytes/sec.
ftp> quit
221
```

Step 3:   **Stop the Wireshark capture.**

Step 4:   **View the Wireshark Main Window.**

Wireshark captured many packets during the FTP session to ftp.cdc.gov. To limit the amount of data for analysis, type **tcp and ip.addr == 198.246.112.54** in the **Filter: entry** area and click **Apply**. The IP address, 198.246.112.54, is the address for ftp.cdc.gov.

Step 5: **Analyze the TCP fields.**

After the TCP filter has been applied, the first three frames in the packet list pane (top section) displays the transport layer protocol TCP creating a reliable session. The sequence of [SYN], [SYN, ACK], and [ACK] illustrates the three-way handshake.

```
5 1.136716000  192.168.1.17    198.246.112.54    TCP      66 49243 > ftp [SYN] Seq=0 Win=8192 L
7 1.226502000  198.246.112.54  192.168.1.17      TCP      66 ftp > 49243 [SYN, ACK] Seq=0 Ack=1
8 1.226627000  192.168.1.17    198.246.112.54    TCP      54 49243 > ftp [ACK] Seq=1 Ack=1 Win=8
```

TCP is routinely used during a session to control datagram delivery, verify datagram arrival, and manage window size. For each data exchange between the FTP client and FTP server, a new TCP session is started. At the conclusion of the data transfer, the TCP session is closed. Finally, when the FTP session is finished, TCP performs an orderly shutdown and termination.

In Wireshark, detailed TCP information is available in the packet details pane (middle section). Highlight the first TCP datagram from the host computer, and expand the TCP record. The expanded TCP datagram appears similar to the packet detail pane shown below.

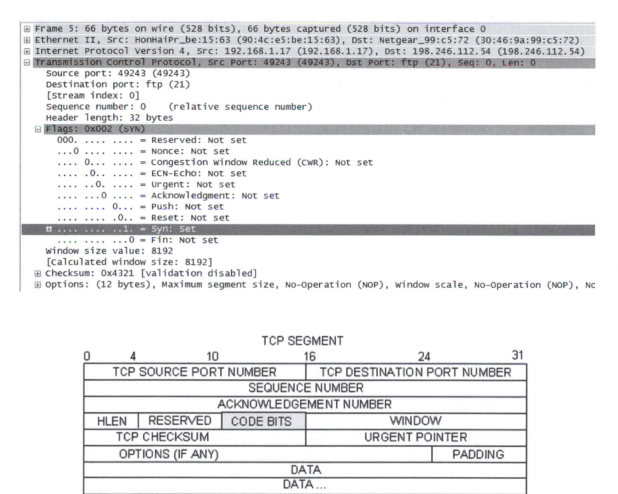

```
⊞ Frame 5: 66 bytes on wire (528 bits), 66 bytes captured (528 bits) on interface 0
⊞ Ethernet II, Src: HonHaiPr_be:15:63 (90:4c:e5:be:15:63), Dst: Netgear_99:c5:72 (30:46:9a:99:c5:72)
⊞ Internet Protocol Version 4, Src: 192.168.1.17 (192.168.1.17), Dst: 198.246.112.54 (198.246.112.54)
⊟ Transmission Control Protocol, Src Port: 49243 (49243), Dst Port: ftp (21), Seq: 0, Len: 0
    Source port: 49243 (49243)
    Destination port: ftp (21)
    [Stream index: 0]
    Sequence number: 0     (relative sequence number)
    Header length: 32 bytes
  ⊟ Flags: 0x002 (SYN)
      000. .... .... = Reserved: Not set
      ...0 .... .... = Nonce: Not set
      .... 0... .... = Congestion window Reduced (CWR): Not set
      .... .0.. .... = ECN-Echo: Not set
      .... ..0. .... = Urgent: Not set
      .... ...0 .... = Acknowledgment: Not set
      .... .... 0... = Push: Not set
      .... .... .0.. = Reset: Not set
      ⊞ .... .... ..1. = Syn: Set
      .... .... ...0 = Fin: Not set
    Window size value: 8192
    [Calculated window size: 8192]
  ⊞ Checksum: 0x4321 [validation disabled]
  ⊞ Options: (12 bytes), Maximum segment size, No-Operation (NOP), Window scale, No-Operation (NOP), No
```

TCP SEGMENT

0 4 10	16 24 31
TCP SOURCE PORT NUMBER	TCP DESTINATION PORT NUMBER
SEQUENCE NUMBER	
ACKNOWLEDGEMENT NUMBER	
HLEN / RESERVED / CODE BITS	WINDOW
TCP CHECKSUM	URGENT POINTER
OPTIONS (IF ANY)	PADDING
DATA	
DATA ...	

CODE BITS: URG ACK RST PSH SYN FIN

The image above is a TCP datagram diagram. An explanation of each field is provided for reference:

- The **TCP source port number** belongs to the TCP session host that opened a connection. The value is normally a random value above 1,023.

- The **TCP destination port number** is used to identify the upper layer protocol or application on the remote site. The values in the range 0–1,023 represent the "well-known ports" and are associated with popular services and applications (as described in RFC 1700, such as Telnet, FTP, HTTP, and so on). The combination of the source IP address, source port, destination IP address, and destination port uniquely identifies the session to both sender and receiver.

Note: In the Wireshark capture below, the destination port is 21, which is FTP. FTP servers listen on port 21 for FTP client connections.

- The **Sequence number** specifies the number of the last octet in a segment.

- The **Acknowledgment number** specifies the next octet expected by the receiver.

- The **Code bits** have a special meaning in session management and in the treatment of segments. Among interesting values are:

  - ACK — Acknowledgement of a segment receipt.

  - SYN — Synchronize, only set when a new TCP session is negotiated during the TCP three-way handshake.

  - FIN — Finish, request to close the TCP session.

- The **Window size** is the value of the sliding window; determines how many octets can be sent before waiting for an acknowledgement.

- The **Urgent pointer** is only used with an Urgent (URG) flag when the sender needs to send urgent data to the receiver.

- The **Options** has only one option currently, and it is defined as the maximum TCP segment size (optional value).

Using the Wireshark capture of the first TCP session startup (SYN bit set to 1), fill in information about the TCP header:

From the PC to CDC server (only the SYN bit is set to 1):

Source IP Address:	
Destination IP Address:	
Source port number:	
Destination port number:	
Sequence number:	
Acknowledgement number:	
Header length:	
Window size:	

In the second Wireshark filtered capture, the CDC FTP server acknowledges the request from the PC. Note the values of the SYN and ACK bits.

```
⊞ Frame 7: 66 bytes on wire (528 bits), 66 bytes captured (528 bits) on interface 0
⊞ Ethernet II, Src: Netgear_99:c5:72 (30:46:9a:99:c5:72), Dst: HonHaiPr_be:15:63 (90:4c:e5:be:15:63)
⊞ Internet Protocol Version 4, Src: 198.246.112.54 (198.246.112.54), Dst: 192.168.1.17 (192.168.1.17)
⊟ Transmission Control Protocol, Src Port: ftp (21), Dst Port: 49243 (49243), Seq: 0, Ack: 1, Len: 0
    Source port: ftp (21)
    Destination port: 49243 (49243)
    [Stream index: 0]
    Sequence number: 0    (relative sequence number)
    Acknowledgment number: 1    (relative ack number)
    Header length: 32 bytes
  ⊟ Flags: 0x012 (SYN, ACK)
      000. .... .... = Reserved: Not set
      ...0 .... .... = Nonce: Not set
      .... 0... .... = Congestion Window Reduced (CWR): Not set
      .... .0.. .... = ECN-Echo: Not set
      .... ..0. .... = Urgent: Not set
      .... ...1 .... = Acknowledgment: Set
      .... .... 0... = Push: Not set
      .... .... .0.. = Reset: Not set
    ⊞ .... .... ..1. = Syn: Set
      .... .... ...0 = Fin: Not set
    Window size value: 64240
    [Calculated window size: 64240]
  ⊞ Checksum: 0x05bb [validation disabled]
  ⊞ Options: (12 bytes), Maximum segment size, No-Operation (NOP), Window scale, No-Operation (NOP), N
  ⊞ [SEQ/ACK analysis]
```

Fill in the following information regarding the SYN-ACK message.

Source IP address:	
Destination IP address:	
Source port number:	
Destination port number:	
Sequence number:	
Acknowledgement number:	
Header length:	
Window size:	

In the final stage of the negotiation to establish communications, the PC sends an acknowledgement message to the server. Notice only the ACK bit is set to 1, and the Sequence number has been incremented to 1.

```
⊞ Frame 8: 54 bytes on wire (432 bits), 54 bytes captured (432 bits) on interface 0
⊞ Ethernet II, Src: HonHaiPr_be:15:63 (90:4c:e5:be:15:63), Dst: Netgear_99:c5:72 (30:46:9a:99:c5:72)
⊞ Internet Protocol Version 4, Src: 192.168.1.17 (192.168.1.17), Dst: 198.246.112.54 (198.246.112.54)
⊟ Transmission Control Protocol, Src Port: 49243 (49243), Dst Port: ftp (21), Seq: 1, Ack: 1, Len: 0
      Source port: 49243 (49243)
      Destination port: ftp (21)
      [Stream index: 0]
      Sequence number: 1    (relative sequence number)
      Acknowledgment number: 1    (relative ack number)
      Header length: 20 bytes
   ⊟ Flags: 0x010 (ACK)
      000. .... .... = Reserved: Not set
      ...0 .... .... = Nonce: Not set
      .... 0... .... = Congestion Window Reduced (CWR): Not set
      .... .0.. .... = ECN-Echo: Not set
      .... ..0. .... = Urgent: Not set
      .... ...1 .... = Acknowledgment: Set
      .... .... 0... = Push: Not set
      .... .... .0.. = Reset: Not set
      .... .... ..0. = Syn: Not set
      .... .... ...0 = Fin: Not set
      Window size value: 8192
      [Calculated window size: 8192]
      [Window size scaling factor: 1]
   ⊞ Checksum: 0x2127 [validation disabled]
   ⊞ [SEQ/ACK analysis]
```

Fill in the following information regarding the ACK message.

Source IP address:	
Destination IP address:	
Source port number:	
Destination port number:	
Sequence number:	
Acknowledgement number:	
Header length:	
Window size:	

How many other TCP datagrams contained a SYN bit?

_____

After a TCP session is established, FTP traffic can occur between the PC and FTP server. The FTP client and server communicate between each other, unaware that TCP has control and management over the session. When the FTP server sends a Response: 220 to the FTP client, the TCP session on the FTP client sends an acknowledgment to the TCP session on the server. This sequence is visible in the Wireshark capture below.

```
   9 1.314568000  198.246.112.54   192.168.1.17      FTP       81 Response: 220 Microsoft FTP Service
  10 1.523372000  192.168.1.17     198.246.112.54    TCP       54 49243 > ftp [ACK] Seq=1 Ack=28 win=
  12 4.585185000  192.168.1.17     198.246.112.54    FTP       70 Request: USER anonymous
  13 4.675040000  198.246.112.54   192.168.1.17      FTP       126 Response: 331 Anonymous access allo
```

```
⊞ Frame 9: 81 bytes on wire (648 bits), 81 bytes captured (648 bits) on interface 0
⊞ Ethernet II, Src: Netgear_99:c5:72 (30:46:9a:99:c5:72), Dst: HonHaiPr_be:15:63 (90:4c:e5:be:15:63)
⊞ Internet Protocol Version 4, Src: 198.246.112.54 (198.246.112.54), Dst: 192.168.1.17 (192.168.1.17)
⊞ Transmission Control Protocol, Src Port: ftp (21), Dst Port: 49243 (49243), Seq: 1, Ack: 1, Len: 27
⊟ File Transfer Protocol (FTP)
    ⊟ 220 Microsoft FTP Service\r\n
        Response code: Service ready for new user (220)
        Response arg: Microsoft FTP Service
```

When the FTP session has finished, the FTP client sends a command to "quit". The FTP server acknowledges the FTP termination with a Response: 221 Goodbye. At this time, the FTP server TCP session sends a TCP datagram to the FTP client, announcing the termination of the TCP session. The FTP client TCP session acknowledges receipt of the termination datagram, then sends its own TCP session termination. When the originator of the TCP termination, FTP server, receives a duplicate termination, an ACK datagram is sent to acknowledge the termination and the TCP session is closed. This sequence is visible in the diagram and capture below.

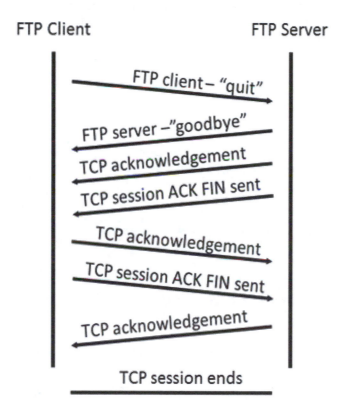

By applying an **ftp** filter, the entire sequence of the FTP traffic can be examined in Wireshark. Notice the sequence of the events during this FTP session. The username anonymous was used to retrieve the Readme file. After the file transfer completed, the user ended the FTP session.

Filter:	ftp			▼ Expression... Clear Apply Save	

No.	Time	Source	Destination	Protocol	Length	Info
9	1.314568000	198.246.112.54	192.168.1.17	FTP	81	Response: 220 Microsoft FTP Service
12	4.585185000	192.168.1.17	198.246.112.54	FTP	70	Request: USER anonymous
13	4.675040000	198.246.112.54	192.168.1.17	FTP	126	Response: 331 Anonymous access allowe
19	5.961514000	192.168.1.17	198.246.112.54	FTP	61	Request: PASS
20	6.048929000	198.246.112.54	192.168.1.17	FTP	85	Response: 230 Anonymous user logged i
25	8.855225000	192.168.1.17	198.246.112.54	FTP	80	Request: PORT 192,168,1,17,192,92
26	8.945530000	198.246.112.54	192.168.1.17	FTP	84	Response: 200 PORT command successful
27	8.955549000	192.168.1.17	198.246.112.54	FTP	60	Request: NLST
29	9.053034000	198.246.112.54	192.168.1.17	FTP	109	Response: 150 Opening ASCII mode data
39	9.347432000	198.246.112.54	192.168.1.17	FTP	78	Response: 226 Transfer complete.
42	12.621720000	192.168.1.17	198.246.112.54	FTP	80	Request: PORT 192,168,1,17,192,93
43	12.709658000	198.246.112.54	192.168.1.17	FTP	84	Response: 200 PORT command successful
44	12.722592000	192.168.1.17	198.246.112.54	FTP	67	Request: RETR Readme
45	12.811097000	198.246.112.54	192.168.1.17	FTP	118	Response: 150 Opening ASCII mode data
58	13.107294000	198.246.112.54	192.168.1.17	FTP	78	Response: 226 Transfer complete.
61	15.514815000	192.168.1.17	198.246.112.54	FTP	60	Request: QUIT
62	15.601920000	198.246.112.54	192.168.1.17	FTP	61	Response: 221

Apply the TCP filter again in Wireshark to examine the termination of the TCP session. Four packets are transmitted for the termination of the TCP session. Because TCP connection is full-duplex, each direction must terminate independently. Examine the source and destination addresses.

In this example, the FTP server has no more data to send in the stream; it sends a segment with the FIN flag set in frame 63. The PC sends an ACK to acknowledge the receipt of the FIN to terminate the session from the server to the client in frame 64.

In frame 65, the PC sends a FIN to the FTP server to terminate the TCP session. The FTP server responds with an ACK to acknowledge the FIN from the PC in frame 67. Now the TCP session terminated between the FTP server and PC.

61	15.514815000	192.168.1.17	198.246.112.54	FTP	60	Request: QUIT
62	15.601920000	198.246.112.54	192.168.1.17	FTP	61	Response: 221
63	15.602245000	198.246.112.54	192.168.1.17	TCP	54	ftp > 49243 [FIN, ACK] Seq=365 Ack=
64	15.602314000	192.168.1.17	198.246.112.54	TCP	54	49243 > ftp [ACK] Seq=101 Ack=366 ᴠ
65	15.605832000	192.168.1.17	198.246.112.54	TCP	54	49243 > ftp [FIN, ACK] Seq=101 Ack=
67	15.696497000	198.246.112.54	192.168.1.17	TCP	54	ftp > 49243 [ACK] Seq=366 Ack=102 ᴠ

⊞ Frame 63: 54 bytes on wire (432 bits), 54 bytes captured (432 bits) on interface 0
⊞ Ethernet II, Src: Netgear_99:c5:72 (30:46:9a:99:c5:72), Dst: HonHaiPr_be:15:63 (90:4c:e5:be:15:63)
⊞ Internet Protocol Version 4, Src: 198.246.112.54 (198.246.112.54), Dst: 192.168.1.17 (192.168.1.17)
⊞ Transmission Control Protocol, Src Port: ftp (21), Dst Port: 49243 (49243), Seq: 365, Ack: 101, Len

Part 2: Identify UDP Header Fields and Operation Using a Wireshark TFTP Session Capture

In Part 2, you use Wireshark to capture a TFTP session and inspect UDP header fields.

Step 1: Set up this physical topology and prepare for TFTP capture.

a. Establish a console and Ethernet connection between PC-A and Switch S1.

b. If not already done, manually configure the IP address on the PC to 192.168.1.3. It is not required to set the default gateway.

Internet Protocol Version 4 (TCP/IPv4) Properties

General

You can get IP settings assigned automatically if your network supports this capability. Otherwise, you need to ask your network administrator for the appropriate IP settings.

○ Obtain an IP address automatically

● Use the following IP address:

IP address: `192 . 168 . 1 . 3`

Subnet mask: `255 . 255 . 255 . 0`

Default gateway: `.  .  .`

○ Obtain DNS server address automatically

● Use the following DNS server addresses:

Preferred DNS server: `.  .  .`

Alternate DNS server: `.  .  .`

☐ Validate settings upon exit   Advanced...

OK   Cancel

c. Configure the switch. Assign an IP address of 192.168.1.1 to VLAN 1. Verify connectivity with the PC by pinging 192.168.1.3. Troubleshoot as necessary.

```
Switch> enable

Switch# conf t

Enter configuration commands, one per line.  End with CNTL/Z.

Switch(config)# host S1

S1(config)# interface vlan 1

S1(config-if)# ip address 192.168.1.1 255.255.255.0

S1(config-if)# no shut

*Mar  1 00:37:50.166: %LINK-3-UPDOWN: Interface Vlan1, changed state to up

*Mar  1 00:37:50.175: %LINEPROTO-5-UPDOWN: Line protocol on Interface Vlan1,
changed state to up

S1(config-if)# end

S1# ping 192.168.1.3

Type escape sequence to abort.
```

```
Sending 5, 100-byte ICMP Echos to 192.168.1.3, timeout is 2 seconds:
!!!!!
Success rate is 100 percent (5/5), round-trip min/avg/max = 1/203/1007 ms
```

Step 2:   **Prepare the TFTP server on the PC.**

a. If it does not already exist, create a folder on the PC desktop called **TFTP**. The files from the switch will be copied to this location.

b. Start **tftpd32** on the PC.

c. Click **Browse** and change the current directory to **C:\Users\user1\Desktop\TFTP** by replacing user1 with your username.

The TFTP server should look like this:

Notice that in Current Directory, it lists the user and the Server (PC-A) interface as the IP address of **192.168.1.3**.

d. Test the ability to copy a file using TFTP from the switch to the PC. Troubleshoot as necessary.

```
S1# copy start tftp
Address or name of remote host []? 192.168.1.3
Destination filename [s1-confg]?
!!
1638 bytes copied in 0.026 secs (63000 bytes/sec)
```

If you see that the file has copied (as in the above output), then you are ready to go on to the next step. If not, then troubleshoot. If you get the %Error opening tftp (Permission denied) error, first check to make sure your firewall is not blocking TFTP, and that you are copying to a location where your username has adequate permission, such as the desktop.

Step 3:   Capture a TFTP session in Wireshark

a. Open Wireshark. From the **Edit** menu, choose **Preferences** and click the (+) sign to expand **Protocols**.
    Scroll down and select **UDP**. Click the **Validate the UDP checksum if possible** check box and click **Apply**. Then click **OK**.

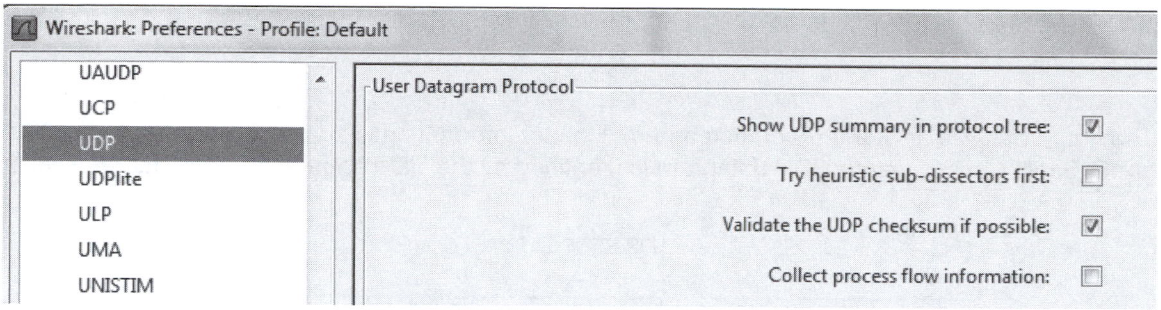

b. Start a Wireshark capture.

c. Run the `copy start tftp` command on the switch.

d. Stop the Wireshark capture.

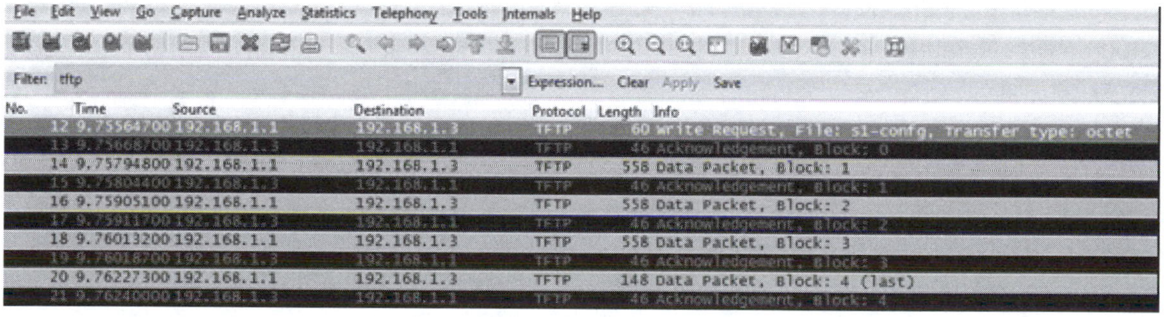

e. Set the filter to **tftp**. Your output should look similar to the output shown above. This TFTP transfer is used
    to analyze transport layer UDP operations.

In Wireshark, detailed UDP information is available in the Wireshark packet details pane. Highlight the
first UDP datagram from the host computer, and move the mouse pointer to the packet details pane. It
may be necessary to adjust the packet details pane and expand the UDP record by clicking the protocol
expand box. The expanded UDP datagram should look similar to the diagram below.

```
                              ⊟ User Datagram Protocol, Src Port: 62513 (62513), Dst Port: tftp (69)
         UDP                       Source port: 62513 (62513)
        Header                     Destination port: tftp (69)
                                   Length: 25
                               ⊞ Checksum: 0x482c [correct]
                              ⊟ Trivial File Transfer Protocol
         UDP                       [DESTINATION File: s1-confg]
         Data                      Opcode: Write Request (2)
                                   DESTINATION File: s1-confg
                                   Type: octet
```

The figure below is a UDP datagram diagram. Header information is sparse, compared to the TCP datagram. Similar to TCP, each UDP datagram is identified by the UDP source port and UDP destination port.

UDP SEGMENT

0	16	31
UDP SOURCE PORT	UDP DESTINATION PORT	
UDP MESSAGE LENGTH	UDP CHECKSUM	
DATA		
DATA ...		

Using the Wireshark capture of the first UDP datagram, fill in information about the UDP header. The checksum value is a hexadecimal (base 16) value, denoted by the preceding 0x code:

Source IP Address:	
Destination IP Address:	
Source Port Number:	
Destination Port Number:	
UDP Message Length:	
UDP Checksum:	

How does UDP verify datagram integrity?

_____

_____

Examine the first frame returned from tftpd server. Fill in the information about the UDP header:

Source IP Address:	
Destination IP Address:	
Source Port Number:	
Destination Port Number:	
UDP Message Length:	
UDP Checksum:	

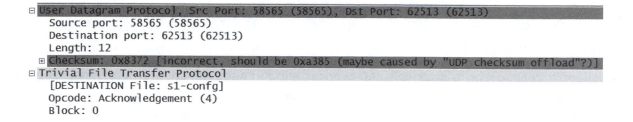

```
⊟ User Datagram Protocol, Src Port: 58565 (58565), Dst Port: 62513 (62513)
    Source port: 58565 (58565)
    Destination port: 62513 (62513)
    Length: 12
  ⊞ Checksum: 0x8372 [incorrect, should be 0xa385 (maybe caused by "UDP checksum offload"?)]
⊟ Trivial File Transfer Protocol
    [DESTINATION File: s1-confg]
    Opcode: Acknowledgement (4)
    Block: 0
```

Notice that the return UDP datagram has a different UDP source port, but this source port is used for the remainder of the TFTP transfer. Because there is no reliable connection, only the original source port used to begin the TFTP session is used to maintain the TFTP transfer.

Also notice that the UDP Checksum is incorrect. This is most likely caused by UDP checksum offload. You can learn more about why this happens by searching for "UDP checksum offload".

Reflection

This lab provided the opportunity to analyze TCP and UDP protocol operations from captured FTP and TFTP sessions. How does TCP manage communication differently than UDP?

_____

_____

Challenge

Because neither FTP nor TFTP are secure protocols, all transferred data is sent in clear text. This includes any user IDs, passwords, or clear-text file contents. Analyzing the upper-layer FTP session will quickly identify the user ID, password, and configuration file passwords. Upper-layer TFTP data examination is a bit more complicated, but the data field can be examined and the configuration user ID and password information extracted.

Cleanup

Unless directed otherwise by your instructor:

Remove the files that were copied to your PC.

Erase the configurations on switch **S1**.

Remove the manual IP address from the PC and restore Internet connectivity.

5.3.1.1 Class Activity — We Need to Talk, Again

Objectives

Explain how transport layer protocols and services support communications across data networks.

In this activity, given a scenario, you will determine whether high-reliability messaging should be used. You will focus on whether the final message is complete, correct, and delivered in a timely manner

Background/Scenario

Note: It is important that the students have completed the Introductory MA for this chapter. This activity works best in medium-sized groups of 6 to 8 students.

Your instructor will whisper a complex message to the first student in a group. An example of the message might be "We are expecting a blizzard tomorrow. It should be arriving in the morning and school will be delayed 2 two hours so bring your homework."

That student whispers the message to the next student in the group. Each group follows this process until all members of each group have heard the whispered message.

Here are the rules to follow:

- You can whisper the message in short parts to your neighbor AND you can repeat the message parts after verifying your neighbor heard the correct message.

- Small parts of the message may be checked and repeated again (clockwise OR counter-clockwise to ensure accuracy of the message parts) by whispering. A student will be assigned to time the entire activity.

- When the message has reached the end of the group, the last student will say aloud what was heard. Small parts of the message may be repeated (i.e., re-sent), and the process can be restarted to ensure that ALL parts of the message are fully delivered and correct.

- Your instructor will repeat the original message to check for quality delivery.

Reflection

1. Would the contents of this message need to be clear and correct when you received them, if you were depending on this message to drive your personal/business calendar, studying schedule, etc.?

   _____

2. Would the length of time taken to deliver the message be an important factor to the sender and recipient?

   _____

3. Compare the Introductory Modeling Activity of this chapter to this activity. What differences do you notice about the delivery of the message?

   _____

Chapter 6 — Network Layer

6.0.1.2 Class Activity — The road less traveled...or is it?

Objectives

Explain how network devices use routing tables to direct packets to a destination network.

In this activity, you will visualize how a hop-by-hop routing paradigm, with correct path selection at each hop, results in a successful delivery of packets. You will recognize that each router on the path must have correct knowledge about the destination network, and that path towards that network, to deliver packets over the shortest path.

Background/Scenario

During the upcoming weekend, you decide to visit a schoolmate who is currently at home sick. You know his street address but you have never been to his town before. Instead of looking up the address on the map, you decide to take it easy and to simply ask town residents for directions after you arrive by train.

The citizens you ask for directions are very helpful. However, they all have an interesting habit. Instead of explaining the entire route to your destination, they all tell you, "Take this road and as soon as you arrive at the nearest crossroad, ask somebody there again." Somewhat bemused at this apparent oddity, you follow these instructions and finally arrive, crossroad by crossroad, and road by road, at your friend's house.

Answer the following questions:

1. Would it have made a significant difference if you were told about the whole route or a larger part of the route instead of just being directed to the nearest crossroad?

2. Would it have been more helpful to ask about the specific street address or just about the street name? What would happen if the person you asked for directions did not know where the destination street was or directed you through an incorrect road?

3. Assuming that on your way back home, you again choose to ask residents for directions. Would it be guaranteed that you would be directed via the same route you took to get to your friend's home? Explain your answer.

4. Is it necessary to explain where you depart from when asking directions to an intended destination?

Reflection

1. Would it have made a significant difference if you were told about the whole route or a larger part of the route instead of just being directed to the nearest crossroad?

2. Would it have been more helpful to ask about the specific street address or just about the street name?

   _____

3. What would happen if the person you asked for directions did not know where the destination street was or directed you through an incorrect road?

   _____

4. Assuming that on your way back home, you again choose to ask residents for directions. Is it guaranteed that you will be directed via the same route you took to get to your friend's home? Explain your answer.

   _____

5. Is it necessary to explain where you depart from when asking directions to an intended destination?

   _____

6.2.2.8 Lab — Viewing Host Routing Tables

Topology

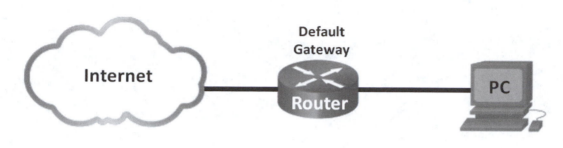

Objectives

Part 1: Access the Host Routing Table

Part 2: Examine IPv4 Host Routing Table Entries

Part 3: Examine IPv6 Host Routing Table Entries

Background / Scenario

To access a resource on a network, your host will determine the route to the destination host using its routing table. The host routing table is similar to that of a router, but is specific to the local host and much less complex. For a packet to reach a local destination, the local host routing table is required. To reach a remote destination, both the local host routing table and the router routing table are required. The **netstat –r** and **route print** commands provide insight into how your local host routes packets to the destination.

In this lab, you will display and examine the information in the host routing table of your PC using the **netstat –r** and **route print** commands. You will determine how packets will be routed by your PC depending on the destination address.

Note: This lab cannot be completed using Netlab. This lab assumes that you have Internet access.

Required Resources

- 1 PC (Windows 7, Vista, or XP with Internet and command prompt access)

Part 1:   Access the Host Routing Table

Step 1:   Record your PC information.

On your PC, open a command prompt window and type the **ipconfig /all** command to display the following information and record it:

IPv4 Address	
MAC Address	
Default Gateway	

Step 2: **Display the routing tables.**

In a command prompt window type the **netstat –r** (or **route print**) command to display the host routing table.

```
C:\Users\user1>netstat -r
===========================================================================
Interface List
 13...90 4c e5 be 15 63 ......Atheros AR9285 802.11b/g/n WiFi Adapter
  1...........................Software Loopback Interface 1
 25...00 00 00 00 00 00 00 e0 Microsoft ISATAP Adapter
 12...00 00 00 00 00 00 00 e0 Microsoft 6to4 Adapter
 26...00 00 00 00 00 00 00 e0 Microsoft ISATAP Adapter #2
 14...00 00 00 00 00 00 00 e0 Teredo Tunneling Pseudo-Interface
===========================================================================

IPv4 Route Table
===========================================================================
Active Routes:
Network Destination        Netmask          Gateway       Interface  Metric
          0.0.0.0          0.0.0.0      192.168.1.1    192.168.1.11     25
        127.0.0.0        255.0.0.0         On-link        127.0.0.1    306
        127.0.0.1  255.255.255.255         On-link        127.0.0.1    306
  127.255.255.255  255.255.255.255         On-link        127.0.0.1    306
      192.168.1.0    255.255.255.0         On-link     192.168.1.11    281
     192.168.1.11  255.255.255.255         On-link     192.168.1.11    281
    192.168.1.255  255.255.255.255         On-link     192.168.1.11    281
        224.0.0.0        240.0.0.0         On-link        127.0.0.1    306
        224.0.0.0        240.0.0.0         On-link     192.168.1.11    281
  255.255.255.255  255.255.255.255         On-link        127.0.0.1    306
  255.255.255.255  255.255.255.255         On-link     192.168.1.11    281
===========================================================================
Persistent Routes:
  None

IPv6 Route Table
===========================================================================
Active Routes:
 If Metric Network Destination      Gateway
 14     58 ::/0                     On-link
  1    306 ::1/128                  On-link
 14     58 2001::/32                On-link
 14    306 2001:0:9d38:6ab8:1863:3bca:3f57:fef4/128
                                    On-link
 14    306 fe80::/64                On-link
 14    306 fe80::1863:3bca:3f57:fef4/128
                                    On-link
  1    306 ff00::/8                 On-link
 14    306 ff00::/8                 On-link
===========================================================================
Persistent Routes:
  None
```

What are the three sections displayed in the output?

_____

Step 3: **Examine the Interface List.**

The first section, Interface List, displays the Media Access Control (MAC) addresses and assigned interface number of every network-capable interface on the host.

```
==============================================================================
Interface List
 13...90 4c e5 be 15 63 ......Atheros AR9285 802.11b/g/n WiFi Adapter
  1...........................Software Loopback Interface 1
 25...00 00 00 00 00 00 00 e0 Microsoft ISATAP Adapter
 12...00 00 00 00 00 00 00 e0 Microsoft 6to4 Adapter
 26...00 00 00 00 00 00 00 e0 Microsoft ISATAP Adapter #2
 14...00 00 00 00 00 00 00 e0 Teredo Tunneling Pseudo-Interface
==============================================================================
```

The first column is the interface number. The second column is the list of MAC addresses associated with the network-capable interfaces on the hosts. These interfaces can include Ethernet, Wi-Fi and Bluetooth adapters. The third column shows the manufacturer and a description of the interface.

In this example, the first line displays the wireless interface that is connected to the local network.

Note: If you have a PC with an Ethernet interface and a Wireless adapter enabled, both interfaces would be listed in the Interface List.

What is the MAC address of the interface connected to your local network? How does the MAC address compare to the recorded MAC address in Step 1?

_____

The second line is loopback interface. The loopback interface is automatically assigned an IP address of 127.0.0.1 when the Transmission Control Protocol/Internet Protocol (TCP/IP) is running on a host.

The last four lines represent transition technology that allows communication in a mixed environment and includes IPv4 and IPv6.

Part 2:   Examine IPv4 Host Routing Table Entries

In Part 2, you will examine the IPv4 host routing table. This table is in the second section as a result of the **netstat –r** output. It lists all the known IPv4 routes, including direct connections, local network, and local default routes.

```
IPv4 Route Table
==============================================================================
Active Routes:
Network Destination        Netmask          Gateway       Interface  Metric
          0.0.0.0          0.0.0.0      192.168.1.1   192.168.1.11      25
        127.0.0.0        255.0.0.0          On-link        127.0.0.1     306
        127.0.0.1  255.255.255.255          On-link        127.0.0.1     306
  127.255.255.255  255.255.255.255          On-link        127.0.0.1     306
      192.168.1.0    255.255.255.0          On-link     192.168.1.11     281
     192.168.1.11  255.255.255.255          On-link     192.168.1.11     281
    192.168.1.255  255.255.255.255          On-link     192.168.1.11     281
        224.0.0.0        240.0.0.0          On-link        127.0.0.1     306
        224.0.0.0        240.0.0.0          On-link     192.168.1.11     281
  255.255.255.255  255.255.255.255          On-link        127.0.0.1     306
  255.255.255.255  255.255.255.255          On-link     192.168.1.11     281
==============================================================================
Persistent Routes:
  None
```

The output is divided in five columns: Network Destination, Netmask, Gateway, Interface, and Metric.

- The Network Destination column lists the reachable network. The Network Destination is used with Netmask to match the destination IP address.

- The Netmask lists the subnet mask that the host uses to determine the network and host portions of the IP address.

- The Gateway column lists the address that the host uses to send the packets to a remote network destination. If a destination is directly connected, the gateway is listed as On-link in the output.

- The Interface column lists the IP address that is configured on the local network adaptor. This is used to forward a packet on the network.

- The Metric column lists the cost of using a route. It is used to calculate the best route to a destination. A preferred route has a lower metric number than other routes listed.

The output displays five different types of active routes:

- The local default route 0.0.0.0 is used when the packet does not match other specified addresses in the routing table. The packet will be sent to the gateway from the PC for further processing. In this example, the packet will be sent to 192.168.1.1 from 192.168.1.11.

- The loopback addresses, 127.0.0.0 – 127.255.255.255, are related to direct connection and provide services to the local host.

- The addresses for the subnet, 192.168.1.0 – 192.168.1.255, are all related to the host and the local network. If the final destination of the packet is in the local network, the packet will exit 192.168.1.11 interface.

    - The local route address 192.168.1.0 represents all devices on the 192.168.1.0/24 network.

    - The address of the local host is 192.168.1.11.

    - The network broadcast address 192.168.1.255 is used to send messages to all the hosts on the local network.

- The special multicast class D addresses 224.0.0.0 are reserved for use through either the loopback interface (127.0.0.1) or the host (192.168.1.11).

- The local broadcast address 255.255.255.255 can be used through either the loopback interface (127.0.0.1) or host (192.168.1.11).

Based on the contents of the IPv4 routing table, if the PC wanted to send a packet to 192.168.1.15, what would it do and where would it send the packet?

_____

_____

_____

_____

If the PC wanted to send a packet to a remote host located at 172.16.20.23, what would it do and where would it send the packet?

_____

_____

_____

_____

_____

Part 3:   Examine IPv6 Host Routing Table Entries

In Part 3, you will examine the IPv6 routing table. This table is in the third section displayed in the **netstat –r** output. It lists all the known IPv6 routes including direct connections, local network and local default routes.

```
IPv6 Route Table
===========================================================================
Active Routes:
 If Metric Network Destination      Gateway
 14     58 ::/0                     On-link
  1    306 ::1/128                  On-link
 14     58 2001::/32                On-link
 14    306 2001:0:9d38:6ab8:1863:3bca:3f57:fef4/128
                                    On-link
 14    306 fe80::/64                On-link
 14    306 fe80::1863:3bca:3f57:fef4/128
                                    On-link
  1    306 ff00::/8                 On-link
 14    306 ff00::/8                 On-link
===========================================================================
Persistent Routes:
  None
```

The output of the IPv6 Route Table differs in column headings and format because the IPv6 addresses are 128 bits versus only 32 bits for IPv4 addresses. The IPv6 Route Table section displays four columns:

- The If column lists the interface numbers of the IPv6-enabled network interfaces from the Interface List section of the **netstat –r** command.

- The Metric column lists the cost of each route to a destination. The lower cost is the preferred route, and the metric is used to select between multiple routes with the same prefix.

- The Network Destination column lists the address prefix for the route.

- The Gateway lists the next-hop IPv6 address to reach the destination. On-link is listed as the next-hop address if it is directly connected to the host.

In this example, the figure displays the IPv6 Route Table section generated by the **netstat –r** command to reveal the following network destinations:

- ::/0: This is the IPv6 equivalent of the local default route. The Gateway column provides the link-local address of the default router.

- ::1/128: This is equivalent to the IPv4 loopback address and provides services to the local host.

- 2001::/32: This is the global unicast network prefix.

- 2001:0:9d38:6ab8:1863:3bca:3f57:fef4/128: This is the global unicast IPv6 address of the local computer.

- fe80::/64: This is the local link network route address and represents all computers on the local-link IPv6 network.

- fe80::1863:3bca:3f57:fef4/128: This is the link-local IPv6 address of the local computer.

- ff00::/8: These are special reserved multicast class D addresses equivalent to the IPv4 224.x.x.x addresses.

The host routing table for IPv6 has similar information as the IPv4 routing table. What is the local default route for IPv4 and what is it for IPv6?

What is the loopback address and subnet mask for IPv4? What is the loopback IP address for IPv6?

_____

How many IPv6 addresses have been assigned to this PC?

_____

How many broadcast addresses does the IPv6 routing table contain?

_____

Reflection

1. How is the number of bits for the network indicated for IPv4. How is it done for IPv6?

    _____

2. Why is there both IPv4 and IPv6 information in the host routing tables?

    _____

6.3.1.9 Lab — Exploring Router Physical Characteristics

Topology

Objectives

Part 1: Examine Router External Characteristics

- Identify the various parts of a Cisco router, including:
  - Management ports
  - LAN interfaces
  - WAN interfaces
  - Module expansion slots
  - Compact Flash memory expansion slots
  - USB ports
- Examine the router activity and status lights.

Part 2: Examine Router Internal Characteristics Using Show Commands

- Establish a console connection to the router using Tera Term.
- Identify router internal characteristics using the **show version** command.
- Identify router interface characteristics using **show interface** commands.

Background / Scenario

In this lab, you will examine the outside of the router to become familiar with its characteristics and components, such as its power switch, management ports, LAN and WAN interfaces, indicator lights, network expansion slots, memory expansion slots, and USB ports.

You will also identify the internal components and characteristics of the IOS by consoling into the router and issuing various commands, such as **show version** and **show interfaces**, from the CLI.

Note: The routers used with CCNA hands-on labs are Cisco 1941 Integrated Services Routers (ISRs) with Cisco IOS Release 15.2(4)M3 (universalk9 image). Other routers and Cisco IOS versions can be used. Depending on the model and Cisco IOS version, the commands available and output produced might vary from what is shown in the labs.

Note: Make sure that the routers have been erased and have no startup configurations. If you are unsure, contact your instructor.

Required Resources

- 1 Router (Cisco 1941 with Cisco IOS Release 15.2(4)M3 universal image or comparable)

- 1 PC (Windows 7, Vista, or XP with terminal emulation program, such as Tera Term)

- Console cables to configure the Cisco IOS devices via the console ports

Part 1:   Examine Router External Characteristics

Use the images below, as well as your own direct inspection of the backplane of a Cisco router, to answer the following questions. Feel free to draw arrows and circle the areas of the image that correctly identify the parts.

Note: The router depicted in the images below is a Cisco 1941 router, which may be different from the make and model of the routers in your particular academy. You can find device information and specifications for the Cisco 1941 series routers at the Cisco.com website. Additional information, including answers to many of the questions below can be found here:

http://www.cisco.com/en/US/prod/collateral/routers/ps10538/data_sheet_c78_556319.html

Step 1:   Identify the various parts of a Cisco router.

The image shown in this step is of the backplane of a Cisco 1941 ISR. Use it to answer the questions in this step. In addition, if you are examining a different model router, a space has been provided here for you to draw the backplane and identify components and interfaces as specified in the questions that follow.

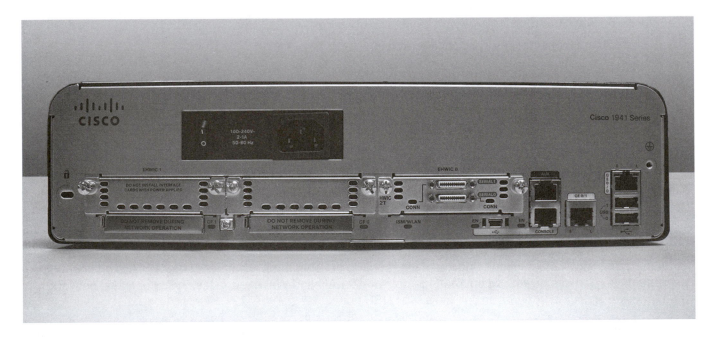

a. Circle and label the router's power switch. Is the power switch on your router in the same area as the router depicted in the image?

_____

b. Circle and label the management ports. What are the built-in management ports? Are the management ports the same on your router? If not, how are they different?

_____

c. Circle and label the router's LAN interfaces. How many LAN interfaces does the router in the image have and what is the interface technology type? Are the LAN interfaces the same on your router? If not, how are they different?

_____

d. Circle and label the router's WAN interfaces. How many WAN interfaces does the router in the image have and what is the interface technology type? Are the WAN interfaces the same on your router? If not, how are they different?

_____

e. The Cisco 1941 ISR is a modular platform and comes with module expansion slots for varied network connectivity requirements. Circle and label the module slots. How many module slots are there? How many are used? What type of module expansion slots are they? Are the module slots the same on your router? If not, how are they different?

_____

f. The Cisco 1941 router comes with CompactFlash memory slots for high speed storage. Circle and label the CompactFlash memory slots. How many memory slots are there? How many are used? How much memory can they hold? Are the memory slots the same on your router? If not, how are they different?

_____

g. The Cisco 1941 router comes with USB 2.0 ports. The built-in USB ports support eToken devices and USB flash memory. The USB eToken device feature provides device authentication and secure configuration of Cisco routers. The USB flash feature provides optional secondary storage capability and an additional boot device. Circle and label the USB ports. How many USB ports are there? Are there USB ports on your router?

h. The Cisco 1941 router also comes with a mini-B USB console port. Circle and label the mini-B USB console port.

Step 2: **Examine the router activity and status lights.**

The following images highlight the activity and status lights of the front panel and backplane of a powered up and connected Cisco 1941 ISR.

Note: Some of the indicator lights are obscured from view in the image of the backplane of the Cisco 1941 router below.

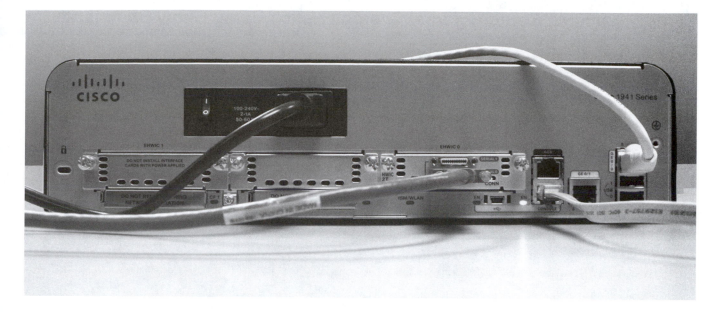

a. In the top image above, examine the indicator lights on the front panel of the router? The lights are labeled SYS, ACT, and POE. What do the labels refer to? What do the lights in the image indicate about the status of the router? These labels would be readable if they were not lit.

_____

_____

_____

b. In the backplane image above, examine the indicator lights on the router. There are three visible activity lights, one for each of the connected interfaces and management ports. Examine the interface lights on your router. How are the lights labeled, and what is their meaning?

_____

_____

_____

c. Aside from the management ports and network interfaces, what other indicator lights are on the backplane of the router and what might their purpose be?

_____

_____

_____

___

Part 2: Examine Router Internal Characteristics Using Show Commands

Step 1: Establish a console connection to the router and use the show version command.

a. Using Tera Term, console into the router and enter privileged EXEC mode using the **enable** command:

```
Router> enable
Router#
```

b. Display information about the router by using the **show version** command. Use the Spacebar on the keyboard to page through the output.

```
Router# show version
Cisco IOS Software, C1900 Software (C1900-UNIVERSALK9-M), Version 15.2(4)M3, RELEASE
SOFTWARE (fc1)

Technical Support: http://www.cisco.com/techsupport

Copyright (c) 1986-2011 by Cisco Systems, Inc.

Compiled Thu 26-Jul-12 19:34 by prod_rel_team


ROM: System Bootstrap, Version 15.0(1r)M15, RELEASE SOFTWARE (fc1)


Router uptime is 1 day, 14 hours, 46 minutes

System returned to ROM by power-on

System restarted at 07:26:55 UTC Mon Dec 3 2012

System image file is "flash0:c1900-universalk9-mz.SPA.152-4.M3.bin"

Last reload type: Normal Reload

Last reload reason: power-on


<output omitted>


If you require further assistance please contact us by sending email to

export@cisco.com.


Cisco CISCO1941/K9 (revision 1.0) with 487424K/36864K bytes of memory.

Processor board ID FGL16082318

2 Gigabit Ethernet interfaces

2 Serial(sync/async) interfaces

1 terminal line

1 Virtual Private Network (VPN) Module

DRAM configuration is 64 bits wide with parity disabled.

255K bytes of non-volatile configuration memory.

250880K bytes of ATA System CompactFlash 0 (Read/Write)

<output omitted>
```

```
Technology Package License Information for Module:'c1900'

---------------------------------------------------------------
Technology    Technology-package           Technology-package
              Current      Type            Next reboot
---------------------------------------------------------------
ipbase        ipbasek9     Permanent       ipbasek9

security      securityk9   Permanent       securityk9

data          None         None            None


Configuration register is 0x2102
```

c. Based on the output of the **show version** command, answer the following questions about the router. If you are examining a different model router, include the information about it here.

   1) What is the version of the Cisco IOS and what is the system image filename?

   _____

   2) What is the Bootstrap program version in ROM BIOS?

   _____

   3) How long has the router been running without a restart (also known as its uptime)?

   _____

   4) How much dynamic random-access memory (DRAM) memory does the router have?

   _____

   5) What is the router's processor board ID number?

   _____

   6) What network interfaces does the router have?

   _____

   7) How much CompactFlash memory for IOS storage is there?

   _____

8) How much nonvolatile random-access memory (NVRAM) memory for configuration file storage is there?

_____

9) What is the setting of the configuration register?

_____

Step 2:   Use the show interface command to examine the network interfaces.

a. Use the **show interface gigabitEthernet 0/0** command to see the status of the Gigabit Ethernet 0/0 interface.

Note: After typing part of the command, for example, **show interface g**, you can use the **Tab** key on your keyboard to complete the gigabitEthernet command parameter.

```
Router# show interface gigabitEthernet 0/0
GigabitEthernet0/0 is administratively down, line protocol is down
  Hardware is CN Gigabit Ethernet, address is 442b.031a.b9a0 (bia 442b.031a.b9a0)
  MTU 1500 bytes, BW 100000 Kbit/sec, DLY 100 usec,
     reliability 255/255, txload 1/255, rxload 1/255
  Encapsulation ARPA, loopback not set
  Keepalive set (10 sec)
  Full Duplex, 100Mbps, media type is RJ45
  output flow-control is unsupported, input flow-control is unsupported
  ARP type: ARPA, ARP Timeout 04:00:00
  Last input never, output never, output hang never
  Last clearing of "show interface" counters never
  Input queue: 0/75/0/0 (size/max/drops/flushes); Total output drops: 0
  Queueing strategy: fifo
  Output queue: 0/40 (size/max)
  5 minute input rate 0 bits/sec, 0 packets/sec
  5 minute output rate 0 bits/sec, 0 packets/sec
     3 packets input, 276 bytes, 0 no buffer
     Received 0 broadcasts (0 IP multicasts)
     0 runts, 0 giants, 0 throttles
     0 input errors, 0 CRC, 0 frame, 0 overrun, 0 ignored
     0 watchdog, 0 multicast, 0 pause input
     0 packets output, 0 bytes, 0 underruns
     0 output errors, 0 collisions, 0 interface resets
     0 unknown protocol drops
```

```
   0 babbles, 0 late collision, 0 deferred
   0 lost carrier, 0 no carrier, 0 pause output
   0 output buffer failures, 0 output buffers swapped out
```

b. Given the output of the **show interface gigabitEthernet 0/0** command depicted above, or using the output from your router, answer the following questions:

What is the hardware type and MAC address of the Gigabit Ethernet interface?

_____

What is the interface media type? Is the interface up or down?

_____

c. Use the **show interfaces serial 0/0/0** command to view the status of the Serial 0/0/0 interface.

```
Router# show interface serial 0/0/0
Serial0/0/0 is administratively down, line protocol is down
  Hardware is WIC MBRD Serial
  MTU 1500 bytes, BW 1544 Kbit/sec, DLY 20000 usec,
     reliability 255/255, txload 1/255, rxload 1/255
  Encapsulation HDLC, loopback not set
  Keepalive set (10 sec)
  Last input 07:41:21, output never, output hang never
  Last clearing of "show interface" counters never
  Input queue: 0/75/0/0 (size/max/drops/flushes); Total output drops: 0
  Queueing strategy: fifo
  Output queue: 0/40 (size/max)
  5 minute input rate 0 bits/sec, 0 packets/sec
  5 minute output rate 0 bits/sec, 0 packets/sec
     1 packets input, 24 bytes, 0 no buffer
     Received 1 broadcasts (0 IP multicasts)
     0 runts, 0 giants, 0 throttles
     0 input errors, 0 CRC, 0 frame, 0 overrun, 0 ignored, 0 abort
     0 packets output, 0 bytes, 0 underruns
     0 output errors, 0 collisions, 2 interface resets
     0 unknown protocol drops
     0 output buffer failures, 0 output buffers swapped out
     1 carrier transitions
  DCD=down  DSR=down  DTR=down  RTS=down  CTS=down
```

d. Given the output command depicted above, answer the following questions:

What is the frame encapsulation type?

_____

What is the hardware type? Is the interface up or down?

_____

Reflection

1. Why might you need to use an EHWIC expansion slot?

_____

2. Why might you need to upgrade the Flash memory?

_____

3. What is the purpose of the mini-USB port?

_____

_____

_____

4. What is the purpose of the ISM/WLAN indicator light on the backplane of the router? What does it refer to?

_____

_____

_____

_____

6.4.3.5 Lab — Building a Switch and Router Network

Topology

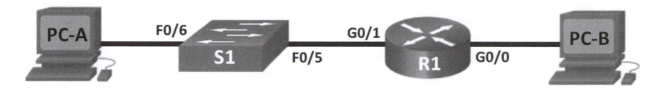

Addressing Table

Device	Interface	IP Address	Subnet Mask	Default Gateway
R1	G0/0	192.168.0.1	255.255.255.0	N/A
	G0/1	192.168.1.1	255.255.255.0	N/A
S1	VLAN 1	N/A	N/A	N/A
PC-A	NIC	192.168.1.3	255.255.255.0	192.168.1.1
PC-B	NIC	192.168.0.3	255.255.255.0	192.168.0.1

Objectives

Part 1: Set Up the Topology and Initialize Devices

- Set up equipment to match the network topology.
- Initialize and restart the router and switch.

Part 2: Configure Devices and Verify Connectivity

- Assign static IP information to the PC interfaces.
- Configure the router.
- Verify network connectivity.

Part 3: Display Device Information

- Retrieve hardware and software information from the network devices.
- Interpret the output from the routing table.
- Display interface information on the router.
- Display a summary list of the interfaces on the router and switch.

Background / Scenario

This is a comprehensive lab to review previously covered IOS commands. In this lab, you will cable the equipment as shown in the topology diagram. You will then configure the devices to match the addressing table. After the configurations have been saved, you will verify your configurations by testing for network connectivity.

After the devices have been configured and network connectivity has been verified, you will use IOS commands to retrieve information from the devices to answer questions about your network equipment.

This lab provides minimal assistance with the actual commands necessary to configure the router. However, the required commands are provided in Appendix A. Test your knowledge by trying to configure the devices without referring to the appendix.

Note: The routers used with CCNA hands-on labs are Cisco 1941 Integrated Services Routers (ISRs) with Cisco IOS Release 15.2(4)M3 (universalk9 image). The switches used are Cisco Catalyst 2960s with Cisco IOS Release 15.0(2) (lanbasek9 image). Other routers, switches, and Cisco IOS versions can be used. Depending on the model and Cisco IOS version, the commands available and output produced might vary from what is shown in the labs. Refer to the Router Interface Summary Table at the end of this lab for the correct interface identifiers.

Note: Ensure that the routers and switches have been erased and have no startup configurations. Refer to Appendix B for the procedure to initialize and reload a router and switch.

Required Resources

- 1 Router (Cisco 1941 with Cisco IOS Release 15.2(4)M3 universal image or comparable)
- 1 Switch (Cisco 2960 with Cisco IOS Release 15.0(2) lanbasek9 image or comparable)
- 2 PCs (Windows 7, Vista, or XP with terminal emulation program, such as Tera Term)
- Console cables to configure the Cisco IOS devices via the console ports
- Ethernet cables as shown in the topology

Note: The Gigabit Ethernet interfaces on Cisco 1941 routers are autosensing and an Ethernet straight-through cable may be used between the router and PC-B. If using another model Cisco router, it may be necessary to use an Ethernet crossover cable.

Part 1: Set Up Topology and Initialize Devices

Step 1: Cable the network as shown in the topology.

a. Attach the devices shown in the topology diagram, and cable, as necessary.

b. Power on all the devices in the topology.

Step 2: Initialize and reload the router and switch.

If configuration files were previously saved on the router and switch, initialize and reload these devices back to their basic configurations. For information on how to initialize and reload these devices, refer to Appendix B.

Part 2: Configure Devices and Verify Connectivity

In Part 2, you will set up the network topology and configure basic settings, such as the interface IP addresses, device access, and passwords. Refer to the Topology and Addressing Table at the beginning of this lab for device names and address information.

Note: Appendix A provides configuration details for the steps in Part 2. You should attempt to complete Part 2 prior to reviewing this appendix.

Step 1: Assign static IP information to the PC interfaces.

a. Configure the IP address, subnet mask, and default gateway settings on PC-A.

b. Configure the IP address, subnet mask, and default gateway settings on PC-B.

c. Ping PC-B from a command prompt window on PC-A.

Why were the pings not successful?

_____

Step 2:   **Configure the router.**

a. Console into the router and enable privileged EXEC mode.

b. Enter configuration mode.

c. Assign a device name to the router.

d. Disable DNS lookup to prevent the router from attempting to translate incorrectly entered commands as though they were host names.

e. Assign **class** as the privileged EXEC encrypted password.

f. Assign **cisco** as the console password and enable login.

g. Assign **cisco** as the VTY password and enable login.

h. Encrypt the clear text passwords.

i. Create a banner that warns anyone accessing the device that unauthorized access is prohibited.

j. Configure and activate both interfaces on the router.

k. Configure an interface description for each interface indicating which device is connected to it.

l. Save the running configuration to the startup configuration file.

m. Set the clock on the router.

Note: Use the question mark (**?**) to help with the correct sequence of parameters needed to execute this command.

n. Ping PC-B from a command prompt window on PC-A.

Were the pings successful? Why?

_____

_____

_____

Part 3:   Display Device Information

In Part 3, you will use **show** commands to retrieve information from the router and switch.

Step 1:   Retrieve hardware and software information from the network devices.

a.   Use the **show version** command to answer the following questions about the router.

What is the name of the IOS image that the router is running?

_____

How much DRAM memory does the router have?

_____

_____

How much NVRAM memory does the router have?

_____

How much Flash memory does the router have?

_____

b.   Use the **show version** command to answer the following questions about the switch.

What is the name of the IOS image that the switch is running?

_____

How much dynamic random access memory (DRAM) does the switch have?

_____

How much nonvolatile random-access memory (NVRAM) does the switch have?

_____

What is the model number of the switch?

_____

Step 2:   **Display the routing table on the router.**

Use the **show ip route** command on the router to answer the following questions.

What code is used in the routing table to indicate a directly connected network? _____

How many route entries are coded with a C code in the routing table? _____

What interface types are associated to the C coded routes?

_____

Step 3:   **Display interface information on the router.**

Use the **show interface g0/1** to answer the following questions.

What is the operational status of the G0/1 interface?

_____

What is the Media Access Control (MAC) address of the G0/1 interface?

_____

How is the Internet address displayed in this command?

_____

Step 4:   **Display a summary list of the interfaces on the router and switch.**

There are several commands that can be used to verify an interface configuration. One of the most useful of these is the **show ip interface brief** command. The command output displays a summary list of the interfaces on the device and provides immediate feedback to the status of each interface.

a.   Enter the **show ip interface brief** command on the router.

```
R1# show ip interface brief
Interface                  IP-Address      OK? Method Status                Protocol
Embedded-Service-Engine0/0 unassigned      YES unset  administratively down down
GigabitEthernet0/0         192.168.0.1     YES manual up                    up
GigabitEthernet0/1         192.168.1.1     YES manual up                    up
Serial0/0/0                unassigned      YES unset  administratively down down
Serial0/0/1                unassigned      YES unset  administratively down down
R1#
```

b.   Enter the **show ip interface brief** command on the switch.

```
Switch# show ip interface brief
Interface                  IP-Address      OK? Method Status    Protocol
Vlan1                      unassigned      YES manual up        up
FastEthernet0/1            unassigned      YES unset  down      down
FastEthernet0/2            unassigned      YES unset  down      down
FastEthernet0/3            unassigned      YES unset  down      down
FastEthernet0/4            unassigned      YES unset  down      down
FastEthernet0/5            unassigned      YES unset  up        up
FastEthernet0/6            unassigned      YES unset  up        up
FastEthernet0/7            unassigned      YES unset  down      down
FastEthernet0/8            unassigned      YES unset  down      down
FastEthernet0/9            unassigned      YES unset  down      down
FastEthernet0/10           unassigned      YES unset  down      down
FastEthernet0/11           unassigned      YES unset  down      down
FastEthernet0/12           unassigned      YES unset  down      down
FastEthernet0/13           unassigned      YES unset  down      down
FastEthernet0/14           unassigned      YES unset  down      down
FastEthernet0/15           unassigned      YES unset  down      down
FastEthernet0/16           unassigned      YES unset  down      down
FastEthernet0/17           unassigned      YES unset  down      down
FastEthernet0/18           unassigned      YES unset  down      down
FastEthernet0/19           unassigned      YES unset  down      down
FastEthernet0/20           unassigned      YES unset  down      down
FastEthernet0/21           unassigned      YES unset  down      down
FastEthernet0/22           unassigned      YES unset  down      down
FastEthernet0/23           unassigned      YES unset  down      down
```

```
FastEthernet0/24      unassigned      YES unset  down          down

GigabitEthernet0/1    unassigned      YES unset  down          down

GigabitEthernet0/2    unassigned      YES unset  down          down

Switch#
```

Reflection

1. If the G0/1 interface showed administratively down, what interface configuration command would you use to turn the interface up?

    _____

2. What would happen if you had incorrectly configured interface G0/1 on the router with an IP address of 192.168.1.2?

    _____

    _____

Router Interface Summary Table

Router Interface Summary				
Router Model	Ethernet Interface #1	Ethernet Interface #2	Serial Interface #1	Serial Interface #2
1800	Fast Ethernet 0/0 (F0/0)	Fast Ethernet 0/1 (F0/1)	Serial 0/0/0 (S0/0/0)	Serial 0/0/1 (S0/0/1)
1900	Gigabit Ethernet 0/0 (G0/0)	Gigabit Ethernet 0/1 (G0/1)	Serial 0/0/0 (S0/0/0)	Serial 0/0/1 (S0/0/1)
2801	Fast Ethernet 0/0 (F0/0)	Fast Ethernet 0/1 (F0/1)	Serial 0/1/0 (S0/1/0)	Serial 0/1/1 (S0/1/1)
2811	Fast Ethernet 0/0 (F0/0)	Fast Ethernet 0/1 (F0/1)	Serial 0/0/0 (S0/0/0)	Serial 0/0/1 (S0/0/1)
2900	Gigabit Ethernet 0/0 (G0/0)	Gigabit Ethernet 0/1 (G0/1)	Serial 0/0/0 (S0/0/0)	Serial 0/0/1 (S0/0/1)

Note: To find out how the router is configured, look at the interfaces to identify the router type and how many interfaces the router has. There is no way to effectively list all the combinations of configurations for each router class. This table includes identifiers for the possible combinations of Ethernet and Serial interfaces in the device. The table does not include any other type of interface, even though a specific router may contain one. An example of this might be an ISDN BRI interface. The string in parenthesis is the legal abbreviation that can be used in Cisco IOS commands to represent the interface.

Appendix A: Configuration Details for Steps in Part 2

Step 1:   **Configure the PC interfaces.**

a.   Configure the IP address, subnet mask, and default gateway settings on PC-A.

Internet Protocol Version 4 (TCP/IPv4) Properties   ? ✕

General

You can get IP settings assigned automatically if your network supports
this capability. Otherwise, you need to ask your network administrator
for the appropriate IP settings.

○ Obtain an IP address automatically
⦿ Use the following IP address:

IP address: 192 . 168 . 1 . 3

Subnet mask: 255 . 255 . 255 . 0

Default gateway: 192 . 168 . 1 . 1

b. Configure the IP address, subnet mask, and default gateway settings on PC-B.

Internet Protocol Version 4 (TCP/IPv4) Properties   ? ✕

General

You can get IP settings assigned automatically if your network supports
this capability. Otherwise, you need to ask your network administrator
for the appropriate IP settings.

○ Obtain an IP address automatically
⦿ Use the following IP address:

IP address: 192 . 168 . 0 . 3

Subnet mask: 255 . 255 . 255 . 0

Default gateway: 192 . 168 . 0 . 1

c. Ping PC-B from a command prompt window on PC-A.

```
C:\>ping 192.168.0.3

Pinging 192.168.0.3 with 32 bytes of data:
Reply from 192.168.1.3: Destination host unreachable.
Reply from 192.168.1.3: Destination host unreachable.
Reply from 192.168.1.3: Destination host unreachable.
Reply from 192.168.1.3: Destination host unreachable.

Ping statistics for 192.168.0.3:
    Packets: Sent = 4, Received = 4, Lost = 0 (0% loss),

C:\>
```

Step 2: **Configure the router.**

a. Console into the router and enable privileged EXEC mode.

```
Router> enable
Router#
```

b. Enter configuration mode.

```
Router# conf t
Enter configuration commands, one per line.  End with CNTL/Z.
Router(config)#
```

c. Assign a device name to the router.

```
Router(config)# hostname R1
```

d. Disable DNS lookup to prevent the router from attempting to translate incorrectly entered commands as though they were host names.

```
R1(config)# no ip domain-lookup
```

e. Assign **class** as the privileged EXEC encrypted password.

```
R1(config)# enable secret class
```

f. Assign **cisco** as the console password and enable login.

```
R1(config)# line con 0
R1(config-line)# password cisco
R1(config-line)# login
R1(config-line)# exit
R1(config)#
```

g. Assign **cisco** as the vty password and enable login.

```
R1(config)# line vty 0 4
R1(config-line)# password cisco
R1(config-line)# login
R1(config-line)# exit
R1(config)#
```

h. Encrypt the clear text passwords.

```
R1(config)# service password-encryption
```

i. Create a banner that warns anyone accessing the device that unauthorized access is prohibited.

```
R1(config)# banner motd #
Enter TEXT message.  End with the character '#'.
  Unauthorized access prohibited!
#
R1(config)#
```

j. Configure and activate both interfaces on the router.

```
R1(config)# int g0/0
R1(config-if)# description Connection to PC-B.
R1(config-if)# ip address 192.168.0.1 255.255.255.0
R1(config-if)# no shut
```

```
R1(config-if)#

*Nov 29 23:49:44.195: %LINK-3-UPDOWN: Interface GigabitEthernet0/0, changed state to
down

*Nov 29 23:49:47.863: %LINK-3-UPDOWN: Interface GigabitEthernet0/0, changed state to
up

*Nov 29 23:49:48.863: %LINEPROTO-5-UPDOWN: Line protocol on Interface GigabitEther-
net0/0, changed state to up

R1(config-if)# int g0/1

R1(config-if)# description Connection to S1.

R1(config-if)# ip address 192.168.1.1 255.255.255.0

R1(config-if)# no shut

R1(config-if)# exit

R1(config)# exit

*Nov 29 23:50:15.283: %LINK-3-UPDOWN: Interface GigabitEthernet0/1, changed state to
down

*Nov 29 23:50:18.863: %LINK-3-UPDOWN: Interface GigabitEthernet0/1, changed state to
up

*Nov 29 23:50:19.863: %LINEPROTO-5-UPDOWN: Line protocol on Interface GigabitEther-
net0/1, changed state to up

R1#
```

k. Save the running configuration to the startup file.

```
R1# copy running-config startup-config

Destination filename [startup-config]?

Building configuration...

[OK]

R1#
```

l. Set the clock on the router.

```
R1# clock set 17:00:00 29 Nov 2012

R1#

*Nov 29 17:00:00.000: %SYS-6-CLOCKUPDATE: System clock has been updated from 23:55:46
UTC Thu Nov 29 2012 to 17:00:00 UTC Thu Nov 29 2012, configured from console by con-
sole.

R1#
```

Note: Use the question mark (**?**) to help determine the correct sequence of the parameters needed to execute this command.

m. Ping PC-B from a command prompt window on PC-A.

```
C:\>ping 192.168.0.3

Pinging 192.168.0.3 with 32 bytes of data:
Reply from 192.168.0.3: bytes=32 time<1ms TTL=127
Reply from 192.168.0.3: bytes=32 time<1ms TTL=127
Reply from 192.168.0.3: bytes=32 time<1ms TTL=127
Reply from 192.168.0.3: bytes=32 time<1ms TTL=127

Ping statistics for 192.168.0.3:
    Packets: Sent = 4, Received = 4, Lost = 0 (0% loss),
Approximate round trip times in milli-seconds:
    Minimum = 0ms, Maximum = 0ms, Average = 0ms

C:\>
```

Appendix B: Initializing and Reloading a Router and Switch

Part 1:   Initialize the Router and Reload

Step 1:   Connect to the router.

Console into the router and enter privileged EXEC mode using the **enable** command.

```
Router> enable
Router#
```

Step 2:   Erase the startup configuration file from NVRAM.

Type the **erase startup-config** command to remove the startup configuration from nonvolatile random-access memory (NVRAM).

```
Router# erase startup-config
Erasing the nvram filesystem will remove all configuration files! Continue? [confirm]
[OK]
Erase of nvram: complete
Router#
```

Step 3:   Reload the router.

Issue the **reload** command to remove an old configuration from memory. When prompted to Proceed with reload, press Enter to confirm the reload. Pressing any other key will abort the reload.

```
Router# reload
Proceed with reload? [confirm]


*Nov 29 18:28:09.923: %SYS-5-RELOAD: Reload requested by console. Reload Reason: Re-
load Command.
```

Note: You may receive a prompt to save the running configuration prior to reloading the router. Respond by typing **no** and press Enter.

```
System configuration has been modified. Save? [yes/no]: no
```

Step 4: **Bypass the initial configuration dialog.**

After the router reloads, you are prompted to enter the initial configuration dialog. Enter **no** and press Enter.

```
Would you like to enter the initial configuration dialog? [yes/no]: no
```

Step 5: **Terminate the autoinstall program.**

You will be prompted to terminate the autoinstall program. Respond **yes** and then press Enter.

```
Would you like to terminate autoinstall? [yes]: yes
Router>
```

Part 2: Initialize the Switch and Reload

Step 1: **Connect to the switch.**

Console into the switch and enter privileged EXEC mode.

```
Switch> enable
Switch#
```

Step 2: **Determine if there have been any virtual local-area networks (VLANs) created.**

Use the **show flash** command to determine if any VLANs have been created on the switch.

```
Switch# show flash

Directory of flash:/

    2  -rwx        1919   Mar 1 1993 00:06:33 +00:00  private-config.text
    3  -rwx        1632   Mar 1 1993 00:06:33 +00:00  config.text
    4  -rwx       13336   Mar 1 1993 00:06:33 +00:00  multiple-fs
    5  -rwx    11607161   Mar 1 1993 02:37:06 +00:00  c2960-lanbasek9-mz.150-2.SE.bin
    6  -rwx         616   Mar 1 1993 00:07:13 +00:00  vlan.dat


32514048 bytes total (20886528 bytes free)
Switch#
```

Step 3: **Delete the VLAN file.**

a. If the **vlan.dat** file was found in flash, then delete this file.

```
Switch# delete vlan.dat
Delete filename [vlan.dat]?
```

You will be prompted to verify the file name. At this point, you can change the file name or just press Enter if you have entered the name correctly.

b. When you are prompted to delete this file, press Enter to confirm the deletion. (Pressing any other key will abort the deletion.)

```
Delete flash:/vlan.dat? [confirm]
Switch#
```

Step 4:   Erase the startup configuration file.

Use the **erase startup-config** command to erase the startup configuration file from NVRAM. When you are prompted to remove the configuration file, press Enter to confirm the erase. (Pressing any other key will abort the operation.)

```
Switch# erase startup-config
Erasing the nvram filesystem will remove all configuration files! Continue? [confirm]
[OK]
Erase of nvram: complete
Switch#
```

Step 5:   Reload the switch.

Reload the switch to remove any old configuration information from memory. When you are prompted to re-load the switch, press Enter to proceed with the reload. (Pressing any other key will abort the reload.)

```
Switch# reload
Proceed with reload? [confirm]
```

Note: You may receive a prompt to save the running configuration prior to reloading the switch. Type **no** and press Enter.

```
System configuration has been modified. Save? [yes/no]: no
```

Step 6:   Bypass the initial configuration dialog.

After the switch reloads, you should see a prompt to enter the initial configuration dialog. Type **no** at the prompt and press Enter.

```
Would you like to enter the initial configuration dialog? [yes/no]: no
Switch>
```

6.5.1.1 Class Activity — Can you read this map?

Objectives

Explain how network devices use routing tables to direct packets to a destination network.

In this activity, given a scenario, you will determine whether high-reliability messaging should be used. You will focus on whether the final message is complete, correct, and delivered in a timely manner.

Background/Scenario

Note: It is suggested that students work in pairs; however, if preferred, students can complete this activity individually.

Your instructor will provide you with output generated by a router's **show ip route** command. Use Packet Tracer to build a topology model using this routing information.

At a minimum, the following should be used in your topology model:

- One Catalyst 2960 switch
- One Cisco Series 1941 Router with one HWIC-4ESW switching port modular card and IOS Version 15.1 or higher
- Three PCs (can be servers, generic PCs, laptops, etc.)

Use the note tool in Packet Tracer to indicate the addresses of the router interfaces and possible addresses for the end devices you chose for your model.

Label all end devices, ports, and addresses ascertained from the **show ip route** output/routing table information in your Packet Tracer file. Save your work in hard or soft copy to share with the class.

Required Resources

- Packet Tracer software program.
- Routing **Table 1** - You can use the table to assist one another as you read the information provided, and then construct the model using Packet Tracer.

Table 1

```
R1# show ip route
Codes: L - local, C - connected, S - static, R - RIP, M - mobile, B -
BGP
D - EIGRP, EX - EIGRP external, O - OSPF, IA - OSPF inter area
N1 - OSPF NSSA external type 1, N2 - OSPF NSSA external type 2
E1 - OSPF external type 1, E2 - OSPF external type 2
i - IS-IS, su - IS-IS summary, L1 - IS-IS level-1, L2 - IS-IS level-2
ia - IS-IS inter area, * - candidate default, U - per-user static
route
o - ODR, P - periodic downloaded static route, H - NHRP, l - LISP
+ - replicated route, % - next hop override

Gateway of last resort is not set

      192.168.0.0/24 is variably subnetted, 2 subnets, 2 masks
C     192.168.0.0/24 is directly connected, GigabitEthernet0/0
L     192.168.0.1/32 is directly connected, GigabitEthernet0/0
      192.168.1.0/24 is variably subnetted, 2 subnets, 2 masks
C     192.168.1.0/24 is directly connected, GigabitEthernet0/1
L     192.168.1.1/32 is directly connected, GigabitEthernet0/1
```

Reflection

1. What was the hardest part of designing this network model? Explain your answer.

Chapter 7 — IP Addressing

7.0.1.2 Class Activity — The Internet of Everything (IoE)

Objectives

Explain how network devices use routing tables to direct packets to a destination network.

IPv6 is important to help manage the data traffic identification, which will be needed in the future. Many addresses will assist in this endeavor, and IPv6 helps to alleviate this need.

Background /Scenario

Today, more than 99% of our world remains unconnected. Tomorrow, we will be connected to almost everything. 37 billion devices will be connected to the Internet by 2020. From trees to water to cars, the organic and the digital will work together for a more intelligent and connected world. This tomorrow of networking is known as "The Internet of Everything" or "IoE."

If traffic, transportation, networking and space exploration depend on digital information sharing, how will that information be identified from its source to its destination?

In this activity, you will begin to think about not only what will be identified in the IoE world, but how everything will be addressed in the same world!

Activity directions for class or individual students:

1. Read the blog/news source, "Internet of Everything: Fueling an Amazing Future #TomorrowStartsHere" authored by John Chambers regarding the Internet of Everything (IoE). This blog is located at http://blogs.cisco.com/news/internet-of-everything-2.

2. Then view the video, "Cisco Commercial: Tomorrow Starts Here" located halfway down the page.

3. Next, navigate to the IoE main page located at http://www.cisco.com/web/tomorrow-starts-here/index.html.Then click on a category that interests you from within the graphic collage.

4. Next, watch the video or read through the blog or .pdf that belongs to your IoE category of interest.

5. Write 5 comments or questions about what you saw or read. Be prepared to share with the class.

Required Resources

- Internet connectivity for research on the cisco.com site. Headphones may also be useful if students are individually completing this activity within a group setting.
- Recording capabilities (paper, tablet, etc.) for comments or questions regarding the videos, blogs and/or .pdfs read or viewed for Step 3.

Reflection

1. Why do you think there is a need to address trees? Windmills? Cars? Refrigerators? Why will just about anything be able to use an IP address?

7.1.2.7 Lab — Using the Windows Calculator with Network Addresses

Objectives

Part 1: Access the Windows Calculator

Part 2: Convert between Numbering Systems

Part 3: Convert Host IPv4 Addresses and Subnet Masks into Binary

Part 4: Determine the Number of Hosts in a Network Using Powers of 2

Part 5: Convert MAC Addresses and IPv6 Addresses to Binary

Background / Scenario

Network technicians use binary, decimal, and hexadecimal numbers when working with computers and networking devices. Microsoft provides a built-in Calculator application as part of the operating system. The Windows 7 version of Calculator includes a Standard view that can be used to perform basic arithmetic tasks such as addition, subtract, multiplication, and division. The Calculator application also has advanced programming, scientific, and statistical capabilities.

In this lab, you will use the Windows 7 Calculator application Programmer view to convert between the binary, decimal, and hexadecimal number systems. You will also use the Scientific view powers function to determine the number of hosts that can be addressed based on the number of host bits available.

Required Resources

- 1 PC (Windows 7, Vista, or XP)

Note: If using an operating system other than Windows 7, the Calculator application views and functions available may vary from those shown in this lab. However, you should be able to perform the calculations.

Part 1:   Access the Windows Calculator

In Part 1, you will become familiar with the Microsoft Windows built-in calculator application and view the available modes.

Step 1:   Click the Windows Start button and select All Programs.

Step 2:   Click the Accessories folder and select Calculator.

Step 3:   After Calculator opens, click the View menu.

What are the four available modes?

_____

Note: The Programmer and Scientific modes are used in this lab.

Part 2:   Convert between Numbering Systems

In the Windows Calculator Programmer view, several number system modes are available: Hex (Hexadecimal or base 16), Dec (Decimal or base 10), Oct (Octal or base 8), and Bin (Binary or base 2).

We are accustomed to using the decimal number system that uses the digits 0 to 9. The decimal numbering system is used in everyday life for all counting, money, and financial transactions. Computers and other electronic devices use the binary numbering system with only the digits 0 and 1 for data storage, data transmission and numerical calculations. All computer calculations are ultimately performed internally in binary (digital) form, regardless of how they are displayed.

One disadvantage of binary numbers is that the binary number equivalent of a large decimal number can be quite long. This makes them difficult to read and write. One way to overcome this problem is to arrange binary numbers into groups of four as hexadecimal numbers. Hexadecimal numbers are base 16, and a combination of numbers from 0 to 9 and the letters A to F are used to represent the binary or decimal equivalent. Hexadecimal characters are used when writing or displaying IPv6 and MAC addresses.

The octal numbering system is very similar in principle to hexadecimal. Octal numbers represent binary numbers in groups of three. This numbering system uses digits 0 to 7. Octal numbers are also a convenient way to represent a large binary number in smaller groups, but this numbering system is not commonly used.

In this lab, the Windows 7 Calculator is used to convert between different numbering systems in the Programmer mode.

a.   Click the **View** menu and select **Programmer** to switch to Programmer mode.

Note: For Windows XP and Vista, only two modes, Standard and Scientific, are available. If you are using one of these operating systems, you can use the Scientific mode to perform this lab.

Which number system is currently active? _____

Which numbers on the number pad are active in decimal mode? _____

b.   Click the **Bin** (Binary) radio button. Which numbers are active on the number pad now?

_____

Why do you think the other numbers are grayed out?

_____

c. Click the **Hex** (Hexadecimal) radio button. Which characters are activated on the number pad now?

_____

d. Click the **Dec** radio button. Using your mouse, click the number **1** followed by the number **5** on the number pad. The decimal number 15 is now entered.

Note: The numbers and letters on the keyboard can also be used to enter the values. If using the numerical keypad, type the number **15**. If the number does not enter into the calculator, press the **Num Lock** key to enable the numeric keypad.

Click the **Bin** radio button. What happened to the number 15?

_____

e. Numbers are converted from one numbering system to another by selecting the desired number mode. Click the **Dec** radio button again. The number converts back to decimal.

f. Click the **Hex** radio button to **Hex** radio button to change to Hexadecimal mode. Which hexadecimal character (0 through 9 or A to F) represents decimal 15? _____

g. As you were switching between the numbering systems, you may have noticed the binary number 1111 is displayed during the conversion. This assists you in relating the binary digits to other numbering system values. Each set of 4 bits represents a hexadecimal character or potentially multiple decimal characters.

h. Clear the values in the window by clicking **C** above the 9 on the calculator keypad. Convert the following numbers between the binary, decimal, and hexadecimal numbering systems.

Decimal	Binary	Hexadecimal
86		
175		
204		
	0001 0011	
	0100 1101	
	0010 1010	
		38
		93
		E4

i. As you record the values in the table above, do you see a pattern between the binary and hexadecimal numbers?

_____

_____

Part 3: Convert Host IPv4 Addresses and Subnet Masks into Binary

Internet Protocol version 4 (IPv4) addresses and subnet masks are represented in a dotted decimal format (four octets), such as 192.168.1.10 and 255.255.255.0, respectively. This makes these addresses more readable to humans. Each of the decimal octets in the address or a mask can be converted to 8 binary bits. An octet is always 8 binary bits. If all 4 octets were converted to binary, how many bits would there be?

_____

a. Use the Windows Calculator application to convert the IP address 192.168.1.10 into binary and record the binary numbers in the following table:

Decimal	Binary
192	
168	
1	
10	

b. Subnet masks, such as 255.255.255.0, are also represented in a dotted decimal format. A subnet mask will always consist of four 8-bit octets, each represented as a decimal number. Using the Windows Calculator, convert the 8 possible decimal subnet mask octet values to binary numbers and record the binary numbers in the following table:

Decimal	Binary
0	
128	
192	
224	
240	
248	
252	
254	
255	

c. With the combination of IPv4 address and the subnet mask, the network portion can be determined and the number of hosts available in a given IPv4 subnet can also be calculated. The process is examined in Part 4.

Part 4: Determine the Number of Hosts in a Network Using Powers of 2

Given an IPv4 network address and a subnet mask, the network portion can be determined along with the number of hosts available in the network.

a. To calculate the number of hosts on a network, you must determine the network and host portion of the address.

Using the example of 192.168.1.10 with a subnet of 255.255.248.0, the address and subnet mask are converted to binary numbers. Align the bits as you record your conversions to binary numbers.

Decimal IP Address and Subnet Mask	Binary IP Address and Subnet Mask
192.168.1.10	
255.255.248.0	

Because the first 21 bits in the subnet mask are consecutive numeral ones, the corresponding first 21 bits in the IP address in binary is 110000001010100000000; these represent the network portion of the address. The remaining 11 bits are 00100001010 and represent the host portion of the address.

What is the decimal and binary network number for this address?

_____

What is the decimal and binary host portion for this address?

_____

Because the network number and the broadcast address use two addresses out of the subnet, the formula to determine the number of hosts available in an IPv4 subnet is the number 2 to the power of the number of host bits available, minus 2:

$$\text{Number of available hosts} = 2^{(\text{number of host bits})} - 2$$

b. Using the Windows Calculator application, switch to the Scientific mode by clicking the **View** menu, then select **Scientific**.

c. Input **2**. Click the **x^y** key. This key raises a number to a power.

d. Input **11**. Click **=**, or press Enter on the keyboard for the answer.

e. Subtract **2** from the answer by using the calculator if desired.

f. In this example, there are 2046 hosts are available on this network (2^{11}-2).

g. If given the number of host bits, determine the number of hosts available and record the number in the following table.

Number of Available Host Bits	Number of Available Hosts
5	
14	
24	
10	

h. For a given subnet mask, determine the number of hosts available and record the answer in the following table.

Subnet Mask	Binary Subnet Mask	Number of Available Host Bits	Number of Available Hosts
255.255.255.0	11111111.11111111.11111111.00000000		
255.255.240.0	11111111.11111111.11110000.00000000		
255.255.255.128	11111111.11111111.11111111.10000000		
255.255.255.252	11111111.11111111.11111111.11111100		
255.255.0.0	11111111.11111111.00000000.00000000		

Part 5:   Convert MAC Addresses and IPv6 Addresses to Binary

Both Media Access Control (MAC) and Internet Protocol version 6 (IPv6) addresses are represented as hexadecimal digits for readability. However, computers only understand binary digits and use these binary digits for computations. In this part, you will convert these hexadecimal addresses to binary addresses.

Step 1:   **Convert MAC addresses to binary digits.**

a. The MAC or physical address is normally represented as 12 hexadecimal characters, grouped in pairs and separated by hyphens (-). Physical addresses on a Windows-based computer are displayed in a format of xx-xx-xx-xx-xx-xx, where each x is a number from 0 to 9 or a letter from A to F. Each of the hex characters in the address can be converted to 4 binary bits, which is what the computer understands. If all 12 hex characters were converted to binary, how many bits would there be?

_____

b. Record the MAC address for your PC.

_____

c. Convert the MAC address into binary digits using the Windows Calculator application.

_____

Step 2:   **Convert an IPv6 address into binary digits.**

IPv6 addresses are also written in hexadecimal characters for human convenience. These IPv6 addresses can be converted to binary numbers for computer use.

a. IPv6 addresses are binary numbers represented in human-readable notations: 2001:0DB8:AC AD:0001:0000:0000:0000:0001 or in a shorter format: 2001:DB8:ACAD:1::1.

b. An IPv6 address is 128 bits long. Using the Windows Calculator application, convert the sample IPv6 address into binary numbers and record it in the table below.

Hexadecimal	Binary
2001	
0DB8	
ACAD	
0001	
0000	
0000	
0000	
0001	

Reflection

1. Can you perform all the conversions without the assistance of the calculator? What can you do to make it happen?

_____

2. For most IPv6 addresses, the network portion of the address is usually 64 bits. How many hosts are available on a subnet where the first 64 bits represent the network? Hint: All host addresses are available in the subnet for hosts.

_____

7.1.2.8 Lab — Converting IPv4 Addresses to Binary

Objectives

Part 1: Convert IPv4 Addresses from Dotted Decimal to Binary

Part 2: Use Bitwise ANDing Operation to Determine Network Addresses

Part 3: Apply Network Address Calculations

Background / Scenario

Every IPv4 address is comprised of two parts: a network portion and a host portion. The network portion of an address is the same for all devices that reside in the same network. The host portion identifies a specific host within a given network. The subnet mask is used to determine the network portion of an IP address. Devices on the same network can communicate directly; devices on different networks require an intermediary Layer 3 device, such as a router, to communicate.

To understand the operation of devices on a network, we need to look at addresses the way devices do—in binary notation. To do this, we must convert the dotted decimal form of an IP address and its subnet mask to binary notation. After this has been done, we can use the bitwise ANDing operation to determine the network address.

This lab provides instructions on how to determine the network and host portion of IP addresses by converting addresses and subnet masks from dotted decimal to binary, and then using the bitwise ANDing operation. You will then apply this information to identify addresses in the network.

Part 1: Convert IPv4 Addresses from Dotted Decimal to Binary

In Part 1, you will convert decimal numbers to their binary equivalent. After you have mastered this activity, you will convert IPv4 addresses and subnet masks from dotted decimal to their binary form.

Step 1: Convert decimal numbers to their binary equivalent.

Fill in the following table by converting the decimal number to an 8-bit binary number. The first number has been completed for your reference. Recall that the eight binary bit values in an octet are based on the powers of 2, and from left to right are 128, 64, 32, 16, 8, 4, 2, and 1.

Decimal	Binary
192	11000000
168	
10	
255	
2	

Step 2: Convert the IPv4 addresses to their binary equivalent.

An IPv4 address can be converted using the same technique you used above. Fill in the table below with the binary equivalent of the addresses provided. To make your answers easier to read, separate the binary octets with a period.

Decimal	Binary
192.168.10.10	11000000.10101000.00001010.00001010
209.165.200.229	
172.16.18.183	
10.86.252.17	
255.255.255.128	
255.255.192.0	

Part 2:   Use Bitwise ANDing Operation to Determine Network Addresses

In Part 2, you will use the bitwise ANDing operation to calculate the network address for the provided host addresses. You will first need to convert an IPv4 decimal address and subnet mask to their binary equivalent. Once you have the binary form of the network address, convert it to its decimal form.

Note: The ANDing process compares the binary value in each bit position of the 32-bit host IP with the corresponding position in the 32-bit subnet mask. If there two 0s or a 0 and a 1, the ANDing result is 0. If there are two 1s, the result is a 1, as shown in the example here.

Step 1:   Determine the number of bits to use to calculate the network address.

Description	Decimal	Binary
IP Address	192.168.10.131	11000000.10101000.00001010.10000011
Subnet Mask	255.255.255.192	11111111.11111111.11111111.11000000
Network Address	192.168.10.128	11000000.10101000.00001010.10000000

How do you determine what bits to use to calculate the network address?

_____

In the example above, how many bits are used to calculate the network address?

_____

Step 2:   Use the ANDing operation to determine the network address.

a.   Enter the missing information into the table below:

Description	Decimal	Binary
IP Address	172.16.145.29	
Subnet Mask	255.255.0.0	
Network Address		

b.   Enter the missing information into the table below:

Description	Decimal	Binary
IP Address	192.168.10.10	
Subnet Mask	255.255.255.0	
Network Address		

c.   Enter the missing information into the table below:

Description	Decimal	Binary
IP Address	192.168.68.210	
Subnet Mask	255.255.255.128	
Network Address		

d.   Enter the missing information into the table below:

Description	Decimal	Binary
IP Address	172.16.188.15	
Subnet Mask	255.255.240.0	
Network Address		

e.   Enter the missing information into the table below:

Description	Decimal	Binary
IP Address	10.172.2.8	
Subnet Mask	255.224.0.0	
Network Address		

Part 3:   **Apply Network Address Calculations**

In Part 3, you must calculate the network address for the given IP addresses and subnet masks. After you have the network address, you should be able to determine the responses needed to complete the lab.

Step 1:   **Determine whether IP addresses are on same network.**

a.   You are configuring two PCs for your network. PC-A is given an IP address of 192.168.1.18, and PC-B is given an IP address of 192.168.1.33. Both PCs receive a subnet mask of 255.255.255.240.

What is the network address for PC-A? _____

What is the network address for PC-B? _____

Will these PCs be able to communicate directly with each other? _____

What is the highest address that can be given to PC-B that allows it to be on the same network as PC-A?

_____

b.   You are configuring two PCs for your network. PC-A is given an IP address of 10.0.0.16, and PC-B is given an IP address of 10.1.14.68. Both PCs receive a subnet mask of 255.254.0.0.

What is the network address for PC-A? _____

What is the network address for PC-B? _____

Will these PCs be able to communicate directly with each other? _____

What is the lowest address that can be given to PC-B that allows it to be on the same network as PC-A?

_____

Step 2:   Identify the default gateway address.

a. Your company has a policy to use the first IP address in a network as the default gateway address.
    A host on the local-area network (LAN) has an IP address of 172.16.140.24 and a subnet mask of
    255.255.192.0.

    What is the network address for this network?

    _____

    What is the default gateway address for this host?

    _____

b. Your company has a policy to use the first IP address in a network as the default gateway address. You
    have been instructed to configure a new server with an IP address of 192.168.184.227 and a subnet
    mask of 255.255.255.248.

    What is the network address for this network?

    _____

    What is the default gateway for this server?

    _____

Reflection

Why is the subnet mask important in determining the network address?

_____

_____

7.1.4.8 Lab — Identifying IPv4 Addresses

Objectives

Part 1: Identify IPv4 Addresses

- Identify the network and host portion of an IP address.
- Identify the range of host addresses given a network/prefix mask pair.

Part 2: Classify IPv4 Addresses

- Identify the type of address (network, host, multicast, or broadcast).
- Identify whether an address is public or private.
- Determine if an address assignment is a valid host address.

Background / Scenario

Addressing is an important function of network layer protocols because it enables data communication between hosts on the same network, or on different networks. In this lab, you will examine the structure of Internet Protocol version 4 (IPv4) addresses. You will identify the various types of IPv4 addresses and the components that help comprise the address, such as network portion, host portion, and subnet mask. Types of addresses covered include public, private, unicast, and multicast.

Required Resources

- Device with Internet access
- Optional: IPv4 address calculator

Part 1: Identify IPv4 Addresses

In Part 1, you will be given several examples of IPv4 addresses and will complete tables with appropriate information.

Step 1: Analyze the table shown below and identify the network portion and host portion of the given IPv4 addresses.

The first two rows show examples of how the table should be completed.

Key for table:

N = all 8 bits for an octet are in the network portion of the address

n = a bit in the network portion of the address

H = all 8 bits for an octet are in the host portion of the address

h = a bit in the host portion of the address

IP Address/Prefix	Network/Host N,n = Network H,h = Host	Subnet Mask	Network Address
192.168.10.10/24	N.N.N.H	255.255.255.0	192.168.10.0
10.101.99.17/23	N.N.nnnnnnnh.H	255.255.254.0	10.101.98.0
209.165.200.227/27			
172.31.45.252/24			
10.1.8.200/26			
172.16.117.77/20			
10.1.1.101/25			
209.165.202.140/27			
192.168.28.45/28			

Step 2:   Analyze the table below and list the range of host and broadcast addresses given a network/prefix mask pair.

The first row shows an example of how the table should be completed.

IP Address/Prefix	First Host Address	Last Host Address	Broadcast Address
192.168.10.10/24	192.168.10.1	192.168.10.254	192.168.10.255
10.101.99.17/23			
209.165.200.227/27			
172.31.45.252/24			
10.1.8.200/26			
172.16.117.77/20			
10.1.1.101/25			
209.165.202.140/27			
192.168.28.45/28			

Part 2: Classify IPv4 Addresses

In Part 2, you will identify and classify several examples of IPv4 addresses.

Step 1:   Analyze the table shown below and identify the type of address (network, host, multicast, or broadcast address).

The first row shows an example of how the table should be completed.

IP Address	Subnet Mask	Address Type
10.1.1.1	255.255.255.252	host
192.168.33.63	255.255.255.192	
239.192.1.100	255.252.0.0	
172.25.12.52	255.255.255.0	
10.255.0.0	255.0.0.0	
172.16.128.48	255.255.255.240	
209.165.202.159	255.255.255.224	
172.16.0.255	255.255.0.0	
224.10.1.11	255.255.255.0	

Step 2: **Analyze the table shown below and identify the address as public or private.**

IP Address/Prefix	Public or Private
209.165.201.30/27	
192.168.255.253/24	
10.100.11.103/16	
172.30.1.100/28	
192.31.7.11/24	
172.20.18.150/22	
128.107.10.1/16	
192.135.250.10/24	
64.104.0.11/16	

Step 3: **Analyze the table shown below and identify whether the address/prefix pair is a valid host address.**

IP Address/Prefix	Valid Host Address?	Reason
127.1.0.10/24		
172.16.255.0/16		
241.19.10.100/24		
192.168.0.254/24		
192.31.7.255/24		
64.102.255.255/14		
224.0.0.5/16		
10.0.255.255/8		
198.133.219.8/24		

Reflection

Why should we continue to study and learn about IPv4 addressing if the available IPv4 address space is depleted?

_____

_____

7.2.5.4 Lab — Identifying IPv6 Addresses

Topology

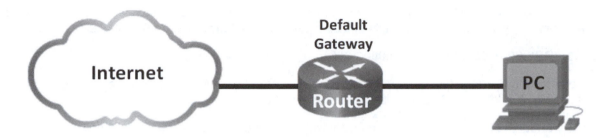

Objectives

Part 1: Identify the Different Types of IPv6 Addresses

- Review the different types of IPv6 addresses.
- Match the IPv6 address with the correct type.

Part 2: Examine a Host IPv6 Network Interface and Address

- Check PC IPv6 network address settings.

Part 3: Practice IPv6 Address Abbreviation

- Study and review the rules for IPv6 address abbreviation.
- Practice compressing and decompressing IPv6 addresses.

Part 4: Identify the Hierarchy of the IPv6 Global Unicast Address Network Prefix

- Study and review the hierarchy of the IPv6 network prefix.
- Practice deriving network prefix information from an IPv6 address.

Background / Scenario

With the depletion of the Internet Protocol version 4 (IPv4) network address space and the adoption and transition to IPv6, networking professionals must understand how both IPv4 and IPv6 networks function. Many devices and applications already support IPv6. This includes extensive Cisco device Internetwork Operating System (IOS) support and workstation/server operating system support, such as that found in Windows and Linux.

This lab focuses on IPv6 addresses and the components of the address. In Part 1, you will identify the IPv6 address types, and in Part 2, you will view the IPv6 settings on a PC. In Part 3, you will practice IPv6 address abbreviation, and in Part 4, you will identify the parts of the IPv6 network prefix with a focus on global unicast addresses.

Required Resources

- 1 PC (Windows 7 or Vista with Internet access)

Note: The IPv6 protocol is enabled in Windows 7 and Vista by default. The Windows XP operating system does not enable IPv6 by default and is not recommended for use with this lab. This lab uses Windows 7 PC hosts.

Part 1: Identify the Different Types of IPv6 Addresses

In Part 1, you will review the characteristics of IPv6 addresses to identify the different types of IPv6 addresses.

Step 1: Review the different types of IPv6 addresses.

An IPv6 address is 128 bits long. It is most often presented as 32 hexadecimal characters. Each hexadecimal character is the equivalent of 4 bits (4 x 32 = 128). A non-abbreviated IPv6 host address is shown here:

2001:0DB8:0001:0000:0000:0000:0000:0001

A hextet is the hexadecimal, IPv6 version of an IPv4 octet. An IPv4 address is 4 octets long, separated by dots. An IPv6 address is 8 hextets long, separated by colons.

An IPv4 address is 4 octets and is commonly written or displayed in decimal notation.

255.255.255.255

An IPv6 address is 8 hextets and is commonly written or displayed in hexadecimal notation.

FFFF:FFFF:FFFF:FFFF:FFFF:FFFF:FFFF:FFFF

In an IPv4 address, each individual octet is 8 binary digits (bits). Four octets equals one 32-bit IPv4 address.

11111111 = 255

11111111.11111111.11111111.11111111 = 255.255.255.255

In an IPv6 address, each individual hextet is 16 bits long. Eight hextets equals one 128-bit IPv6 address.

1111111111111111 = FFFF

**1111111111111111.1111111111111111.1111111111111111.1111111111111111. 1111111111111111.11111111
1111111.1111111111111111.1111111111111111 = FFFF:FFFF:FFFF:FFFF:FFFF:FFFF:FFFF:FFFF**

If we read an IPv6 address starting from the left, the first (or far left) hextet identifies the IPv6 address type. For example, if the IPv6 address has all zeros in the far left hextet, then the address is possibly a loopback address.

0000:0000:0000:0000:0000:0000:0000:0001 = loopback address

::1 = loopback address abbreviated

As another example, if the IPv6 address has FE80 in the first hextet, then the address is a link-local address.

FE80:0000:0000:0000:C5B7:CB51:3C00:D6CE = link-local address

FE80::C5B7:CB51:3C00:D6CE = link-local address abbreviated

Study the chart below to help you identify the different types of IPv6 address based on the numbers in the first hextet.

First Hextet (Far Left)	Type of IPv6 Address
0000 to 00FF	Loopback address, any address, unspecified address, or IPv4-compatible
2000 to 3FFF	Global unicast address (a routable address in a range of addresses that is currently being handed out by the Internet Assigned Numbers Authority [IANA])
FE80 to FEBF	Link-local (a unicast address which identifies the host computer on the local network)
FC00 to FCFF	Unique-local (a unicast address which can be assigned to a host to identify it as being part of a specific subnet on the local network)
FF00 to FFFF	Multicast address

There are other IPv6 address types that are either not yet widely implemented, or have already become deprecated, and are no longer supported. For instance, an **anycast address** is new to IPv6 and can be used by routers to facilitate load sharing and provide alternate path flexibility if a router becomes unavailable. Only routers should respond to an anycast address. Alternatively, **site-local addresses** have been deprecated and replaced by unique-local addresses. Site-local addresses were identified by the numbers FEC0 in the initial hextet.

In IPv6 networks, there are no network (wire) addresses or broadcast addresses as there are in IPv4 networks.

Step 2: Match the IPv6 address to its type.

Match the IPv6 addresses to their corresponding address type. Notice that the addresses have been compressed to their abbreviated notation and that the slash network prefix number is not shown. Some answer choices must be used more than once.

IPv6 Address	Answer
2001:0DB8:1:ACAD::FE55:6789:B210	1. _____
::1	2. _____
FC00:22:A:2::CD4:23E4:76FA	3. _____
2033:DB8:1:1:22:A33D:259A:21FE	4. _____
FE80::3201:CC01:65B1	5. _____
FF00::	6. _____
FF00::DB7:4322:A231:67C	7. _____
FF02::2	8. _____

Answer Choices

a. Loopback address

b. Global unicast address

c. Link-local address

d. Unique-local address

e. Multicast address

Part 2: Examine a Host IPv6 Network Interface and Address

In Part 2, you will check the IPv6 network settings of your PC to identify your network interface IPv6 address.

Step 1: Check your PC IPv6 network address settings.

a. Verify that the IPv6 protocol is installed and active on your PC-A (check your Local Area Connection settings).

b. Click the Windows **Start** button and then **Control Panel** and change **View by: Category** to **View by: Small icons**.

c. Click the **Network and Sharing Center** icon.

d. On the left side of the window, click **Change adapter settings**. You should now see icons representing your installed network adapters. Right-click your active network interface (it may be a **Local Area Connection** or a **Wireless Network Connection**), and then click **Properties**.

e. You should now see your Network Connection Properties window. Scroll through the list of items to determine whether IPv6 is present, which indicates that it is installed, and if it is also check marked, which indicates that it is active.

f. Select the item **Internet Protocol Version 6 (TCP/IPv6)** and click **Properties**. You should see the IPv6 settings for your network interface. Your IPv6 properties window is likely set to **Obtain an IPv6 address automatically**. This does not mean that IPv6 relies on the Dynamic Host Configuration Protocol (DHCP). Instead of using DHCP, IPv6 looks to the local router for IPv6 network information and then auto-configures its own IPv6 addresses. To manually configure IPv6, you must provide the IPv6 address, the subnet prefix length, and the default gateway.

Note: The local router can refer host requests for IPv6 information, especially Domain Name System (DNS) information, to a DHCPv6 server on the network.

```
┌─────────────────────────────────────────────────────────────────────────────────┐
│ Internet Protocol Version 6 (TCP/IPv6) Properties                        [?] [x]  │
├─────────────────────────────────────────────────────────────────────────────────┤
│ ┌─────────┐                                                                       │
│ │ General │                                                                       │
│ ├─────────┘                                                                       │
│                                                                                   │
│  You can get IPv6 settings assigned automatically if your network supports this   │
│  capability. Otherwise, you need to ask your network administrator for the        │
│  appropriate IPv6 settings.                                                       │
│                                                                                   │
│     (•) Obtain an IPv6 address automatically                                      │
│     ( ) Use the following IPv6 address:                                           │
│          IPv6 address:            ┌────────────────────────────┐                  │
│                                   └────────────────────────────┘                  │
│          Subnet prefix length:    ┌────┐                                          │
│                                   └────┘                                          │
│          Default gateway:         ┌────────────────────────────┐                  │
│                                   └────────────────────────────┘                  │
│                                                                                   │
│     (•) Obtain DNS server address automatically                                   │
│     ( ) Use the following DNS server addresses:                                   │
│          Preferred DNS server:    ┌────────────────────────────┐                  │
│                                   └────────────────────────────┘                  │
│          Alternate DNS server:    ┌────────────────────────────┐                  │
│                                   └────────────────────────────┘                  │
│                                                                                   │
│     [ ] Validate settings upon exit                        [  Advanced...  ]      │
│                                                                                   │
│                                                      [  OK  ]    [  Cancel  ]      │
└─────────────────────────────────────────────────────────────────────────────────┘
```

g.   After you have verified that IPv6 is installed and active on your PC, you should check your IPv6 address information. To do this, click the **Start** button, type **cmd** in the *Search programs and files* form box, and press Enter. This opens a Windows command prompt window.

h.   Type **ipconfig /all** and press Enter. Your output should look similar to this:

```
C:\Users\user> ipconfig /all


Windows IP Configuration


<output omitted>


Wireless LAN adapter Wireless Network Connection:


    Connection-specific DNS Suffix  . :

    Description . . . . . . . . . . . : Intel(R) Centrino(R) Advanced-N 6200 AGN

    Physical Address. . . . . . . . . : 02-37-10-41-FB-48

    DHCP Enabled. . . . . . . . . . . : Yes

    Autoconfiguration Enabled . . . . : Yes

    Link-local IPv6 Address . . . . . : fe80::8d4f:4f4d:3237:95e2%14(Preferred)

    IPv4 Address. . . . . . . . . . . : 192.168.2.106(Preferred)

    Subnet Mask . . . . . . . . . . . : 255.255.255.0

    Lease Obtained. . . . . . . . . . : Sunday, January 06, 2013 9:47:36 AM

    Lease Expires . . . . . . . . . . : Monday, January 07, 2013 9:47:38 AM

    Default Gateway . . . . . . . . . : 192.168.2.1

    DHCP Server . . . . . . . . . . . : 192.168.2.1

    DHCPv6 IAID . . . . . . . . . . . : 335554320
```

```
DHCPv6 Client DUID. . . . . . . . : 00-01-00-01-14-57-84-B1-1C-C1-DE-91-C3-5D


DNS Servers . . . . . . . . . . . : 192.168.1.1
                                    8.8.4.4
```

i. You can see from the output that the client PC has an IPv6 link-local address with a randomly generated interface ID. What does it indicate about the network regarding IPv6 global unicast address, IPv6 unique-local address, or IPv6 gateway address?

_____

_____

j. What kind of IPv6 addresses did you find when using **ipconfig /all**?

_____

_____

Part 3: **Practice IPv6 Address Abbreviation**

In Part 3, you will study and review rules for IPv6 address abbreviation to correctly compress and decompress IPv6 addresses.

Step 1: **Study and review the rules for IPv6 address abbreviation.**

Rule 1: In an IPv6 address, a string of four zeros (0s) in a hextet can be abbreviated as a single zero.

2001:0404:0001:1000:**0000:0000**:0EF0:BC00

2001:0404:0001:1000:**0:0**:0EF0:BC00 (abbreviated with single zeros)

Rule 2: In an IPv6 address, the leading zeros in each hextet can be omitted, trailing zeros cannot be omitted.

2001:**0404:000**1:1000:0000:0000:**0**EF0:BC00

2001:404:1:1000:0:0:EF0:BC00 (abbreviated with leading zeros omitted)

Rule 3: In an IPv6 address, a single continuous string of four or more zeros can be abbreviated as a double colon (::). The double colon abbreviation can only be used one time in an IP address.

2001:0404:0001:1000:**0000:0000**:0EF0:BC00

2001:404:1:1000**::**EF0:BC00 (abbreviated with leading zeroes omitted and continuous zeros replaced with a double colon)

The image below illustrates these rules of IPv6 address abbreviation:

```
  FF01:0000:0000:0000:0000:0000:0000:1
= FF01:0:0:0:0:0:0:1
= FF01::1
```

```
  E3D7:0000:0000:0000:51F4:00C8:C0A8:6420
= E3D7::51F4:C8:C0A8:6420
```

```
  3FFE:0501:0008:0000:0260:97FF:FE40:EFAB
= 3FFE:501:8:0:260:97FF:FE40:EFAB
= 3FFE:501:8::260:97FF:FE40:EFAB
```

Step 2: **Practice compressing and decompressing IPv6 addresses.**

Using the rules of IPv6 address abbreviation, either compress or decompress the following addresses:

1) 2002:0EC0:0200:0001:0000:04EB:44CE:08A2

_____

2) FE80:0000:0000:0001:0000:60BB:008E:7402

_____

3) FE80::7042:B3D7:3DEC:84B8

_____

4) FF00::

_____

5) 2001:0030:0001:ACAD:0000:330E:10C2:32BF

_____

Part 4:   Identify the Hierarchy of the IPv6 Global Unicast Address Network Prefix

In Part 4, you will study and review the characteristics of the IPv6 network prefix to identify the hierarchical network components of the IPv6 network prefix.

Step 1:   Study and review the hierarchy of IPv6 network prefix.

An IPv6 address is a 128-bit address made up of two parts, the network portion, identified by the first 64 bits, or first four hextets, and the host portion, which is identified by the last 64 bits, or last four hextets. Remember that each number, or character, in an IPv6 address is written in hexadecimal, which is equivalent to four bits. The following is a typical global unicast address:

> **The network portion**:   **2001:DB8:0001:ACAD**:xxxx:xxxx:xxxx:xxxx
>
> **The host portion**:   xxxx:xxxx:xxxx:xxxx:**0000:0000:0000:0001**

Most global unicast (routable) addresses use a 64-bit network prefix and a 64-bit host address. However, the network portion of an IPv6 address is not restricted to 64 bits in length and its length is identified at the end of the address by slash notation, followed by a decimal number indicating its length. If the network prefix is /64, then the network portion of the IPv6 address is 64 bits long from left to right. The host portion, or interface ID, which is the last 64 bits, is the remaining length of the IPv6 address. In some cases, as with a loopback address, the network prefix can be /128, or one hundred and twenty eight bits long. In this case, there are no bits left over for the interface identifier, and therefore, the network is restricted to a single host. Here are some examples of IPv6 addresses with different network prefix lengths:

Global unicast address:	2001:DB8:0001:ACAD:0000:0000:0000:0001/64
Loopback address:	::1/128
Multicast address:	FF00::/8
All networks address:	::/0 (similar to a quad zero address in IPv4)
Link-local address	fe80::8d4f:4f4d:3237:95e2%14 (notice that the slash fourteen at the end of the address is represented by a percent sign and the decimal number of fourteen. This address was taken from the output of an ipconfig /all command in the Windows Command Prompt)

From left to right, the network portion of an IPv6 global unicast address has a hierarchical structure that will give the following information:

1)   IANA Global Routing Number (the first three binary bits are fixed as 001)

> **200**::/12

2)   Regional Internet Registry (RIR) Prefix (bits /12 to /23)

> 200**1:0D**::/23 (the hexadecimal D character is 1101 in binary. Bits 21 to 23 are 110, and the last bit is part of the ISP Prefix)

3)   Internet service provider (ISP) Prefix (the bits up to /32)

> 2001:0D**B8**::/32

4)   Site Prefix or Site Level Aggregator (SLA) which is assigned to the customer by the ISP (the bits up to /48)

> 2001:0DB8:**0001**::/48

5)   Subnet Prefix (assigned by the customer; the bits up to /64)

2001:0DB8:0001:**ACAD**::/64

6)   Interface ID (the host is identified by the last 64 bits in the address)

2001:DB8:0001:ACAD:**8D4F:4F4D:3237:95E2**/64

The image below shows that the IPv6 address can be grouped into four basic parts:

1)   Global Routing Prefix /32

2)   Site Level Aggregator (SLA) /48

3)   Subnet ID (LAN) /64

4)   Interface ID (last 64 bits)

The host portion of the IPv6 address is called the Interface ID, because it does not identify the actual host, but rather the host's network interface card. Each network interface can have multiple IPv6 addresses, and therefore, can also have multiple interface IDs.

Step 2:   **Practice deriving network prefix information from an IPv6 address.**

Given the following address, answer the following questions:

2000:1111:aaaa:0:50a5:8a35:a5bb:66e1/64

a.   What is the interface ID?

_____

b.   What is the subnet number?

_____

c.   What is the site number?

_____

d. What is the ISP number?

_____

e. What is the ISP number in binary?

_____

f. What is the Registry number?

_____

g. What is the Registry number in binary?

_____

h. What is the IANA global number?

_____

i. What is the global routing prefix?

_____

Reflection

1. How do you think you must support IPv6 in the future?

_____

_____

2. Do you think IPv4 networks continue on, or will everyone eventually switch over to IPv6? How long do you think it will take?

_____

_____

7.2.5.5 Lab — Configuring IPv6 Addresses on Network Devices

Topology

Addressing Table

Device	Interface	IPv6 Address	Prefix Length	Default Gateway
R1	G0/0	2001:DB8:ACAD:A::1	64	N/A
	G0/1	2001:DB8:ACAD:1::1	64	N/A
S1	VLAN 1	2001:DB8:ACAD:1::B	64	N/A
PC-A	NIC	2001:DB8:ACAD:1::3	64	FE80::1
PC-B	NIC	2001:DB8:ACAD:A::3	64	FE80::1

Objectives

Part 1: Set Up Topology and Configure Basic Router and Switch Settings

Part 2: Configure IPv6 Addresses Manually

Part 3: Verify End-to-End Connectivity

Background / Scenario

Knowledge of the Internet Protocol version 6 (IPv6) multicast groups can be helpful when assigning IPv6 addresses manually. Understanding how the all-router multicast group is assigned and how to control address assignments for the Solicited Nodes multicast group can prevent IPv6 routing issues and help ensure best practices are implemented.

In this lab, you will configure hosts and device interfaces with IPv6 addresses and explore how the all-router multicast group is assigned to a router. You will use **show** commands to view IPv6 unicast and multicast addresses. You will also verify end-to-end connectivity using the **ping** and **traceroute** commands.

Note: The routers used with CCNA hands-on labs are Cisco 1941 ISRs with Cisco IOS Release 15.2(4)M3 (universalk9 image). The switches used are Cisco Catalyst 2960s with Cisco IOS Release 15.0(2) (lanbasek9 image). Other routers, switches and Cisco IOS versions can be used. Depending on the model and Cisco IOS version, the commands available and output produced might vary from what is shown in the labs. Refer to the Router Interface Summary table at the end of the lab for the correct interface identifiers.

Note: Make sure that the routers and switches have been erased and have no startup configurations. If you are unsure, contact your instructor.

Required Resources

- 1 Router (Cisco 1941 with Cisco IOS software, Release 15.2(4)M3 universal image or comparable)
- 1 Switch (Cisco 2960 with Cisco IOS Release 15.0(2) lanbasek9 image or comparable)
- 2 PCs (Windows 7 with terminal emulation program, such as Tera Term)
- Console cables to configure the Cisco IOS devices via the console ports
- Ethernet cables as shown in the topology

Note: The Gigabit Ethernet interfaces on Cisco 1941 routers are autosensing and an Ethernet straight-through cable may be used between the router and PC-B. If using another model Cisco router, it may be necessary to use an Ethernet crossover cable.

Note: The IPv6 protocol is enabled in Windows 7 and Vista by default. The Windows XP operating system does not enable IPv6 by default and is not recommended for use with this lab. This lab uses Windows 7 PC hosts.

Part 1:   Set Up Topology and Configure Basic Router and Switch Settings

Step 1:   Cable the network as shown in the topology.

Step 2:   Initialize and reload the router and switch.

Step 3:   Verify that the PC interfaces are configured to use the IPv6 protocol.

Verify that the IPv6 protocol is active on both PCs by ensuring that the **Internet Protocol Version 6 (TCP/IPv6)** check box is selected in the Local Area Connection Properties window.

Step 4:   **Configure the router.**

a.   Console into the router and enable privileged EXEC mode.

b.   Assign the device name to the router.

c.   Disable DNS lookup to prevent the router from attempting to translate incorrectly entered commands as though they were hostnames.

d.   Assign **class** as the privileged EXEC encrypted password.

e.   Assign **cisco** as the console password and enable login.

f.   Assign **cisco** as the VTY password and enable login.

g.   Encrypt the clear text passwords.

h.   Create a banner that warns anyone accessing the device that unauthorized access is prohibited.

i.   Save the running configuration to the startup configuration file.

Step 5:   **Configure the switch.**

a.   Console into the switch and enable privileged EXEC mode.

b.   Assign the device name to the switch.

c.   Disable DNS lookup to prevent the router from attempting to translate incorrectly entered commands as though they were hostnames.

d.   Assign **class** as the privileged EXEC encrypted password.

e.   Assign **cisco** as the console password and enable login.

f.   Assign **cisco** as the VTY password and enable login.

g.   Encrypt the clear text passwords.

h.   Create a banner that warns anyone accessing the device that unauthorized access is prohibited.

i.   Save the running configuration to the startup configuration file.

Part 2:   **Configure IPv6 Addresses Manually**

Step 1:   **Assign the IPv6 addresses to Ethernet interfaces on R1.**

a.   Assign the IPv6 global unicast addresses, listed in the Addressing Table, to both Ethernet interfaces on R1.

```
R1(config)# interface g0/0
R1(config-if)# ipv6 address 2001:db8:acad:a::1/64
R1(config-if)# no shutdown
R1(config-if)# interface g0/1
R1(config-if)# ipv6 address 2001:db8:acad:1::1/64
```

```
R1(config-if)# no shutdown
R1(config-if)# end
R1#
```

b. Issue the **show ipv6 interface brief** command to verify that the correct IPv6 unicast address is assigned to each interface.

```
R1# show ipv6 interface brief
Em0/0                    [administratively down/down]
    unassigned
GigabitEthernet0/0       [up/up]
    FE80::D68C:B5FF:FECE:A0C0
    2001:DB8:ACAD:A::1
GigabitEthernet0/1       [up/up]
    FE80::D68C:B5FF:FECE:A0C1
    2001:DB8:ACAD:1::1
Serial0/0/0              [administratively down/down]
    unassigned
Serial0/0/1              [administratively down/down]
    unassigned
R1#
```

c. Issue the **show ipv6 interface g0/0** command. Notice that the interface is listing two Solicited Nodes multicast groups, because the IPv6 link-local (FE80) Interface ID was not manually configured to match the IPv6 unicast Interface ID.

Note: The link-local address displayed is based on EUI-64 addressing, which automatically uses the interface Media Access Control (MAC) address to create a 128-bit IPv6 link-local address.

```
R1# show ipv6 interface g0/0
GigabitEthernet0/0 is up, line protocol is up
  IPv6 is enabled, link-local address is FE80::D68C:B5FF:FECE:A0C0
  No Virtual link-local address(es):
  Global unicast address(es):
    2001:DB8:ACAD:A::1, subnet is 2001:DB8:ACAD:A::/64
  Joined group address(es):
    FF02::1
    FF02::1:FF00:1
    FF02::1:FFCE:A0C0
  MTU is 1500 bytes
  ICMP error messages limited to one every 100 milliseconds
  ICMP redirects are enabled
  ICMP unreachables are sent
  ND DAD is enabled, number of DAD attempts: 1
```

```
ND reachable time is 30000 milliseconds (using 30000)

ND advertised reachable time is 0 (unspecified)

ND advertised retransmit interval is 0 (unspecified)

ND router advertisements are sent every 200 seconds

ND router advertisements live for 1800 seconds

ND advertised default router preference is Medium

Hosts use stateless autoconfig for addresses.

R1#
```

d. To get the link-local address to match the unicast address on the interface, manually enter the link-local addresses on each of the Ethernet interfaces on R1.

```
R1# config t

Enter configuration commands, one per line.  End with CNTL/Z.

R1(config)# interface g0/0

R1(config-if)# ipv6 address fe80::1 link-local

R1(config-if)# interface g0/1

R1(config-if)# ipv6 address fe80::1 link-local

R1(config-if)# end

R1#
```

Note: Each router interface belongs to a separate network. Packets with a link-local address never leave the local network; therefore, you can use the same link-local address on both interfaces.

e. Re-issue the **show ipv6 interface g0/0** command. Notice that the link-local address has been changed to **FE80::1** and that there is only one Solicited Nodes multicast group listed.

```
R1# show ipv6 interface g0/0

GigabitEthernet0/0 is up, line protocol is up

  IPv6 is enabled, link-local address is FE80::1

  No Virtual link-local address(es):

  Global unicast address(es):

    2001:DB8:ACAD:A::1, subnet is 2001:DB8:ACAD:A::/64

  Joined group address(es):

    FF02::1

    FF02::1:FF00:1

  MTU is 1500 bytes

  ICMP error messages limited to one every 100 milliseconds

  ICMP redirects are enabled

  ICMP unreachables are sent

  ND DAD is enabled, number of DAD attempts: 1

  ND reachable time is 30000 milliseconds (using 30000)

  ND advertised reachable time is 0 (unspecified)

  ND advertised retransmit interval is 0 (unspecified)

  ND router advertisements are sent every 200 seconds

  ND router advertisements live for 1800 seconds
```

```
    ND advertised default router preference is Medium

    Hosts use stateless autoconfig for addresses.

R1#
```

What multicast groups have been assigned to interface G0/0?

Step 2: **Enable IPv6 routing on R1.**

a. On a PC-B command prompt, enter the **ipconfig** command to examine IPv6 address information assigned to the PC interface.

```
C:\>ipconfig

Windows IP Configuration


Ethernet adapter Local Area Connection:

    Connection-specific DNS Suffix  . :
    Link-local IPv6 Address . . . . . : fe80::dd0e:67fb:d14f:1288%11
    Autoconfiguration IPv4 Address. . : 169.254.18.136
    Subnet Mask . . . . . . . . . . . : 255.255.0.0
    Default Gateway . . . . . . . . . :

Tunnel adapter isatap.{E2FC1866-B195-460A-BF40-F04F42A38FFE}:

    Media State . . . . . . . . . . . : Media disconnected
    Connection-specific DNS Suffix  . :

Tunnel adapter Local Area Connection* 11:

    Media State . . . . . . . . . . . : Media disconnected
    Connection-specific DNS Suffix  . :

C:\>_
```

Has an IPv6 unicast address been assigned to the network interface card (NIC) on PC-B? _____

b. Enable IPv6 routing on R1 using the **IPv6 unicast-routing** command.

```
R1 # configure terminal

R1(config)# ipv6 unicast-routing

R1(config)# exit

R1#

*Dec 17 18:29:07.415: %SYS-5-CONFIG_I: Configured from console by console
```

c. Use the **show ipv6 interface g0/0** command to see what multicast groups are assigned to interface G0/0. Notice that the all-router multicast group (FF02::2) now appears in the group list for interface G0/0.

Note: This will allow the PCs to obtain their IP address and default gateway information automatically using Stateless Address Autoconfiguration (SLAAC).

```
R1# show ipv6 interface g0/0

GigabitEthernet0/0 is up, line protocol is up

  IPv6 is enabled, link-local address is FE80::1
```

```
        No Virtual link-local address(es):
        Global unicast address(es):
          2001:DB8:ACAD:A::1, subnet is 2001:DB8:ACAD:A::/64 [EUI]
        Joined group address(es):
          FF02::1
          FF02::2
          FF02::1:FF00:1
      MTU is 1500 bytes
      ICMP error messages limited to one every 100 milliseconds
      ICMP redirects are enabled
      ICMP unreachables are sent
      ND DAD is enabled, number of DAD attempts: 1
      ND reachable time is 30000 milliseconds (using 30000)
      ND advertised reachable time is 0 (unspecified)
      ND advertised retransmit interval is 0 (unspecified)
      ND router advertisements are sent every 200 seconds
      ND router advertisements live for 1800 seconds
      ND advertised default router preference is Medium
      Hosts use stateless autoconfig for addresses.
    R1#
```

d. Now that R1 is part of the all-router multicast group, re-issue the **ipconfig** command on PC-B. Examine the IPv6 address information.

```
C:\>ipconfig

Windows IP Configuration


Ethernet adapter Local Area Connection:

   Connection-specific DNS Suffix  . :
   IPv6 Address. . . . . . . . . . . : 2001:db8:acad:a:dd0e:67fb:d14f:1288
   Temporary IPv6 Address. . . . . . : 2001:db8:acad:a:6082:dcb0:5fb2:3ece
   Link-local IPv6 Address . . . . . : fe80::dd0e:67fb:d14f:1288%11
   Autoconfiguration IPv4 Address. . : 169.254.18.136
   Subnet Mask . . . . . . . . . . . : 255.255.0.0
   Default Gateway . . . . . . . . . : fe80::1%11

Tunnel adapter isatap.{E2FC1866-B195-460A-BF40-F04F42A38FFE}:

   Media State . . . . . . . . . . . : Media disconnected
   Connection-specific DNS Suffix  . :

Tunnel adapter Local Area Connection* 11:

   Media State . . . . . . . . . . . : Media disconnected
   Connection-specific DNS Suffix  . :

C:\>
```

Why did PC-B receive the Global Routing Prefix and Subnet ID that you configured on R1?

_____

_____

Step 3: **Assign IPv6 addresses to the management interface (SVI) on S1.**

  a. Assign the IPv6 address listed in the Addressing Table to the management interface (VLAN 1) on S1. Also assign a link-local address for this interface. IPv6 command syntax is the same as on the router.

  b. Verify that the IPv6 addresses are properly assigned to the management interface using the **show ipv6 interface vlan1** command.

Step 4: **Assign static IPv6 addresses to the PCs.**

  a. Open the Local Area Connection Properties window on PC-A. Select **Internet Protocol Version 6 (TCP/IPv6)** and click **Properties**.

  b. Click the **Use the following IPv6 address** radio button. Refer to the Addressing Table and enter the **IPv6 address**, **Subnet prefix length**, and **Default gateway** information. Click **OK**.

c.   Click **Close** to close the Local Area Connection Properties window.

d.   Repeat Steps 4a to c to enter the static IPv6 information on PC-B. For the correct IPv6 address information, refer to the Addressing Table.

e.   Issue the **ipconfig** command from the command line on PC-B to verify the IPv6 address information.

```
C:\>ipconfig

Windows IP Configuration


Ethernet adapter Local Area Connection:

   Connection-specific DNS Suffix  . :
   IPv6 Address. . . . . . . . . . . : 2001:db8:acad:a::3
   IPv6 Address. . . . . . . . . . . : 2001:db8:acad:a:d428:7de2:997c:b05a
   Temporary IPv6 Address. . . . . . : 2001:db8:acad:a:e19e:db9f:e38e:9252
   Link-local IPv6 Address . . . . . : fe80::d428:7de2:997c:b05a%11
   Default Gateway . . . . . . . . . : fe80::1%11

Tunnel adapter isatap.{E2FC1866-B195-460A-BF40-F04F42A38FFE}:

   Media State . . . . . . . . . . . : Media disconnected
   Connection-specific DNS Suffix  . :

Tunnel adapter Local Area Connection* 11:

   Media State . . . . . . . . . . . : Media disconnected
   Connection-specific DNS Suffix  . :

C:\>
```

Part 3:   **Verify End-to-End Connectivity**

a.   From PC-A, ping **FE80::1**. This is the link-local address assigned to G0/1 on R1.

```
C:\>ping fe80::1

Pinging fe80::1 with 32 bytes of data:
Reply from fe80::1: time<1ms
Reply from fe80::1: time<1ms
Reply from fe80::1: time<1ms
Reply from fe80::1: time<1ms

Ping statistics for fe80::1:
    Packets: Sent = 4, Received = 4, Lost = 0 (0% loss),
Approximate round trip times in milli-seconds:
    Minimum = 0ms, Maximum = 0ms, Average = 0ms

C:\>
```

Note: You can also test connectivity by using the global unicast address, instead of the link-local address.

b.   Ping the S1 management interface from PC-A.

```
C:\>ping 2001:db8:acad:1::b

Pinging 2001:db8:acad:1::b with 32 bytes of data:
Reply from 2001:db8:acad:1::b: time=14ms
Reply from 2001:db8:acad:1::b: time=2ms
Reply from 2001:db8:acad:1::b: time=2ms
Reply from 2001:db8:acad:1::b: time=3ms

Ping statistics for 2001:db8:acad:1::b:
    Packets: Sent = 4, Received = 4, Lost = 0 (0% loss),
Approximate round trip times in milli-seconds:
    Minimum = 2ms, Maximum = 14ms, Average = 5ms

C:\>
```

c.   Use the **tracert** command on PC-A to verify that you have end-to-end connectivity to PC-B.

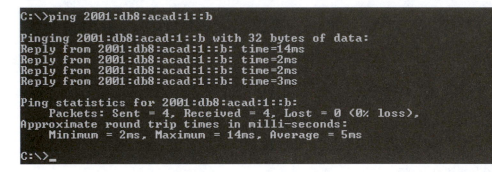

```
C:\>tracert 2001:db8:acad:a::3

Tracing route to 2001:db8:acad:a::3 over a maximum of 30 hops

  1    <1 ms    <1 ms    <1 ms  2001:db8:acad:1::1
  2     5 ms    <1 ms    <1 ms  2001:db8:acad:a::3

Trace complete.

C:\>
```

d.   From PC-B, ping PC-A.

```
C:\>ping 2001:db8:acad:1::3

Pinging 2001:db8:acad:1::3 with 32 bytes of data:
Reply from 2001:db8:acad:1::3: time<1ms
Reply from 2001:db8:acad:1::3: time<1ms
Reply from 2001:db8:acad:1::3: time<1ms
Reply from 2001:db8:acad:1::3: time<1ms

Ping statistics for 2001:db8:acad:1::3:
    Packets: Sent = 4, Received = 4, Lost = 0 (0% loss),
Approximate round trip times in milli-seconds:
    Minimum = 0ms, Maximum = 0ms, Average = 0ms

C:\>
```

e. From PC-B, ping the link-local address for G0/0 on R1.

```
C:\>ping fe80::1

Pinging fe80::1 with 32 bytes of data:
Reply from fe80::1: time<1ms
Reply from fe80::1: time<1ms
Reply from fe80::1: time<1ms
Reply from fe80::1: time<1ms

Ping statistics for fe80::1:
    Packets: Sent = 4, Received = 4, Lost = 0 (0% loss),
Approximate round trip times in milli-seconds:
    Minimum = 0ms, Maximum = 0ms, Average = 0ms

C:\>
```

Note: If end-to-end connectivity is not established, troubleshoot your IPv6 address assignments to verify that you entered the addresses correctly on all devices.

Reflection

1. Why can the same link-local address, FE80::1, be assigned to both Ethernet interfaces on R1?

    _____

    _____

2. What is the Subnet ID of the IPv6 unicast address 2001:db8:acad::aaaa:1234/64?

    _____

Router Interface Summary Table

Router Interface Summary				
Router Model	Ethernet Interface #1	Ethernet Interface #2	Serial Interface #1	Serial Interface #2
1800	Fast Ethernet 0/0 (F0/0)	Fast Ethernet 0/1 (F0/1)	Serial 0/0/0 (S0/0/0)	Serial 0/0/1 (S0/0/1)
1900	Gigabit Ethernet 0/0 (G0/0)	Gigabit Ethernet 0/1 (G0/1)	Serial 0/0/0 (S0/0/0)	Serial 0/0/1 (S0/0/1)
2801	Fast Ethernet 0/0 (F0/0)	Fast Ethernet 0/1 (F0/1)	Serial 0/1/0 (S0/0/0)	Serial 0/1/1 (S0/0/1)
2811	Fast Ethernet 0/0 (F0/0)	Fast Ethernet 0/1 (F0/1)	Serial 0/0/0 (S0/0/0)	Serial 0/0/1 (S0/0/1)
2900	Gigabit Ethernet 0/0 (G0/0)	Gigabit Ethernet 0/1 (G0/1)	Serial 0/0/0 (S0/0/0)	Serial 0/0/1 (S0/0/1)

Note: To find out how the router is configured, look at the interfaces to identify the type of router and how many interfaces the router has. There is no way to effectively list all the combinations of configurations for each router class. This table includes identifiers for the possible combinations of Ethernet and Serial interfaces in the device. The table does not include any other type of interface, even though a specific router may contain one. An example of this might be an ISDN BRI interface. The string in parenthesis is the legal abbreviation that can be used in Cisco IOS commands to represent the interface.

7.3.2.7 Lab — Testing Network Connectivity with Ping and Traceroute

Topology

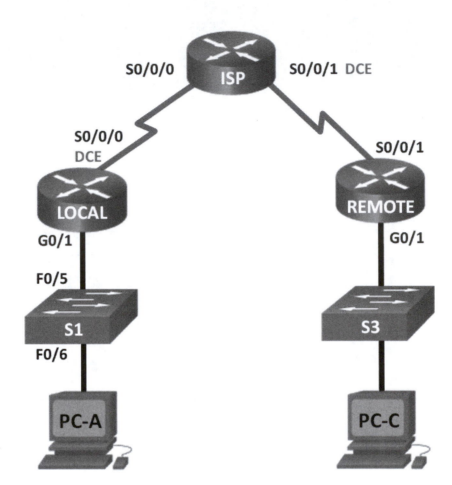

Addressing Table

Device	Interface	IP Address	Subnet Mask	Default Gateway
LOCAL	G0/1	192.168.1.1	255.255.255.0	N/A
	S0/0/0 (DCE)	10.1.1.1	255.255.255.252	N/A
ISP	S0/0/0	10.1.1.2	255.255.255.252	N/A
	S0/0/1 (DCE)	10.2.2.2	255.255.255.252	N/A
REMOTE	G0/1	192.168.3.1	255.255.255.0	N/A
	S0/0/1	10.2.2.1	255.255.255.252	N/A
S1	VLAN 1	192.168.1.11	255.255.255.0	192.168.1.1
S3	VLAN 1	192.168.3.11	255.255.255.0	192.168.3.1
PC-A	NIC	192.168.1.3	255.255.255.0	192.168.1.1
PC-C	NIC	192.168.3.3	255.255.255.0	192.168.3.1

Objectives

Part 1: Build and Configure the Network

- Cable the network.
- Configure the PCs.
- Configure the routers.
- Configure the switches.

Part 2: Use Ping Command for Basic Network Testing

- Use ping from a PC.
- Use ping from Cisco devices.

Part 3: Use Tracert and Traceroute Commands for Basic Network Testing

- Use tracert from a PC.
- Use traceroute from Cisco devices.

Part 4: Troubleshoot the Topology

Background / Scenario

Ping and traceroute are two tools that are indispensable when testing TCP/IP network connectivity. Ping is a network administration utility used to test the reachability of a device on an IP network. This utility also measures the round-trip time for messages sent from the originating host to a destination computer. The ping utility is available on Windows, Unix-like operating systems (OS), and the Cisco Internetwork Operating System (IOS).

The traceroute utility is a network diagnostic tool for displaying the route and measuring the transit delays of packets travelling an IP network. The tracert utility is available on Windows, and a similar utility, traceroute, is available on Unix-like OS and Cisco IOS.

In this lab, the **ping** and **traceroute** commands are examined and command options are explored to modify the command behavior. Cisco devices and PCs are used in this lab for command exploration. Cisco routers will use Enhanced Interior Gateway Routing Protocol (EIGRP) to route packets between networks. The necessary Cisco device configurations are provided in this lab.

Note: The routers used with CCNA hands-on labs are Cisco 1941 Integrated Services Routers (ISRs) with Cisco IOS Release 15.2(4)M3 (universalk9 image). The switches used are Cisco Catalyst 2960s with Cisco IOS Release 15.0(2) (lanbasek9 image). Other routers, switches and Cisco IOS versions can be used. Depending on the model and Cisco IOS version, the commands available and output produced might vary from what is shown in the labs. Refer to the Router Interface Summary Table at the end of this lab for the correct interface identifiers.

Note: Make sure that the routers and switches have been erased and have no startup configurations. If you are unsure, contact your instructor.

Required Resources

- 3 Routers (Cisco 1941 with Cisco IOS Release 15.2(4)M3 universal image or comparable)
- 2 Switches (Cisco 2960 with Cisco IOS Release 15.0(2) lanbasek9 image or comparable)
- 2 PCs (Windows 7, Vista, or XP with terminal emulation program, such as Tera Term)
- Console cables to configure the Cisco IOS devices via the console ports
- Ethernet and serial cables as shown in the topology

Part 1: Build and Configure the Network

In Part 1, you will set up the network in the topology and configure the PCs and Cisco devices. The initial configurations for the routers and switches are provided for your reference. In this topology, EIGRP is used to route packets between networks.

Step 1: **Cable the network as shown in the topology.**

Step 2: **Erase the configurations on the routers and switches, and reload the devices.**

Step 3: **Configure PC IP addresses and default gateways according to the Addressing Table.**

Step 4: **Configure the LOCAL, ISP, and REMOTE routers using the initial configurations provided below.**

At the switch or router global config mode prompt, copy and paste the configuration for each device. Save the configuration to startup-config.

Initial configurations for the LOCAL router:

```
hostname LOCAL
no ip domain-lookup
interface s0/0/0
 ip address 10.1.1.1 255.255.255.252
 clock rate 56000
 no shutdown
interface g0/1
 ip add 192.168.1.1 255.255.255.0
 no shutdown
router eigrp 1
 network 10.1.1.0 0.0.0.3
 network 192.168.1.0 0.0.0.255
 no auto-summary
```

Initial configurations for ISP:

```
hostname ISP
no ip domain-lookup
interface s0/0/0
 ip address 10.1.1.2 255.255.255.252
 no shutdown
interface s0/0/1
 ip add 10.2.2.2 255.255.255.252
 clock rate 56000
 no shutdown
router eigrp 1
 network 10.1.1.0 0.0.0.3
 network 10.2.2.0 0.0.0.3
```

```
 no auto-summary
end
```

Initial configurations for REMOTE:

```
hostname REMOTE
no ip domain-lookup
interface s0/0/1
 ip address 10.2.2.1 255.255.255.252
 no shutdown
interface g0/1
 ip add 192.168.3.1 255.255.255.0
 no shutdown
router eigrp 1
 network 10.2.2.0 0.0.0.3
 network 192.168.3.0 0.0.0.255
 no auto-summary
end
```

Step 5: **Configure the S1 and S3 switches with the initial configurations.**

Initial configurations for S1:

```
hostname S1
no ip domain-lookup
interface vlan 1
 ip add 192.168.1.11 255.255.255.0
 no shutdown
 exit
ip default-gateway 192.168.1.1
end
```

Initial configurations for S3:

```
hostname S3
no ip domain-lookup
interface vlan 1
 ip add 192.168.3.11 255.255.255.0
 no shutdown
 exit
ip default-gateway 192.168.3.1
end
```

Step 6:   **Configure an IP host table on the LOCAL router.**

The IP host table allows you to use a hostname to connect to a remote device rather than an IP address. The host table provides name resolution for the device with the following configurations. Copy and paste the following configurations for the LOCAL router. The configurations will allow you to use the hostnames for **ping** and **traceroute** commands on the LOCAL router.

```
ip host REMOTE 10.2.2.1 192.168.3.1

ip host ISP 10.1.1.2 10.2.2.2

ip host LOCAL 192.168.1.1 10.1.1.1

ip host PC-C 192.168.3.3

ip host PC-A 192.168.1.3

ip host S1 192.168.1.11

ip host S3 192.168.3.11

end
```

Part 2:   Use Ping Command for Basic Network Testing

In Part 2 of this lab, use the **ping** command to verify end-to-end connectivity. Ping operates by sending Internet Control Message Protocol (ICMP) echo request packets to the target host and then waiting for an ICMP response. It can record the round trip time and any packet loss.

You will examine the results with the **ping** command and the additional ping options that are available on Windows-based PCs and Cisco devices.

Step 1:   **Test network connectivity from the LOCAL network using PC-A.**

All the pings from PC-A to other devices in the topology should be successful. If they are not, check the topology and the cabling, as well as the configuration of the Cisco devices and the PCs.

a. Ping from PC-A to its default gateway (LOCAL's GigabitEthernet 0/1 interface).

```
C:\Users\User1> ping 192.168.1.1

Pinging 192.168.1.1 with 32 bytes of data:

Reply from 192.168.1.1: bytes=32 time<1ms TTL=255

Reply from 192.168.1.1: bytes=32 time<1ms TTL=255

Reply from 192.168.1.1: bytes=32 time<1ms TTL=255

Reply from 192.168.1.1: bytes=32 time<1ms TTL=255


Ping statistics for 192.168.1.1:

    Packets: Sent = 4, Received = 4, Lost = 0 (0% loss),

Approximate round trip times in milli-seconds:

    Minimum = 0ms, Maximum = 0ms, Average = 0ms
```

In this example, four (4) ICMP requests, 32 bytes each, were sent and the responses were received in less than one millisecond with no packet loss. The transmission and reply time increases as the ICMP requests and responses are processed by more devices during the journey to and from the final destination.

b. From PC-A, ping the addresses listed in the following table and record the average round trip time and Time to Live (TTL).

Destination	Average Round Trip Time (ms)	TTL
192.168.1.1 (LOCAL)		
192.168.1.11 (S1)		
10.1.1.1 (LOCAL)		
10.1.1.2 (ISP)		
10.2.2.2 (ISP)		
10.2.2.1 (REMOTE)		
192.168.3.1 (REMOTE)		
192.168.3.11 (S3)		
192.168.3.3 (PC-C)		

Notice the average round trip time to 192.168.3.3 (PC-C). The time increased because the ICMP requests were processed by three routers before PC-A received the reply from PC-C.

```
C:\Users\User1> ping 192.168.3.3

Pinging 192.168.3.3 with 32 bytes of data:

Reply from 192.168.3.3: bytes=32 time=41ms TTL=125

Reply from 192.168.3.3: bytes=32 time=41ms TTL=125

Reply from 192.168.3.3: bytes=32 time=40ms TTL=125

Reply from 192.168.3.3: bytes=32 time=41ms TTL=125


Ping statistics for 192.168.3.3:
    Packets: Sent = 4, Received = 4, Lost = 0 (0% loss),
Approximate round trip times in milli-seconds:
    Minimum = 40ms, Maximum = 41ms, Average = 40ms
```

Step 2:   Use extended ping commands on a PC.

The default **ping** command sends four requests at 32 bytes each. It waits 4,000 milliseconds (4 seconds) for each response to be returned before displaying the "Request timed out" message. The **ping** command can be fine tuned for troubleshooting a network.

a. At the command prompt, type **ping** and press Enter.

```
C:\Users\User1> ping

Usage: ping [-t] [-a] [-n count] [-l size] [-f] [-i TTL] [-v TOS]
            [-r count] [-s count] [[-j host-list] | [-k host-list]]
            [-w timeout] [-R] [-S srcaddr] [-4] [-6] target_name


Options:
    -t              Ping the specified host until stopped.

                    To see statistics and continue - type Control-Break;

                    To stop - type Control-C.
    -a              Resolve addresses to hostnames.
```

```
-n count        Number of echo requests to send.

-l size         Send buffer size.

-f              Set Don't Fragment flag in packet (IPv4-only).

-i TTL          Time To Live.

-v TOS          Type Of Service (IPv4-only. This setting has been deprecated
                and has no effect on the type of service field in the IP Header).

-r count        Record route for count hops (IPv4-only).

-s count        Timestamp for count hops (IPv4-only).

-j host-list    Loose source route along host-list (IPv4-only).

-k host-list    Strict source route along host-list (IPv4-only).

-w timeout      Timeout in milliseconds to wait for each reply.

-R              Use routing header to test reverse route also (IPv6-only).

-S srcaddr      Source address to use.

-4              Force using IPv4.

-6              Force using IPv6.
```

b.   Using the **–t** option, ping PC-C to verify that PC-C is reachable.

```
C:\Users\User1> ping -t 192.168.3.3

Reply from 192.168.3.3: bytes=32 time=41ms TTL=125

Reply from 192.168.3.3: bytes=32 time=40ms TTL=125
```

To illustrate the results when a host is unreachable, disconnect the cable between the REMOTE router and the S3 switch, or shut down the GigabitEthernet 0/1 interface on the REMOTE router.

```
Reply from 192.168.3.3: bytes=32 time=41ms TTL=125

Reply from 192.168.1.3: Destination host unreachable.

Reply from 192.168.1.3: Destination host unreachable.
```

While the network is functioning correctly, the **ping** command can determine whether the destination responded and how long it took to receive a reply from the destination. If a network connectivity problem exists, the **ping** command displays an error message.

c.   Reconnect the Ethernet cable or enable the GigabitEthernet interface on the REMOTE router (using the **no shutdown** command) before moving onto the next step. After about 30 seconds, the ping should be successful again.

```
Request timed out.

Request timed out.

Request timed out.

Request timed out.

Reply from 192.168.3.3: bytes=32 time=41ms TTL=125

Reply from 192.168.3.3: bytes=32 time=40ms TTL=125
```

d.   Press **Ctrl+C** to stop the ping command.

Step 3:   **Test network connectivity from the LOCAL network using Cisco devices.**

The **ping** command is also available on Cisco devices. In this step, the **ping** command is examined using the LOCAL router and the S1 switch.

a. Ping PC-C on the REMOTE network using the IP address of 192.168.3.3 from the LOCAL router.

    ```
    LOCAL# ping 192.168.3.3

    Type escape sequence to abort.

    Sending 5, 100-byte ICMP Echos to 192.168.3.3, timeout is 2 seconds:

    !!!!!

    Success rate is 100 percent (5/5), round-trip min/avg/max = 60/64/68 ms
    ```

    The exclamation point (!) indicates that the ping was successful from the LOCAL router to PC-C. The round trip takes an average of 64 ms with no packet loss, as indicated by a 100% success rate.

b. Because a local host table was configured on the LOCAL router, you can ping PC-C on the REMOTE network using the hostname configured from the LOCAL router.

    ```
    LOCAL# ping PC-C

    Type escape sequence to abort.

    Sending 5, 100-byte ICMP Echos to 192.168.3.3, timeout is 2 seconds:

    !!!!!

    Success rate is 100 percent (5/5), round-trip min/avg/max = 60/63/64 ms
    ```

c. There are more options available for the **ping** command. At the CLI, type **ping** and press Enter. Input **192.168.3.3** or **PC-C** for the Target IP address. Press Enter to accept the default value for other options.

    ```
    LOCAL# ping

    Protocol [ip]:

    Target IP address: PC-C

    Repeat count [5]:

    Datagram size [100]:

    Timeout in seconds [2]:

    Extended commands [n]:

    Sweep range of sizes [n]:

    Type escape sequence to abort.

    Sending 5, 100-byte ICMP Echos to 192.168.3.3, timeout is 2 seconds:

    !!!!!

    Success rate is 100 percent (5/5), round-trip min/avg/max = 60/63/64 ms
    ```

d. You can use an extended ping to observe when there is a network issue. Start the **ping** command to 192.168.3.3 with a repeat a count of 500. Then, disconnect the cable between the REMOTE router and the S3 switch or shut down the GigabitEthernet 0/1 interface on the REMOTE router.

    Reconnect the Ethernet cable or enable the GigabitEthernet interface on the REMOTE router after the exclamation points (!) have replaced by the letter U and periods (.). After about 30 seconds, the ping should be successful again. Press **Ctrl+Shift+6** to stop the **ping** command if desired.

    ```
    LOCAL# ping

    Protocol [ip]:

    Target IP address: 192.168.3.3

    Repeat count [5]: 500

    Datagram size [100]:

    Timeout in seconds [2]:

    Extended commands [n]:
    ```

```
Sweep range of sizes [n]:

Type escape sequence to abort.

Sending 500, 100-byte ICMP Echos to 192.168.3.3, timeout is 2 seconds:

!!!!!!!!!!!!!!!!!!!!!!!!!!!!!!!!!!!!!!!!!!!!!!!!!!!!!!!!!!!!!!!!!!!!!!!!!!!

!!!!!!!!!!!!!!!!!!!!!!!!!!!!!!!!!!!!!!!!!!!!!!!!!!!!!!!!!!!!!!!!!!!!!!!!!!!

!!!!!!!!!!!!!!!!!!!!!!!!!!!!!!!!!!!!!!!!!!!!!!!!!!!!!U..................

....!!!!!!!!!!!!!!!!!!!!!!!!!!!!!!!!!!!!!!!!!!!!!!!!!!!!!!!!!!!!!!!!!!!!!

!!!!!!!!!!!!!!!!!!!!!!!!!!!!!!!!!!!!!!!!!!!!!!!!!!!!!!!!!!!!!!!!!!!!!!!!!!!

!!!!!!!!!!!!!!!!!!!!!!!!!!!!!!!!!!!!!!!!!!!!!!!!!!!!!!!!!!!!!!!!!!!!!!!!!!!

!!!!!!!!!!!!!!!!!!!!!!!!!!!!!!!!!!!!!!!!!!!!!!!!!!!!!!!!!!!!!!!!!!!!!!!!!!!

!!!!!!!!!!!

Success rate is 95 percent (479/500), round-trip min/avg/max = 60/63/72 ms
```

The letter U in the results indicates that a destination is unreachable. An error protocol data unit (PDU) was received by the LOCAL router. Each period (.) in the output indicates that the ping timed out while waiting for a reply from PC-C. In this example, 5% of the packets were lost during the simulated network outage.

Note: You can also use the following command for the same results:

```
LOCAL# ping 192.168.3.3 repeat 500
```

or

```
LOCAL# ping PC-C repeat 500
```

e. You can also test network connectivity with a switch. In this example, the S1 switch pings the S3 switch on the REMOTE network.

```
S1# ping 192.168.3.11

Type escape sequence to abort.

Sending 5, 100-byte ICMP Echos to 192.168.3.11, timeout is 2 seconds:

!!!!!

Success rate is 100 percent (5/5), round-trip min/avg/max = 67/67/68 ms
```

The **ping** command is extremely useful when troubleshooting network connectivity. However, ping cannot indicate the location of problem when a ping is not successful. The **tracert** (or **traceroute**) command can display network latency and path information.

Part 3: Use Tracert and Traceroute Commands for Basic Network Testing

The commands for tracing routes can be found on PCs and network devices. For a Windows-based PC, the **tracert** command uses ICMP messages to trace the path to the final destination. The **traceroute** command utilizes the User Datagram Protocol (UDP) datagrams for tracing routes to the final destination for Cisco devices and other Unix-like PCs.

In Part 3, you will examine the traceroute commands and determine the path that a packet travels to its final destination. You will use the **tracert** command from the Windows PCs and the **traceroute** command from the Cisco devices. You will also examine the options that are available for fine tuning the traceroute results.

Step 1: Use the tracert command from PC-A to PC-C.

a. At the command prompt, type **tracert 192.168.3.3**.

```
C:\Users\User1> tracert 192.168.3.3

Tracing route to PC-C [192.168.3.3]

Over a maximum of 30 hops:


    1     <1 ms     <1 ms     <1 ms      192.168.1.1

    2     24 ms     24 ms     24 ms      10.1.1.2

    3     48 ms     48 ms     48 ms      10.2.2.1

    4     59 ms     59 ms     59 ms      PC-C [192.168.3.3]


Trace complete.
```

The tracert results indicates the path from PC-A to PC-C is from PC-A to LOCAL to ISP to REMOTE to PC-C. The path to PC-C traveled through three router hops to the final destination of PC-C.

Step 2:   Explore additional options for the tracert command.

a.   At the command prompt, type **tracert** and press Enter.

```
C:\Users\User1> tracert


Usage: tracert [-d] [-h maximum_hops] [-j host-list] [-w timeout]
               [-R] [-S srcaddr] [-4] [-6] target_name


Options:
    -d                     Do not resolve addresses to hostnames.
    -h maximum_hops        Maximum number of hops to search for target.
    -j host-list           Loose source route along host-list (IPv4-only).
    -w timeout             Wait timeout milliseconds for each reply.
    -R                     Trace round-trip path (IPv6-only).
    -S srcaddr             Source address to use (IPv6-only).
    -4                     Force using IPv4.
    -6                     Force using IPv6.
```

b.   Use the **-d** option. Notice that the IP address of 192.168.3.3 is not resolved as PC-C.

```
C:\Users\User1> tracert -d 192.168.3.3

Tracing route to 192.168.3.3 over a maximum of 30 hops:


    1     <1 ms     <1 ms     <1 ms      192.168.1.1

    2     24 ms     24 ms     24 ms      10.1.1.2

    3     48 ms     48 ms     48 ms      10.2.2.1

    4     59 ms     59 ms     59 ms      192.168.3.3


Trace complete.
```

Step 3: **Use the traceroute command from the LOCAL router to PC-C.**

a. At the command prompt, type **traceroute 192.168.3.3** or **traceroute PC-C** on the LOCAL router. The hostnames are resolved because a local IP host table was configured on the LOCAL router.

```
LOCAL# traceroute 192.168.3.3
Type escape sequence to abort.
Tracing the route to PC-C (192.168.3.3)
VRF info: (vrf in name/id, vrf out name/id)
  1 ISP (10.1.1.2) 16 msec 16 msec 16 msec
  2 REMOTE (10.2.2.1) 28 msec 32 msec 28 msec
  3 PC-C (192.168.3.3) 32 msec 28 msec 32 msec


LOCAL# traceroute PC-C
Type escape sequence to abort.
Tracing the route to PC-C (192.168.3.3)
VRF info: (vrf in name/id, vrf out name/id)
  1 ISP (10.1.1.2) 16 msec 16 msec 16 msec
  2 REMOTE (10.2.2.1) 28 msec 32 msec 28 msec
  3 PC-C (192.168.3.3) 32 msec 32 msec 28 msec
```

Step 4: **Use the traceroute command from the S1 switch to PC-C.**

a. On the S1 switch, type **traceroute 192.168.3.3**. The hostnames are not displayed in the traceroute results because a local IP host table was not configured on this switch.

```
S1# traceroute 192.168.3.3
Type escape sequence to abort.
Tracing the route to 192.168.3.3
VRF info: (vrf in name/id, vrf out name/id)
  1 192.168.1.1 1007 msec 0 msec 0 msec
  2 10.1.1.2 17 msec 17 msec 16 msec
  3 10.2.2.1 34 msec 33 msec 26 msec
  4 192.168.3.3 33 msec 34 msec 33 msec
```

The **traceroute** command has additional options. You can use the **?** or just press Enter after typing **traceroute** at the prompt to explore these options.

The following link provides more information regarding the **ping** and **traceroute** commands for a Cisco device:

http://www.cisco.com/en/US/products/sw/iosswrel/ps1831/products_tech_note09186a00800a6057.shtml

Part 4: Troubleshoot the Topology

Step 1:   Erase the configurations on the REMOTE router.

Step 2:   Reload the REMOTE router.

Step 3:   Copy and paste the following configuration into the REMOTE router.

```
hostname REMOTE
no ip domain-lookup
interface s0/0/1
 ip address 10.2.2.1 255.255.255.252
 no shutdown
interface g0/1
 ip add 192.168.8.1 255.255.255.0
 no shutdown
router eigrp 1
 network 10.2.2.0 0.0.0.3
 network 192.168.3.0 0.0.0.255
 no auto-summary
end
```

Step 4:   From the LOCAL network, use ping and tracert or traceroute commands to trouble-shoot and correct the problem on the REMOTE network.

a. Use the **ping** and **tracert** commands from PC-A.

You can use the **tracert** command to determine end-to-end network connectivity. This tracert result indicates that PC-A can reach its default gateway of 192.168.1.1, but PC-A does not have network connectivity with PC-C.

```
C:\Users\User1> tracert 192.168.3.3


Tracing route to 192.168.3.3 over a maximum of 30 hops
  1    <1 ms    <1 ms    <1 ms   192.168.1.1
  2  192.168.1.1  reports: Destination host unreachable.


Trace complete.
```

One way to locate the network issue is to ping each hop in the network to PC-C. First determine if PC-A can reach the ISP router Serial 0/0/1 interface with an IP address of 10.2.2.2.

```
C:\Users\Utraser1> ping 10.2.2.2


Pinging 10.2.2.2 with 32 bytes of data:
Reply from 10.2.2.2: bytes=32 time=41ms TTL=254
Reply from 10.2.2.2: bytes=32 time=41ms TTL=254
```

```
Reply from 10.2.2.2: bytes=32 time=41ms TTL=254

Reply from 10.2.2.2: bytes=32 time=41ms TTL=254


Ping statistics for 10.2.2.2:

    Packets: Sent = 4, Received = 4, Lost = 0 (0% loss),

Approximate round trip times in milli-seconds:

    Minimum = 20ms, Maximum = 21ms, Average = 20ms
```

The ping was successful to the ISP router. The next hop in the network is the REMOTE router. Ping the REMOTE router Serial 0/0/1 interface with an IP address of 10.2.2.1.

```
C:\Users\User1> ping 10.2.2.1


Pinging 10.2.2.1 with 32 bytes of data:

Reply from 10.2.2.1: bytes=32 time=41ms TTL=253

Reply from 10.2.2.1: bytes=32 time=41ms TTL=253

Reply from 10.2.2.1: bytes=32 time=41ms TTL=253

Reply from 10.2.2.1: bytes=32 time=41ms TTL=253


Ping statistics for 10.2.2.1:

    Packets: Sent = 4, Received = 4, Lost = 0 (0% loss),

Approximate round trip times in milli-seconds:

    Minimum = 40ms, Maximum = 41ms, Average = 40ms
```

PC-A can reach the REMOTE router. Based on the successful ping results from PC-A to the REMOTE router, the network connectivity issue is with 192.168.3.0/24 network. Ping the default gateway to PC-C, which is the GigabitEthernet 0/1 interface of the REMOTE router.

```
C:\Users\User1> ping 192.168.3.1


Pinging 192.168.3.1 with 32 bytes of data:

Reply from 192.168.1.1: Destination host unreachable.

Reply from 192.168.1.1: Destination host unreachable.

Reply from 192.168.1.1: Destination host unreachable.

Reply from 192.168.1.1: Destination host unreachable.


Ping statistics for 192.168.3.1:

    Packets: Sent = 4, Received = 4, Lost = 0 (0% loss),
```

PC-A cannot reach the GigabitEthernet 0/1 interface of the REMOTE router, as displayed by the results from the **ping** command.

The S3 switch can also be pinged from PC-A to verify the location of the networking connectivity issue by typing **ping 192.168.3.11** at the command prompt. Because PC-A cannot reach GigabitEthernet 0/1 of the REMOTE router, PC-A probably cannot ping the S3 switch successfully, as indicated by the results below.

```
C:\Users\User1> ping 192.168.3.11


Pinging 192.168.3.11 with 32 bytes of data:
```

```
Reply from 192.168.1.1: Destination host unreachable.
Reply from 192.168.1.1: Destination host unreachable.
Reply from 192.168.1.1: Destination host unreachable.
Reply from 192.168.1.1: Destination host unreachable.


Ping statistics for 192.168.3.11:
    Packets: Sent = 4, Received = 4, Lost = 0 (0% loss),
```

The tracert and ping results conclude that PC-A can reach the LOCAL, ISP, and REMOTE routers, but not PC-C or the S3 switch, nor the default gateway for PC-C.

b. Use the **show** commands to examine the running configurations for the the REMOTE router.

```
REMOTE# show ip interface brief
Interface                  IP-Address      OK? Method Status                Protocol
Embedded-Service-Engine0/0 unassigned      YES unset  administratively down down
GigabitEthernet0/0         unassigned      YES unset  administratively down down
GigabitEthernet0/1         192.168.8.1     YES manual up                    up
Serial0/0/0                unassigned      YES unset  administratively down down
Serial0/0/1                10.2.2.1        YES manual up                    up


REMOTE# show run
<output omitted>
interface GigabitEthernet0/0
 no ip address
 shutdown
 duplex auto
 speed auto
!
interface GigabitEthernet0/1
 ip address 192.168.8.1 255.255.255.0
 duplex auto
 speed auto
!
interface Serial0/0/0
 no ip address
 shutdown
 clock rate 2000000
!
interface Serial0/0/1
 ip address 10.2.2.1 255.255.255.252
<output omitted>
```

The outputs of the **show run** and **show ip interface brief** commands indicate that the GigabitEthernet 0/1 interface is up/up, but was configured with an incorrect IP address.

c. Correct the IP address for GigabitEthernet 0/1.

```
REMOTE# configure terminal
Enter configuration commands, one per line.  End with CNTL/Z.
REMOTE(config)# interface GigabitEthernet 0/1
REMOTE(config-if)# ip address 192.168.3.1 255.255.255.0
```

d. Verify that PC-A can ping and tracert to PC-C.

```
C:\Users\User1> ping 192.168.3.3
Pinging 192.168.3.3 with 32 bytes of data:
Reply from 192.168.3.3: bytes=32 time=44ms TTL=125
Reply from 192.168.3.3: bytes=32 time=41ms TTL=125
Reply from 192.168.3.3: bytes=32 time=40ms TTL=125
Reply from 192.168.3.3: bytes=32 time=41ms TTL=125


Ping statistics for 192.168.3.3:
    Packets: Sent = 4, Received = 4, Lost = 0 (0% loss),
Approximate round trip times in milli-seconds:
    Minimum = 40ms, Maximum = 44ms, Average = 41ms


C:\Users\User1> tracert 192.168.3.3


Tracing route to PC-C [192.168.3.3]
Over a maximum of 30 hops:


  1    <1 ms     <1 ms     <1 ms     192.168.1.1
  2    24 ms     24 ms     24 ms     10.1.1.2
  3    48 ms     48 ms     48 ms     10.2.2.1
  4    59 ms     59 ms     59 ms     PC-C [192.168.3.3]


Trace complete.
```

Note: This can also be accomplished using **ping** and **traceroute** commands from the CLI on the the LOCAL router and the S1 switch after verifying that there are no network connectivity issues on the 192.168.1.0/24 network.

Reflection

1. What could prevent ping or traceroute responses from reaching the originating device beside network connectivity issues?

_____

_____

2. If you ping a non-existent address on the remote network, such as 192.168.3.4, what is the message displayed by the **ping** command? What does this mean? If you ping a valid host address and receive this response, what should you check?

_____

_____

3. If you ping an address that does not exist in any network in your topology, such as 192.168.5.3, from a Windows-based PC, what is the message displayed by the **ping** command? What does this message indicate?

_____

_____

Router Interface Summary Table

Router Interface Summary				
Router Model	**Ethernet Interface #1**	**Ethernet Interface #2**	**Serial Interface #1**	**Serial Interface #2**
1800	Fast Ethernet 0/0 (F0/0)	Fast Ethernet 0/1 (F0/1)	Serial 0/0/0 (S0/0/0)	Serial 0/0/1 (S0/0/1)
1900	Gigabit Ethernet 0/0 (G0/0)	Gigabit Ethernet 0/1 (G0/1)	Serial 0/0/0 (S0/0/0)	Serial 0/0/1 (S0/0/1)
2801	Fast Ethernet 0/0 (F0/0)	Fast Ethernet 0/1 (F0/1)	Serial 0/1/0 (S0/1/0)	Serial 0/1/1 (S0/1/1)
2811	Fast Ethernet 0/0 (F0/0)	Fast Ethernet 0/1 (F0/1)	Serial 0/0/0 (S0/0/0)	Serial 0/0/1 (S0/0/1)
2900	Gigabit Ethernet 0/0 (G0/0)	Gigabit Ethernet 0/1 (G0/1)	Serial 0/0/0 (S0/0/0)	Serial 0/0/1 (S0/0/1)

Note: To find out how the router is configured, look at the interfaces to identify the type of router and how many interfaces the router has. There is no way to effectively list all the combinations of configurations for each router class. This table includes identifiers for the possible combinations of Ethernet and Serial interfaces in the device. The table does not include any other type of interface, even though a specific router may contain one. An example of this might be an ISDN BRI interface. The string in parenthesis is the legal abbreviation that can be used in Cisco IOS commands to represent the interface.

7.4.1.1 Class Activity — The Internet of Everything...Naturally!

Objectives

Explain the need for IPv6 network addresses.

This is an application-based activity. You will develop a plan to show how IoE subnets, unicasts, and multicasts could be used in our daily lives to affect data communication.

Background/Scenario

Note: This activity may be completed individually or in small/large groups.

This chapter discussed the ways in which small to medium-sized businesses are connected to networks in groups. The IoE was introduced in the activity at the beginning of this chapter.

Choose one of the following:

- Online banking
- World news
- Weather forecasting/climate
- Traffic conditions

Devise an IPv6 addressing scheme for the area you have chosen. Your addressing scheme should include how you would plan for:

- Subnetting
- Unicasts
- Multicasts

Keep a copy of your scheme to share with the class or learning community. Be prepared to explain:

- How subnetting, unicasts, and multicasts could be incorporated
- Where your addressing scheme could be used
- How small to medium-size businesses would be affected by using your plan

Required Resources

- Paper, pens, pencils, or tablets
- Packet Tracer (if you would like to display how your network would physically look)
- Hard- or soft-copy of the final network topology with IPv6 addressing indicated for sharing with the class.

Reflection

1. What was the hardest part of designing this network model? Explain your answer.

Chapter 8 — Subnetting IP Networks

8.0.1.2 Class Activity — Call me!

Objectives

Explain why routing is necessary for hosts on different subnets to communicate.

In this activity, you will:

- Recognize that data is delivered quicker if group addressing identifiers are used.

- Visualize how communication is facilitated through providing large groups and then splitting those groups into more manageable parts. After reflecting on how your smartphone or landline telephone numbers are divided, you can draw inferences to how networking employs the same practices.

Background/Scenario

In this chapter, you will learn how devices can be grouped into subnets, or smaller network groups, from a large network.

In this modeling activity, you are asked to think about a number you probably use every day, a number such as your telephone number. As you complete the activity, think about how your telephone number compares to strategies that network administrators might use to identify hosts for efficient data communication.

Complete the two sections listed below and record your answers. Save the two sections in either hard- or soft-copy format to use later for class discussion purposes.

- Explain how your smartphone or landline telephone number is divided into identifying groups of numbers. Does your telephone number use an area code? An Internet service provider (ISP) identifier? A city, state, or country code?

- In what ways does separating your telephone number into managed parts assist in contacting or communicating with others?

Required Resources

Recording capabilities (paper, tablet, etc.) for reflective comments to be shared with the class

Reflection

1. Why do you think ISPs need your telephone number when setting up your account parameters?

8.1.3.8 Lab — Calculating IPv4 Subnets

Objectives

Part 1: Determine IPv4 Address Subnetting

- Determine the network address.
- Determine the broadcast address.
- Determine the number of hosts.

Part 2: Calculate IPv4 Address Subnetting

- Determine the number of subnets created.
- Determine number of hosts per subnet.
- Determine the subnet address.
- Determine the host range for the subnet.
- Determine the broadcast address for the subnet.

Background / Scenario

The ability to work with IPv4 subnets and determine network and host information based on a given IP address and subnet mask is critical to understanding how IPv4 networks operate. The first part is designed to reinforce how to compute network IP address information from a given IP address and subnet mask. When given an IP address and subnet mask, you will be able to determine other information about the subnet such as:

- Network address
- Broadcast address
- Total number of host bits
- Number of hosts per subnet

In the second part of the lab, for a given IP address and subnet mask, you will determine such information as follows:

- Network address of this subnet
- Broadcast address of this subnet
- Range of host addresses for this subnet
- Number of subnets created
- Number of hosts for each subnet

Required Resources

- 1 PC (Windows 7, Vista, or XP with Internet access)
- Optional: IPv4 address calculator

Part 1:   Determine IPv4 Address Subnetting

In Part 1, you will determine the network and broadcast addresses, as well as the number of hosts, given an IPv4 address and subnet mask.

REVIEW: To determine the network address, perform binary ANDing on the IPv4 address using the subnet mask provided. The result will be the network address. Hint: If the subnet mask has decimal value 255 in an octet, the result will ALWAYS be the original value of that octet. If the subnet mask has decimal value 0 in an octet, the result will ALWAYS be 0 for that octet.

Example:

IP Address	192.168.10.10
Subnet Mask	255.255.255.0
	==========
Result (Network)	192.168.10.0

Knowing this, you may only have to perform binary ANDing on an octet that does not have 255 or 0 in its subnet mask portion.

Example:

IP Address	172.30.239.145
Subnet Mask	255.255.192.0

Analyzing this example, you can see that you only have to perform binary ANDing on the third octet. The first two octets will result in 172.30 due to the subnet mask. The fourth octet will result in 0 due to the subnet mask.

IP Address	172.30.239.145
Subnet Mask	255.255.192.0
	==========
Result (Network)	172.30.**?**.0

Perform binary ANDing on the third octet.

	Decimal	**Binary**
	239	11101111
	192	11000000
		=======
Result	**192**	11000000

Analyzing this example again produces the following result:

IP Address	172.30.239.145
Subnet Mask	255.255.192.0
	==========
Result (Network)	172.30.192.0

Continuing with this example, determining the number of hosts per network can be calculated by analyzing the subnet mask. The subnet mask will be represented in dotted decimal format, such as 255.255.192.0, or in network prefix format, such as /18. An IPv4 address always has 32 bits. Subtracting the number of bits used for the network portion (as represented by the subnet mask) gives you the number of bits used for hosts.

Using our example above, the subnet mask 255.255.192.0 is equivalent to /18 in prefix notation. Subtracting 18 network bits from 32 bits results in 14 bits left for the host portion. From there, it is a simple calculation:

$$2^{(number\ of\ host\ bits)} - 2 = Number\ of\ hosts$$

$$2^{14} = 16,384 - 2 = 16,382\ hosts$$

Determine the network and broadcast addresses and number of host bits and hosts for the given IPv4 addresses and prefixes in the following table.

IPv4 Address/Prefix	Network Address	Broadcast Address	Total Number of Host Bits	Total Number of Hosts
192.168.100.25/28				
172.30.10.130/30				
10.1.113.75/19				
198.133.219.250/24				
128.107.14.191/22				
172.16.104.99/27				

Part 2:   Calculate IPv4 Address Subnetting

When given an IPv4 address, the original subnet mask and the new subnet mask, you will be able to determine:

- Network address of this subnet

- Broadcast address of this subnet

- Range of host addresses of this subnet

- Number of subnets created

- Number of hosts per subnet

The following example shows a sample problem along with the solution for solving this problem:

Given:	
Host IP Address:	172.16.77.120
Original Subnet Mask	255.255.0.0
New Subnet Mask:	255.255.240.0
Find:	
Number of Subnet Bits	4
Number of Subnets Created	16
Number of Host Bits per Subnet	12
Number of Hosts per Subnet	4,094
Network Address of this Subnet	172.16.64.0
IPv4 Address of First Host on this Subnet	172.16.64.1
IPv4 Address of Last Host on this Subnet	172.16.79.254
IPv4 Broadcast Address on this Subnet	172.16.79.255

Let's analyze how this table was completed.

The original subnet mask was 255.255.0.0 or /16. The new subnet mask is 255.255.240.0 or /20. The resulting difference is 4 bits. Because 4 bits were borrowed, we can determine that 16 subnets were created because $2^4 = 16$.

The new mask of 255.255.240.0 or /20 leaves 12 bits for hosts. With 12 bits left for hosts, we use the following formula: $2^{12} = 4,096 - 2 = 4,094$ hosts per subnet.

Binary ANDing will help you determine the subnet for this problem, which results in the network 172.16.64.0.

Finally, you need to determine the first host, last host, and broadcast address for each subnet. One method to determine the host range is to use binary math for the host portion of the address. In our example, the last 12 bits of the address is the host portion. The first host would have all significant bits set to zero and the least significant bit set to 1. The last host would have all significant bits set to 1 and the least significant bit set to 0. In this example, the host portion of the address resides in the 3rd and 4th octets.

Description	1st Octet	2nd Octet	3rd Octet	4th Octet	Description
Network/Host	**nnnnnnnn**	**nnnnnnnn**	**nnnn**hhhh	hhhhhhhh	Subnet Mask
Binary	**10101100**	**00010000**	**0100**0000	00000001	First Host
Decimal	172	16	64	1	First Host
Binary	**10101100**	**00010000**	**0100**1111	11111110	Last Host
Decimal	172	16	79	254	Last Host
Binary	**10101100**	**00010000**	**0100**1111	11111111	Broadcast
Decimal	172	16	79	255	Broadcast

Step 1: Fill out the tables below with appropriate answers given the IPv4 address, original subnet mask, and new subnet mask.

a. **Problem 1:**

Given:	
Host IP Address:	192.168.200.139
Original Subnet Mask	255.255.255.0
New Subnet Mask:	255.255.255.224
Find:	
Number of Subnet Bits	
Number of Subnets Created	
Number of Host Bits per Subnet	
Number of Hosts per Subnet	
Network Address of this Subnet	
IPv4 Address of First Host on this Subnet	
IPv4 Address of Last Host on this Subnet	
IPv4 Broadcast Address on this Subnet	

b. **Problem 2**:

Given:	
Host IP Address:	10.101.99.228
Original Subnet Mask	255.0.0.0
New Subnet Mask:	255.255.128.0
Find:	
Number of Subnet Bits	
Number of Subnets Created	
Number of Host Bits per Subnet	
Number of Hosts per Subnet	
Network Address of this Subnet	
IPv4 Address of First Host on this Subnet	
IPv4 Address of Last Host on this Subnet	
IPv4 Broadcast Address on this Subnet	

c. **Problem 3**:

Given:	
Host IP Address:	172.22.32.12
Original Subnet Mask	255.255.0.0
New Subnet Mask:	255.255.224.0
Find:	
Number of Subnet Bits	
Number of Subnets Created	
Number of Host Bits per Subnet	
Number of Hosts per Subnet	
Network Address of this Subnet	
IPv4 Address of First Host on this Subnet	
IPv4 Address of Last Host on this Subnet	
IPv4 Broadcast Address on this Subnet	

d. **Problem 4**:

Given:	
Host IP Address:	192.168.1.245
Original Subnet Mask	255.255.255.0
New Subnet Mask:	255.255.255.252
Find:	
Number of Subnet Bits	
Number of Subnets Created	
Number of Host Bits per Subnet	
Number of Hosts per Subnet	
Network Address of this Subnet	
IPv4 Address of First Host on this Subnet	
IPv4 Address of Last Host on this Subnet	
IPv4 Broadcast Address on this Subnet	

e.   **Problem 5**:

Given:	
Host IP Address:	128.107.0.55
Original Subnet Mask	255.255.0.0
New Subnet Mask:	255.255.255.0
Find:	
Number of Subnet Bits	
Number of Subnets Created	
Number of Host Bits per Subnet	
Number of Hosts per Subnet	
Network Address of this Subnet	
IPv4 Address of First Host on this Subnet	
IPv4 Address of Last Host on this Subnet	
IPv4 Broadcast Address on this Subnet	

f.   **Problem 6**:

Given:	
Host IP Address:	192.135.250.180
Original Subnet Mask	255.255.255.0
New Subnet Mask:	255.255.255.248
Find:	
Number of Subnet Bits	
Number of Subnets Created	
Number of Host Bits per Subnet	
Number of Hosts per Subnet	
Network Address of this Subnet	
IPv4 Address of First Host on this Subnet	
IPv4 Address of Last Host on this Subnet	
IPv4 Broadcast Address on this Subnet	

Reflection

Why is the subnet mask so important when analyzing an IPv4 address?

_____

_____

_____

8.1.3.9 Lab — Subnetting Network Topologies

Objectives

Parts 1 to 5, for each network topology:

- Determine the number of subnets.
- Design an appropriate addressing scheme.
- Assign addresses and subnet mask pairs to device interfaces.
- Examine the use of the available network address space and future growth potential.

Background / Scenario

When given a network topology, it is important to be able to determine the number of subnets required. In this lab, several scenario topologies will be provided, along with a base network address and mask. You will subnet the network address and provide an IP addressing scheme that will accommodate the number of subnets displayed in the topology diagram. You must determine the number of bits to borrow, the number of hosts per subnet, and potential for growth as specified by the instructions.

Part 1: Network Topology A

In Part 1, you have been given the 192.168.10.0/24 network address to subnet, with the following topology. Determine the number of networks needed and then design an appropriate addressing scheme.

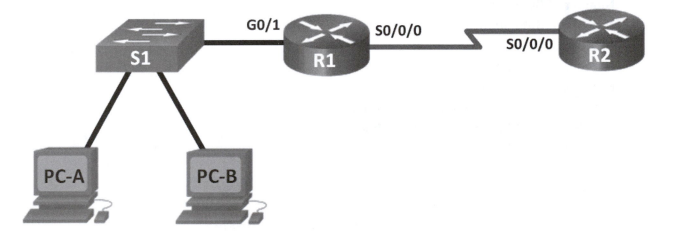

Step 1: **Determine the number of subnets in Network Topology A.**

a. How many subnets are there? _____

b. How many bits should you borrow to create the required number of subnets? _____

c. How many usable host addresses per subnet are in this addressing scheme? _____

d. What is the new subnet mask in dotted decimal format? _____

e. How many subnets are available for future use? _____

Step 2: Record the subnet information.

Fill in the following table with the subnet information:

Subnet Number	Subnet Address	First Usable Host Address	Last Usable Host Address	Broadcast Address
0				
1				
2				
3				
4				
5				

Part 2: Network Topology B

The network topology from Part 1 has expanded to accommodate the addition of router R3 and its accompanying network, as illustrated in the following topology. Use the 192.168.10.0/24 network address to provide addresses to the network devices, and then design a new addressing scheme to support the additional network requirement.

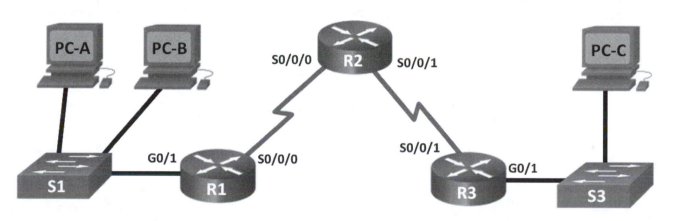

Step 1: Determine the number of subnets in Network Topology B.

a. How many subnets are there? _____

b. How many bits should you borrow to create the required number of subnets? _____

c. How many usable host addresses per subnet are in this addressing scheme? _____

d. What is the new subnet mask in dotted decimal format? _____

e. How many subnets are available for future use? _____

Step 2:   **Record the subnet information.**

Fill in the following table with the subnet information:

Subnet Number	Subnet Address	First Usable Host Address	Last Usable Host Address	Broadcast Address
0				
1				
2				
3				
4				
5				
6				
7				

Part 3:   Network Topology C

The topology has changed again with a new LAN added to R2 and a redundant link between R1 and R3. Use the 192.168.10.0/24 network address to provide addresses to the network devices. Also provide an IP address scheme that will accommodate these additional devices. For this topology, assign a subnet to each network.

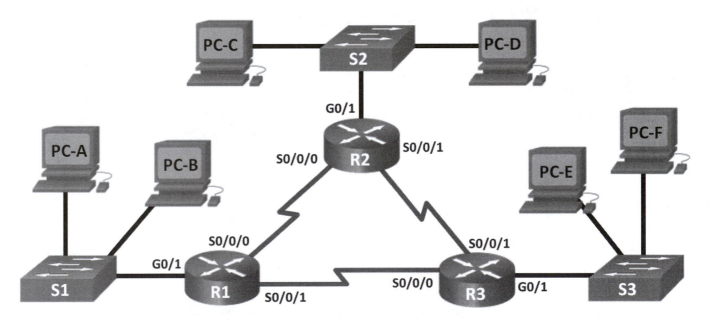

Step 1:   **Determine the number of subnets in Network Topology C.**

a.   How many subnets are there? _____

b.   How many bits should you borrow to create the required number of subnets? _____

c.   How many usable host addresses per subnet are in this addressing scheme? _____

d.   What is the new subnet mask in dotted decimal format? _____

e.   How many subnets are available for future use? _____

Step 2: Record the subnet information.

Fill in the following table with the subnet information:

Subnet Number	Subnet Address	First Usable Host Address	Last Usable Host Address	Broadcast Address
0				
1				
2				
3				
4				
5				
6				
7				
8				
9				
10				

Step 3: Assign addresses to network devices in the subnets.

a. Fill in the following table with IP addresses and subnet masks for the router interfaces:

Device	Interface	IP Address	Subnet Mask
R1	GigabitEthernet 0/1		
	Serial 0/0/0		
	Serial 0/0/1		
R2	GigabitEthernet 0/1		
	Serial 0/0/0		
	Serial 0/0/1		
R3	GigabitEthernet 0/1		
	Serial 0/0/0		
	Serial 0/0/1		

b. Fill in the following table with the IP addresses and subnet masks for devices in the LAN as displayed in topology.

Device	Interface	IP Address	Subnet Mask	Default Gateway
PC-A	NIC			
PC-B	NIC			
S1	VLAN 1			
PC-C	NIC			
PC-D	NIC			
S2	VLAN 1			
PC-E	NIC			
PC-F	NIC			
S3	VLAN 1			

Part 4: Network Topology D

The network was modified to accommodate changes in the organization. The 192.168.10.0/24 network address is used to provide the addresses in the network.

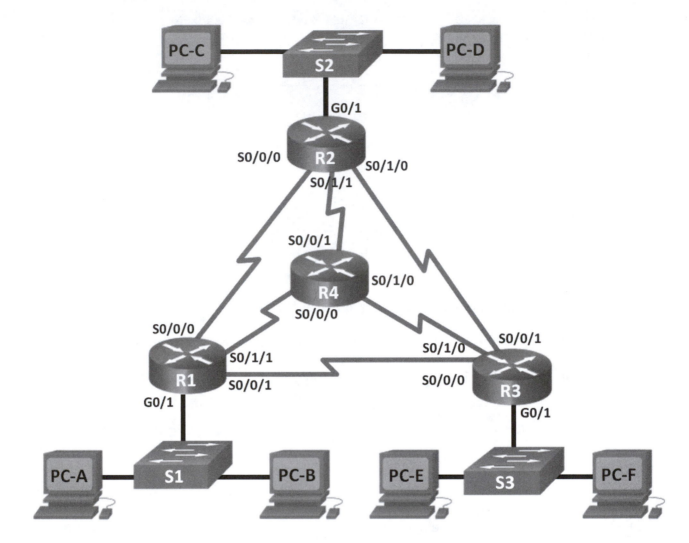

Step 1: Determine the number of subnets in Network Topology D.

a. How many subnets are there? _____

b. How many bits should you borrow to create the required number of subnets? _____

c. How many usable host addresses per subnet are in this addressing scheme? _____

d. What is the new subnet mask in dotted decimal format? _____

e. How many subnets are available for future use? _____

Step 2: Record the subnet information.

Fill in the following table with the subnet information.

Subnet Number	Subnet Address	First Usable Host Address	Last Usable Host Address	Broadcast Address
0				
1				
2				
3				
4				
5				
6				
7				
8				
9				
10				
11				
12				
13				
14				
15				
16				
17				

Part 5:   Network Topology E

The organization has a network address of 172.16.128.0/17 to be divided as illustrated in the following topology. You must choose an addressing scheme that can accommodate the number of networks and hosts in the topology.

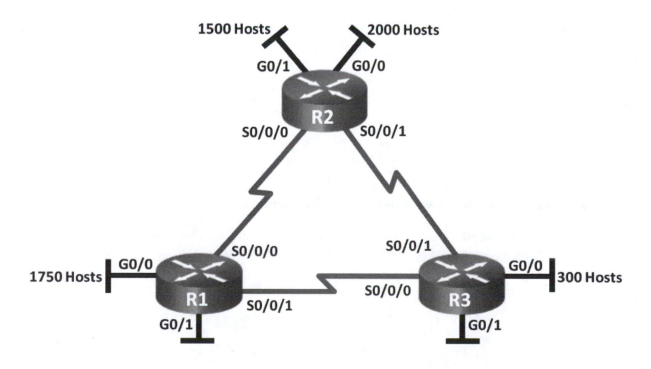

Step 1:   **Determine the number of subnets in Network Topology E.**

a.   How many subnets are there? _____

b.   How many bits should you borrow to create the required number of subnets? _____

c.   How many usable host addresses per subnet are in this addressing scheme? _____

d.   What is the new subnet mask in dotted decimal format? _____

e.   How many subnets are available for future use? _____

Step 2:   **Record the subnet information.**

Fill in the following table with the subnet information:

Subnet Number	Subnet Address	First Usable Host Address	Last Usable Host Address	Broadcast Address
0				
1				
2				
3				
4				
5				
6				
7				
8				
9				
10				
11				
12				
13				
14				
15				
16				
17				

Step 3:   **Assign addresses to network devices in the subnets.**

a.   Fill in the following table with IP addresses and subnet masks for the router interfaces:

Device	Interface	IP Address	Subnet Mask
R1	GigabitEthernet 0/0		
	GigabitEthernet 0/1		
	Serial 0/0/0		
	Serial 0/0/1		
R2	GigabitEthernet 0/0		
	GigabitEthernet 0/1		
	Serial 0/0/0		
	Serial 0/0/1		
R3	GigabitEthernet 0/0		
	GigabitEthernet 0/1		
	Serial 0/0/0		
	Serial 0/0/1		

Reflection

1. What information is needed when determining an appropriate addressing scheme for a network?

_____

_____

2. After the subnets are assigned, will all the host addresses be utilized in each subnet?

_____

_____

8.1.3.10 Lab — Researching Subnet Calculators

Objectives

Part 1: Review Available Subnet Calculators

Part 2: Perform Network Calculations Using a Subnet Calculator

Background / Scenario

While it is important to understand how to convert a decimal IP address to its binary format and apply the bitwise ANDing operation to determine the network address, it is also a tedious and mistake-prone process. To assist with these calculations, many network administrators make use of an IP subnet calculator utility program. A number of these types of programs have been developed that can be downloaded or run directly from the Internet.

In this lab, you will be introduced to a few of the free IP subnet calculators that are available. You will use a web-based IP subnet calculator to perform the network operations in this lab.

Required Resources

Device with Internet access

Part 1:   Review Available Subnet Calculators

In Part 1, you are introduced to two types of subnet calculators: client-based (programs that are downloaded and installed) and web-based (utilities that are run from a browser).

Step 1:   Review client-based subnet calculators.

Solarwinds provides a free subnet calculator that can be downloaded and installed on a PC running a Windows operating system. You will be required to provide personal information (Name, Company, Location, Email Address, and Phone number) to be able to download this program. You can download and install the Solarwinds Subnet Calculator at www.solarwinds.com.

If you have a PC running Linux, it is recommended that you use the **ipcalc** utility (available with most Linux distributions). Use the **apt-get install ipcalc** command to install ipcalc on a PC running Linux.

Step 2:   Use a web-based subnet calculator.

Web-based subnet calculators do not require installation, but you do need Internet access to use them. The following web-based subnet calculator is accessible from any device that has Internet access, including smartphones and tablets.

a.   From your browser, go to www.ipcalc.org and click the **IP Subnet Calculator** link.

Note: Several other useful utilities are also listed on the menu, such as MAC vendor lookup, whois lookup, and DNS lookup.

Note: At the time of this writing, a page formatting issue was encountered when viewing the www.ipcalc.org website using Internet Explorer (Version 9). While the site functioned correctly, you may want to consider using another browser (Firefox or Chrome) when accessing this site.

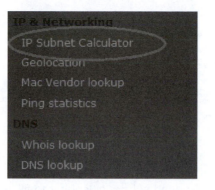

b.   On the IP Subnet Calculator screen, enter an IP address and subnet mask or an IP address and CIDR prefix notation. Examples of how to enter each of these are shown in the Introduction area.

> ## :: IP Subnet Calculator ::
>
> **Introduction:**
>
> A subnet is a logically visible subdivision of an IP network. The practice of dividing a network into subnetworks is called subnetting.
>
> This application will help you to compute information about IP subnetting. It's easy to use.
>
> In the following form you can enter differents address format:
>
> | Description | Format |
> |---|---|
> | IP & CIDR Netmask | 10.0.0.1/22 |
> | IP & Netmask | 10.0.0.1 255.255.252.0 |
> | IP & Wildcard Mask | 10.0.0.1 0.0.3.255 |
>
> The behavior of this application is the same that the *ipcalc* binary of GNU/Linux system's !
>
> **Application:**
>
> Enter IP & Mask or CIDR here !   Calc !

c.   In the Application field, enter **192.168.50.50/27** and click **Calc!**. The next screen displays a table with network information in both decimal and binary formats.

Application:

192.168.50.50/27   Calc !

Description	Value		Extra
Address	192.168.50.50	11000000.10101000.00110010.00110010	
Netmask	255.255.255.224	11111111.11111111.11111111.11100000	/27
Network	192.168.50.32	11000000.10101000.00110010.00100000	
Broadcast	192.168.50.63		
Host min	192.168.50.33	11000000.10101000.00110010.00100001	
Host max	192.168.50.62	11000000.10101000.00110010.00111110	
Host/net	30	Class C, Private Internet	

d. Using the information provided in the example above, answer the following questions.

What is the network address? _____

What is the subnet mask? _____

How many hosts will this network support? _____

What is the lowest host address? _____

What is the highest host address? _____

What is the broadcast address? _____

Part 2: Perform Network Calculations Using a Subnet Calculator

In Part 2, use the www.ipcalc.org web-based subnet calculator to fill in the tables provided.

Step 1: **Fill in the following table for address 10.223.23.136/10:**

Description	Decimal	Binary
Address	10.223.23.136	
Subnet mask		
Network address		
Broadcast address		
First host address		
Last host address		
Number of hosts available	N/A	

What type of address, public, or private? _____

Step 2: **Fill in the following table for the 172.18.255.92 address with a subnet mask of 255.255.224.0:**

Description	Decimal	Binary
Address	172.18.255.92	
Subnet mask	255.255.224.0	
Network address		
Broadcast address		
First host address		
Last host address		
Number of hosts available	N/A	

What is the CIDR prefix notation for this network? _____

What type of address, public, or private? _____

Step 3: **Fill in the following table using the 192.168.184.78 address with a subnet mask of 255.255.255.252:**

Description	Decimal	Binary
Address	192.168.184.78	
Subnet mask		
Network address		
Broadcast address		
First host address		
Last host address		
Number of hosts available		N/A

What is the CIDR prefix notation for this network? _____

What type of address, public, or private? _____

Where would you most likely find a network like this being used?

_____

Step 4: **Fill in the following table for the 209.165.200.225/27 address:**

Description	Decimal	Binary
Address	209.165.200.225	
Subnet mask		
Network address		
Broadcast address		
First host address		
Last host address		
Number of hosts available		N/A

What type of address, public, or private? _____

Step 5: **Fill in the following table for address 64.104.110.7/20:**

Description	Decimal	Binary
Address	64.104.110.7	
Subnet mask		
Network address		
Broadcast address		
First host address		
Last host address		
Number of hosts available		N/A

What type of address, public, or private? _____

Reflection

1. What is an advantage of using a client-based subnet calculator?

   _____

   _____

2. What is an advantage of using a web-based subnet calculator?

   _____

   _____

8.2.1.3 Lab — Designing and Implementing a Subnetted IPv4 Addressing Scheme

Topology

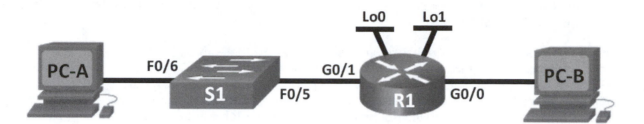

Addressing Table

Device	Interface	IP Address	Subnet Mask	Default Gateway
R1	G0/0			N/A
	G0/1			N/A
	Lo0			N/A
	Lo1			N/A
S1	VLAN 1	N/A	N/A	N/A
PC-A	NIC			
PC-B	NIC			

Objectives

Part 1: Design a Network Subnetting Scheme

- Create a subnetting scheme that meets the required number of subnets and host addresses.
- Complete the diagram, showing where the host IP addresses will be applied.

Part 2: Configure the Devices

- Assign an IP address, subnet mask, and default gateway to the PCs.
- Configure the router Gigabit Ethernet interfaces with an IP address and subnet mask.
- Create two loopback interfaces on the router, and configure each with an IP address and subnet mask.

Part 3: Test and Troubleshoot the Network

- Verify and troubleshoot network connectivity using ping.

Background / Scenario

In this lab, starting from a single network address and network mask, you will subnet the network into multiple subnets. The subnet scheme should be based on the number of host computers required in each subnet, as well as other network considerations, like future network host expansion.

After you have created a subnetting scheme and completed the network diagram by filling in the host and interface IP addresses, you will configure the host PCs and router interfaces, including loopback interfaces. The loopback interfaces are created to simulate additional LANs attached to router R1.

After the network devices and host PCs have been configured, you will use the **ping** command to test for network connectivity.

This lab provides minimal assistance with the actual commands necessary to configure the router. However, the required commands are provided in Appendix A. Test your knowledge by trying to configure the devices without referring to the appendix.

Note: The routers used with CCNA hands-on labs are Cisco 1941 Integrated Services Routers (ISRs) with Cisco IOS Release 15.2(4)M3 (universalk9 image). The switches used are Cisco Catalyst 2960s with Cisco IOS Release 15.0(2) (lanbasek9 image). Other routers, switches and Cisco IOS versions can be used. Depending on the model and Cisco IOS version, the commands available and output produced might vary from what is shown in the labs. Refer to the Router Interface Summary Table at this end of the lab for the correct interface identifiers.

Note: Make sure that the routers and switches have been erased and have no startup configurations. If you are unsure, contact your instructor.

Required Resources

- 1 Router (Cisco 1941 with Cisco IOS Release 15.2(4)M3 universal image or comparable)
- 1 Switch (Cisco 2960 with Cisco IOS Release 15.0(2) lanbasek9 image or comparable)
- 2 PCs (Windows 7, Vista, or XP with terminal emulation program, such as Tera Term)
- Console cables to configure the Cisco IOS devices via the console ports
- Ethernet cables as shown in the topology

Note: The Gigabit Ethernet interfaces on Cisco 1941 routers are autosensing. An Ethernet straight-through cable may be used between the router and PC-B. If using another Cisco router model, it may be necessary to use an Ethernet crossover cable.

Part 1:   Design a Network Subnetting Scheme

Step 1:   Create a subnetting scheme that meets the required number of subnets and required number of host addresses.

In this scenario, you are a network administrator for a small subdivision within a larger company. You must create multiple subnets out of the 192.168.0.0/24 network address space to meet the following requirements:

- The first subnet is the employee network. You need a minimum of 25 host IP addresses.
- The second subnet is the administration network. You need a minimum of 10 IP addresses.
- The third and fourth subnets are reserved as virtual networks on virtual router interfaces, loopback 0 and loopback 1. These virtual router interfaces simulate LANs attached to R1.
- You also need two additional unused subnets for future network expansion.

Note: Variable length subnet masks will not be used. All of the device subnet masks will be the same length.

Answer the following questions to help create a subnetting scheme that meets the stated network requirements:

1)   How many host addresses are needed in the largest required subnet? _____

2) What is the minimum number of subnets required? _____

3) The network that you are tasked to subnet is 192.168.0.0/24. What is the /24 subnet mask in binary?

_____

4) The subnet mask is made up of two portions, the network portion, and the host portion. This is represented in the binary by the ones and the zeros in the subnet mask.

In the network mask, what do the ones represent? _____

In the network mask, what do the zeros represent? _____

5) To subnet a network, bits from the host portion of the original network mask are changed into subnet bits. The number of subnet bits defines the number of subnets. Given each of the possible subnet masks depicted in the following binary format, how many subnets and how many hosts are created in each example?

Hint: Remember that the number of host bits (to the power of 2) defines the number of hosts per subnet (minus 2), and the number of subnet bits (to the power of two) defines the number of subnets. The subnet bits (depicted in bold type face) are the bits that have been borrowed beyond the original network mask of /24. The /24 is the slash prefix notation and corresponds to a dotted decimal mask of 255.255.255.0.

(/25) 11111111.11111111.11111111.**1**0000000

Dotted decimal subnet mask equivalent: _____

Number of subnets? _____, Number of hosts? _____

(/26) 11111111.11111111.11111111.**11**000000

Dotted decimal subnet mask equivalent: _____

Number of subnets? _____, Number of hosts? _____

(/27) 11111111.11111111.11111111.**111**00000

Dotted decimal subnet mask equivalent: _____

Number of subnets? _____ Number of hosts? _____

(/28) 11111111.11111111.11111111.**1111**0000

Dotted decimal subnet mask equivalent: _____

Number of subnets? _____ Number of hosts? _____

(/29) 11111111.11111111.11111111.**11111**000

Dotted decimal subnet mask equivalent: _____

Number of subnets? _____ Number of hosts? _____

(/30) 11111111.11111111.11111111.**111111**00

Dotted decimal subnet mask equivalent: _____

Number of subnets? _____ Number of hosts? _____

6) Considering your answers, which subnet masks meet the required number of minimum host addresses?

_____

7) Considering your answers, which subnet masks meets the minimum number of subnets required?

_____

8) Considering your answers, which subnet mask meets both the required minimum number of hosts and the minimum number of subnets required?

_____

9) When you have determined which subnet mask meets all of the stated network requirements, you will derive each of the subnets starting from the original network address. List the subnets from first to last below. Remember that the first subnet is 192.168.0.0 with the newly acquired subnet mask.

Subnet Address   / Prefix   Subnet Mask (dotted decimal)

_____ / ____ _____

_____ / ____ _____

_____ / ____ _____

_____ / ____ _____

_____ / ____ _____

_____ / ____ _____

_____ / ____ _____

_____ / ____ _____

_____ / ____ _____

_____ / ____ _____

Step 2:   Complete the diagram showing where the host IP addresses will be applied.

On the following lines provided, fill in the IP addresses and subnets masks in slash prefix notation. On the router, use the first usable address in each subnet for each of the interfaces, Gigabit Ethernet 0/0, Gigabit Ethernet 0/1, loopback 0, and loopback 1. Fill in an IP address for both PC-A and PC-B. Also enter this information into the Addressing Table on Page 1.

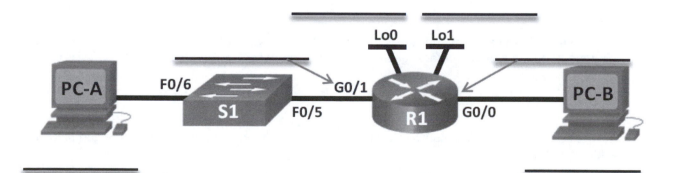

Part 2: **Configure the Devices**

In Part 2, set up the network topology and configure basic settings on the PCs and router, such as the router Gigabit Ethernet interface IP addresses, and the PC's IP addresses, subnet masks, and default gateways. Refer to the Addressing Table for device names and address information.

Note: Appendix A provides configuration details for the steps in Part 2. You should attempt to complete Part 2 prior to reviewing Appendix A.

Step 1: **Configure the router.**

a. Enter into privileged EXEC mode and then global config mode.

b. Assign the **R1** as the hostname for the router.

c. Configure both the **G0/0** and **G0/1** interfaces with IP addresses and subnet masks, and then enable them.

d. Loopback interfaces are created to simulate additional LANs on R1 router. Configure the loopback interfaces with IP addresses and subnet masks. After they are created, loopback interfaces are enabled, by default. (To create the loopback addresses, enter the command **interface loopback 0** at the global config mode)

    Note: You can create additional loopbacks for testing with different addressing schemes, if desired.

e. Save the running configuration to the startup configuration file.

Step 2: **Configure the PC interfaces.**

a. Configure the IP address, subnet mask, and default gateway settings on PC-A.

b. Configure the IP address, subnet mask, and default gateway settings on PC-B.

Part 3: **Test and Troubleshoot the Network**

In Part 3, you will use the **ping** command to test network connectivity.

a. Test to see if PC-A can communicate with its default gateway. From PC-A, open a command prompt and ping the IP address of the router Gigabit Ethernet 0/1 interface. Do you get a reply? _____

b. Test to see if PC-B can communicate with its default gateway. From PC-B, open a command prompt and ping the IP address of the router Gigabit Ethernet 0/0 interface. Do you get a reply? _____

c. Test to see if PC-A can communicate with PC-B. From PC-A, open a command prompt and ping the IP address of PC-B. Do you get a reply? _____

d. If you answered "no" to any of the preceding questions, then you should go back and check all of your IP address and subnet mask configurations, and ensure that the default gateways have been correctly configured on PC-A and PC-B.

e. If you verify that all of the settings are correct, and you can still not ping successfully, then there are a few additional factors that can block ICMP pings. On PC-A and PC-B within Windows, make sure that the Windows Firewall is turned off for the Work, Home, and Public networks.

f. Experiment by purposely misconfiguring the gateway address on PC-A to 10.0.0.1. What happens when you try and ping from PC-B to PC-A? Do you receive a reply?

_____

_____

Reflection

1. Subnetting one larger network into multiple smaller subnetworks allows for greater flexibility and security in network design. However, what do you think some of the drawbacks are when the subnets are limited to being the same size?

_____

_____

2. Why do you think the gateway/router IP address is usually the first usable IP address in the network?

_____

_____

Router Interface Summary Table

Router Interface Summary				
Router Model	**Ethernet Interface #1**	**Ethernet Interface #2**	**Serial Interface #1**	**Serial Interface #2**
1800	Fast Ethernet 0/0 (F0/0)	Fast Ethernet 0/1 (F0/1)	Serial 0/0/0 (S0/0/0)	Serial 0/0/1 (S0/0/1)
1900	Gigabit Ethernet 0/0 (G0/0)	Gigabit Ethernet 0/1 (G0/1)	Serial 0/0/0 (S0/0/0)	Serial 0/0/1 (S0/0/1)
2801	Fast Ethernet 0/0 (F0/0)	Fast Ethernet 0/1 (F0/1)	Serial 0/1/0 (S0/1/0)	Serial 0/1/1 (S0/1/1)
2811	Fast Ethernet 0/0 (F0/0)	Fast Ethernet 0/1 (F0/1)	Serial 0/0/0 (S0/0/0)	Serial 0/0/1 (S0/0/1)
2900	Gigabit Ethernet 0/0 (G0/0)	Gigabit Ethernet 0/1 (G0/1)	Serial 0/0/0 (S0/0/0)	Serial 0/0/1 (S0/0/1)

Note: To find out how the router is configured, look at the interfaces to identify the type of router and how many interfaces the router has. There is no way to effectively list all the combinations of configurations for each router class. This table includes identifiers for the possible combinations of Ethernet and Serial interfaces in the device. The table does not include any other type of interface, even though a specific router may contain one. An example of this might be an ISDN BRI interface. The string in parenthesis is the legal abbreviation that can be used in Cisco IOS commands to represent the interface.

Appendix A: Configuration Details for Steps in Part 2

Step 1:   **Configure the router.**

g.   Console into the router and enable privileged EXEC mode.

```
Router> enable
Router#
```

h.   Enter into configuration mode.

```
Router# conf t
Enter configuration commands, one per line.  End with CNTL/Z.
Router(config)#
```

i.   Assign a device name to the router.

```
Router(config)# hostname R1
R1(config)#
```

j.   Configure both the **G0/0** and **G0/1** interfaces with IP addresses and subnet masks, and enable them.

```
R1(config)# interface g0/0
R1(config-if)# ip address <ip address> <subnet mask>
R1(config-if)# no shutdown
R1(config-if)# interface g0/1
R1(config-if)# ip address <ip address> <subnet mask>
R1(config-if)# no shutdown
```

k.   Loopback interfaces are created to simulate additional LANs off of router R1. Configure the loopback interfaces with IP addresses and subnet masks. When they are created, loopback interfaces are enabled, by default.

```
R1(config)# interface loopback 0
R1(config-if)# ip address <ip address> <subnet mask>
R1(config-if)# interface loopback 1
R1(config-if)# ip address <ip address> <subnet mask>
R1(config-if)# end
```

l.   Save the running configuration to the startup configuration file.

```
R1# copy running-config startup-config
```

Step 2:   **Configure the PC interfaces.**

m. Configure the IP address, subnet mask, and default gateway settings on PC-A.

n. Configure the IP address, subnet mask, and default gateway settings on PC-B.

8.2.1.4 Lab — Designing and Implementing a VLSM Addressing Scheme

Topology

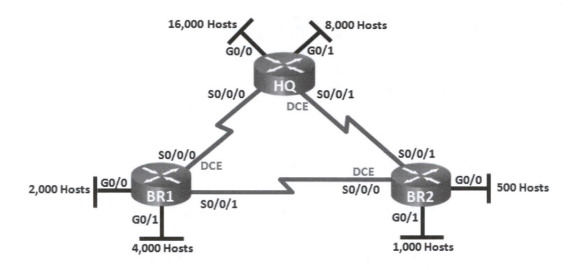

Objectives

Part 1: Examine Network Requirements

Part 2: Design the VLSM Address Scheme

Part 3: Cable and Configure the IPv4 Network

Background / Scenario

Variable Length Subnet Mask (VLSM) was designed to avoid wasting IP addresses. With VLSM, a network is subnetted and then re-subnetted. This process can be repeated multiple times to create subnets of various sizes based on the number of hosts required in each subnet. Effective use of VLSM requires address planning.

In this lab, use the 172.16.128.0/17 network address to develop an address scheme for the network displayed in the topology diagram. VLSM is used to meet the IPv4 addressing requirements. After you have designed the VLSM address scheme, you will configure the interfaces on the routers with the appropriate IP address information.

Note: The routers used with CCNA hands-on labs are Cisco 1941 Integrated Services Routers (ISRs) with Cisco IOS Release 15.2(4)M3 (universalk9 image). Other routers and Cisco IOS versions can be used. Depending on the model and Cisco IOS version, the commands available and output produced might vary from what is shown in the labs. Refer to the Router Interface Summary Table at the end of this lab for the correct interface identifiers.

Note: Make sure that the routers have been erased and have no startup configurations. If you are unsure, contact your instructor.

Required Resources

- 3 routers (Cisco 1941 with Cisco IOS software, Release 15.2(4)M3 universal image or comparable)
- 1 PC (with terminal emulation program, such as Tera Term, to configure routers)
- Console cable to configure the Cisco IOS devices via the console ports
- Ethernet (optional) and serial cables, as shown in the topology
- Windows Calculator (optional)

Part 1:   Examine Network Requirements

In Part 1, you will examine the network requirements to develop a VLSM address scheme for the network displayed in the topology diagram using the 172.16.128.0/17 network address.

Note: You can use the Windows Calculator application and the www.ipcalc.org IP subnet calculator to help with your calculations.

Step 1:   Determine how many host addresses and subnets are available.

How many host addresses are available in a /17 network? _____

What is the total number of host addresses needed in the topology diagram? _____

How many subnets are needed in the network topology? _____

Step 2:   Determine the largest subnet.

What is the subnet description (e.g. BR1 G0/1 LAN or BR1-HQ WAN link)? _____

How many IP addresses are required in the largest subnet? _____

What subnet mask can support that many host addresses?

_____

How many total host addresses can that subnet mask support? _____

Can you subnet the 172.16.128.0/17 network address to support this subnet? _____

What are the two network addresses that would result from this subnetting?

_____

_____

Use the first network address for this subnet.

Step 3:   Determine the second largest subnet.

What is the subnet description? _____

How many IP addresses are required for the second largest subnet? _____

What subnet mask can support that many host addresses?

_____

How many total host addresses can that subnet mask support? _____

Can you subnet the remaining subnet again and still support this subnet? _____

What are the two network addresses that would result from this subnetting?

_____

_____

Use the first network address for this subnet.

Step 4:   **Determine the next largest subnet.**

What is the subnet description? _____

How many IP addresses are required for the next largest subnet? _____

What subnet mask can support that many host addresses?

_____

How many total host addresses can that subnet mask support? _____

Can you subnet the remaining subnet again and still support this subnet? _____

What are the two network addresses that would result from this subnetting?

_____

_____

Use the first network address for this subnet.

Step 5:   **Determine the next largest subnet.**

What is the subnet description? _____

How many IP addresses are required for the next largest subnet? _____

What subnet mask can support that many host addresses?

_____

How many total host addresses can that subnet mask support? _____

Can you subnet the remaining subnet again and still support this subnet? _____

What are the two network addresses that would result from this subnetting?

_____

_____

Use the first network address for this subnet.

Step 6:   **Determine the next largest subnet.**

What is the subnet description? _____

How many IP addresses are required for the next largest subnet? _____

What subnet mask can support that many host addresses?

_____

How many total host addresses can that subnet mask support? _____

Can you subnet the remaining subnet again and still support this subnet? _____

What are the two network addresses that would result from this subnetting?

_____

_____

Use the first network address for this subnet.

Step 7:   **Determine the next largest subnet.**

What is the subnet description? _____

How many IP addresses are required for the next largest subnet? _____

What subnet mask can support that many host addresses?

_____

How many total host addresses can that subnet mask support? _____

Can you subnet the remaining subnet again and still support this subnet? _____

What are the two network addresses that would result from this subnetting?

_____

_____

Use the first network address for this subnet.

Step 8:   **Determine the subnets needed to support the serial links.**

How many host addresses are required for each serial subnet link? _____

What subnet mask can support that many host addresses?

_____

a.   Continue subnetting the first subnet of each new subnet until you have four /30 subnets. Write the first three network addresses of these /30 subnets below.

_____

_____

_____

b. Enter the subnet descriptions for these three subnets below.

_____

_____

_____

Part 2:   Design the VLSM Address Scheme

Step 1:   Calculate the subnet information.

Use the information that you obtained in Part 1 to fill in the following table.

Subnet Description	Number of Hosts Needed	Network Address /CIDR	First Host Address	Broadcast Address
HQ G0/0	16,000			
HQ G0/1	8,000			
BR1 G0/1	4,000			
BR1 G0/0	2,000			
BR2 G0/1	1,000			
BR2 G0/0	500			
HQ S0/0/0 – BR1 S0/0/1	2			
HQ S0/0/1 – BR2 S0/0/1	2			
BR1 S0/0/1 – BR2 S0/0/0	2			

Step 2:   Complete the device interface address table.

Assign the first host address in the subnet to the Ethernet interfaces. HQ should be given the first host address on the Serial links to BR1 and BR2. BR1 should be given the first host address for the serial link to BR2.

Device	Interface	IP Address	Subnet Mask	Device Interface
HQ	G0/0			16,000 Host LAN
	G0/1			8,000 Host LAN
	S0/0/0			BR1 S0/0/0
	S0/0/1			BR2 S0/0/1
BR1	G0/0			2,000 Host LAN
	G0/1			4,000 Host LAN
	S0/0/0			HQ S0/0/0
	S0/0/1			BR2 S0/0/0
BR2	G0/0			500 Host LAN
	G0/1			1,000 Host LAN
	S0/0/0			BR1 S0/0/1
	S0/0/1			HQ S0/0/1

Part 3: Cable and Configure the IPv4 Network

In Part 3, you will cable the network topology and configure the three routers using the VLSM address scheme that you developed in Part 2.

Step 1: Cable the network as shown in the topology.

Step 2: Configure basic settings on each router.

a. Assign the device name to the router.

b. Disable DNS lookup to prevent the router from attempting to translate incorrectly entered commands as though they were hostnames.

c. Assign **class** as the privileged EXEC encrypted password.

d. Assign **cisco** as the console password and enable login.

e. Assign **cisco** as the VTY password and enable login.

f. Encrypt the clear text passwords.

g. Create a banner that will warn anyone accessing the device that unauthorized access is prohibited.

Step 3: Configure the interfaces on each router.

a. Assign an IP address and subnet mask to each interface using the table that you completed in Part 2.

b. Configure an interface description for each interface.

c. Set the clocking rate on all DCE serial interfaces to 128000.

    HQ(config-if)# clock rate 128000

d. Activate the interfaces.

Step 4: Save the configuration on all devices.

Step 5: Test Connectivity.

a. From HQ, ping BR1's S0/0/0 interface address.

b. From HQ, ping BR2's S0/0/1 interface address.

c. From BR1, ping BR2's S0/0/0 interface address.

d. Troubleshoot connectivity issues if pings were not successful.

Note: Pings to the GigabitEthernet interfaces on other routers will not be successful. The LANs defined for the GigabitEthernet interfaces are simulated. Because no devices are attached to these LANs they will be in down/down state. A routing protocol needs to be in place for other devices to be aware of those subnets. The GigabitEthernet interfaces also need to be in an up/up state before a routing protocol can add the subnets to the routing table. These interfaces will remain in a down/down state until a device is connected to the other end of the Ethernet interface cable. The focus of this lab is on VLSM and configuring the interfaces.

Reflection

Can you think of a shortcut for calculating the network addresses of consecutive /30 subnets?

_____

_____

_____

_____

Router Interface Summary Table

Router Interface Summary				
Router Model	**Ethernet Interface #1**	**Ethernet Interface #2**	**Serial Interface #1**	**Serial Interface #2**
1800	Fast Ethernet 0/0 (F0/0)	Fast Ethernet 0/1 (F0/1)	Serial 0/0/0 (S0/0/0)	Serial 0/0/1 (S0/0/1)
1900	Gigabit Ethernet 0/0 (G0/0)	Gigabit Ethernet 0/1 (G0/1)	Serial 0/0/0 (S0/0/0)	Serial 0/0/1 (S0/0/1)
2801	Fast Ethernet 0/0 (F0/0)	Fast Ethernet 0/1 (F0/1)	Serial 0/1/0 (S0/1/0)	Serial 0/1/1 (S0/1/1)
2811	Fast Ethernet 0/0 (F0/0)	Fast Ethernet 0/1 (F0/1)	Serial 0/0/0 (S0/0/0)	Serial 0/0/1 (S0/0/1)
2900	Gigabit Ethernet 0/0 (G0/0)	Gigabit Ethernet 0/1 (G0/1)	Serial 0/0/0 (S0/0/0)	Serial 0/0/1 (S0/0/1)
Note: To find out how the router is configured, look at the interfaces to identify the type of router and how many interfaces the router has. There is no way to effectively list all the combinations of configurations for each router class. This table includes identifiers for the possible combinations of Ethernet and Serial interfaces in the device. The table does not include any other type of interface, even though a specific router may contain one. An example of this might be an ISDN BRI interface. The string in parenthesis is the legal abbreviation that can be used in Cisco IOS commands to represent the interface.				

8.4.1.1 Class Activity — Can you call me now?

Objectives

Calculate the necessary subnet mask to accommodate a given number of hosts.

Subnetting is hierarchical and can help deliver network traffic more easily if small groups of IP addresses are designed to serve network needs.

Background/Scenario

Note: This activity may be completed individually or in small or large groups using Packet Tracer software.

- You are setting up a dedicated, computer addressing scheme for patient rooms in a hospital. The switch will be centrally located in the nurses' station, as each of the five rooms will be wired so that patients can just connect to an RJ45 port built into the wall of their room. Devise a physical and logical topology for only one of the six floors using the following addressing scheme requirements: There are six floors with five patient rooms on each floor for a total of 30 connections. Each room needs a network connection.

- Subnetting must be incorporated into your scheme.

- Use one router, one switch, and five host stations for addressing purposes.

- Validate that all PCs can connect to the hospital's in-house services.

Keep a copy of your scheme to share later with the class or learning community. Be prepared to explain how subnetting, unicasts, multicasts, and broadcasts would be incorporated, and where your addressing scheme could be used.

.

Required Resources

Packet Tracer software

Reflection

1. How would you change your addressing scheme if you were going to add an additional network connection to the hospital rooms with a total of 10 connections per floor or 2 ports per room?

_____

Chapter 9 — Network Access

9.0.1.2 Class Activity — Let Me Tell You What I Heard at a Conference...

Objectives

Describe the purpose and function of the data link layer in preparing communication for transmission on specific media.

In this activity, you will discuss how communication within a single data-link layer domain can be performed immediately by addressing the intended node directly. You will also consider the increasing difficulty of communication if multiple nodes in a single domain need to communicate.

Background/Scenario

You and your colleague are attending a networking conference. There are many lectures and presentations held during this event, and because they overlap, each of you can attend only a limited set of sessions. Therefore, you decide to split up, each of you attending a separate set of presentations, and after the event ends, you share the slides and the knowledge each of you gained during the event.

Answer the following questions:

- How would you personally organize a conference where multiple sessions are held at the same time? Would you put all of them into a single conference room, or would you use multiple rooms? Explain your answer.

- Assume that the conference room is properly fitted with audiovisual equipment to display large-size video and amplify the speaker's voice. If a person wanted to attend a specific session, does it matter which seat the person takes, or is it sufficient for the person to sit anywhere as long as it is in an appropriate conference room?

- What are the potential consequences or benefits if the speech from one conference room somehow leaked into another?

- If questions or inquiries arise during a presentation, should an attendee simply shout out a question, or should there be some process of assuring that attendees are given an opportunity to ask questions that everyone can hear? What would happen without this process?

- Can a session run out of time without going through the entire intended content if an interesting topic elicits a larger discussion where many attendees have questions? If you did not want this to happen, what would be the best way to ensure that it does not occur?

- Imagine that the session is in a panel format, which allows more free discussion of attendees with the panelists and among themselves. If a person wants to address another person within the same room, can it be done directly? If so, how is this possible? How would a panelist invite another person to join who is not presently in the room?

- What benefit, if any, was achieved by the isolation of multiple sessions into separate conference rooms if, after the event, people could meet and share the information?

Required Resources

Recording capabilities (paper, tablet, etc.) for reflective comments to be shared with the class.

Reflection

1. How would you personally organize a conference where multiple sessions are held at the same time? Would you put all of them into a single conference room, or would you use multiple rooms? What would be the reason? Explain your answer.

   _____

2. Assume that the conference room is properly fitted with audiovisual equipment to display large-size video and amplify the speaker's voice. If a person wanted to attend a specific session, does it matter which seat will the person takes, or is it sufficient for the person to sit anywhere as long as it is in appropriate conference room?

   _____

3. What are the potential consequences or benefits if the speech from one conference room somehow leaked into another?

   _____

4. If questions or inquiries arise during a presentation, should an attendee simply shout out his/her question, or should there be some process of assuring that attendees are given an opportunity to ask questions that everyone can hear? What would happen without this process?

   _____

   Can a session run out of time without going through the entire intended content if an interesting topic elicits a larger discussion where many attendees have questions? If you did not want this to happen, what would be the best way to ensure that it does not occur? _____

   _____

5. Imagine that the session is in a panel format, which allows more free discussion of attendees with the panelists and among themselves. If a person wants to address another person within the same room, can he/she do it directly? If so, how is this possible? How would a panelist invite another person to join who is not presently in the room?

   _____

6. What benefit, if any, was achieved by the isolation of multiple sessions into separate conference rooms if, after the event, people could meet and share the information?

   _____

9.3.1.4 Lab A — Identifying Network Devices and Cabling

Objectives

Part 1: Identify Network Devices

- Describe the functions and physical characteristics of the network device.

Part 2: Identify Network Media

- Describe the functions and physical characteristics of the media.

Background / Scenario

As a member of the networking support staff, you must be able to identify different networking equipment. You must also understand the function of equipment in the appropriate part of the network. In this lab, you will have access to network devices and media. You will identify the type and characteristics of the network equipment and media.

Part 1:   Identify Network Devices

Your instructor will provide various network devices for identification. Each will be tagged with an ID number.

Fill in the table below with the device tag ID number, manufacturer, device model, type (hub, switch, and router), functionality (wireless, router, switch, or combination), and other physical characteristics, such as number of interface types. The first line is filled out as a reference.

ID	Manufacturer	Model	Type	Functionality	Physical Characteristics
1	Cisco	1941	Router	Router	2 GigabitEthernet Ports 2 EHWIC slots 2 CompactFlash slots 1 ISM slot 2 Console ports: USB, RJ-45
2					
3					
4					
5					
6					

Part 2:   **Identify Network Media**

Your instructor will provide various network media for identification. You will name the network media, identify the media type (copper, fiber optic, or wireless), and provide a short media description including what device types it connects. Use the table below to record your findings. The first line in the table has been filled out as a reference.

ID	Network Media	Type	Description and to What It Connects
1	UTP	Copper	Connect wired NIC and Ethernet ports on network devices Cat 5 straight-through wired. Connects PCs and routers to switches and wiring panels.
2			
3			
4			
5			
6			

Reflection

After you have identified the network equipment, where would you find more information about the equipment?

_____

_____

_____

9.4.2.8 Lab — Building an Ethernet Crossover Cable

Topology

Addressing Table

Device	Interface	IP Address	Subnet Mask	Default Gateway
PC-A	NIC	192.168.10.1	255.255.255.0	N/A
PC-B	NIC	192.168.10.2	255.255.255.0	N/A

Objectives

Part 1: Analyze Ethernet Cabling Standards and Pinouts

- Analyze diagrams and tables for the TIA/EIA 568-A standard Ethernet cable.
- Analyze diagrams and tables for the TIA/EIA 568-B standard Ethernet cable.

Part 2: Build an Ethernet Crossover Cable

- Build and terminate a TIA/EIA 568-A cable end.
- Build and terminate a TIA/EIA 568-B cable end.

Part 3: Test an Ethernet Crossover Cable

- Test an Ethernet crossover cable with a cable tester.
- Connect two PCs together using an Ethernet crossover cable.

Background / Scenario

In this lab, you will build and terminate an Ethernet crossover cable and test it by connecting two PCs together and pinging between them. You will first analyze the Telecommunications Industry Association/Electronic Industries Association (TIA/EIA) 568-A and 568-B standards and how they apply to Ethernet cables. You will then construct an Ethernet crossover cable and test it. Finally, you will use the cable you just constructed to connect two PCs together and test it by pinging between them.

Note: With autosensing capabilities available on many devices, such as the Cisco 1941 Integrated Services Router (ISR) switch, you may see straight-through cables connecting like devices.

Required Resources

- One length of cable, either Category 5 or 5e. Cable length should be 0.6 to 0.9m (2 to 3 ft.)

- 2 RJ-45 connectors

- RJ-45 crimping tool

- Wire cutter

- Wire stripper

- Ethernet cable tester (optional)

- 2 PCs (Windows 7, Vista, or XP)

Part 1:   Analyze Ethernet Cabling Standards and Pinouts

The TIA/EIA has specified unshielded twisted pair (UTP) cabling standards for use in LAN cabling environments. TIA/EIA 568-A and 568-B stipulates the commercial cabling standards for LAN installations; these are the standards most commonly used in LAN cabling for organizations and they determine which color wire is used on each pin.

With a crossover cable, the second and third pairs on the RJ-45 connector at one end of the cable are reversed at the other end, which reverses the send and receive pairs. The cable pinouts are the 568-A standard on one end and the 568-B standard on the other end. Crossover cables are normally used to connect hubs to hubs or switches to switches, but they can also be used to directly connect two hosts to create a simple network.

Note: With modern networking devices, a straight-through cable can often be used even when connecting like devices because of their autosensing feature. With autosensing, the interfaces detect whether the send and receive circuit pairs are correctly connected. If they are not, the interfaces reverse one end of the connection. Autosensing also alters the speed of the interfaces to match the slowest one. For example, if connecting a Gigabit Ethernet (1000 Mb/s) router interface to a Fast Ethernet (100 Mb/s) switch interface, the connection uses Fast Ethernet.

The Cisco 2960 switch has autosensing turned on, by default; therefore, connecting two 2960 switches together works with either a crossover or a straight-through cable. With some older switches, this is not the case and a crossover cable must be used.

In addition, the Cisco 1941 router Gigabit Ethernet interfaces are autosensing and a straight-through cable may be used to connect a PC directly to the router interface (bypassing the switch). With some older routers, this is not the case and a crossover cable must be used.

When directly connecting two hosts, it is generally advisable to use a crossover cable.

Step 1:   Analyze diagrams and tables for the TIA/EIA 568-A standard Ethernet cable.

The following table and diagrams display the color scheme and pinouts, as well as the function of the four pairs of wires used for the 568-A standard.

Note: In LAN installations using 100Base-T (100 Mb/s), only two pairs out of the four are used.

568-A 10/100/1000Base-TX Ethernet

Pin Number	Pair Number	Wire Color	10Base-T Signal 100Base-TX Signal	1000Base-T Signal
1	2	White/Green	Transmit	BI_DA+
2	2	Green	Transmit	BI_DA-
3	3	White/Orange	Receive	BI_DB+
4	1	Blue	Not Used	BI_DC+
5	1	White/Blue	Not Used	BI_DC-
6	3	Orange	Receive	BI_DB-
7	4	White/Brown	Not Used	BI_DD+
8	4	Brown	Not Used	BI_DD-

The following diagrams display how the wire color and pinouts align with an RJ-45 jack for the 568-A standard.

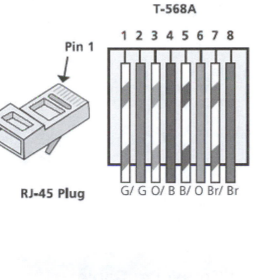

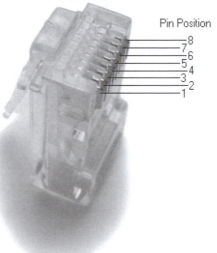

Step 2: **Analyze diagrams and tables for the TIA/EIA 568-B standard Ethernet cable.**

The following table and diagram display the color scheme and pinouts for the 568-B standard.

568-B 10/100/1000-BaseTX Ethernet

Pin Number	Pair Number	Wire Color	10Base-T Signal 100Base-TX Signal	1000Base-T Signal
1	2	White/Orange	Transmit	BI_DA+
2	2	Orange	Transmit	BI_DA-
3	3	White/Green	Receive	BI_DB+
4	1	Blue	Not Used	BI_DC+
5	1	White/Blue	Not Used	BI_DC-
6	3	Green	Receive	BI_DB-
7	4	White/Brown	Not Used	BI_DD+
8	4	Brown	Not Used	BI_DD-

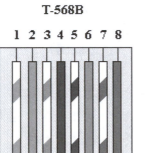

T-568B

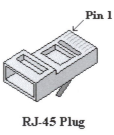

RJ-45 Plug

Part 2: **Build an Ethernet Crossover Cable**

A crossover cable has the second and third pairs on the RJ-45 connector at one end, reversed at the other end (refer to the table in Part 1, Step 2). The cable pinouts are the 568-A standard on one end and the 568-B standard on the other end. The two following diagrams illustrate this concept.

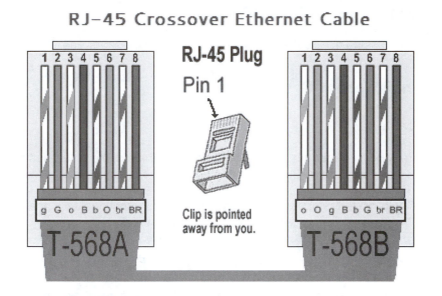

RJ-45 Crossover Ethernet Cable

RJ-45 Plug
Pin 1

Clip is pointed
away from you.

T-568A

T-568B

Step 1: **Build and terminate a TIA/EIA 568-A cable end.**

a. Determine the cable length required. (Your instructor will let you know the cable length you should make.)

    Note: If you were making a cable in a production environment, the general guideline is to add another 12 in. (30.48 cm) to the length.

b. Cut off a piece of cable to the desired length and using your wire stripper, remove 5.08 cm (2 in.) of the cable jacket from both ends.

c. Hold the four pairs of twisted cables tightly where the jacket was cut away. Reorganize the cable pairs into the order of the 568-A wiring standard. Refer to the diagrams, if necessary. Take as much care as possible to maintain the twists in the cable; this provides noise cancellation.

d. Flatten, straighten, and line up the wires using your thumb and forefinger.

e. Ensure that the cable wires are still in the correct order for the 568-A standard. Using your wire cutters, trim the four pairs in a straight line to within 1.25 to 1.9 cm (1/2 to 3/4 in.).

f. Place an RJ-45 connector on the end of your cable, with the prong on the underside pointing downward. Firmly insert the wires into the RJ-45 connector. All wires should be seen at the end of the connector in their proper positions. If the wires are not extending to the end of the connector, take the cable out, rearrange the wires as necessary, and reinsert the wires back into the RJ-45 connector.

g. If everything is correct, insert the RJ-45 connector with cable into the crimper. Crimp down hard enough to force the contacts on the RJ-45 connector through the insulation on the wires, thus completing the conducting path. See the following diagram for an example.

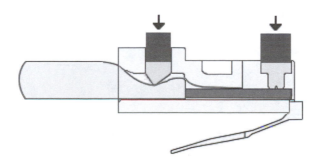

Step 2:   **Build and terminate a TIA/EIA 568-B cable end.**

Repeat steps 1a to 1g using the 568-B color wiring scheme for the other end.

Part 3:   **Test an Ethernet Crossover Cable**

Step 1:   **Test the cable.**

Many cable testers will test for length and mapping of wires. If the cable tester has a wire map feature, it verifies which pins on one end of the cable are connected to which pins on the other end.

If your instructor has a cable tester, test the crossover cable for functionality. If it fails, check with your instructor first as to whether you should re-cable the ends and re-test.

Step 2:   **Connect two PCs together via NICs using your Ethernet crossover cable.**

a.   Working with a lab partner, set your PC to one of the IP addresses shown in the Addressing Table (see page 1). For example, if your PC is **PC-A**, your IP address should be set to **192.168.10.1** with a **24-bit subnet mask**. You partner's IP address should be **192.168.10.2**. The default gateway address can be left empty.

b.   Using the crossover cable you made, connect the two PCs together via their NICs.

c.   On the PC-A command prompt, ping the PC-B IP address.

Note: The Windows firewall may have to be temporarily disabled for pings to be successful. If the firewall is disabled, make sure you re-enable it at the conclusion of this lab.

d.   Repeat the process and ping from PC-B to PC-A.

Assuming IP addressing and firewall are not issues, your pings should be successful if the cables were properly made.

Reflection

1.   Which part of making cables did you find the most difficult?

_____

2.   Why do you have to learn how to make a cable if you can easily buy pre-made cables?

_____

9.4.4.6 Lab — Viewing Wireless and Wired NIC Information

Objectives

Part 1: Identify and Work with PC NICs

Part 2: Identify and Use the System Tray Network Icons

Background / Scenario

This lab requires you to determine the availability and status of the network interface cards (NICs) on the PC that you use. Windows provides a number of ways to view and work with your NICs.

In this lab, you will access the NIC information of your PC and change the status of these cards.

Required Resources

* 1 PC (Windows 7, Vista, or XP with two NICs, wired and wireless, and a wireless connection)

   Note: At the start of this lab, the wired Ethernet NIC in the PC was cabled to one of the integrated switch ports on a wireless router and the Local Area Connection (wired) was enabled. The wireless NIC was disabled initially. If the wired and wireless NICs are both enabled the PC will receive two different IP addresses and the wireless NIC will take precedence.

Part 1:   Identify and Work with PC NICs

In Part 1, you will identify the NIC types in the PC that you are using. You will explore different ways to extract information about these NICs and how to activate and deactivate them.

Note: This lab was performed using a PC running on the Windows 7 operating system. You should be able to perform the lab with one of the other Windows operating systems listed; however, menu selections and screens may vary.

Step 1:   Use the Network and Sharing Center.

a.   Open the **Network and Sharing Center** by clicking the Windows **Start** button > **Control Panel** > **View network status and tasks** under Network and Internet heading in the Category View.

b.   In the left pane, click the **Change adapter settings** link.

c.   The Network Connections window displays, which provides the list of NICs available on this PC. Look for your Local Area Connection and Wireless Network Connection adapters in this window.

Note: Virtual Private Network (VPN) adapters and other types of network connections may also be displayed in this window.

Step 2:   **Work with your wireless NIC.**

a. Select the **Wireless Network Connection** option and right-click it to bring up a drop-down list. If your wireless NIC is disabled, you will have an option to **Enable** it. If your NIC was already enabled, then **Disable** would be the first option on this drop-down menu. If your **Wireless Network Connection** is currently disabled, then click **Enable**.

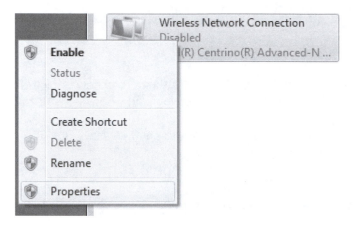

b. Right-click the **Wireless Network Connection**, and then click **Status**.

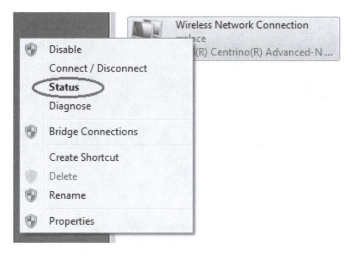

c. The Wireless Network Connection Status window displays where you can view information about your wireless connection.

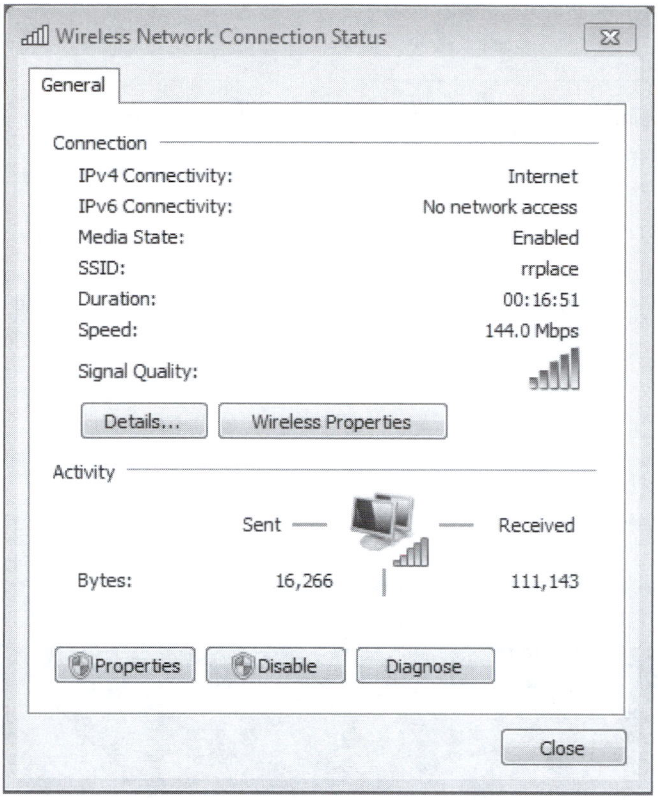

What is the Service Set Identifier (SSID) for the wireless router of your connection?

_____

What is the speed of your wireless connection?

_____

d. Click **Details** to display the Network Connection Details window.

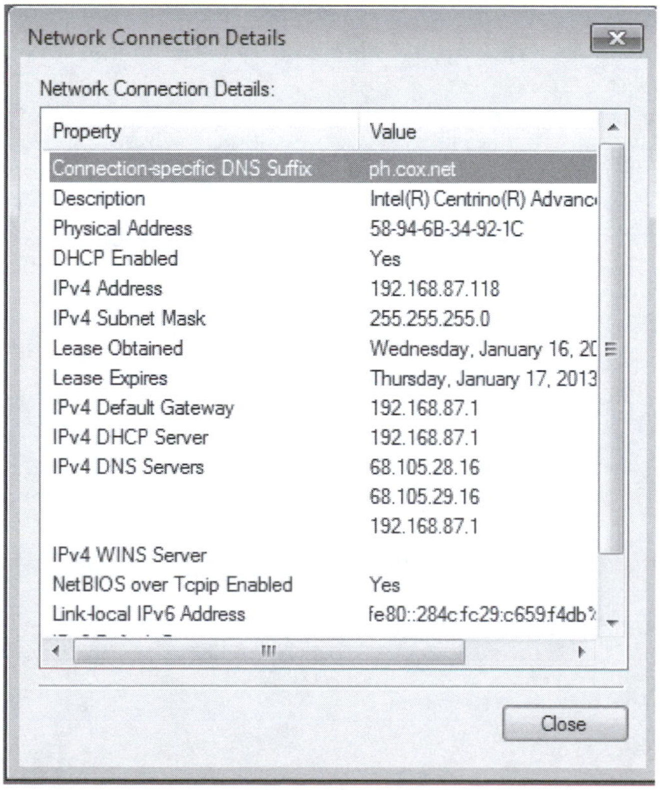

What is the MAC address of your wireless NIC?

_____

Do you have multiple IPv4 DNS Servers listed?

_____

Why would multiple DNS Servers be listed?

_____

_____

e.   When you have reviewed the network connection details, click **Close**.

f.   Open a command window prompt and type **ipconfig /all**.

```
Wireless LAN adapter Wireless Network Connection:

   Connection-specific DNS Suffix  . : ph.cox.net
   Description . . . . . . . . . . . : Intel(R) Centrino(R) Advanced-N 6200 AGN
   Physical Address. . . . . . . . . : 58-94-6B-34-92-1C
   DHCP Enabled. . . . . . . . . . . : Yes
   Autoconfiguration Enabled . . . . : Yes
   Link-local IPv6 Address . . . . . : fe80::284c:fc29:c659:f4db%11(Preferred)
   IPv4 Address. . . . . . . . . . . : 192.168.87.118(Preferred)
   Subnet Mask . . . . . . . . . . . : 255.255.255.0
   Lease Obtained. . . . . . . . . . : Thursday, January 17, 2013 8:30:40 AM
   Lease Expires . . . . . . . . . . : Friday, January 18, 2013 8:30:41 AM
   Default Gateway . . . . . . . . . : 192.168.87.1
   DHCP Server . . . . . . . . . . . : 192.168.87.1
   DHCPv6 IAID . . . . . . . . . . . : 307795051
   DHCPv6 Client DUID. . . . . . . . : 00-01-00-01-14-AC-22-0A-5C-26-0A-24-2A-60
   DNS Servers . . . . . . . . . . . : 68.105.28.16
                                       68.105.29.16
                                       192.168.87.1
   NetBIOS over Tcpip. . . . . . . . : Enabled
```

Notice that the information displayed here is the same information that was displayed in the Network Connection Details window in Step d.

g.   Close the command window and the Network Connection Details windows. This should bring you back to the Wireless Network Connection Status window. Click **Wireless Properties**.

h.   In the **Wireless Network Properties** window, click the **Security** tab.

i. The type of security the connected wireless router has implemented displays. Click the **Show characters** check box to display the actual Network security key, instead of the hidden characters, and then click **OK**.

j. Close the Wireless Network Properties and the Network Connection Status windows. Select and right-click the **Wireless Network Connection** option > **Connect/Disconnect**. A pop-up window should appear at the bottom right corner of your desktop that displays your current connections, along with a list of SSIDs that are in range of the wireless NIC of your PC. If a scrollbar appears on the right side of this window, you can use it to display additional SSIDs.

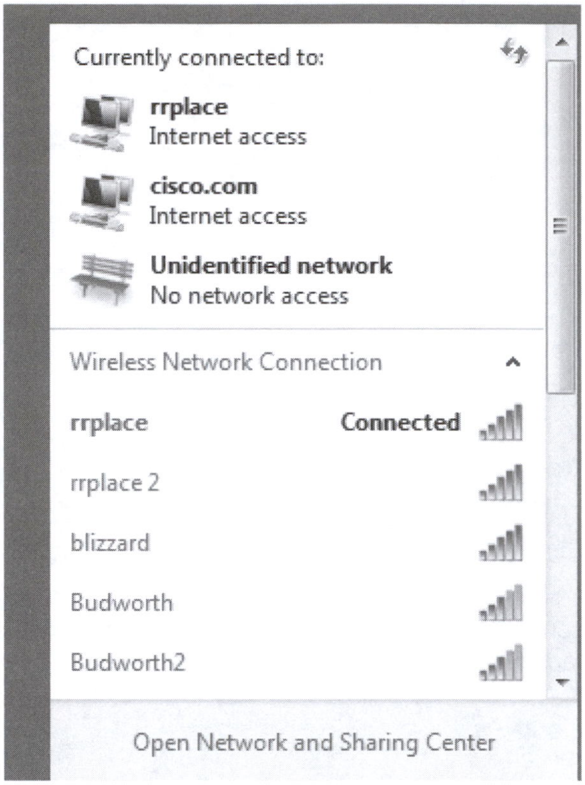

k. To join one of the other wireless network SSIDs listed, click the SSID that you want to join, and then click **Connect**.

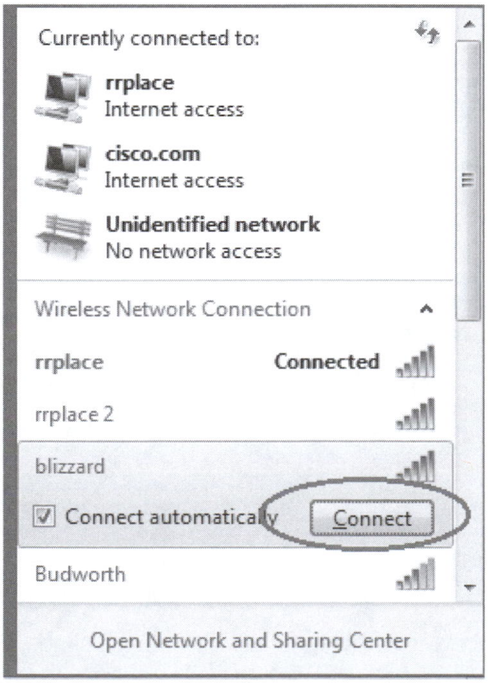

l.   If you have selected a secure SSID, you are prompted to enter the **Security key** for the SSID. Type the security key for that SSID and click **OK**. You can click the **Hide characters** check box to prevent people from seeing what you type in the **Security key** field.

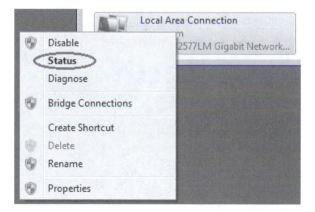

Step 3:   **Work with your wired NIC.**

a.   On the Network Connections window, select and right-click the **Local Area Connection** option to display the drop-down list. If the NIC is disabled, enable it, and then click the **Status** option.

Note: You must have an Ethernet cable attaching your PC NIC to a switch or similar device to see the status. Many wireless routers have a small 4-port Ethernet switch built-in. You can connect to one of the ports using a straight-through Ethernet patch cable.

b.   The Local Area Connection Status window will open. This window displays information about your wired connection to the LAN.

Click **Details...** to view the address information for your LAN connection.

c.   Open a command window prompt and type **ipconfig /all**. Find your Local Area Connection information and compare this with the information displayed in the Network Connection Details window.

```
Ethernet adapter Local Area Connection:

   Connection-specific DNS Suffix  . : ph.cox.net
   Description . . . . . . . . . . . : Intel(R) 82577LM Gigabit Network Connection
   Physical Address. . . . . . . . . : 5C-26-0A-24-2A-60
   DHCP Enabled. . . . . . . . . . . : Yes
   Autoconfiguration Enabled . . . . : Yes
   Link-local IPv6 Address . . . . . : fe80::b875:731b:3c7b:c0b1%10(Preferred)
   IPv4 Address. . . . . . . . . . . : 192.168.87.127(Preferred)
   Subnet Mask . . . . . . . . . . . : 255.255.255.0
   Lease Obtained. . . . . . . . . . : Thursday, January 17, 2013 10:38:14 AM
   Lease Expires . . . . . . . . . . : Friday, January 18, 2013 10:38:14 AM
   Default Gateway . . . . . . . . . : 192.168.87.1
   DHCP Server . . . . . . . . . . . : 192.168.87.1
   DHCPv6 IAID . . . . . . . . . . . : 240920074
   DHCPv6 Client DUID. . . . . . . . : 00-01-00-01-14-AC-22-0A-5C-26-0A-24-2A-60
   DNS Servers . . . . . . . . . . . : 68.105.28.16
                                       68.105.29.16
                                       192.168.87.1
   NetBIOS over Tcpip. . . . . . . . : Enabled
```

d.   Close all windows on your desktop.

Part 2:   Identify and Use the System Tray Network Icons

In Part 2, you will use the network icons in your system tray to determine and control the NICs on your PC.

Step 1:   Use the Wireless Network icon.

a.   Click the system tray **Wireless Network** icon to view the pop-up window that displays the SSIDs that are in-range of your wireless NIC. When the system tray displays the Wireless Network icon, the wireless NIC is active.

b.   Click the **Open Network and Sharing Center** link. **Note:** This is a shortcut way to bring up this window.

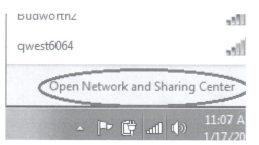

c.   In the left pane, click the **Change adapter settings** link to display the Network Connections window.

d.   Select and right-click the **Wireless Network Connection**, and then click **Disable** to disable your wireless NIC.

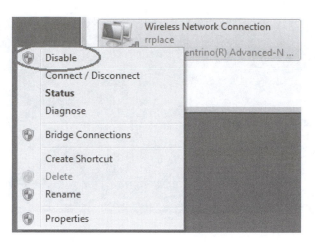

e. Examine your system tray. The **Wireless Network Connection** icon should be replaced by the **Wired Network** icon, which indicates that you are using your wired NIC for network connectivity.

Note: If both NICs are active, the **Wireless Network** icon is the one that is displayed.

Step 2:   Use the Wired Network icon.

a. Click the **Wired Network** icon. Notice that the Wireless SSIDs are no longer displayed in this pop-up window, but you still have the ability to get to the Network and Sharing Center window from here.

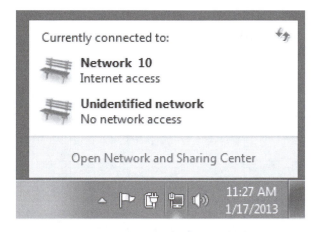

b. Click the **Open Network and Sharing Center** link > **Change adapter settings** and **Enable** your **Wireless Network Connection**. The **Wireless Network** icon should replace the **Wired Network** icon in your system tray.

Step 3:   **Identify the Network Problem icon.**

    a.   On the Network Connections window, disable both the **Wireless Network Connection** and the **Local Area Connection**.

    b.   The system tray now displays the **Network Disabled** icon, which indicates that network connectivity has been disabled.

    c.   You can click this icon to return to the Network and Sharing Center window (examine the network diagram at the top).

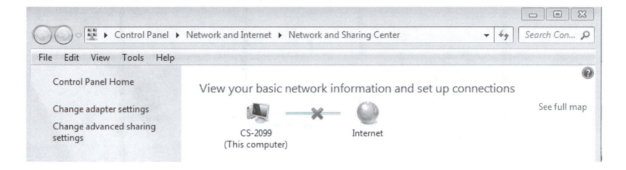

        You can click the red   to have the PC troubleshoot the problem with the network connection. Troubleshooting attempts to resolve the network issue for you.

    d.   If troubleshooting did not enable one of your NICs, then you should do this manually to restore the network connectivity of your PC.

        Note: If a network adapter is enabled and the NIC is unable to establish network connectivity, then the **Network Problem** icon appears in the system tray.

If this icon appears, you can troubleshoot this issue just like you did in Step 3c.

Reflection

Why would you activate more than one NIC on a PC?

9.5.1.1 Class Activity — Linked In!

Objectives

Connect devices using wired and wireless media.

In this activity, you will map your network cabling or technology type ideas to a physical topology. Because this chapter focuses on the network access layer, you should be able to prepare a basic physical model. No logical (IP addressing) schemes are required for this activity.

Physical Topology

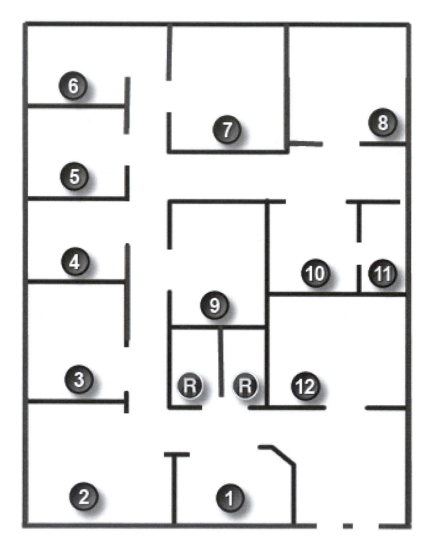

Background/Scenario

Note: This activity is best completed in groups of 2-3 students.

Your small business is moving to a new location! Your building is brand new and you must come up with a physical topology so that network port installation can begin.

Your instructor will provide you with a blueprint created for this activity. The area on the blueprint, indicated by Number 1, is the reception area and the area labeled "RR" is the restroom area.

All rooms are within Category 6 UTP specifications (328 ft. [100 m]), so you have no concerns about hard-wiring the building to code. Each room in the diagram must have at least one network connection available for users/intermediary devices.

With your teammate(s), indicate on the drawing:

- Where would you locate your network main distribution facility, while keeping security in mind?

- How many intermediary devices would you use and where would you place them?

- What kind of cabling you would use (UTP, STP, wireless, fiber optics, etc.) and where would the ports be placed?

- What types of end devices you would use (wired, wireless, laptops, desktops, tablets, etc.)?

Do not go into excessive detail on your design. Just use the content from the chapter to be able to justify your decisions to the class.

Required Resources

Packet Tracer software

Reflection

1. Where would you locate your network main distribution facility, while keeping security in mind?

   _____

2. How many intermediary devices would you use and where would you place them?

   _____

3. What kind of cabling you would use (UTP, STP, wireless, fiber optics, etc.) and where would the ports be placed?

   _____

4. What types of end devices you would use (wired, wireless, laptops, desktops, tablets, etc.)?

   _____

Chapter 10 — Ethernet

10.0.1.2 Class Activity — Join my social circle!

Objectives

Describe the impact of ARP requests on network and host performance.

In this activity, you will discuss the ways in which local addressing (source and destination) is critical to data communication identification when using messaging, conferencing, emailing, and even gaming.

Background/Scenario

Note: This activity can be completed individually in class or outside of class.

Much of our network communication takes the form of email, messaging (text or instant), video contact, and social media postings.

For this activity, choose one of the following types of network communications:

- Text or instant messaging

- Audio/video conferencing

- Emailing

- Online gaming

Now that you have selected a network communication type, record your answers to the following questions:

1. Is there a procedure you must follow to register others and yourself so that you form a communications account? Why do you think that a procedure is needed?

2. How do you initiate contact with the person or people with whom you wish to communicate?

3. How do you ensure that your conversations are received only by those with whom you wish to communicate? Be prepared to discuss your answers in class.

Required Resources

Recording capabilities (paper, tablet, etc.) for reflective comments to be shared with the class

Reflection

1. Is there a procedure you must follow to register others and yourself so that you form a communications account? Why do you think that a procedure is needed?

   _____

2. How do you initiate contact with the person or people with whom you wish to communicate?

   _____

3. How do you ensure that your conversations are received only by those with whom you wish to communicate?

   _____

10.1.3.6 Lab — Viewing Network Device MAC Addresses

Topology

Addressing Table

Device	Interface	IP Address	Subnet Mask	Default Gateway
R1	G0/1	192.168.1.1	255.255.255.0	N/A
S1	VLAN 1	N/A	N/A	N/A
PC-A	NIC	192.168.1.3	255.255.255.0	192.168.1.1

Objectives

Part 1: Set Up the Topology and Initialize Devices

- Set up equipment to match the network topology.
- Initialize and restart (if necessary) the router and switch.

Part 2: Configure Devices and Verify Connectivity

- Assign static IP address to PC-A NIC.
- Configure basic information on R1.
- Assign a static IP address to R1.
- Verify network connectivity.

Part 3: Display, Describe, and Analyze Ethernet MAC Addresses

- Analyze MAC address for PC-A.
- Analyze MAC addresses for router R1.
- Display the MAC address table on switch S1.

Background / Scenario

Every device on an Ethernet LAN is identified by a Layer-2 MAC address. This address is burned into the NIC. This lab will explore and analyze the components that make up a MAC address, and how you can find this information on various networking devices, such as a router, switch, and PC.

You will cable the equipment as shown in the topology. You will then configure the router and PC to match the addressing table. You will verify your configurations by testing for network connectivity.

After the devices have been configured and network connectivity has been verified, you will use various commands to retrieve information from the devices to answer questions about your network equipment.

Note: The routers used with CCNA hands-on labs are Cisco 1941 Integrated Services Routers (ISRs) with Cisco IOS Release 15.2(4)M3 (universalk9 image). The switches used are Cisco Catalyst 2960s with Cisco IOS Release 15.0(2) (lanbasek9 image). Other routers, switches, and Cisco IOS versions can be used. Depending on the model and Cisco IOS version, the commands available and output produced might vary from what is shown in the labs. Refer to the Router Interface Summary Table at the end of this lab for the correct interface identifiers.

Note: Make sure that the routers and switches have been erased and have no startup configurations. If you are unsure, contact your instructor.

Required Resources

- 1 Router (Cisco 1941 with Cisco IOS Release 15.2(4)M3 universal image or comparable)
- 1 Switch (Cisco 2960 with Cisco IOS Release 15.0(2) lanbasek9 image or comparable)
- 1 PC (Windows 7, Vista, or XP with terminal emulation program, such as Tera Term)
- Console cables to configure the Cisco IOS devices via the console ports
- Ethernet cables as shown in the topology

Part 1: Set Up the Topology and Initialize Devices

In Part 1, you will set up the network topology, clear any configurations, if necessary, and configure basic settings, such as the interface IP addresses on the router and PC.

Step 1: Cable the network as shown in the topology.

a. Attach the devices shown in the topology and cable as necessary.

b. Power on all the devices in the topology.

Step 2: Initialize and reload the router and switch.

Part 2: Configure Devices and Verify Connectivity

In Part 2, you will set up the network topology and configure basic settings, such as the interface IP addresses and device access. For device names and address information, refer to the Topology and Addressing Table.

Step 1: Configure the IPv4 address for the PC.

a. Configure the IPv4 address, subnet mask, and default gateway address for PC-A.

b. Ping the default gateway address of R1 from a PC-A command prompt.

Were the pings successful? Why or why not?

_____

_____

Step 2:   **Configure the router.**

    a. Console into the router and enter global configuration mode.

    b. Assign a hostname to the router based on the Addressing Table.

    c. Disable DNS lookup.

    d. Configure and enable the G0/1 interface on the router.

Step 3:   **Verify network connectivity.**

    a. Ping the default gateway address of R1 from PC-A.

    Were the pings successful?

Part 3:   Display, Describe, and Analyze Ethernet MAC Addresses

Every device on an Ethernet LAN has a Media Access Control (MAC) address that is burned into the Network Interface Card (NIC). Ethernet MAC addresses are 48-bits long. They are displayed using six sets of hexadecimal digits usually separated by dashes, colons, or periods. The following example shows the same MAC address using the three different notation methods:

        00-05-9A-3C-78-00   **00:05:9A:3C:78:00**   **0005.9A3C.7800**

Note: MAC addresses are also called physical addresses, hardware addresses, or Ethernet hardware addresses.

In Part 3, you will issue commands to display the MAC addresses on a PC, router, and switch, and you will analyze the properties of each one.

Step 1:   Analyze the MAC address for the PC-A NIC.

Before you analyze the MAC address on PC-A, look at an example from a different PC NIC. You can issue the **ipconfig /all** command to view the MAC address of your NICs. An example screen output is shown below. When using the **ipconfig /all** command, notice that MAC addresses are referred to as physical addresses. Reading the MAC address from left to right, the first six hex digits refer to the vendor (manufacturer) of this device. These first six hex digits (3 bytes) are also known as the organizationally unique identifier (OUI). This 3-byte code is assigned to the vendor by the IEEE organization. To find the manufacturer, you can use a tool such as www.macvendorlookup.com or go to the IEEE web site to find the registered OUI vendor codes. The IEEE web site address for OUI information is http://standards.ieee.org/develop/regauth/oui/public.html. The last six digits are the NIC serial number assigned by the manufacturer.

    a. Using the output from the **ipconfig /all** command, answer the following questions.

```
Ethernet adapter Local Area Connection:

    Connection-specific DNS Suffix  . :
    Description . . . . . . . . . . . : Realtek PCIe GBE Family Controller
    Physical Address. . . . . . . . . : C8-0A-A9-FA-DE-0D
    DHCP Enabled. . . . . . . . . . . : No
    Autoconfiguration Enabled . . . . : Yes
    IPv4 Address. . . . . . . . . . . : 192.168.1.3(Preferred)
    Subnet Mask . . . . . . . . . . . : 255.255.255.0
    Default Gateway . . . . . . . . . : 192.168.1.1
    NetBIOS over Tcpip. . . . . . . . : Enabled
```

What is the OUI portion of the MAC address for this device?

_____

What is the serial number portion of the MAC address for this device?

_____

Using the example above, find the name of the vendor that manufactured this NIC.

_____

b. From the command prompt on PC-A, issue the **ipconfig /all** command and identify the OUI portion of the MAC address for the NIC of PC-A.

_____

_____

Identify the name of the vendor that manufactured the NIC of PC-A.

_____

Step 2: Analyze the MAC address for the R1 G0/1 interface.

You can use a variety of commands to display MAC addresses on the router.

a. Console into R1 and use the **show interfaces g0/1** command to find the MAC address information. A sample is shown below. Use output generated by your router to answer the questions.

```
R1> show interfaces g0/1
GigabitEthernet0/1 is up, line protocol is up
  Hardware is CN Gigabit Ethernet, address is 30f7.0da3.1821 (bia 30f7.0da3.1821)
  Internet address is 192.168.1.1/24
  MTU 1500 bytes, BW 100000 Kbit/sec, DLY 100 usec,
```

```
        reliability 255/255, txload 1/255, rxload 1/255
   Encapsulation ARPA, loopback not set
   Keepalive set (10 sec)
   Full Duplex, 100Mbps, media type is RJ45
   output flow-control is unsupported, input flow-control is unsupported
   ARP type: ARPA, ARP Timeout 04:00:00
   Last input 00:00:00, output 00:00:00, output hang never
   Last clearing of "show interface" counters never
   Input queue: 0/75/0/0 (size/max/drops/flushes); Total output drops: 0
   Queueing strategy: fifo
   Output queue: 0/40 (size/max)
   5 minute input rate 3000 bits/sec, 4 packets/sec
   5 minute output rate 0 bits/sec, 0 packets/sec
      15183 packets input, 971564 bytes, 0 no buffer
      Received 13559 broadcasts (0 IP multicasts)
      0 runts, 0 giants, 0 throttles
      0 input errors, 0 CRC, 0 frame, 0 overrun, 0 ignored
      0 watchdog, 301 multicast, 0 pause input
      1396 packets output, 126546 bytes, 0 underruns
      0 output errors, 0 collisions, 1 interface resets
      195 unknown protocol drops
      0 babbles, 0 late collision, 0 deferred
      0 lost carrier, 0 no carrier, 0 pause output
      0 output buffer failures, 0 output buffers swapped out
```

What is the MAC address for G0/1 on R1?

_____

What is the MAC serial number for G0/1?

_____

What is the OUI for G0/1?

_____

Based on this OUI, what is the name of the vendor?

_____

What does bia stand for?

_____

Why does the output show the same MAC address twice?

_____

_____

b. Another way to display the MAC addresses on the router is to use the **show arp** command. Use the **show arp** command to display MAC address information. This command maps the Layer 2 address to its corresponding Layer 3 address. A sample is shown below. Use output generated by your router to answer the questions.

```
R1> show arp

Protocol  Address          Age (min)  Hardware Addr   Type   Interface

Internet  192.168.1.1            -    30f7.0da3.1821  ARPA   GigabitEthernet0/1

Internet  192.168.1.3            0    c80a.a9fa.de0d  ARPA   GigabitEthernet0/1
```

What Layer 2 addresses are displayed on R1?

_____

_____

What Layer 3 addresses are displayed on R1?

_____

_____

Why do you think there is no information showing for the switch with the **show arp** command?

_____

_____

Step 3: **View the MAC addresses on the switch.**

a. Console into the switch and use the **show interfaces** command for ports 5 and 6 to display MAC address information. A sample is shown below. Use output generated by your switch to answer the questions.

```
Switch> show interfaces f0/5

FastEthernet0/5 is up, line protocol is up (connected)
  Hardware is Fast Ethernet, address is 0cd9.96e8.7285 (bia 0cd9.96e8.7285)
  MTU 1500 bytes, BW 100000 Kbit, DLY 100 usec,
     reliability 255/255, txload 1/255, rxload 1/255
  Encapsulation ARPA, loopback not set
  Keepalive set (10 sec)
  Full-duplex, 100Mb/s, media type is 10/100BaseTX
  input flow-control is off, output flow-control is unsupported
  ARP type: ARPA, ARP Timeout 04:00:00
  Last input 00:00:45, output 00:00:00, output hang never
  Last clearing of "show interface" counters never
  Input queue: 0/75/0/0 (size/max/drops/flushes); Total output drops: 0
```

```
Queueing strategy: fifo

Output queue: 0/40 (size/max)

5 minute input rate 0 bits/sec, 0 packets/sec

5 minute output rate 0 bits/sec, 0 packets/sec

    3362 packets input, 302915 bytes, 0 no buffer

    Received 265 broadcasts (241 multicasts)

    0 runts, 0 giants, 0 throttles

    0 input errors, 0 CRC, 0 frame, 0 overrun, 0 ignored

    0 watchdog, 241 multicast, 0 pause input

    0 input packets with dribble condition detected

    38967 packets output, 2657748 bytes, 0 underruns

    0 output errors, 0 collisions, 1 interface resets

    0 babbles, 0 late collision, 0 deferred

    0 lost carrier, 0 no carrier, 0 PAUSE output

    0 output buffer failures, 0 output buffers swapped out
```

What is the MAC address for F0/5 on your switch?

_____

Issue the same command and write down the MAC address for F0/6.

_____

Are the OUIs shown on the switch the same as those that were displayed on the router?

_____

The switch keeps track of devices by their Layer 2 MAC addresses. In our topology, the switch has knowledge of both MAC address of R1 and the MAC address of PC-A.

b.   Issue the **show mac address-table** command on the switch. A sample is shown below. Use output generated by your switch to answer the questions.

```
Switch> show mac address-table
        Mac Address Table
-------------------------------------------


Vlan    Mac Address      Type        Ports
----    -----------      --------    -----
All     0100.0ccc.cccc   STATIC      CPU

All     0100.0ccc.cccd   STATIC      CPU

All     0180.c200.0000   STATIC      CPU
```

```
All      0180.c200.0001      STATIC      CPU
All      0180.c200.0002      STATIC      CPU
All      0180.c200.0003      STATIC      CPU
All      0180.c200.0004      STATIC      CPU
All      0180.c200.0005      STATIC      CPU
All      0180.c200.0006      STATIC      CPU
All      0180.c200.0007      STATIC      CPU
All      0180.c200.0008      STATIC      CPU
All      0180.c200.0009      STATIC      CPU
All      0180.c200.000a      STATIC      CPU
All      0180.c200.000b      STATIC      CPU
All      0180.c200.000c      STATIC      CPU
All      0180.c200.000d      STATIC      CPU
All      0180.c200.000e      STATIC      CPU
All      0180.c200.000f      STATIC      CPU
All      0180.c200.0010      STATIC      CPU
All      ffff.ffff.ffff      STATIC      CPU
  1      30f7.0da3.1821      DYNAMIC     Fa0/5
  1      c80a.a9fa.de0d      DYNAMIC     Fa0/6
Total Mac Addresses for this criterion: 22
```

Did the switch display the MAC address of PC-A? If you answered yes, what port was it on?

_____

Did the switch display the MAC address of R1? If you answered yes, what port was it on?

_____

Reflection

1. Can you have broadcasts at the Layer 2 level? If so, what would the MAC address be?

_____

2. Why would you need to know the MAC address of a device?

_____

Router Interface Summary Table

Router Interface Summary				
Router Model	**Ethernet Interface #1**	**Ethernet Interface #2**	**Serial Interface #1**	**Serial Interface #2**
1800	Fast Ethernet 0/0 (F0/0)	Fast Ethernet 0/1 (F0/1)	Serial 0/0/0 (S0/0/0)	Serial 0/0/1 (S0/0/1)
1900	Gigabit Ethernet 0/0 (G0/0)	Gigabit Ethernet 0/1 (G0/1)	Serial 0/0/0 (S0/0/0)	Serial 0/0/1 (S0/0/1)
2801	Fast Ethernet 0/0 (F0/0)	Fast Ethernet 0/1 (F0/1)	Serial 0/1/0 (S0/1/0)	Serial 0/1/1 (S0/1/1)
2811	Fast Ethernet 0/0 (F0/0)	Fast Ethernet 0/1 (F0/1)	Serial 0/0/0 (S0/0/0)	Serial 0/0/1 (S0/0/1)
2900	Gigabit Ethernet 0/0 (G0/0)	Gigabit Ethernet 0/1 (G0/1)	Serial 0/0/0 (S0/0/0)	Serial 0/0/1 (S0/0/1)

Note: To find out how the router is configured, look at the interfaces to identify the type of router and how many interfaces the router has. There is no way to effectively list all the combinations of configurations for each router class. This table includes identifiers for the possible combinations of Ethernet and Serial interfaces in the device. The table does not include any other type of interface, even though a specific router may contain one. An example of this might be an ISDN BRI interface. The string in parenthesis is the legal abbreviation that can be used in Cisco IOS commands to represent the interface.

10.1.4.3 Lab — Using Wireshark to Examine Ethernet Frames

Topology

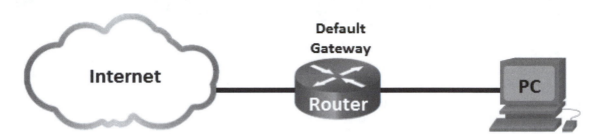

Objectives

Part 1: Examine the Header Fields in an Ethernet II Frame

Part 2: Use Wireshark to Capture and Analyze Ethernet Frames

Background / Scenario

When upper layer protocols communicate with each other, data flows down the Open Systems Interconnection (OSI) layers and is encapsulated into a Layer 2 frame. The frame composition is dependent on the media access type. For example, if the upper layer protocols are TCP and IP and the media access is Ethernet, then the Layer 2 frame encapsulation will be Ethernet II. This is typical for a LAN environment.

When learning about Layer 2 concepts, it is helpful to analyze frame header information. In the first part of this lab, you will review the fields contained in an Ethernet II frame. In Part 2, you will use Wireshark to capture and analyze Ethernet II frame header fields for local and remote traffic.

Required Resources

- 1 PC (Windows 7, Vista, or XP with Internet access with Wireshark installed)

Part 1: Examine the Header Fields in an Ethernet II Frame

In Part 1, you will examine the header fields and content in an Ethernet II Frame. A Wireshark capture will be used to examine the contents in those fields.

Step 1: Review the Ethernet II header field descriptions and lengths.

Preamble	Destination Address	Source Address	Frame Type	Data	FCS
8 Bytes	6 Bytes	6 Bytes	2 Bytes	46 – 1500 Bytes	4 Bytes

Step 2: Examine the network configuration of the PC.

This PC host IP address is 10.20.164.22 and the default gateway has an IP address of 10.20.164.17.

```
Ethernet adapter Local Area Connection:

   Connection-specific DNS Suffix   . : cisco.com
   Link-local IPv6 Address . . . . . : fe80::b875:731b:3c7b:c0b1%10
   IPv4 Address. . . . . . . . . . . : 10.20.164.22
   Subnet Mask . . . . . . . . . . . : 255.255.255.240
   Default Gateway . . . . . . . . . : 10.20.164.17
```

Step 3:   **Examine Ethernet frames in a Wireshark capture.**

The Wireshark capture below shows the packets generated by a ping being issued from a PC host to its default gateway. A filter has been applied to Wireshark to view the ARP and ICMP protocols only. The session begins with an ARP query for the MAC address of the gateway router, followed by four ping requests and replies.

Step 4:   **Examine the Ethernet II header contents of an ARP request.**

The following table takes the first frame in the Wireshark capture and displays the data in the Ethernet II header fields.

Field	Value	Description
Preamble	Not shown in capture	This field contains synchronizing bits, processed by the NIC hardware.
Destination Address	Broadcast (ff:ff:ff:ff:ff:ff)	Layer 2 addresses for the frame. Each address is 48 bits long, or 6 octets, expressed as 12 hexadecimal digits, `0-9,A-F`. A common format is `12:34:56:78:9A:BC`.
Source Address	Dell_24:2a:60 (5c:26:0a:24:2a:60)	The first six hex numbers indicate the manufacturer of the network interface card (NIC), the last six hex numbers are the serial number of the NIC.
		The destination address may be a broadcast, which contains all ones, or a unicast. The source address is always unicast.

Frame Type	0x0806	For Ethernet II frames, this field contains a hexadecimal value that is used to indicate the type of upper-layer protocol in the data field. There are numerous upper-layer protocols supported by Ethernet II. Two common frame types are:
		Value Description
		`0x0800` IPv4 Protocol
		`0x0806` Address resolution protocol (ARP)
Data	ARP	Contains the encapsulated upper-level protocol. The data field is between 46 – 1,500 bytes.
FCS	Not shown in capture	Frame Check Sequence, used by the NIC to identify errors during transmission. The value is computed by the sending machine, encompassing frame addresses, type, and data field. It is verified by the receiver.

What is significant about the contents of the destination address field?

_____

_____

Why does the PC send out a broadcast ARP prior to sending the first ping request?

_____

_____

_____

What is the MAC address of the source in the first frame? _____

What is the Vendor ID (OUI) of the Source's NIC? _____

What portion of the MAC address is the OUI?

_____

What is the Source's NIC serial number? _____

Part 2: Use Wireshark to Capture and Analyze Ethernet Frames

In Part 2, you will use Wireshark to capture local and remote Ethernet frames. You will then examine the information that is contained in the frame header fields.

Step 1: Determine the IP address of the default gateway on your PC.

Open a command prompt window and issue the **ipconfig** command.

What is the IP Address of the PC Default Gateway? _____

Step 2: **Start capturing traffic on your PC's NIC.**

    a. Open Wireshark.

    b. On the Wireshark Network Analyzer toolbar, click the **Interface List** icon.

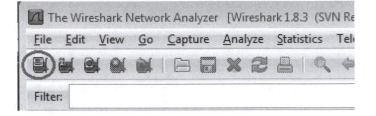

    c. On the Wireshark: Capture Interfaces window, select the interface to start traffic capturing by clicking the appropriate check box, and then click **Start**. If you are uncertain of what interface to check, click **Details** for more information about each interface listed.

    d. Observe the traffic that appears in the Packet List window.

Step 3: **Filter Wireshark to display only ICMP traffic.**

You can use the filter in Wireshark to block visibility of unwanted traffic. The filter does not block the capture of unwanted data; it only filters what to display on the screen. For now, only ICMP traffic is to be displayed.

In the Wireshark **Filter** box, type **icmp**. The box should turn green if you typed the filter correctly. If the box is green, click **Apply** to apply the filter.

Step 4: **From the command prompt window, ping the default gateway of your PC.**

From the command window, ping the default gateway using the IP address that you recorded in Step 1.

Step 5: Stop capturing traffic on the NIC.

Click the **Stop Capture** icon to stop capturing traffic.

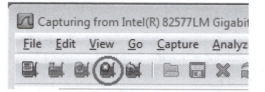

Step 6: Examine the first Echo (ping) request in Wireshark.

The Wireshark main window is divided into three sections: the Packet List pane (top), the Packet Details pane (middle), and the Packet Bytes pane (bottom). If you selected the correct interface for packet capturing in Step 3, Wireshark should display the ICMP information in the Packet List pane of Wireshark, similar to the following example.

a. In the Packet List pane (top section), click the first frame listed. You should see **Echo (ping) request** under the **Info** heading. This should highlight the line blue.

b. Examine the first line in the Packet Details pane (middle section). This line displays the length of the frame; 74 bytes in this example.

c. The second line in the Packet Details pane shows that it is an Ethernet II frame. The source and destination MAC addresses are also displayed.

What is the MAC address of the PC's NIC? _____

What is the default gateway's MAC address? _____

d. You can click the plus (+) sign at the beginning of the second line to obtain more information about the Ethernet II frame. Notice that the plus sign changes to a minus (-) sign.

What type of frame is displayed? _____

e.   The last two lines displayed in the middle section provide information about the data field of the frame. Notice that the data contains the source and destination IPv4 address information.

What is the source IP address? _____

What is the destination IP address? _____

f.   You can click any line in the middle section to highlight that part of the frame (hex and ASCII) in the Packet Bytes pane (bottom section). Click the **Internet Control Message Protocol** line in the middle section and examine what is highlighted in the Packet Bytes pane.

```
⊞ Frame 7: 74 bytes on wire (592 bits), 74 bytes captured (592 bits) on interface 0
⊞ Ethernet II, Src: Dell_24:2a:60 (5c:26:0a:24:2a:60), Dst: Cisco_7a:ec:84 (30:f7:0d:7a:ec:84)
⊞ Internet Protocol Version 4, Src: 10.20.164.22 (10.20.164.22), Dst: 10.20.164.17 (10.20.164.17)
⊟ Internet Control Message Protocol
    Type: 8 (Echo (ping) request)
    Code: 0
    Checksum: 0x4d4e [correct]

0000  30 f7 0d 7a ec 84 5c 26  0a 24 2a 60 08 00 45 00   0..z..\& .$*`..E.
0010  00 3c 03 48 00 00 80 01  db 29 0a 14 a4 16 0a 14   .<.H.... .).....
0020  a4 11 08 00 4d 4e 00 01  00 0d 61 62 63 64 65 66   ....MN.. ..abcdef
0030  67 68 69 6a 6b 6c 6d 6e  6f 70 71 72 73 74 75 76   ghijklmn opqrstuv
0040  77 61 62 63 64 65 66 67  68 69                     wabcdefg hi
```

What do the last two highlighted octets spell? _____

g.   Click the next frame in the top section and examine an Echo reply frame. Notice that the source and destination MAC addresses have reversed, because this frame was sent from the default gateway router as a reply to the first ping.

What device and MAC address is displayed as the destination address?

_____

Step 7:   Restart packet capture in Wireshark.

Click the **Start Capture** icon to start a new Wireshark capture. You will receive a popup window asking if you would like to save the previous captured packets to a file before starting a new capture. Click **Continue without Saving**.

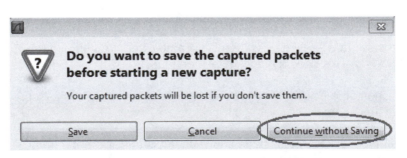

Step 8:   **In the command prompt window, ping www.cisco.com.**

Step 9:   **Stop capturing packets.**

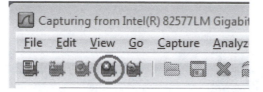

Step 10: **Examine the new data in the packet list pane of Wireshark.**

In the first echo (ping) request frame, what are the source and destination MAC addresses?

Source: _____

Destination: _____

What are the source and destination IP addresses contained in the data field of the frame?

Source: _____

Destination: _____

Compare these addresses to the addresses you received in Step 7. The only address that changed is the destination IP address. Why has the destination IP address changed, while the destination MAC address remained the same?

_____

_____

_____

_____

Reflection

Wireshark does not display the preamble field of a frame header. What does the preamble contain?

_____

_____

10.2.1.8 Lab — Observing ARP with the Windows CLI, IOS CLI, and Wireshark

Topology

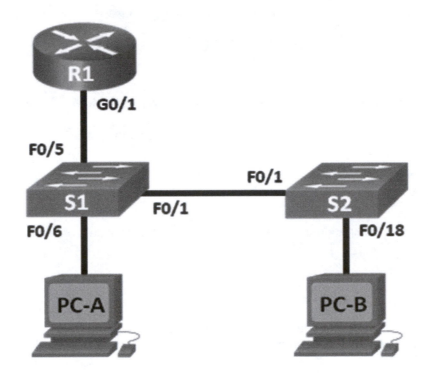

Addressing Table

Device	Interface	IP Address	Subnet Mask	Default Gateway
R1	G0/1	192.168.1.1	255.255.255.0	N/A
S1	VLAN 1	192.168.1.11	255.255.255.0	192.168.1.1
S2	VLAN 1	192.168.1.12	255.255.255.0	192.168.1.1
PC-A	NIC	192.168.1.3	255.255.255.0	192.168.1.1
PC-B	NIC	192.168.1.2	255.255.255.0	192.168.1.1

Objectives

Part 1: Build and Configure the Network

Part 2: Use the Windows ARP Command

Part 3: Use the IOS Show ARP Command

Part 4: Use Wireshark to Examine ARP Exchanges

Background / Scenario

The Address Resolution Protocol (ARP) is used by TCP/IP to map a Layer 3 IP address to a Layer 2 MAC address. When a frame is placed on the network, it must have a destination MAC address. To dynamically discover the MAC address for the destination device, an ARP request is broadcast on the LAN. The device that contains the destination IP address responds, and the MAC address is recorded in the ARP cache. Every device on the LAN keeps its own ARP cache, or small area in RAM that holds ARP results. An ARP cache timer removes ARP entries that have not been used for a certain period of time.

ARP is an excellent example of performance tradeoff. With no cache, ARP must continually request address translations each time a frame is placed on the network. This adds latency to the communication and could congest the LAN. Conversely, unlimited hold times could cause errors with devices that leave the network or change the Layer 3 address.

A network administrator should be aware of ARP, but may not interact with the protocol on a regular basis. ARP is a protocol that enables network devices to communicate with the TCP/IP protocol. Without ARP, there is no efficient method to build the datagram Layer 2 destination address. Also, ARP is a potential security risk. ARP spoofing, or ARP poisoning, is a technique used by an attacker to inject the wrong MAC address association in a network. An attacker forges the MAC address of a device, and frames are sent to the wrong destination. Manually configuring static ARP associations is one way to prevent ARP spoofing. Finally, an authorized MAC address list may be configured on Cisco devices to restrict network access to only approved devices.

In this lab, you will use the ARP commands in both Windows and Cisco routers to display the ARP table. You will also clear the ARP cache and add static ARP entries.

Note: The routers used with CCNA hands-on labs are Cisco 1941 Integrated Services Routers (ISRs) with Cisco IOS Release 15.2(4)M3 (universalk9 image). The switches used are Cisco Catalyst 2960s with Cisco IOS Release 15.0(2) (lanbasek9 image). Other routers, switches, and Cisco IOS versions can be used. Depending on the model and Cisco IOS version, the commands available and output produced might vary from what is shown in the labs. Refer to the Router Interface Summary Table at the end of this lab for the correct interface identifiers.

Note: Make sure that the routers and switches have been erased and have no startup configurations. If you are unsure, contact your instructor.

Required Resources

- 1 Router (Cisco 1941 with Cisco IOS Release 15.2(4)M3 universal image or comparable)
- 2 Switches (Cisco 2960 with Cisco IOS Release 15.0(2) lanbasek9 image or comparable)
- 2 PCs (Windows 7, Vista, or XP with terminal emulation program, such as Tera Term and Wireshark installed)
- Console cables to configure the Cisco IOS devices via the console ports
- Ethernet cables as shown in the topology

Note: The Fast Ethernet interfaces on Cisco 2960 switches are autosensing and an Ethernet straight-through cable may be used between switches S1 and S2. If using another Cisco switch model, it may be necessary to use an Ethernet crossover cable.

Part 1: Build and Configure the Network

Step 1: Cable the network according to the topology.

Step 2: Configure the IP addresses for the devices according to the Addressing Table.

Step 3: Verify network connectivity by pinging all the devices from PC-B.

Part 2: Use the Windows ARP Command

The **arp** command allows the user to view and modify the ARP cache in Windows. You access this command from the Windows command prompt.

Step 1: Display the ARP cache.

a. Open a command window on PC-A and type **arp**.

```
C:\Users\User1> arp


Displays and modifies the IP-to-Physical address translation tables used by
address resolution protocol (ARP).


ARP -s inet_addr eth_addr [if_addr]
ARP -d inet_addr [if_addr]
ARP -a [inet_addr] [-N if_addr] [-v]


  -a            Displays current ARP entries by interrogating the current
                protocol data.  If inet_addr is specified, the IP and Physical
                addresses for only the specified computer are displayed.  If
                more than one network interface uses ARP, entries for each ARP
                table are displayed.
  -g            Same as -a.
  -v            Displays current ARP entries in verbose mode.  All invalid
                entries and entries on the loop-back interface will be shown.
  inet_addr     Specifies an internet address.
  -N if_addr    Displays the ARP entries for the network interface specified
                by if_addr.
  -d            Deletes the host specified by inet_addr. inet_addr may be
                wildcarded with * to delete all hosts.
  -s            Adds the host and associates the Internet address inet_addr
                with the Physical address eth_addr.  The Physical address is
                given as 6 hexadecimal bytes separated by hyphens. The entry
                is permanent.
  eth_addr      Specifies a physical address.
  if_addr       If present, this specifies the Internet address of the
```

```
                  interface whose address translation table should be modified.
                  If not present, the first applicable interface will be used.
    Example:
      > arp -s 157.55.85.212   00-aa-00-62-c6-09  .... Adds a static entry.
      > arp -a                                    .... Displays the arp table.
```

b. Examine the output.

What command would be used to display all entries in the ARP cache?

What command would be used to delete all ARP cache entries (flush ARP cache)?

What command would be used to delete the ARP cache entry for 192.168.1.11?

c. Type **arp –a** to display the ARP table.

```
C:\Users\User1> arp -a

Interface: 192.168.1.3 --- 0xb
  Internet Address      Physical Address      Type
  192.168.1.1           d4-8c-b5-ce-a0-c1     dynamic
  192.168.1.255         ff-ff-ff-ff-ff-ff     static
  224.0.0.22            01-00-5e-00-00-16     static
  224.0.0.252           01-00-5e-00-00-fc     static
  239.255.255.250       01-00-5e-7f-ff-fa     static
```

Note: The ARP table is empty if you use Windows XP (as displayed below).

```
C:\Documents and Settings\User1> arp -a
No ARP Entries Found.
```

d. Ping from PC-A to PC-B to dynamically add entries in the ARP cache.

```
C:\Documents and Settings\User1> ping 192.168.1.2

Interface: 192.168.1.3 --- 0xb
  Internet Address      Physical Address      Type
  192.168.1.2           00-50-56-be-f6-db     dynamic
```

What is the physical address for the host with IP address of 192.168.1.2?

Step 2: **Adjust entries in the ARP cache manually.**

To delete entries in ARP cache, issue the command **arp –d {inet-addr | *}**. Addresses can be deleted individually by specifying the IP address, or all entries can be deleted with the wildcard *.

Verify that the ARP cache contains the following entries: the R1 G0/1 default gateway (192.168.1.1), PC-B (192.168.1.2) and both switches (192.168.1.11 and 192.168.1.12).

a. From PC-A, ping all the addresses in the Address Table.

b. Verify that all the addresses have been added to the ARP cache. If the address is not in ARP cache, ping the destination address and verify that the address was added to the ARP cache.

```
C:\Users\User1> arp -a


Interface: 192.168.1.3 --- 0xb
  Internet Address       Physical Address      Type
  192.168.1.1            d4-8c-b5-ce-a0-c1     dynamic
  192.168.1.2            00-50-56-be-f6-db     dynamic
  192.168.1.11           0c-d9-96-e8-8a-40     dynamic
  192.168.1.12           0c-d9-96-d2-40-40     dynamic
  192.168.1.255          ff-ff-ff-ff-ff-ff     static
  224.0.0.22             01-00-5e-00-00-16     static
  224.0.0.252            01-00-5e-00-00-fc     static
  239.255.255.250        01-00-5e-7f-ff-fa     static
```

c. As an administrator, access the command prompt. Click the **Start** icon, and in the *Search programs and file* box, type **cmd**. When the **cmd** icon appears, right-click the icon and select **Run as administrator**. Click **Yes** to allow this program to make changes.

Note: For Windows XP users, it is not necessary to have administrator privileges to modify ARP cache entries.

d. In the Administrator command prompt window, type **arp –d ***. This command deletes all the ARP cache entries. Verify that all the ARP cache entries are deleted by typing **arp –a** at the command prompt.

```
C:\windows\system32> arp –d *

C:\windows\system32> arp –a

No ARP Entries Found.
```

e. Wait a few minutes. The Neighbor Discovery protocol starts to populate the ARP cache again.

```
C:\Users\User1> arp –a


Interface: 192.168.1.3 --- 0xb
  Internet Address      Physical Address      Type
  192.168.1.255         ff-ff-ff-ff-ff-ff     static
```

Note: The Neighbor Discovery protocol is not implemented in Windows XP.

f. From PC-A, ping PC-B (192.168.1.2) and the switches (192.168.1.11 and 192.168.1.12) to add the ARP entries. Verify that the ARP entries have been added to the cache.

```
C:\Users\User1> arp –a
```

```
Interface: 192.168.1.3 --- 0xb
  Internet Address      Physical Address      Type
   192.168.1.2          00-50-56-be-f6-db     dynamic
   192.168.1.11         0c-d9-96-e8-8a-40     dynamic
   192.168.1.12         0c-d9-96-d2-40-40     dynamic
   192.168.1.255        ff-ff-ff-ff-ff-ff     static
```

g. Record the physical address for switch S2.

_____

h. Delete a specific ARP cache entry by typing **arp –d** *inet-addr*. At the command prompt, type **arp -d 192.168.1.12** to delete the ARP entry for S2.

```
C:\windows\system32> arp –d 192.168.1.12
```

i. Type **arp –a** to verify that the ARP entry for S2 has been removed from the ARP cache.

```
C:\Users\User1> arp –a
```

```
Interface: 192.168.1.3 --- 0xb
  Internet Address      Physical Address      Type
   192.168.1.2          00-50-56-be-f6-db     dynamic
   192.168.1.11         0c-d9-96-e8-8a-40     dynamic
   192.168.1.255        ff-ff-ff-ff-ff-ff     static
```

j. You can add a specific ARP cache entry by typing **arp –s** *inet_addr mac_addr*. The IP address and MAC address for S2 will be used in this example. Use the MAC address recorded in step g.

```
C:\windows\system32> arp –s 192.168.1.12 0c-d9-96-d2-40-40
```

k. Verify that the ARP entry for S2 has been added to the cache.

Part 3:   Use the IOS show arp Command

The Cisco IOS can also display the ARP cache on routers and switches with the **show arp** or **show ip arp** command.

Step 1:   Display ARP entries on router R1.

```
R1# show arp
Protocol  Address        Age (min)  Hardware Addr    Type   Interface
Internet  192.168.1.1           -    d48c.b5ce.a0c1   ARPA   GigabitEthernet0/1
Internet  192.168.1.2           0    0050.56be.f6db   ARPA   GigabitEthernet0/1
Internet  192.168.1.3           0    0050.56be.768c   ARPA   GigabitEthernet0/1
R1#
```

Notice there is no Age (-) for the first entry, router interface G0/1 (the LAN default gateway). The Age is the number of minutes (min) that the entry has been in ARP cache and is incremented for the other entries. The Neighbor Discovery protocol populates the PC-A and PC-B IP and MAC address ARP entries.

Step 2: Add ARP entries on router R1.

You can add ARP entries to the ARP table of the router by pinging other devices.

a. Ping switch S1.

```
R1# ping 192.168.1.11
Type escape sequence to abort.
Sending 5, 100-byte ICMP Echos to 192.168.1.11, timeout is 2 seconds:
.!!!!
Success rate is 80 percent (4/5), round-trip min/avg/max = 1/2/4 ms
```

b. Verify that an ARP entry for switch S1 has been added to the ARP table of R1.

```
R1# show ip arp
Protocol   Address          Age (min)   Hardware Addr    Type    Interface
Internet   192.168.1.1            -     d48c.b5ce.a0c1   ARPA    GigabitEthernet0/1
Internet   192.168.1.2            6     0050.56be.f6db   ARPA    GigabitEthernet0/1
Internet   192.168.1.3            6     0050.56be.768c   ARPA    GigabitEthernet0/1
Internet   192.168.1.11           0     0cd9.96e8.8a40   ARPA    GigabitEthernet0/1
R1#
```

Step 3: Display ARP entries on switch S1.

```
S1# show ip arp
Protocol   Address          Age (min)   Hardware Addr    Type    Interface
Internet   192.168.1.1           46     d48c.b5ce.a0c1   ARPA    Vlan1
Internet   192.168.1.2            8     0050.56be.f6db   ARPA    Vlan1
Internet   192.168.1.3            8     0050.56be.768c   ARPA    Vlan1
Internet   192.168.1.11           -     0cd9.96e8.8a40   ARPA    Vlan1
S1#
```

Step 4: Add ARP entries on switch S1.

By pinging other devices, ARP entries can also be added to the ARP table of the switch.

a. From switch S1, ping switch S2.

```
S1# ping 192.168.1.12
Type escape sequence to abort.
Sending 5, 100-byte ICMP Echos to 192.168.1.12, timeout is 2 seconds:
.!!!!
Success rate is 80 percent (4/5), round-trip min/avg/max = 1/2/8 ms
```

b. Verify that the ARP entry for switch S2 has been added to ARP table of S1.

```
S1# show ip arp
Protocol   Address          Age (min)   Hardware Addr    Type    Interface
Internet   192.168.1.1            5     d48c.b5ce.a0c1   ARPA    Vlan1
Internet   192.168.1.2           11     0050.56be.f6db   ARPA    Vlan1
Internet   192.168.1.3           11     0050.56be.768c   ARPA    Vlan1
```

```
Internet  192.168.1.11              -   0cd9.96e8.8a40  ARPA  Vlan1
Internet  192.168.1.12              2   0cd9.96d2.4040  ARPA  Vlan1
S1#
```

Part 4: Use Wireshark to Examine ARP Exchanges

In Part 4, you will examine ARP exchanges by using Wireshark to capture and evaluate the ARP exchange. You will also examine network latency caused by ARP exchanges between devices.

Step 1: Configure Wireshark for packet captures.

a. Start Wireshark.

b. Choose the network interface to use for capturing the ARP exchanges.

Step 2: Capture and evaluate ARP communications.

a. Start capturing packets in Wireshark. Use the filter to display only ARP packets.

b. Flush the ARP cache by typing the **arp –d** * command at the command prompt.

c. Verify that the ARP cache has been cleared.

d. Send a ping to the default gateway, using the **ping 192.168.1.1** command.

e. Stop the Wireshark capture after pinging to the default gateway is finished.

f. Examine the Wireshark captures for the ARP exchanges in the packet details pane.

What was the first ARP packet? _____

```
File  Edit  View  Go  Capture  Analyze  Statistics  Telephony  Tools  Internals  Help

Filter: arp                                          ▼ Expression...  Clear  Apply  Save

No.  Time          Source          Destination     Protocol  Length  Info
  6 1.795609000  Dell_19:55:92   Broadcast       ARP          42  who has 192.168.1.1?  Tell 192.168.1.3
  7 1.796075000  Cisco_45:73:a1  Dell_19:55:92   ARP          60  192.168.1.1 is at c4:71:fe:45:73:a1

⊞ Frame 6: 42 bytes on wire (336 bits), 42 bytes captured (336 bits) on interface 0
⊞ Ethernet II, Src: Dell_19:55:92 (5c:26:0a:19:55:92), Dst: Broadcast (ff:ff:ff:ff:ff:ff)
⊟ Address Resolution Protocol (request)
    Hardware type: Ethernet (1)
    Protocol type: IP (0x0800)
    Hardware size: 6
    Protocol size: 4
    Opcode: request (1)
    Sender MAC address: Dell_19:55:92 (5c:26:0a:19:55:92)
    Sender IP address: 192.168.1.3 (192.168.1.3)
    Target MAC address: 00:00:00_00:00:00 (00:00:00:00:00:00)
    Target IP address: 192.168.1.1 (192.168.1.1)

0000  ff ff ff ff ff ff 5c 26  0a 19 55 92 08 06 00 01   ......\& ..U.....
0010  08 00 06 04 00 01 5c 26  0a 19 55 92 c0 a8 01 03   ......\& ..U.....
0020  00 00 00 00 00 00 c0 a8  01 01                     ........ ..
```

Fill in the following table with information about your first captured ARP packet.

Field	Value
Sender MAC address	
Sender IP address	
Target MAC address	
Target IP address	

What was the second ARP packet? _____

Fill in the following table with information about your second captured ARP packet.

Field	Value
Sender MAC address	
Sender IP address	
Target MAC address	
Target IP address	

Step 3:   Examine network latency caused by ARP.

a.   Clear the ARP entries on PC-A.

b.   Start a Wireshark capture.

c.   Ping switch S2 (192.168.1.12). The ping should be successful after the first echo request.

   Note: If all the pings were successful, S1 should be reloaded to observe network latency with ARP.

```
C:\Users\User1> ping 192.168.1.12

Request timed out.

Reply from 192.168.1.12: bytes=32 time=2ms TTL=255

Reply from 192.168.1.12: bytes=32 time=2ms TTL=255

Reply from 192.168.1.12: bytes=32 time=2ms TTL=255


Ping statistics for 192.168.1.12:
    Packets: Sent = 4, Received = 3, Lost = 1 (25% loss),
Approximate round trip times in milli-seconds:
    Minimum = 1ms, Maximum = 3ms, Average = 2ms
```

d. Stop the Wireshark capture after the pinging is finished. Use the Wireshark filter to display only ARP and ICMP outputs. In Wireshark, type **arp or icmp** in the **Filter:** entry area.

e. Examine the Wireshark capture. In this example, frame 10 is the first ICMP request sent by PC-A to S1. Because there is no ARP entry for S1, an ARP request was sent to the management IP address of S1 asking for the MAC address. During the ARP exchanges, the echo request did not receive a reply before the request was timed out. (frames 8 – 12)

After the ARP entry for S1 was added to the ARP cache, the last three ICMP exchanges were successful, as displayed in frames 26, 27 and 30 – 33.

As displayed in the Wireshark capture, ARP is an excellent example of performance tradeoff. With no cache, ARP must continually request address translations each time a frame is placed on the network. This adds latency to the communication and could congest the LAN.

```
File  Edit  View  Go  Capture  Analyze  Statistics  Telephony  Tools  Internals  Help

Filter:  arp or icmp                                    ▼  Expression...  Clear  Apply  Save

No.  Time          Source          Destination     Protocol  Length  Info
 8 1.649929000  Dell_19:55:92   Broadcast       ARP           42  who has 192.168.1.12?  Tell 192.168.1.3
 9 1.651202000  Cisco_59:91:c0  Dell_19:55:92   ARP           60  192.168.1.12 is at 00:23:5d:59:91:c0
10 1.651489000  192.168.1.3     192.168.1.12    ICMP          74  Echo (ping) request  id=0x0001, seq=187:
11 1.653790000  Cisco_59:91:c0  Broadcast       ARP           60  who has 192.168.1.3?  Tell 192.168.1.12
12 1.653999000  Dell_19:55:92   Cisco_59:91:c0  ARP           42  192.168.1.3 is at 5c:26:0a:19:55:92
26 6.562409000  192.168.1.3     192.168.1.12    ICMP          74  Echo (ping) request  id=0x0001, seq=1874
27 6.564426000  192.168.1.12    192.168.1.3     ICMP          74  Echo (ping) reply    id=0x0001, seq=1874
30 7.560977000  192.168.1.3     192.168.1.12    ICMP          74  Echo (ping) request  id=0x0001, seq=187!
31 7.563586000  192.168.1.12    192.168.1.3     ICMP          74  Echo (ping) reply    id=0x0001, seq=187!
32 8.559352000  192.168.1.3     192.168.1.12    ICMP          74  Echo (ping) request  id=0x0001, seq=187(
33 8.560466000  192.168.1.12    192.168.1.3     ICMP          74  Echo (ping) reply    id=0x0001, seq=187(

⊞ Frame 8: 42 bytes on wire (336 bits), 42 bytes captured (336 bits) on interface 0
⊞ Ethernet II, Src: Dell_19:55:92 (5c:26:0a:19:55:92), Dst: Broadcast (ff:ff:ff:ff:ff:ff)
⊟ Address Resolution Protocol (request)
    Hardware type: Ethernet (1)
    Protocol type: IP (0x0800)
    Hardware size: 6
    Protocol size: 4
    Opcode: request (1)
    Sender MAC address: Dell_19:55:92 (5c:26:0a:19:55:92)
    Sender IP address: 192.168.1.3 (192.168.1.3)
    Target MAC address: 00:00:00_00:00:00 (00:00:00:00:00:00)
    Target IP address: 192.168.1.12 (192.168.1.12)

0000  ff ff ff ff ff ff 5c 26  0a 19 55 92 08 06 00 01   ......\& ..U.....
0010  08 00 06 04 00 01 5c 26  0a 19 55 92 c0 a8 01 03   ......\& ..U.....
0020  00 00 00 00 00 00 c0 a8  01 0c                     ........ ..
```

Reflection

1. How and when are static ARP entries removed?

    _____

2. Why do you want to add static ARP entries in the cache?

    _____

3. If ARP requests can cause network latency, why is it a bad idea to have unlimited hold times for ARP entries?

    _____

Router Interface Summary Table

Router Interface Summary				
Router Model	**Ethernet Interface #1**	**Ethernet Interface #2**	**Serial Interface #1**	**Serial Interface #2**
1800	Fast Ethernet 0/0 (F0/0)	Fast Ethernet 0/1 (F0/1)	Serial 0/0/0 (S0/0/0)	Serial 0/0/1 (S0/0/1)
1900	Gigabit Ethernet 0/0 (G0/0)	Gigabit Ethernet 0/1 (G0/1)	Serial 0/0/0 (S0/0/0)	Serial 0/0/1 (S0/0/1)
2801	Fast Ethernet 0/0 (F0/0)	Fast Ethernet 0/1 (F0/1)	Serial 0/1/0 (S0/1/0)	Serial 0/1/1 (S0/1/1)
2811	Fast Ethernet 0/0 (F0/0)	Fast Ethernet 0/1 (F0/1)	Serial 0/0/0 (S0/0/0)	Serial 0/0/1 (S0/0/1)
2900	Gigabit Ethernet 0/0 (G0/0)	Gigabit Ethernet 0/1 (G0/1)	Serial 0/0/0 (S0/0/0)	Serial 0/0/1 (S0/0/1)
Note: To find out how the router is configured, look at the interfaces to identify the type of router and how many interfaces the router has. There is no way to effectively list all the combinations of configurations for each router class. This table includes identifiers for the possible combinations of Ethernet and Serial interfaces in the device. The table does not include any other type of interface, even though a specific router may contain one. An example of this might be an ISDN BRI interface. The string in parenthesis is the legal abbreviation that can be used in Cisco IOS commands to represent the interface.				

10.3.1.10 Lab — Using IOS CLI with Switch MAC Address Tables

Topology

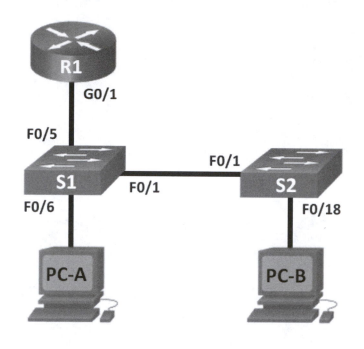

Addressing Table

Device	Interface	IP Address	Subnet Mask	Default Gateway
R1	G0/1	192.168.1.1	255.255.255.0	N/A
S1	VLAN 1	192.168.1.11	255.255.255.0	192.168.1.1
S2	VLAN 1	192.168.1.12	255.255.255.0	192.168.1.1
PC-A	NIC	192.168.1.3	255.255.255.0	192.168.1.1
PC-B	NIC	192.168.1.2	255.255.255.0	192.168.1.1

Objectives

Part 1: Build and Configure the Network

- Cable the network according to the topology diagram.
- Configure the network devices according to the Addressing Table.

Part 2: Examine the Switch MAC Address Table

- Use **show** commands to observe the process of building the switch MAC address table.

Background / Scenario

The purpose of a Layer 2 LAN switch is to deliver Ethernet frames to host devices on the local network. The switch records host MAC addresses that are visible on the network, and maps those MAC addresses to its own Ethernet switch ports. This process is called building the MAC address table. When a switch receives a frame from a PC, it examines the frame's source and destination MAC addresses. The source MAC address is recorded and mapped to the switch port from which it arrived. Then the destination MAC address is looked up in the MAC address table. If the destination MAC address is a known address, then the frame is forwarded out of the corresponding switch port of the MAC address. If the MAC address is unknown, then the frame is broadcast out of all switch ports, except the one from which it came. It is important to observe and understand the function of a switch and how it delivers data on the network. The way a switch operates has implications for network administrators whose job it is to ensure secure and consistent network communication.

Switches are used to interconnect and deliver information to computers on local area networks. Switches deliver Ethernet frames to host devices identified by network interface card MAC addresses.

In Part 1, you will build a multi-switch and router topology with a trunk linking the two switches. In Part 2, you will ping various devices and observe how the two switches build their MAC address tables.

Note: The routers used with CCNA hands-on labs are Cisco 1941 Integrated Services Routers (ISRs) with Cisco IOS Release 15.2(4)M3 (universalk9 image). The switches used are Cisco Catalyst 2960s with Cisco IOS Release 15.0(2) (lanbasek9 image). Other routers, switches and Cisco IOS versions can be used. Depending on the model and Cisco IOS version, the commands available and output produced might vary from what is shown in the labs. Refer to the Router Interface Summary Table at the end of this lab for the correct interface identifiers.

Note: Make sure that the routers and switches have been erased and have no startup configurations. If you are unsure contact your instructor.

Required Resources

- 1 Router (Cisco 1941 with Cisco IOS Release 15.2(4)M3 universal image or comparable)
- 2 Switches (Cisco 2960 with Cisco IOS Release 15.0(2) lanbasek9 image or comparable)
- 2 PCs (Windows 7, Vista, or XP with terminal emulation program, such as Tera Term)
- Console cables to configure the Cisco IOS devices via the console ports
- Ethernet cables as shown in the topology

Note: The Fast Ethernet interfaces on Cisco 2960 switches are autosensing and an Ethernet straight-through cable may be used between switches S1 and S2. If using another model Cisco switch, it may be necessary to use an Ethernet crossover cable.

Part 1:   Build and Configure the Network

Step 1:   Cable the network according to the topology.

Step 2:   Configure PC hosts.

Step 3:   Initialize and reload the routers and switches as necessary.

Step 4:   Configure basic settings for each switch.

a.   Configure device name as shown in the topology.

b.   Configure IP address and default gateway as listed in Addressing Table.

c.   Assign **cisco** as the console and vty passwords.

d.   Assign **class** as the privileged EXEC password.

Step 5:   **Configure basic settings for the router.**

    a.   Disable DNS lookup.

    b.   Configure IP address for the router as listed in Addressing Table.

    c.   Configure device name as shown in the topology.

    d.   Assign **cisco** as the console and vty passwords.

    e.   Assign **class** as the privileged EXEC password.

Part 2:   Examine the Switch MAC Address Table

A switch learns MAC addresses and builds the MAC address table, as network devices initiate communication on the network.

Step 1:   **Record network device MAC addresses.**

    a.   Open a command prompt on PC-A and PC-B and type **ipconfig /all**. What are the Ethernet adapter physical addresses?

        PC-A MAC Address: _____

        PC-B MAC Address: _____

    b.   Console into router R1 and type the **show interface G0/1** command. What is the hardware address?

        R1 Gigabit Ethernet 0/1 MAC Address: _____

    c.   Console into switch S1 and S2 and type the **show interface F0/1** command on each switch. On the second line of command output, what is the hardware addresses (or burned-in address [bia])?

        S1 Fast Ethernet 0/1 MAC Address: _____

        S2 Fast Ethernet 0/1 MAC Address: _____

Step 2:   **Display the switch MAC address table.**

Console into switch S2 and view the MAC address table, both before and after running network communication tests with ping.

    a.   Establish a console connection to S2 and enter privileged EXEC mode.

    b.   In privileged EXEC mode, type the **show mac address-table** command and press Enter.

```
S2# show mac address-table
```

Even though there has been no network communication initiated across the network (i.e., no use of ping), it is possible that the switch has learned MAC addresses from its connection to the PC and the other switch.

Are there any MAC addresses recorded in the MAC address table?

_____

What MAC addresses are recorded in the table? To which switch ports are they mapped and to which devices do they belong? Ignore MAC addresses that are mapped to the CPU.

_____

_____

_____

If you had not previously recorded MAC addresses of network devices in Step 1, how could you tell which devices the MAC addresses belong to, using only the output from the **show mac address-table** command? Does it work in all scenarios?

_____

_____

_____

_____

Step 3: Clear the S2 MAC address table and display the MAC address table again.

a. In privileged EXEC mode, type the **clear mac address-table dynamic** command and press Enter.

```
S2# clear mac address-table dynamic
```

b. Quickly type the **show mac address-table** command again. Does the MAC address table have any addresses in it for VLAN 1? Are there other MAC addresses listed?

_____

Wait 10 seconds, type the **show mac address-table** command, and press Enter. Are there new addresses in the MAC address table? _____

Step 4: From PC-B, ping the devices on the network and observe the switch MAC address table.

a. From PC-B, open a command prompt and type **arp -a**. Not including multicast or broadcast addresses, how many device IP-to-MAC address pairs have been learned by ARP?

_____

b. From the PC-B command prompt, ping the router/gateway R1, PC-A, S1, and S2. Did all devices have successful replies? If not, check your cabling and IP configurations.

_____

_____

c. From a console connection to S2, enter the **show mac address-table** command. Has the switch added additional MAC addresses to the MAC address table? If so, which addresses and devices?

_____

_____

From PC-B, open a command prompt and retype **arp -a**. Does the PC-B ARP cache have additional entries for all network devices that were sent pings?

_____

Reflection

On Ethernet networks, data is delivered to devices by their MAC addresses. For this to happen, switches and PCs dynamically build ARP caches and MAC address tables. With only a few computers on the network this process seems fairly easy. What might be some of the challenges on larger networks?

_____

Router Interface Summary Table

Router Interface Summary				
Router Model	**Ethernet Interface #1**	**Ethernet Interface #2**	**Serial Interface #1**	**Serial Interface #2**
1800	Fast Ethernet 0/0 (F0/0)	Fast Ethernet 0/1 (F0/1)	Serial 0/0/0 (S0/0/0)	Serial 0/0/1 (S0/0/1)
1900	Gigabit Ethernet 0/0 (G0/0)	Gigabit Ethernet 0/1 (G0/1)	Serial 0/0/0 (S0/0/0)	Serial 0/0/1 (S0/0/1)
2801	Fast Ethernet 0/0 (F0/0)	Fast Ethernet 0/1 (F0/1)	Serial 0/1/0 (S0/1/0)	Serial 0/1/1 (S0/1/1)
2811	Fast Ethernet 0/0 (F0/0)	Fast Ethernet 0/1 (F0/1)	Serial 0/0/0 (S0/0/0)	Serial 0/0/1 (S0/0/1)
2900	Gigabit Ethernet 0/0 (G0/0)	Gigabit Ethernet 0/1 (G0/1)	Serial 0/0/0 (S0/0/0)	Serial 0/0/1 (S0/0/1)
Note: To find out how the router is configured, look at the interfaces to identify the type of router and how many interfaces the router has. There is no way to effectively list all the combinations of configurations for each router class. This table includes identifiers for the possible combinations of Ethernet and Serial interfaces in the device. The table does not include any other type of interface, even though a specific router may contain one. An example of this might be an ISDN BRI interface. The string in parenthesis is the legal abbreviation that can be used in Cisco IOS commands to represent the interface.				

10.4.1.1 Class Activity — MAC and Choose…

Objectives

Explain basic switching concepts.

In this activity, you will indicate your knowledge of Ethernet technology by successfully comparing legacy to current standards. You will speculate on potential future Ethernet technology standards, and explain why MAC addresses and framing formats have stayed basically the same, in order to assist data transmission, during Ethernet's evolution.

Background/Scenario

Note: This activity is best completed in groups of 2-3 students.

Please view the video, The History of Ethernet, located at the following link:

http://www.netevents.tv/video/bob-metcalfe-the-history-of-ethernet

Topics discussed in the video include not only where we have come from in Ethernet development, but where we are going with Ethernet technology in the future!

1. After viewing the video and comparing its contents to what you read in the chapter, go to the web and search for information about Ethernet:

    *   How was Ethernet used when it was first developed?

    *   How has Ethernet stayed the same over the past 25 years? What changes are being made to make it more useful and applicable to today's data transmission methods?

2. Collect three pictures of old, current, and possible future Ethernet physical media and devices. Focus your search on switches if possible. Share these pictures with the class and discuss:

    *   How have Ethernet physical media and intermediary devices changed?

    *   How have Ethernet physical media and intermediary devices stayed the same?

    *   How do you think the Ethernet will change in the future? What factors could influence these changes?

Required Resources

*   Internet access to video, The History of Ethernet, located at: http://www.netevents.tv/video/bob-metcalfe-the-history-of-ethernet

*   Hard- or soft-copy media for recording answers to questions and for in-class sharing.

Reflection

1. How was Ethernet used when it was first developed?

    _____

2. How has Ethernet stayed the same over the past 25 years? What changes are being made to make it more useful and applicable to today's data transmission methods?

    _____

3.   How have Ethernet physical media and intermediary devices changed?

   _____

4.   How have Ethernet physical media and intermediary devices stayed the same?

   _____

5.   How do you think the Ethernet will change in the future? What factors could influence these changes?

   _____

Chapter 11 — It's a Network

11.0.1.2 Class Activity — Did you notice...?

Objectives

Explain how a small network of directly connected segments is created, configured and verified.

In this activity, you will note how networks differ, both in size and in function. You will identify how networks provide different networking solutions based upon their cost, speed, ports, expandability, and manageability, related to the needs of a small-to-medium-sized business.

Topology

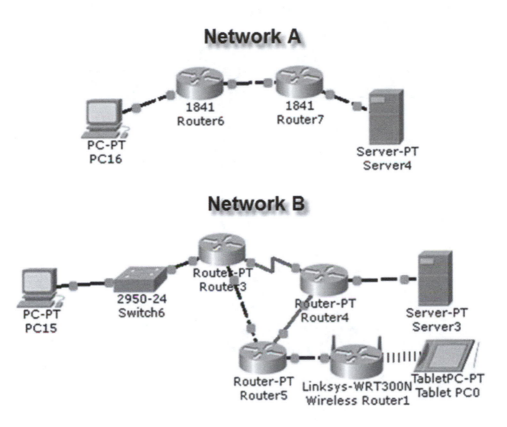

Background/Scenario

Using the two networks in the topology diagram as reference, answer the following questions and record your answers to share with the class.

- Visually compare and contrast Network A and Network B. How are the two networks the same?

- Make note of the devices used in <u>each</u> network design. Because the devices are labeled, you already know what types of end and intermediary devices they are. How are the two networks different? Is the number of devices present in one network the only differentiating factor? Justify your answer.

- Which network you would select if you owned a small-to-medium-sized business. Justify your selected network based on cost, speed, ports, expandability, and manageability.

Required Resources

Recording capabilities (paper, tablet, etc.) for reflective comments to be shared with the class.

Reflection

1. Reflect upon your comparisons of the two network scenarios. What are some things you noted as points of interest?

_____

Identify elements of the model that map to real-world content:

Cost, speed, ports, expandability, and manageability are all factors to consider when designing a small to medium-sized network.

11.2.2.6 Lab — Researching Network Security Threats

Objectives

Part 1: Explore the SANS Website

- Navigate to the SANS website and identify resources.

Part 2: Identify Recent Network Security Threats

- Identify several recent network security threats using the SANS site.
- Identify sites beyond SANS that provide network security threat information.

Part 3: Detail a Specific Network Security Threat

- Select and detail a specific recent network threat.
- Present information to the class.

Background / Scenario

To defend a network against attacks, an administrator must identify external threats that pose a danger to the network. Security websites can be used to identify emerging threats and provide mitigation options for defending a network.

One of the most popular and trusted sites for defending against computer and network security threats is SysAdmin, Audit, Network, Security (SANS). The SANS site provides multiple resources, including a list of the top 20 Critical Security Controls for Effective Cyber Defense and the weekly @Risk: The Consensus Security Alert newsletter. This newsletter details new network attacks and vulnerabilities.

In this lab, you will navigate to and explore the SANS site, use the SANS site to identify recent network security threats, research other websites that identify threats, and research and present the details about a specific network attack.

Required Resources

- Device with Internet access
- Presentation computer with PowerPoint or other presentation software installed

Part 1:   Exploring the SANS Website

In Part 1, navigate to the SANS website and explore the available resources.

Step 1:   Locate SANS resources.

Using a web browser, navigate to www.SANS.org. From the home page, highlight the **Resources** menu.

List three available resources.

_____

_____

Step 2:   **Locate the Top 20 Critical Controls.**

The **Twenty Critical Security Controls for Effective Cyber Defense** listed on the SANS website are the culmination of a public-private partnership involving the Department of Defense (DoD), National Security Association, Center for Internet Security (CIS), and the SANS Institute. The list was developed to prioritize the cyber security controls and spending for DoD. It has become the centerpiece for effective security programs for the United States government. From the **Resources** menu, select **Top 20 Critical Controls**.

Select one of the 20 Critical Controls and list three of the implementation suggestions for this control.

_____

_____

_____

_____

_____

_____

Step 3:   **Locate the Newsletters menu.**

Highlight the **Resources** menu, select **Newsletters**. Briefly describe each of the three newsletters available.

_____

_____

_____

_____

_____

_____

Part 2:   Identify Recent Network Security Threats

In Part 2, you will research recent network security threats using the SANS site and identify other sites containing security threat information.

Step 1:   **Locate the @Risk: Consensus Security Alert Newsletter Archive.**

From the **Newsletters** page, select **Archive** for the @RISK: The Consensus Security Alert. Scroll down to **Archives Volumes** and select a recent weekly newsletter. Review the **Notable Recent Security Issues and Most Popular Malware Files** sections.

List some recent attacks. Browse multiple recent newsletters, if necessary.

_____

_____

_____

Step 2:   **Identify sites providing recent security threat information.**

Besides the SANS site, identify some other websites that provide recent security threat information.

_____

_____

_____

List some of the recent security threats detailed on these websites.

_____

_____

_____

Part 3:   Detail a Specific Network Security Attack

In Part 3, you will research a specific network attack that has occurred and create a presentation based on your findings. Complete the form below based on your findings.

Step 1:   **Complete the following form for the selected network attack.**

Name of attack:	
Type of attack:	
Dates of attacks:	
Computers / Organizations affected:	
How it works and what it did:	
Mitigation options:	
References and info links:	

Step 2: **Follow the instructor's guidelines to complete the presentation.**

Reflection

1. What steps can you take to protect your own computer?

    _____

    _____

    _____

2. What are some important steps that organizations can take to protect their resources?

    _____

    _____

    _____

11.2.4.5 Lab — Accessing Network Devices with SSH

Topology

Addressing Table

Device	Interface	IP Address	Subnet Mask	Default Gateway
R1	G0/1	192.168.1.1	255.255.255.0	N/A
S1	VLAN 1	192.168.1.11	255.255.255.0	192.168.1.1
PC-A	NIC	192.168.1.3	255.255.255.0	192.168.1.1

Objectives

Part 1: Configure Basic Device Settings

Part 2: Configure the Router for SSH Access

Part 3: Examine a Telnet Session with Wireshark

Part 4: Examine a SSH Session with Wireshark

Part 5: Configure the Switch for SSH Access

Part 6: SSH from the CLI on the Switch

Background / Scenario

In the past, Telnet was the most common network protocol used to remotely configure network devices. However, protocols such as Telnet do not authenticate or encrypt the information between the client and server. This allows a network sniffer to intercept passwords and configuration information.

Secure Shell (SSH) is a network protocol that establishes a secure terminal emulation connection to a router or other networking device. SSH encrypts all information that passes over the network link and provides authentication of the remote computer. SSH is rapidly replacing Telnet as the remote login tool of choice for network professionals. SSH is most often used to log in to a remote device and execute commands; however, it can also transfer files using the associated Secure FTP (SFTP) or Secure Copy (SCP) protocols.

For SSH to function, the network devices communicating must be configured to support it. In this lab, you will enable the SSH server on a router and then connect to that router using a PC with an SSH client installed. On a local network, the connection is normally made using Ethernet and IP.

In this lab, you will configure a router to accept SSH connectivity, and use Wireshark to capture and view Telnet and SSH sessions. This will demonstrate the importance of encryption with SSH. You will also be challenged to configure a switch for SSH connectivity on your own.

Note: The routers used with CCNA hands-on labs are Cisco 1941 Integrated Services Routers (ISRs) with Cisco IOS Release 15.2(4)M3 (universalk9 image). The switches used are Cisco Catalyst 2960s with Cisco IOS Release 15.0(2) (lanbasek9 image). Other routers, switches, and Cisco IOS versions can be used. Depending on the model and Cisco IOS version, the commands available and output produced might vary from what is shown in the labs. Refer to the Router Interface Summary Table at the end of this lab for the correct interface identifiers.

Note: Make sure that the routers and switches have been erased and have no startup configurations. If you are unsure, contact your instructor.

Required Resources

- 1 Router (Cisco 1941 with Cisco IOS Release 15.2(4)M3 universal image or comparable)
- 1 Switch (Cisco 2960 with Cisco IOS Release 15.0(2) lanbasek9 image or comparable)
- 1 PC (Windows 7, Vista, or XP with terminal emulation program, such as Tera Term, and Wireshark installed)
- Console cables to configure the Cisco IOS devices via the console ports
- Ethernet cables as shown in the topology

Part 1: Configure Basic Device Settings

In Part 1, you will set up the network topology and configure basic settings, such as the interface IP addresses, device access, and passwords on the router.

Step 1: **Cable the network as shown in the topology.**

Step 2: **Initialize and reload the router and switch.**

Step 3: **Configure the router.**

a. Console into the router and enable privileged EXEC mode.

b. Enter configuration mode.

c. Disable DNS lookup to prevent the router from attempting to translate incorrectly entered commands as though they were host names.

d. Assign **class** as the privileged EXEC encrypted password.

e. Assign **cisco** as the console password and enable login.

f. Assign **cisco** as the vty password and enable login.

g. Encrypt the plain text passwords.

h. Create a banner that will warn anyone accessing the device that unauthorized access is prohibited.

i. Configure and activate the G0/1 interface on the router using the information contained in the Addressing Table.

j. Save the running configuration to the startup configuration file.

Step 4:   **Configure PC-A.**

    a.   Configure PC-A with an IP address and subnet mask.

    b.   Configure a default gateway for PC-A.

Step 5:   **Verify network connectivity.**

Ping R1 from PC-A. If the ping fails, troubleshoot the connection.

Part 2:   Configure the Router for SSH Access

Using Telnet to connect to a network device is a security risk, because all information is transmitted in a clear text format. SSH encrypts the session data and provides device authentication, which is why SSH is recommended for remote connections. In Part 2, you will configure the router to accept SSH connections over the VTY lines.

Step 1:   **Configure device authentication.**

The device name and domain are used as part in the crypto key when it is generated. Therefore, these names must be entered prior to issuing the **crypto key** command.

    a.   Configure device name.

```
Router(config)# hostname R1
```

    b.   Configure the domain for the device.

```
R1(config)# ip domain-name ccna-lab.com
```

Step 2:   **Configure the encryption key method.**

```
R1(config)# crypto key generate rsa modulus 1024
The name for the keys will be: R1.ccna-lab.com

% The key modulus size is 1024 bits
% Generating 1024 bit RSA keys, keys will be non-exportable...
[OK] (elapsed time was 1 seconds)

R1(config)#
*Jan 28 21:09:29.867: %SSH-5-ENABLED: SSH 1.99 has been enabled
```

Step 3:   **Configure a local database username.**

```
R1(config)# username admin privilege 15 secret adminpass
R1(config)#
*Feb  6 23:24:43.971: End->Password:QHjxdsVkjtoP7VxKIcPsLdTiMIvyLkyjT1HbmYxZigc
R1(config)#
```

Note: A privilege level of 15 gives the user administrator rights.

Step 4: **Enable SSH on the VTY lines.**

a. Enable Telnet and SSH on the inbound VTY lines using the **transport input** command.

```
R1(config)# line vty 0 4
R1(config-line)# transport input telnet ssh
```

b. Change the login method to use the local database for user verification.

```
R1(config-line)# login local
R1(config-line)# end
R1#
```

Step 5: **Save the running configuration to the startup configuration file.**

```
R1# copy running-config startup-config
Destination filename [startup-config]?
Building configuration...
[OK]
R1#
```

Part 3: **Examine a Telnet Session with Wireshark**

In Part 3, you will use Wireshark to capture and view the transmitted data of a Telnet session on the router. You will use Tera Term to telnet to R1, sign in, and then issue the show run command on the router.

Note: If a Telnet/SSH client software package is not installed on your PC, you must install one before continuing. Two popular freeware Telnet/SSH packages are Tera Term (http://download.cnet.com/Tera-Term/3000-20432_4-75766675.html) and PuTTy (www.putty.org).

Note: Telnet is not available from the command prompt in Windows 7, by default. To enable Telnet for use in the command prompt window, click **Start** > **Control Panel** > **Programs** > **Programs and Features** > **Turn Windows features on or off**. Click the **Telnet Client** check box, and then click **OK**.

Step 1: **Open Wireshark and start capturing data on the LAN interface.**

Note: If you are unable to start the capture on the LAN interface, you may need to open Wireshark using the **Run as Administrator** option.

Step 2: **Start a Telnet session to the router.**

a. Open Tera Term and select the **Telnet** Service radio button and in the Host field, enter **192.168.1.1**.

What is the default TCP port for Telnet sessions? _____

b. At the Username: prompt, enter **admin** and at the Password: prompt, enter **adminpass**. These prompts are generated because you configured the VTY lines to use the local database with the **login local** command.

c. Issue the **show run** command.

    R1# **show run**

d. Enter **exit** to exit the Telnet session and out of Tera Term.

    R1# **exit**

Step 3:   Stop the Wireshark capture.

Step 4:   Apply a Telnet filter on the Wireshark capture data.

Filter: | telnet   ▼ | Expression...   Clear   Apply

Step 5:   **Use the Follow TCP Stream feature in Wireshark to view the Telnet session.**

a. Right-click one of the **Telnet** lines in the **Packet list** section of Wireshark, and in the drop-down list, select **Follow TCP Stream**.

b. The Follow TCP Stream window displays the data for your Telnet session with the router. The entire session is displayed in clear text, including your password. Notice that the username and **show run** command that you entered are displayed with duplicate characters. This is caused by the echo setting in Telnet to allow you to view the characters that you type on the screen.

c. After you have finished reviewing your Telnet session in the **Follow TCP Stream** window, click **Close**.

Part 4: Examine an SSH session with Wireshark

In Part 4, you will use the Tera Term software to establish an SSH session with the router. Wireshark will be used to capture and view the data of this SSH session.

Step 1: Open Wireshark and start capturing data on the LAN interface.

Step 2: Start an SSH session on the router.

a. Open Tera Term and enter the G0/1 interface IP address of R1 in the Host: field of the Tera Term: New Connection window. Ensure that the **SSH** radio button is selected and then click **OK** to connect to the router.

```
Tera Term: New connection                              [X]

  (•) TCP/IP      Host: |192.168.1.1|                    [▼]
                     ☑ History
                  Service:  ( ) Telnet        TCP port#: |22|
                            (•) SSH       SSH version: |SSH2| [▼]
                            ( ) Other
                                           Protocol: |UNSPEC| [▼]

  ( ) Serial      Port: |COM1: Communications Port (COM1)| [▼]

            [  OK  ]    [ Cancel ]    [  Help  ]
```

What is the default TCP port used for SSH sessions? _____

b. The first time you establish a SSH session to a device, a **SECURITY WARNING** is generated to let you know that you have not connected to this device before. This message is part of the authentication process. Read the security warning and then click **Continue**.

SECURITY WARNING

There is no entry for the server "192.168.1.1" in your list
of known hosts. The machine you have contacted may
be a hostile machine pretending to be the server.

If you choose to add this machine to the known hosts list
and continue, then you will not receive this warning
again.

The server's host key fingerprint is:

f5:b1:e7:f8:c6:74:89:88:79:1c:24:8f:2c:6e:6e:39

```
+--[ RSA 1024]-----+
|                  |
|           . .    |
|          . *     |
|       . + + o    |
|      . S + = o   |
|       o o + =... |
|      o . . .o..  |
|       E     .o   |
|      . .     ..  |
+------------------+
```

☑ Add this machine and its key to the known hosts list

Continue   Disconnect

c. In the SSH Authentication window, enter **admin** for the username and **adminpass** for the passphrase.
    Click **OK** to sign into the router.

SSH Authentication

Logging in to 192.168.1.1

Authentication required.

User name: admin

Passphrase: •••••••••

☑ Remember password in memory

☐ Forward agent

⦿ Use plain password to log in

◯ Use RSA/DSA/ECDSA key to log in   Private key file:

◯ Use rhosts to log in (SSH1)   Local user name:

Host private key file:

◯ Use challenge/response to log in(keyboard-interactive)

◯ Use Pageant

OK   Disconnect

d. You have established a SSH session on the router. The Tera Term software looks very similar to a command window. At the command prompt, issue the **show run** command.

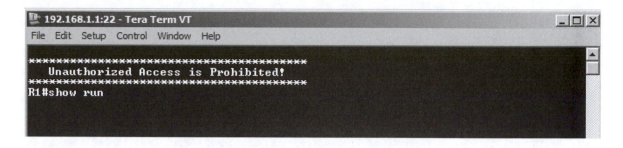

e. Exit the SSH session and out of Tera Term by issuing the **exit** command.

    R1# **exit**

Step 3:   **Stop the Wireshark capture.**

Step 4:   **Apply an SSH filter on the Wireshark Capture data.**

| Filter: | ssh | ▼ | Expression... | Clear | Apply |

Step 5:   **Use the Follow TCP Stream feature in Wireshark to view the Telnet session.**

a. Right-click one of the **SSHv2** lines in the **Packet list** section of Wireshark, and in the drop-down list, select the **Follow TCP Stream** option.

b. Examine the **Follow TCP Stream** window of your SSH session. The data has been encrypted and is unreadable. Compare the data in your SSH session to the data of your Telnet session.

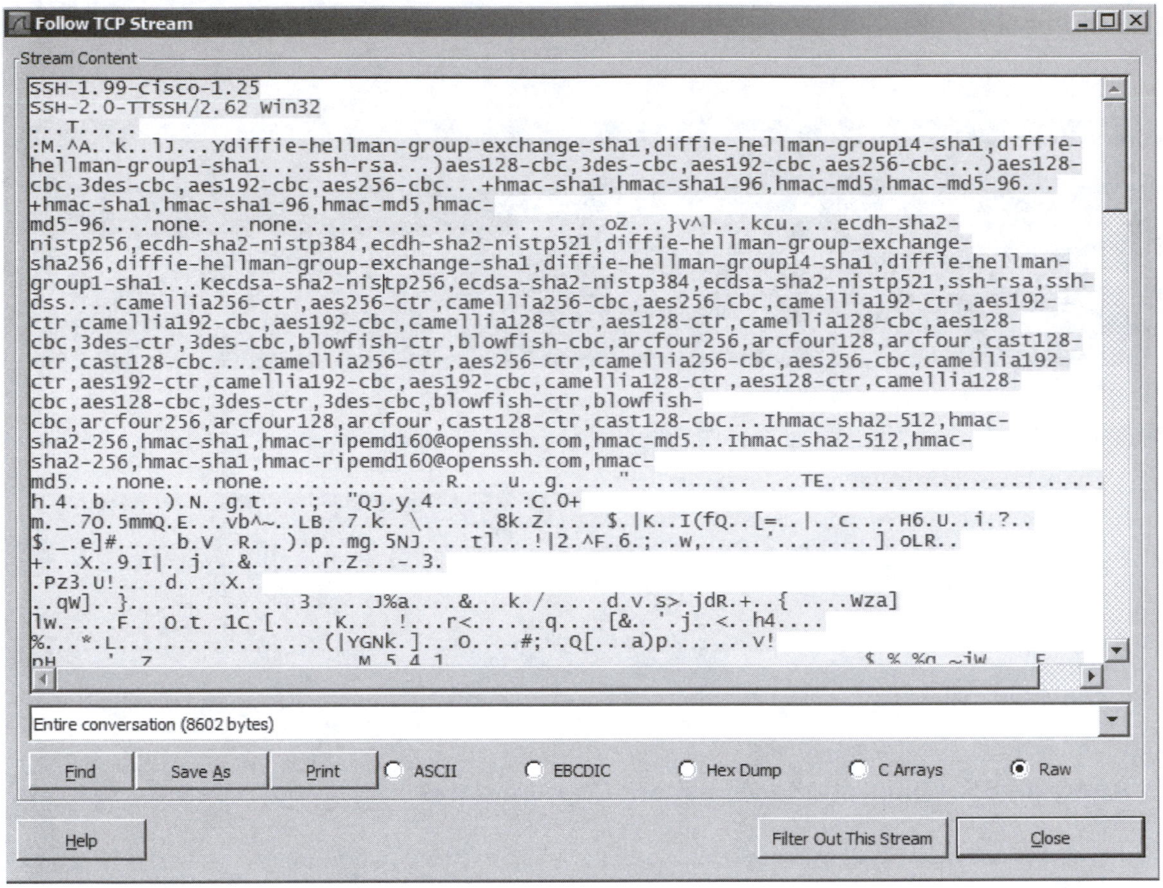

Why is SSH preferred over Telnet for remote connections?

_____

_____

_____

    c.   After examining your SSH session, click **Close**.

    d.   Close Wireshark.

Part 5: Configure the Switch for SSH Access

In Part 5, you are to configure the switch in the topology to accept SSH connections. Once the switch has been configured, establish a SSH session on it using Tera Term.

Step 1: Configure the basic settings on the switch.

Step 2: Configure the switch for SSH connectivity.

Use the same commands that you used to configure SSH on the router in Part 2 to configure SSH for the switch.

Step 3: Establish a SSH connection to the switch.

Start Tera Term from PC-A, and then SSH to the SVI interface on the S1.

Step 4:   **Troubleshoot as necessary.**

Are you able to establish a SSH session with the switch?

_____

Part 6:   SSH From the CLI on the Switch

The SSH client is built into the Cisco IOS and can be run from the CLI. In Part 6, you will SSH to the router from the CLI on the switch.

Step 1:   **View the parameters available for the Cisco IOS SSH client.**

Use the question mark (**?**) to display the parameter options available with the **ssh** command.

```
S1# ssh ?
   -c     Select encryption algorithm
   -l     Log in using this user name
   -m     Select HMAC algorithm
   -o     Specify options
   -p     Connect to this port
   -v     Specify SSH Protocol Version
   -vrf   Specify vrf name
   WORD   IP address or hostname of a remote system
```

Step 2:   **SSH to router R1 from S1.**

a.   You must use the **–l admin** option when you SSH to R1. This allows you to log in as user **admin**. When prompted, enter **adminpass** for the password.

```
S1# ssh -l admin 192.168.1.1

Password:

* * * * * * * * * * * * * * * * * * * * * * * * * * * * * * * * * * * * * * * * * * * *

   Warning: Unauthorized Access is Prohibited!

* * * * * * * * * * * * * * * * * * * * * * * * * * * * * * * * * * * * * * * * * * * * *


R1#
```

b.   You can return to S1 without closing your SSH session to R1 by pressing **Ctrl+Shift+6**. Release the **Ctrl+Shift+6** keys and press **x**. You should see the switch privilege EXEC prompt display.

```
R1#

S1#
```

c. To return to the SSH session on R1, press Enter on a blank CLI line. You may need to press Enter a second time to see the router CLI prompt.

```
S1#

[Resuming connection 1 to 192.168.1.1 ... ]


R1#
```

d. To end the SSH session on R1, type **exit** at the router prompt.

```
R1# exit


[Connection to 192.168.1.1 closed by foreign host]

S1#
```

What versions of SSH are supported from the CLI?

_____

_____

Reflection

How would you provide multiple users, each with their own username, access to a network device?

_____

Router Interface Summary Table

Router Interface Summary				
Router Model	**Ethernet Interface #1**	**Ethernet Interface #2**	**Serial Interface #1**	**Serial Interface #2**
1800	Fast Ethernet 0/0 (F0/0)	Fast Ethernet 0/1 (F0/1)	Serial 0/0/0 (S0/0/0)	Serial 0/0/1 (S0/0/1)
1900	Gigabit Ethernet 0/0 (G0/0)	Gigabit Ethernet 0/1 (G0/1)	Serial 0/0/0 (S0/0/0)	Serial 0/0/1 (S0/0/1)
2801	Fast Ethernet 0/0 (F0/0)	Fast Ethernet 0/1 (F0/1)	Serial 0/1/0 (S0/1/0)	Serial 0/1/1 (S0/1/1)
2811	Fast Ethernet 0/0 (F0/0)	Fast Ethernet 0/1 (F0/1)	Serial 0/0/0 (S0/0/0)	Serial 0/0/1 (S0/0/1)
2900	Gigabit Ethernet 0/0 (G0/0)	Gigabit Ethernet 0/1 (G0/1)	Serial 0/0/0 (S0/0/0)	Serial 0/0/1 (S0/0/1)
Note: To find out how the router is configured, look at the interfaces to identify the type of router and how many interfaces the router has. There is no way to effectively list all the combinations of configurations for each router class. This table includes identifiers for the possible combinations of Ethernet and Serial interfaces in the device. The table does not include any other type of interface, even though a specific router may contain one. An example of this might be an ISDN BRI interface. The string in parenthesis is the legal abbreviation that can be used in Cisco IOS commands to represent the interface.				

11.2.4.6 Lab — Securing Network Devices

Topology

Addressing Table

Device	Interface	IP Address	Subnet Mask	Default Gateway
R1	G0/1	192.168.1.1	255.255.255.0	N/A
S1	VLAN 1	192.168.1.11	255.255.255.0	192.168.1.1
PC-A	NIC	192.168.1.3	255.255.255.0	192.168.1.1

Objectives

Part 1: Configure Basic Device Settings

Part 2: Configure Basic Security Measures on the Router

Part 3: Configure Basic Security Measures on the Switch

Background / Scenario

It is recommended that all network devices be configured with, at least, a minimum set of best practice security commands. This includes end user devices, servers, and network devices, such as routers and switches.

In this lab, you will configure the network devices in the topology to accept SSH sessions for remote management. You will also use the IOS CLI to configure common, basic best practice security measures. You will then test the security measures to verify that they are properly implemented and working correctly.

Note: The routers used with CCNA hands-on labs are Cisco 1941 Integrated Services Routers (ISRs) with Cisco IOS Release 15.2(4)M3 (universalk9 image). The switches used are Cisco Catalyst 2960s with Cisco IOS Release 15.0(2) (lanbasek9 image). Other routers, switches, and Cisco IOS versions can be used. Depending on the model and Cisco IOS version, the commands available and output produced might vary from what is shown in the labs. Refer to the Router Interface Summary Table at the end of this lab for the correct interface identifiers.

Note: Make sure that the routers and switches have been erased and have no startup configurations. If you are unsure, contact your instructor.

Required Resources

- 1 Router (Cisco 1941 with Cisco IOS Release 15.2(4)M3 universal image or comparable)
- 1 Switch (Cisco 2960 with Cisco IOS Release 15.0(2) lanbasek9 image or comparable)
- 1 PC (Windows 7, Vista, or XP with terminal emulation program, such as Tera Term)
- Console cables to configure the Cisco IOS devices via the console ports
- Ethernet cables as shown in the topology

Part 1:   Configure Basic Device Settings

In Part 1, you will set up the network topology and configure basic settings, such as the interface IP address-es, device access, and passwords on the router.

Step 1:   Cable the network as shown in the topology.

Attach the devices as shown in the topology and cable as necessary.

Step 2:   Initialize and reload the router and switch.

Step 3:   Configure the router.

Please refer to the previous lab for help with the commands needed for SSH.

a.   Console into the router and enable privileged EXEC mode.

b.   Enter configuration mode.

c.   Assign the name of the router as R1.

d.   Disable DNS lookup.

e.   Assign **class** as the privileged EXEC encrypted password.

f.   Assign **cisco** as the console password and enable login.

g.   Assign **cisco** as the vty password and enable login.

h.   Encrypt the plain text passwords.

i.   Create a banner that warns anyone accessing the device that unauthorized access is prohibited.

j.   Configure and activate the G0/1 interface on the router using the information contained in the Addressing Table.

k.   Save the running configuration to the startup configuration file.

Step 4:   Configure the switch.

a.   Console into the switch and enable privileged EXEC mode.

b.   Enter configuration mode.

c.   Assign the name of the switch as S1.

d.   Disable DNS lookup to prevent the router from attempting to translate incorrectly entered commands as though they were hostnames.

e.   Assign **class** as the privileged EXEC encrypted password.

f.   Assign **cisco** as the console password and enable login.

g.   Assign **cisco** as the vty password and enable login.

h. Encrypt the plain text passwords.

i. Create a banner that warns anyone accessing the device that unauthorized access is prohibited.

j. Configure the default SVI with the IP address information contained in the Addressing Table.

k. Save the running configuration to the startup configuration file.

Part 2: Configure Basic Security Measures on the Router

Step 1: Strengthen passwords.

An administrator should ensure that passwords meet the standard guidelines for strong passwords. These guidelines could include mixing letters, numbers, and special characters in the password and setting a minimum length.

Note: Best practice guidelines require the use of strong passwords, such as those shown here, in a production environment. However, the other labs in this course use the cisco and class passwords for ease in performing the labs.

a. Change the privileged EXEC encrypted password to meet guidelines.

```
R1(config)# enable secret Enablep@55
```

b. Require that a minimum of 10 characters be used for all passwords.

```
R1(config)# security passwords min-length 10
```

Step 2: Enable SSH connections.

a. Assign the domain name as **CCNA-lab.com**.

```
R1(config)# ip domain-name CCNA-lab.com
```

b. Create a local user database entry to use when connecting to the router via SSH. The password should meet strong password standards, and the user should have administrator-level access.

```
R1(config)# username admin privilege 15 secret Admin15p@55
```

c. Configure the transport input for the vty lines so that they accept SSH connections, but do not allow Telnet connections.

```
R1(config)# line vty 0 4
R1(config-line)# transport input ssh
```

d. The vty lines should use the local user database for authentication.

```
R1(config-line)# login local
R1(config-line)# exit
```

e. Generate a RSA crypto key using a modulus of 1024 bits.

```
R1(config)# crypto key generate rsa modulus 1024
The name for the keys will be: R1.CCNA-lab.com


% The key modulus size is 1024 bits
% Generating 1024 bit RSA keys, keys will be non-exportable...
```

```
[OK] (elapsed time was 2 seconds)


R1(config)#

*Jan 31 17:54:16.127: %SSH-5-ENABLED: SSH 1.99 has been enabled
```

Step 3: Secure the console and VTY lines.

a. You can set the router to log out of a connection that has been idle for a specified time. If a network administrator was logged into a networking device and was suddenly called away, this command automatically logs the user out after the specified time. The following commands cause the line to log out after five minutes of inactivity.

```
R1(config)# line console 0

R1(config-line)# exec-timeout 5 0

R1(config-line)# line vty 0 4

R1(config-line)# exec-timeout 5 0

R1(config-line)# exit

R1(config)#
```

b. The following command impedes brute force login attempts. The router blocks login attempts for 30 seconds if someone fails two attempts within 120 seconds. This timer is set especially low for the purpose of this lab.

```
R1(config)# login block-for 30 attempts 2 within 120
```

What does the **2 within 120** mean in the above command?

_____

What does the **block-for 30** mean in the above command?

_____

Step 4: Verify that all unused ports are disabled.

Router ports are disabled, by default, but it is always prudent to verify that all unused ports are in an administratively down state. This can be quickly checked by issuing the **show ip interface brief** command. Any unused ports that are not in an administratively down state should be disabled using the **shutdown** command in interface configuration mode.

```
R1# show ip interface brief
Interface                  IP-Address      OK? Method Status                Protocol
Embedded-Service-Engine0/0 unassigned      YES NVRAM  administratively down down
GigabitEthernet0/0         unassigned      YES NVRAM  administratively down down
GigabitEthernet0/1         192.168.1.1     YES manual up                    up
Serial0/0/0                unassigned      YES NVRAM  administratively down down
Serial0/0/1                unassigned      YES NVRAM  administratively down down
R1#
```

Step 5:   Verify that your security measures have been implemented correctly.

a. Use Tera Term to telnet to R1.

Does R1 accept the Telnet connection? _____

Why or why not?

_____

b. Use Tera Term to SSH to R1.

Does R1 accept the SSH connection? _____

c. Intentionally mistype the user and password information to see if login access is blocked after two attempts.

What happened after you failed to login the second time?

_____

_____

d. From your console session on the router, issue the **show login** command to view the login status. In the example below, the **show login** command was issued within the 30 second login blocking period and shows that the router is in Quiet-Mode. The router will not accept any login attempts for 14 more seconds.

```
R1# show login
      A default login delay of 1 second is applied.
      No Quiet-Mode access list has been configured.


      Router enabled to watch for login Attacks.
      If more than 2 login failures occur in 120 seconds or less,
      logins will be disabled for 30 seconds.


      Router presently in Quiet-Mode.
      Will remain in Quiet-Mode for 14 seconds.
      Denying logins from all sources.
R1#
```

e. After the 30 seconds has expired, SSH to R1 again and login using the **admin** username and **Admin15p@55** for the password.

After you successfully logged in, what was displayed? _____

f. Enter privileged EXEC mode and use **Enablep@55** for the password.

If you mistype this password, are you disconnected from your SSH session after two failed attempts within 120 seconds? _____

Why or why not?

_____

g. Issue the **show running-config** command at the privileged EXEC prompt to view the security settings you have applied.

Part 3: Configure Basic Security Measures on the Switch

Step 1: Strengthen Passwords on the switch.

Change the privileged EXEC encrypted password to meet strong password guidelines.

```
S1(config)# enable secret Enablep@55
```

Note: The security **password min-length** command is not available on the 2960 switch.

Step 2: Enable SSH Connections.

a. Assign the domain-name as **CCNA-lab.com**

```
S1(config)# ip domain-name CCNA-lab.com
```

b. Create a local user database entry for use when connecting to the router via SSH. The password should meet strong password standards, and the user should have administrative level access.

```
S1(config)# username admin privilege 15 secret Admin15p@55
```

c. Configure the transport input for the vty lines to allow SSH connections but not allow Telnet connections.

```
S1(config)# line vty 0 15
S1(config-line)# transport input ssh
```

d. The vty lines should use the local user database for authentication.

```
S1(config-line)# login local
S1(config-line)# exit
```

e. Generate a RSA crypto key using a modulus of 1024 bits.

```
S1(config)# crypto key generate rsa modulus 1024
```

Step 3: Secure the console and VTY lines.

a. Have the switch log out a line that has been idle for 10 minutes.

```
S1(config)# line console 0
S1(config-line)# exec-timeout 10 0
S1(config-line)# line vty 0 15
S1(config-line)# exec-timeout 10 0
S1(config-line)# exit
S1(config)#
```

b. To impede brute force login attempts, configure the switch to block login access for 30 seconds if there are 2 failed attempts within 120 seconds. This timer is set especially low for the purpose of this lab.

```
S1(config)# login block-for 30 attempts 2 within 120
S1(config)# end
```

Step 4: Verify that all unused ports are disabled.

Switch ports are enabled, by default. Shut down all ports that are not in use on the switch.

a. You can verify the switch port status using the **show ip interface brief** command.

```
S1# show ip interface brief
```

Interface	IP-Address	OK? Method Status		Protocol
Vlan1	192.168.1.11	YES	manual up	up
FastEthernet0/1	unassigned	YES	unset down	down
FastEthernet0/2	unassigned	YES	unset down	down
FastEthernet0/3	unassigned	YES	unset down	down
FastEthernet0/4	unassigned	YES	unset down	down
FastEthernet0/5	unassigned	YES	unset up	up
FastEthernet0/6	unassigned	YES	unset up	up
FastEthernet0/7	unassigned	YES	unset down	down
FastEthernet0/8	unassigned	YES	unset down	down
FastEthernet0/9	unassigned	YES	unset down	down
FastEthernet0/10	unassigned	YES	unset down	down
FastEthernet0/11	unassigned	YES	unset down	down
FastEthernet0/12	unassigned	YES	unset down	down
FastEthernet0/13	unassigned	YES	unset down	down
FastEthernet0/14	unassigned	YES	unset down	down
FastEthernet0/15	unassigned	YES	unset down	down
FastEthernet0/16	unassigned	YES	unset down	down
FastEthernet0/17	unassigned	YES	unset down	down
FastEthernet0/18	unassigned	YES	unset down	down
FastEthernet0/19	unassigned	YES	unset down	down
FastEthernet0/20	unassigned	YES	unset down	down
FastEthernet0/21	unassigned	YES	unset down	down
FastEthernet0/22	unassigned	YES	unset down	down
FastEthernet0/23	unassigned	YES	unset down	down
FastEthernet0/24	unassigned	YES	unset down	down
GigabitEthernet0/1	unassigned	YES	unset down	down
GigabitEthernet0/2	unassigned	YES	unset down	down

```
S1#
```

b. Use the **interface range** command to shut down multiple interfaces at a time.

```
S1(config)# interface range f0/1-4 , f0/7-24 , g0/1-2
S1(config-if-range)# shutdown
S1(config-if-range)# end
S1#
```

c. Verify that all inactive interfaces have been administratively shut down.

```
S1# show ip interface brief
```

Interface	IP-Address	OK? Method Status		Protocol
Vlan1	192.168.1.11	YES	manual up	up

```
FastEthernet0/1        unassigned     YES unset  administratively down down
FastEthernet0/2        unassigned     YES unset  administratively down down
FastEthernet0/3        unassigned     YES unset  administratively down down
FastEthernet0/4        unassigned     YES unset  administratively down down
FastEthernet0/5        unassigned     YES unset  up                      up
FastEthernet0/6        unassigned     YES unset  up                      up
FastEthernet0/7        unassigned     YES unset  administratively down down
FastEthernet0/8        unassigned     YES unset  administratively down down
FastEthernet0/9        unassigned     YES unset  administratively down down
FastEthernet0/10       unassigned     YES unset  administratively down down
FastEthernet0/11       unassigned     YES unset  administratively down down
FastEthernet0/12       unassigned     YES unset  administratively down down
FastEthernet0/13       unassigned     YES unset  administratively down down
FastEthernet0/14       unassigned     YES unset  administratively down down
FastEthernet0/15       unassigned     YES unset  administratively down down
FastEthernet0/16       unassigned     YES unset  administratively down down
FastEthernet0/17       unassigned     YES unset  administratively down down
FastEthernet0/18       unassigned     YES unset  administratively down down
FastEthernet0/19       unassigned     YES unset  administratively down down
FastEthernet0/20       unassigned     YES unset  administratively down down
FastEthernet0/21       unassigned     YES unset  administratively down down
FastEthernet0/22       unassigned     YES unset  administratively down down
FastEthernet0/23       unassigned     YES unset  administratively down down
FastEthernet0/24       unassigned     YES unset  administratively down down
GigabitEthernet0/1     unassigned     YES unset  administratively down down
GigabitEthernet0/2     unassigned     YES unset  administratively down down
S1#
```

Step 5: Verify that your security measures have been implemented correctly.

a. Verify that Telnet has been disabled on the switch.

b. SSH to the switch and intentionally mistype the user and password information to see if login access is blocked.

c. After the 30 seconds has expired, SSH to S1 again and log in using the **admin** username and **Admin15p@55** for the password.

Did the banner appear after you successfully logged in? _____

d. Enter privileged EXEC mode using **Enablep@55** as the password.

e. Issue the **show running-config** command at the privileged EXEC prompt to view the security settings you have applied.

Reflection

1. The **password cisco** command was entered for the console and vty lines in your basic configuration in Part 1. When is this password used after the best practice security measures have been applied?

   _____

   _____

   _____

2. Are preconfigured passwords, shorter than 10 characters, affected by the **security passwords min-length 10** command?

   _____

   _____

   _____

Router Interface Summary Table

Router Interface Summary				
Router Model	**Ethernet Interface #1**	**Ethernet Interface #2**	**Serial Interface #1**	**Serial Interface #2**
1800	Fast Ethernet 0/0 (F0/0)	Fast Ethernet 0/1 (F0/1)	Serial 0/0/0 (S0/0/0)	Serial 0/0/1 (S0/0/1)
1900	Gigabit Ethernet 0/0 (G0/0)	Gigabit Ethernet 0/1 (G0/1)	Serial 0/0/0 (S0/0/0)	Serial 0/0/1 (S0/0/1)
2801	Fast Ethernet 0/0 (F0/0)	Fast Ethernet 0/1 (F0/1)	Serial 0/1/0 (S0/1/0)	Serial 0/1/1 (S0/1/1)
2811	Fast Ethernet 0/0 (F0/0)	Fast Ethernet 0/1 (F0/1)	Serial 0/0/0 (S0/0/0)	Serial 0/0/1 (S0/0/1)
2900	Gigabit Ethernet 0/0 (G0/0)	Gigabit Ethernet 0/1 (G0/1)	Serial 0/0/0 (S0/0/0)	Serial 0/0/1 (S0/0/1)
Note: To find out how the router is configured, look at the interfaces to identify the type of router and how many interfaces the router has. There is no way to effectively list all the combinations of configurations for each router class. This table includes identifiers for the possible combinations of Ethernet and Serial interfaces in the device. The table does not include any other type of interface, even though a specific router may contain one. An example of this might be an ISDN BRI interface. The string in parenthesis is the legal abbreviation that can be used in Cisco IOS commands to represent the interface.				

11.3.2.3 Lab — Testing Network Latency with Ping and Traceroute

Topology

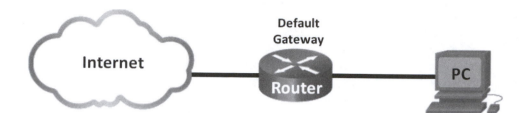

Objectives

Part 1: Use Ping to Document Network Latency

Part 2: Use Traceroute to Document Network Latency

Background / Scenario

To obtain realistic network latency statistics, this activity must be performed on a live network. Be sure to check with your instructor for any local security restrictions against using the **ping** command on the network.

The purpose of this lab is to measure and evaluate network latency over time, and during different periods of the day to capture a representative sample of typical network activity. This will be accomplished by analyzing the return delay from a distant computer with the **ping** command. Return delay times, measured in milliseconds, will be summarized by computing the average latency (mean) and the range (maximum and minimum) of the delay times.

Required Resources

- 1 PC (Windows 7, Vista, or XP with Internet access)

Part 1: Use Ping to Document Network Latency

In Part 1, you will examine network latency to several websites in different parts of the globe. This process can be used in an enterprise production network to create a performance baseline.

Step 1: Verify connectivity.

Ping the following Regional Internet Registry (RIR) websites to verify connectivity:

```
C:\Users\User1> ping www.arin.net

C:\Users\User1> ping www.lacnic.net

C:\Users\User1> ping www.afrinic.net

C:\Users\User1> ping www.apnic.net
```

Note: Because www.ripe.net does not reply to ICMP requests, it cannot be used for this lab.

Step 2: **Collect network data.**

You will collect a sufficient amount of data to compute statistics on the **ping** output by sending out 25 echo requests to each address listed in Step 1. Record the results for each website to text files.

a. At the command prompt, type **ping** to list the available options.

```
C:\Users\User1> ping
```

```
Usage: ping [-t] [-a] [-n count] [-l size] [-f] [-i TTL] [-v TOS]
            [-r count] [-s count] [[-j host-list] | [-k host-list]]
            [-w timeout] [-R] [-S srcaddr] [-4] [-6] target_name
```

```
Options:
    -t              Ping the specified host until stopped.
                    To see statistics and continue - type Control-Break;
                    To stop - type Control-C.
    -a              Resolve addresses to hostnames.
    -n count        Number of echo requests to send.
    -l size         Send buffer size.
    -f              Set Don't Fragment flag in packet (IPv4-only).
    -i TTL          Time To Live.
    -v TOS          Type Of Service (IPv4-only. This setting has been deprecated
<output omitted>
```

b. Using the **ping** command with the count option, you can send 25 echo requests to the destination as illustrated below. Furthermore, it will create a text file with filename of **arin.txt** in the current directory. This text file will contain the results of the echo requests.

```
C:\Users\User1> ping -n 25 www.arin.net > arin.txt
```

Note: The terminal remains blank until the command has finished, because the output has been redirected to a text file, **arin.txt**, in this example. The **>** symbol is used to redirect the screen output to the file and overwrite the file if it already exists. If appending more results to the file is desired, replace **>** with **>>** in the command.

c. Repeat the **ping** command for the other websites.

```
C:\Users\User1> ping -n 25 www.afrinic.net > afrinic.txt
C:\Users\User1> ping -n 25 www.apnic.net > apnic.txt
C:\Users\User1> ping -n 25 www.lacnic.net > lacnic.txt
```

Step 3:   Verify data collection.

To see the results in the file created, use the **more** command at the command prompt.

```
C:\Users\User1> more arin.txt


Pinging www.arin.net [192.149.252.76] with 32 bytes of data:
Reply from 192.149.252.76: bytes=32 time=108ms TTL=45
Reply from 192.149.252.76: bytes=32 time=114ms TTL=45
Reply from 192.149.252.76: bytes=32 time=112ms TTL=45
<output omitted>
Reply from 192.149.252.75: bytes=32 time=111ms TTL=45
Reply from 192.149.252.75: bytes=32 time=112ms TTL=45
Reply from 192.149.252.75: bytes=32 time=112ms TTL=45


Ping statistics for 192.149.252.75:
    Packets: Sent = 25, Received = 25, Lost = 0 (0% loss),
Approximate round trip times in milli-seconds:
    Minimum = 107ms, Maximum = 121ms, Average = 111ms
```

Note: Press the Spacebar to display the rest of the file or press **q** to exit.

To verify that the files have been created, use the **dir** command to list the files in the directory. Also the wild-card * can be used to filter only the text files.

```
C:\Users\User1> dir *.txt
Volume in drive C is OS
 Volume Serial Number is 0A97-D265


 Directory of C:\Users\User1


02/07/2013  12:59 PM              1,642 afrinic.txt
02/07/2013  01:00 PM              1,615 apnic.txt
02/07/2013  12:40 PM              1,641 arin.txt
02/07/2013  12:58 PM              1,589 lacnic.txt
               4 File(s)          6,487 bytes
               0 Dir(s)   34,391,453,696 bytes free
```

Record your results in the following table.

	Minimum	Maximum	Average
www.afrinic.net			
www.apnic.net			
www.arin.net			
www.lacnic.net			

Compare the delay results. How is delay affected by geographical location?

_____

_____

Part 2: Use Traceroute to Document Network Latency

The routes traced may go through many hops and a number of different ISPs depending on the size of the ISPs and the location of the source and destination hosts. The **traceroute** commands can also be used to observe network latency. In Part 2, the **tracert** command is used to trace the path to the same destinations in Part 1.

The **tracert** command uses ICMP TTL Exceed packets and ICMP echo replies to trace the path.

Step 1: Use the tracert command and record the output to text files.

Copy the following commands to create the traceroute files:

```
C:\Users\User1> tracert www.arin.net > traceroute_arin.txt

C:\Users\User1> tracert www.lacnic.net > traceroute_lacnic.txt

C:\Users\User1> tracert www.afrinic.net > traceroute_afrinic.txt

C:\Users\User1> tracert www.apnic.net > traceroute_apnic.txt
```

Step 2: Use the more command to examine the traced path.

a. Use the **more** command to access the content of these files:

```
C:\Users\User1> more traceroute_arin.txt


Tracing route to www.arin.net [192.149.252.75]
over a maximum of 30 hops:


 1     <1 ms     <1 ms     <1 ms   192.168.1.1

 2     11 ms     12 ms     11 ms   10.39.0.1

 3     10 ms     15 ms     11 ms   172.21.0.116

 4     19 ms     10 ms     11 ms   70.169.73.90

 5     13 ms     10 ms     11 ms   chnddsrj01-ae2.0.rd.ph.cox.net [70.169.76.229]

 6     72 ms     71 ms     70 ms   mrfddsrj02-ae0.0.rd.dc.cox.net [68.1.1.7]

 7     72 ms     71 ms     72 ms   68.100.0.146
```

```
 8     74 ms     83 ms     73 ms  172.22.66.29

 9     75 ms     71 ms     73 ms  172.22.66.29

10     74 ms     75 ms     73 ms  wsip-98-172-152-14.dc.dc.cox.net [98.172.152.14]

11     71 ms     71 ms     71 ms  host-252-131.arin.net [192.149.252.131]

12     73 ms     71 ms     71 ms  www.arin.net [192.149.252.75]


Trace complete.
```

In this example, it took less than 1 ms to receive a reply from the default gateway (192.168.1.1). In hop count 6, the round trip to 68.1.1.7 took an average of 71 ms. For the round trip to the final destination at www.arin.net took an average of 72 ms.

Between lines 5 and 6, there is more network delay as indicated by the round trip time increase from an average of 11 ms to 71 ms

b. Perform the same analysis with the rest of the tracert results.

What can you conclude regarding the relationship between the roundtrip time and geographical location?

_____

_____

Reflection

1. The **tracert** and **ping** results can provide important network latency information. What do you need to do if you want an accurate baseline picture regarding network latency for your network?

_____

2. How can you use the baseline information?

_____

11.3.4.6 Lab — Using the CLI to Gather Network Device Information

Topology

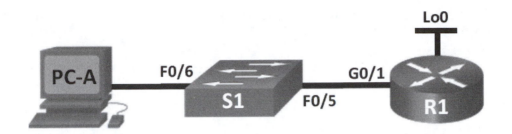

Addressing Table

Device	Interface	IP Address	Subnet Mask	Default Gateway
R1	G0/1	192.168.1.1	255.255.255.0	N/A
	Lo0	209.165.200.225	255.255.255.224	N/A
S1	VLAN 1	192.168.1.11	255.255.255.0	192.168.1.1
PC-A	NIC	192.168.1.3	255.255.255.0	192.168.1.1

Objectives

Part 1: Set Up Topology and Initialize Devices

- Set up equipment to match the network topology.
- Initialize and reload the router and switch.

Part 2: Configure Devices and Verify Connectivity

- Assign a static IP address to PC-A NIC.
- Configure basic settings on R1.
- Configure basic settings on S1.
- Verify network connectivity.

Part 3: Gather Network Device Information

- Gather information on R1 using IOS CLI commands.
- Gather information on S1 using IOS CLI commands.
- Gather information on PC-A using the command prompt CLI.

Background / Scenario

Documenting a working network is one of the most important tasks a network professional can perform. Having proper documentation of IP addresses, model numbers, IOS versions, ports used, and testing security, can go a long way in helping to troubleshoot a network.

In this lab, you will build a small network, configure the devices, add some basic security, and then document the configurations by issuing various commands on the router, switch and PC to gather your information.

Note: The routers used with CCNA hands-on labs are Cisco 1941 Integrated Services Routers (ISRs) with Cisco IOS Release 15.2(4)M3 (universalk9 image). The switches used are Cisco Catalyst 2960s with Cisco IOS Release 15.0(2) (lanbasek9 image). Other routers, switches, and Cisco IOS versions can be used. Depending on the model and Cisco IOS version, the commands available and output produced might vary from what is shown in the labs. Refer to the Router Interface Summary Table at the end of this lab for the correct interface identifiers.

Note: Make sure that the routers and switches have been erased and have no startup configurations. If you are unsure, contact your instructor.

Required Resources

- 1 Router (Cisco 1941 with Cisco IOS Release 15.2(4)M3 universal image or comparable)
- 1 Switch (Cisco 2960 with Cisco IOS Release 15.0(2) lanbasek9 image or comparable)
- 1 PC (Windows 7, Vista, or XP with terminal emulation program, such as Tera Term)
- Console cables to configure the Cisco IOS devices via the console ports
- Ethernet cables as shown in the topology

Part 1: Set Up the Topology and Initialize Devices

In Part 1, you will set up the network topology, clear any configurations if necessary, and configure basic settings on the router and switch.

Step 1: Cable the network as shown in the topology.

a. Attach the devices as shown in the topology and cable as necessary.

b. Power on all devices in the topology.

Step 2: Initialize and reload the router and the switch.

Part 2: Configure Devices and Verify Connectivity

In Part 2, you will set up the network topology and configure basic settings on the router and switch. Refer to the topology and Addressing Table at the beginning of this lab for device names and address information.

Note: Appendix A provides configuration details for the steps in Part 2. You should attempt to complete Part 2 prior to referencing this appendix.

Step 1: Configure the IPv4 address for the PC.

Configure the IPv4 address, subnet mask, and default gateway address for PC-A based on the Addressing Table.

Step 2: Configure the router.

If you need assistance for Step 2, refer to Appendix A for help.

a. Console into the router and enter privileged EXEC mode.

b. Set the correct time on the router.

c. Enter global configuration mode.

    1) Assign a device name to the router based on the topology and Addressing Table.

    2) Disable DNS lookup.

    3) Create a MOTD banner that warns anyone accessing the device that unauthorized access is prohibited.

    4) Assign **class** as the privileged EXEC encrypted password.

    5) Assign **cisco** as the console password and enable console login access.

    6) Encrypt clear text passwords.

    7) Create a domain name of **cisco.com** for SSH access.

    8) Create a user named **admin** with a secret password of **cisco** for SSH access.

    9) Generate a RSA modulus key. Use **512** for the number of bits.

d. Configure vty line access.

    1) Use the local database for authentication for SSH.

    2) Enable SSH only for login access.

e. Return to global configuration mode.

    1) Create the Loopback 0 interface and assign the IP address based on the Addressing Table.

    2) Configure and activate interface G0/1 on the router.

    3) Configure interface descriptions for G0/1 and L0.

    4) Save the running configuration file to the startup configuration file.

Step 3: Configure the switch.

If you need assistance for Step 3, refer to Appendix A for help.

a. Console into the switch and enter privileged EXEC mode.

b. Set the correct time on the switch.

c. Enter global configuration mode.

1)   Assign a device name on the switch based on the topology and Addressing Table.

2)   Disable DNS lookup.

3)   Create a MOTD banner that warns anyone accessing the device that unauthorized access is prohibited.

4)   Assign **class** as the privileged EXEC encrypted password.

5)   Encrypt the clear text passwords.

6)   Create a domain name of **cisco.com** for SSH access.

7)   Create a user named **admin** with a secret password of **cisco** for SSH access.

8)   Generate an RSA modulus key. Use **512** for the number of bits.

9)   Create and activate an IP address on the switch based on the topology and Addressing Table.

10)   Set the default gateway on the switch.

11)   Assign **cisco** as the console password and enable console login access.

d.   Configure vty line access.

1)   Use local database for authentication for SSH.

2)   Enable SSH only for login access.

3)   Enter proper mode to configure interface descriptions for F0/5 and F0/6.

4)   Save the running configuration file to the startup configuration file.

Step 4:   Verify network connectivity.

a.   From a command prompt on PC-A, ping the S1 VLAN 1 IP address. Troubleshoot your physical and logical configurations if the pings were not successful.

b.   From the PC-A command prompt, ping your default gateway IP address on R1. Troubleshoot your physical and logical configurations if the pings were not successful.

c.   From the PC-A command prompt, ping the loopback interface on R1. Troubleshoot your physical and logical configurations if the pings were not successful.

d.   Console back into the switch and ping the G0/1 IP address on R1. Troubleshoot your physical and logical configurations if the pings were not successful.

Part 3:   Gather Network Device Information

In Part 3, you will use a variety of commands to gather information about the devices on your network, as well as some performance characteristics. Network documentation is a very important component of managing your network. Documentation of both physical and logical topologies is important, as is verifying platform models and IOS versions of your network devices. Having knowledge of the proper commands to gather this information is essential for a network professional.

Step 1:   **Gather information on R1 using IOS commands.**

One of the most basic steps is to gather information on the physical device, as well as information on the operating system.

a.   Issue the appropriate command to discover the following information:

Router Model: _____

IOS Version: _____

Total RAM: _____

Total NVRAM: _____

Total Flash Memory: _____

IOS Image File: _____

Configuration Register: _____

Technology Package: _____

What command did you issue to gather the information?

_____

b.   Issue the appropriate command to display a summary of important information about the router interfaces. Write down the command and record your results below.

Note: Only record interfaces that have IP addresses.

_____

_____

_____

_____

c. Issue the appropriate command to display the routing table. Write down the command and record your results below.

_____

_____

_____

_____

_____

_____

_____

d. What command would you use to display the Layer 2 to Layer 3 mapping of addresses on the router? Write down the command and record your results below.

_____

_____

_____

_____

_____

e. What command would you use to see detailed information about all the interfaces on the router or about a specific interface? Write down the command below.

_____

f. Cisco has a very powerful protocol that operates at Layer 2 of the OSI model. This protocol can help you map out how Cisco devices are connected physically, as well as determining model numbers and even IOS versions and IP addressing. What command or commands would you use on router R1 to find out information about switch S1 to help you complete the table below?

Device ID	Local Interface	Capability	Model #	Remote Port ID	IP Address	IOS Version

g. A very elementary test of your network devices is to see if you can telnet into them. Remember, Telnet is not a secure protocol. It should not be enabled in most cases. Using a Telnet client, such as Tera Term or PuTTY, try to telnet to R1 using the default gateway IP address. Record your results below.

_____

h.   From PC-A, test to ensure that SSH is working properly. Using an SSH client, such as Tera Term or PuTTY, SSH into R1 from PC-A. If you get a warning message regarding a different key, click **Continue**. Log in with the appropriate username and password you created in Part 2. Were you successful?

_____

The various passwords configured on your router should be as strong and protected as possible.

Note: The passwords used for our lab (and   ) do not follow the best practices needed for strong passwords. These passwords are used merely for the convenience of performing the labs. By default, the console password and any vty passwords configured would display in clear text in your configuration file.

i.   Verify that all of your passwords in the configuration file are encrypted. Write down the command and record your results below.

Command: _____

Is the console password encrypted? _____

Is the SSH password encrypted? _____

Step 2:   Gather information on S1 using IOS commands.

Many of the commands that you used on R1 can also be used with the switch. However, there are some differences with some of the commands.

a.   Issue the appropriate command to discover the following information:

Switch Model: _____

IOS Version: _____

Total NVRAM: _____

IOS Image File: _____

What command did you issue to gather the information?

_____

b.   Issue the appropriate command to display a summary of key information about the switch interfaces. Write down the command and record your results below.

Note: Only record active interfaces.

_____

_____

_____

_____

_____

c. Issue the appropriate command to display the switch MAC address table. Record the dynamic type MAC addresses only in the space below.

_____

_____

_____

_____

d. Verify that Telnet VTY access is disabled on S1. Using a Telnet client, such as Tera Term or PuTTY, try to telnet to S1 using the 192.168.1.11 address. Record your results below.

_____

e. From PC-A, test to ensure that SSH is working properly. Using an SSH client, such as Tera Term or PuTTY, SSH into S1 from PC-A. If you get a warning message regarding a different key, click **Continue**. Log in with an appropriate username and password. Were you successful?

_____

f. Complete the table below with information about router R1 using the appropriate command or commands necessary on S1.

Device Id	Local Interface	Capability	Model #	Remote Port ID	IP Address	IOS Version

g. Verify that all of your passwords in the configuration file are encrypted. Write down the command and record your results below.

Command: _____

Is the console password encrypted? _____

Step 3: Gather information on PC-A.

Using various Windows utility commands, you will gather information on PC-A.

a. From the PC-A command prompt, issue the **ipconfig /all** command and record your answers below.

What is the PC-A IP address?

_____

What is the PC-A subnet mask?

_____

What is the PC-A default gateway address?

_____

What is the PC-A MAC address?

_____

b. Issue the appropriate command to test the TCP/IP protocol stack with the NIC. What command did you use?

_____

c. Ping the loopback interface of R1 from the PC-A command prompt. Was the ping successful?

_____

d. Issue the appropriate command on PC-A to trace the list of router hops for packets originating from PC-A to the loopback interface on R1. Record the command and output below. What command did you use?

_____

_____

e. Issue the appropriate command on PC-A to find the Layer 2 to Layer 3 address mappings held on your NIC. Record your answers below. Only record answers for the 192.168.1.0/24 network. What command did you use?

_____

_____

_____

_____

Reflection

Why is it important to document your network devices?

_____

_____

_____

_____

_____

Router Interface Summary Table

Router Interface Summary				
Router Model	**Ethernet Interface #1**	**Ethernet Interface #2**	**Serial Interface #1**	**Serial Interface #2**
1800	Fast Ethernet 0/0 (F0/0)	Fast Ethernet 0/1 (F0/1)	Serial 0/0/0 (S0/0/0)	Serial 0/0/1 (S0/0/1)
1900	Gigabit Ethernet 0/0 (G0/0)	Gigabit Ethernet 0/1 (G0/1)	Serial 0/0/0 (S0/0/0)	Serial 0/0/1 (S0/0/1)
2801	Fast Ethernet 0/0 (F0/0)	Fast Ethernet 0/1 (F0/1)	Serial 0/1/0 (S0/1/0)	Serial 0/1/1 (S0/1/1)
2811	Fast Ethernet 0/0 (F0/0)	Fast Ethernet 0/1 (F0/1)	Serial 0/0/0 (S0/0/0)	Serial 0/0/1 (S0/0/1)
2900	Gigabit Ethernet 0/0 (G0/0)	Gigabit Ethernet 0/1 (G0/1)	Serial 0/0/0 (S0/0/0)	Serial 0/0/1 (S0/0/1)

Note: To find out how the router is configured, look at the interfaces to identify the type of router and how many interfaces the router has. There is no way to effectively list all the combinations of configurations for each router class. This table includes identifiers for the possible combinations of Ethernet and Serial interfaces in the device. The table does not include any other type of interface, even though a specific router may contain one. An example of this might be an ISDN BRI interface. The string in parenthesis is the legal abbreviation that can be used in Cisco IOS commands to represent the interface.

Appendix A: Configuration Details for Steps in Part 2

Step 1:   Configure the IPv4 address for the PC.

Configure the IPv4 address, subnet mask, and default gateway address for PC-A based on the Addressing Table at the beginning of this lab.

Step 2:   Configure the router.

a.   Console into the router and enter privileged EXEC mode.

```
Router> enable
Router#
```

f.   Set the correct time on the router.

```
Router# clock set 10:40:30 6 February 2013
Router#
```

g. Enter global configuration mode.

```
Router# config t
Router(config)#
```

Assign a hostname to the router. Use the topology and Addressing Table as guidelines.

```
Router(config)# hostname R1
R1(config)#
```

Disable DNS lookup.

```
R1(config)# no ip domain-lookup
```

Create a MOTD banner that warns anyone accessing the device that unauthorized access is prohibited.

```
R1(config)# banner motd #Warning! Unauthorized Access is prohibited.#
```

Assign **class** as the privileged EXEC encrypted password.

```
R1(config)# enable secret class
```

Assign **cisco** as the console password and enable console login access.

```
R1(config)# line con 0
R1(config-line)# password cisco
R1(config-line)# login
```

Encrypt clear text passwords.

```
R1(config)# service password-encryption
```

Create a domain name of **cisco.com** for SSH access.

```
R1(config)# ip domain-name cisco.com
```

Create a user named **admin** with a secret password of **cisco** for SSH access.

```
R1(config)# username admin secret cisco
```

Generate an RSA modulus key. Use **512** for the number of bits.

```
R1(config)# crypto key generate rsa modulus 512
```

h. Configure vty line access.

Use the local database for authentication for SSH.

```
R1(config)# line vty 0 4
R1(config-line)# login local
```

Enable SSH only for login access.

```
R1(config-line)# transport input ssh
```

i. Return to global configuration mode.

```
R1(config-line)# exit
```

Create the Loopback 0 interface and assign the IP address based on the Address Table.

```
R1(config)# interface loopback 0
```

```
R1(config-if)# ip address 209.165.200.225 255.255.255.224
```

Configure and activate interface G0/1 on the router.

```
R1(config-if)# int g0/1
R1(config-if)# ip address 192.168.1.1 255.255.255.0
R1(config-if)# no shut
```

Configure interface descriptions for G0/1 and L0.

```
R1(config-if)# description Connected to LAN
R1(config-if)# int lo0
R1(config-if)# description Emulate ISP Connection
```

Save the running configuration file to the startup configuration file.

```
R1(config-if)# end
R1# copy run start
```

Step 3:   Configure the switch.

a.   Console into the switch and enter privileged EXEC mode.

```
Switch> enable
Switch#
```

j.   Set the correct time on the switch.

```
Switch# clock set 10:52:30 6 February 2013
```

k.   Enter global configuration mode.

```
Switch# config t
```

Assign a hostname on the switch based on the topology and Addressing Table.

```
Switch(config)# hostname S1
```

Disable DNS lookup.

```
S1(config)# no ip domain-lookup
```

Create a MOTD banner that warns anyone accessing the device that unauthorized access is prohibited.

```
S1(config)# banner motd #Warning! Unauthorized access is prohibited.#
```

Assign **class** as the privileged EXEC encrypted password.

```
S1(config)# enable secret class
```

Encrypt the clear text passwords.

```
S1(config)# service password-encryption
```

Create a domain name of **cisco.com** for SSH access.

```
S1(config)# ip domain-name cisco.com
```

Create a user named **admin** with a secret password of **cisco** for SSH access.

```
S1(config)# username admin secret cisco
```

Generate an RSA modulus key. Use **512** for the number of bits.

```
S1(config)# crypto key generate rsa modulus 512
```

Create and activate an IP address on the switch based on the topology and Addressing Table.

```
S1(config)# interface vlan 1
S1(config-if)# ip address 192.168.1.11 255.255.255.0
S1(config-if)# no shut
```

Set the default gateway on the switch.

```
S1(config)# ip default-gateway 192.168.1.1
```

Assign **cisco** as the console password and enable console login access.

```
S1(config-if)# line con 0
S1(config-line)# password cisco
S1(config-line)# login
```

l. Configure vty line access.

Use local database for authentication for SSH.

```
S1(config-line)# line vty 0 15
S1(config-line)# login local
```

Enable SSH only for login access.

```
S1(config-line)# transport input ssh
```

Enter the appropriate configuration mode to configure interface descriptions for F0/5 and F0/6.

```
S1(config-line)# int f0/5
S1(config-if)# description Connected to R1
S1(config-if)# int f0/6
S1(config-if)# description Connected to PC-A
```

Save the running configuration file to the startup configuration file.

```
S1(config-if)# end
S1# copy run start
```

11.4.2.6 Lab — Managing Router Configuration Files with Terminal Emulation Software

Topology

Addressing Table

Device	Interface	IP Address	Subnet Mask	Default Gateway
R1	G0/1	192.168.1.1	255.255.255.0	N/A
S1	VLAN 1	192.168.1.11	255.255.255.0	192.168.1.1
PC-A	NIC	192.168.1.3	255.255.255.0	192.168.1.1

Objectives

Part 1: Configure Basic Device Settings

Part 2: Use Terminal Emulation Software to Create a Backup Configuration File

Part 3: Use a Backup Configuration File to Restore a Router

Background / Scenario

It is a recommended best practice to maintain backup configuration files for routers and switches in the event that they need to be restored to a previous configuration. Terminal emulation software can be used to easily back up or restore a router or switch configuration file.

In this lab, you will use Tera Term to back up a router running configuration file, erase the router startup configuration file, reload the router, and then restore the missing router configuration from the backup configuration file.

Note: The routers used with CCNA hands-on labs are Cisco 1941 Integrated Services Routers (ISRs) with Cisco IOS Release 15.2(4)M3 (universalk9 image). The switches used are Cisco Catalyst 2960s with Cisco IOS Release 15.0(2) (lanbasek9 image). Other routers, switches, and Cisco IOS versions can be used. Depending on the model and Cisco IOS version, the commands available and output produced might vary from what is shown in the labs. Refer to the Router Interface Summary Table at the end of this lab for the correct interface identifiers.

Note: Make sure that the routers and switches have been erased and have no startup configurations. If you are unsure, contact your instructor.

Required Resources

- 1 Router (Cisco 1941 with Cisco IOS Release 15.2(4)M3 universal image or comparable)
- 1 Switch (Cisco 2960 with Cisco IOS Release 15.0(2) lanbasek9 image or comparable)
- 1 PC (Windows 7, Vista, or XP with terminal emulation program, such as Tera Term)
- Console cables to configure the Cisco IOS devices via the console ports
- Ethernet cables as shown in the topology

Part 1: Configure Basic Device Settings

In Part 1, you will set up the network topology and configure basic settings, such as the interface IP addresses, device access, and passwords on the router.

Step 1: Cable the network as shown in the topology.

Attach the devices as shown in the topology and cable as necessary.

Step 2: Configure the PC-A network settings according to the Addressing Table.

Step 3: Initialize and reload the router and switch.

Step 4: Configure the router.

a. Console into the router and enter global configuration mode.

b. Set the router name to R1.

c. Disable DNS lookup.

d. Assign **class** as the privileged EXEC encrypted password.

e. Assign **cisco** as the console password and enable login.

f. Assign **cisco** as the vty password and enable login.

g. Encrypt the plain text passwords.

h. Create a banner that warns anyone accessing the device that unauthorized access is prohibited.

i. Configure and activate the G0/1 interface on the router using the information contained in the Addressing Table.

j. Save the running configuration to the startup configuration file.

Step 5: Configure the switch.

a. Console into the switch and enter into global configuration mode.

b. Set the switch name to S1.

c. Disable DNS lookup.

d. Assign **class** as the privileged EXEC encrypted password.

e.   Assign **cisco** as the console password and enable login.

f.   Assign **cisco** as the vty password and enable login.

g.   Encrypt the plain text passwords.

h.   Create a banner that warns anyone accessing the device that unauthorized access is prohibited.

i.   Configure the default SVI management interface with the IP address information contained in the Addressing Table.

j.   Configure the switch default gateway.

k.   Save the running configuration to the startup configuration file.

Part 2:   Use Terminal Emulation Software to Create a Backup Configuration File

Step 1:   Establish a Tera Term console session to the router.

Launch the Tera Term Program, and in the New Connection window, select the **Serial** radio button and the appropriate communications port for your PC (i.e., COM1).

Note: If Tera Term is not installed, you can download the latest version from a number of Internet sites. Simply search for a Tera Term download.

a.   In Tera Term, press Enter to connect to the router.

b.   From the **File** menu, choose **Log...**, and save the **teraterm.log** file to the Desktop. Ensure that the **Append** and **Plain text** check boxes are enabled (checked).

c.   The Tera Term log file will create a record of every command issued and every output displayed.

Note: You can use this feature to capture the output from several commands in sequence and use it for network documentation purposes. For example, you could issue the **show version**, **show ip interface brief**, and **show running-config** commands to capture information about the router.

Step 2: Display the router running-configuration.

a. Use the console password to log in to the router.

b. Enter privileged EXEC mode.

c. Enter the **show running-config** command.

d. Continue pressing the space bar when **--More--** is displayed until you see the router R1# prompt return.

e. Click the **Tera Term: Log** icon on the Task bar. Click **Close** to end log session.

Note: You can also copy and paste the text from the Tera Term window directly into a text editor.

Part 3: Use a Backup Configuration File to Restore a Router

Step 1: Erase the router startup-configuration and reload.

a. From privileged EXEC mode erase the startup configuration.

```
R1# erase startup-config
Erasing the nvram filesystem will remove all configuration files! Continue? [confirm]
[OK]
Erase of nvram: complete
```

b. Reload the router.

```
R1# reload
Proceed with reload? [confirm]
```

c. At the System Configuration Dialog prompt, type **no**; a router prompt displays, indicating an unconfigured router.

```
        --- System Configuration Dialog ---


Would you like to enter the initial configuration dialog? [yes/no]:


Press RETURN to get started!

<output omitted>

Router>
```

d. Enter privileged EXEC mode and enter a **show running-config** command to verify that all of the previous configurations were erased.

Step 2: **Edit the saved configuration backup file to prepare it for restoring the router configuration.**

To restore the router configuration from a saved running configuration backup file, you must edit the text.

a. Open the **teraterm.log** text file.

b. Remove each instance of **--More--** in the text file.

Note: The **--More--** was generated by pressing the Spacebar when displaying the running configuration.

c. Delete the initial lines of the backup configuration file, so that the first line starts with the first configuration command as shown below.

```
service timestamps debug datetime msec
service timestamps log datetime msec
service password-encryption
```

d. Replace the encrypted secret password.

```
enable secret 4 06YFDUHH61wAE/kLkDq9BGho1QM5EnRtoyr8cHAUg.2
```

Change to:

```
enable secret class
```

e. In the lines for interface GigabitEthernet0/1, insert a new line to enable the interface.

```
interface GigabitEthernet0/1
 ip address 192.168.1.1 255.255.255.0
 duplex auto
 speed auto
```

Change to:

```
interface GigabitEthernet0/1
 ip address 192.168.1.1 255.255.255.0
 duplex auto
 speed auto
 no shutdown
```

f. Change the message-of-the-day (MOTD) banner configuration to insert the delimiting characters as if you were entering the command at the command line.

```
banner motd ^C Unauthorized Access is Prohibited! ^C
```

Change to:

```
banner motd " Unauthorized Access is Prohibited! "
```

g. In line con 0 and vty 0 4 sections, replace the encrypted password.

```
line con 0
```

```
  password 7 104D000A0618
line vty 0 4
  password 7 104D000A0618
```

Change to:

```
line con 0
  password cisco
line vty 0 4
  password cisco
```

h. After you have made all of the edits to the backup configuration file, save your changes to filename, **R1-config-backup**.

Note: When saving the file, an extension, such as **.txt**, may be added to the filename automatically.

Step 3: Restore the router configuration.

You can restore the edited running configuration directly to the console terminal in router global configuration mode, and the configurations are entered as if they were commands entered individually at the command prompt.

a. From the Tera Term console connection to the router, enter global configuration mode.

b. From the **File** menu, select **Send file…**.

c. Locate **R1-config-backup** and select **Open**.

d. Save the running configuration to the startup configuration file.

```
R1# copy running-config startup-config
```

e. Verify the new running configuration.

Step 4: Back up and restore the switch.

Go back to the beginning of Part 2 and follow the same steps to backup and restore the switch configuration.

Reflection

Why do you think it is important to use a text editor instead of a word processor to copy and save your command configurations?

_____

_____

_____

Router Interface Summary Table

Router Interface Summary				
Router Model	**Ethernet Interface #1**	**Ethernet Interface #2**	**Serial Interface #1**	**Serial Interface #2**
1800	Fast Ethernet 0/0 (F0/0)	Fast Ethernet 0/1 (F0/1)	Serial 0/0/0 (S0/0/0)	Serial 0/0/1 (S0/0/1)
1900	Gigabit Ethernet 0/0 (G0/0)	Gigabit Ethernet 0/1 (G0/1)	Serial 0/0/0 (S0/0/0)	Serial 0/0/1 (S0/0/1)
2801	Fast Ethernet 0/0 (F0/0)	Fast Ethernet 0/1 (F0/1)	Serial 0/1/0 (S0/1/0)	Serial 0/1/1 (S0/1/1)
2811	Fast Ethernet 0/0 (F0/0)	Fast Ethernet 0/1 (F0/1)	Serial 0/0/0 (S0/0/0)	Serial 0/0/1 (S0/0/1)
2900	Gigabit Ethernet 0/0 (G0/0)	Gigabit Ethernet 0/1 (G0/1)	Serial 0/0/0 (S0/0/0)	Serial 0/0/1 (S0/0/1)

Note: To find out how the router is configured, look at the interfaces to identify the type of router and how many interfaces the router has. There is no way to effectively list all the combinations of configurations for each router class. This table includes identifiers for the possible combinations of Ethernet and Serial interfaces in the device. The table does not include any other type of interface, even though a specific router may contain one. An example of this might be an ISDN BRI interface. The string in parenthesis is the legal abbreviation that can be used in Cisco IOS commands to represent the interface.

11.4.2.7 Lab — Managing Device Configuration Files Using TFTP, Flash, and USB

Topology

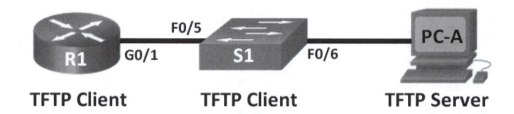

Addressing Table

Device	Interface	IP Address	Subnet Mask	Default Gateway
R1	G0/1	192.168.1.1	255.255.255.0	N/A
S1	VLAN 1	192.168.1.11	255.255.255.0	192.168.1.1
PC-A	NIC	192.168.1.3	255.255.255.0	192.168.1.1

Objectives

Part 1: Build the Network and Configure Basic Device Settings

Part 2: (Optional) Download TFTP Server Software

Part 3: Use TFTP to Back Up and Restore the Switch Running Configuration

Part 4: Use TFTP to Back Up and Restore the Router Running Configuration

Part 5: Back Up and Restore Running Configurations Using Router Flash Memory

Part 6: (Optional) Use a USB Drive to Back Up and Restore the Running Configuration

Background / Scenario

Cisco networking devices are often upgraded or swapped out for a number of reasons. It is important to maintain backups of the latest device configurations, as well as a history of configuration changes. A TFTP server is often used to backup configuration files and IOS images in production networks. A TFTP server is a centralized and secure method used to store the backup copies of the files and restore them as necessary. Using a centralized TFTP server, you can back up files from many different Cisco devices.

In addition to a TFTP server, most of the current Cisco routers can back up and restore files locally from CompactFlash (CF) memory or a USB flash drive. The CF is a removable memory module that has replaced the limited internal flash memory of earlier router models. The IOS image for the router resides in the CF memory, and the router uses this IOS Image for the boot process. With the larger size of the CF memory, additional files can be stored for backup purposes. A removable USB flash drive can also be used for backup purposes.

In this lab, you will use TFTP server software to back up the Cisco device running configuration to the TFTP server or flash memory. You can edit the file using a text editor and copy the new configuration back to a Cisco device.

Note: The routers used with CCNA hands-on labs are Cisco 1941 Integrated Services Routers (ISRs) with Cisco IOS Release 15.2(4)M3 (universalk9 image). The switches used are Cisco Catalyst 2960s with Cisco IOS Release 15.0(2) (lanbasek9 image). Other routers, switches, and Cisco IOS versions can be used. Depending on the model and Cisco IOS version, the commands available and output produced might vary from what is shown in the labs. Refer to the Router Interface Summary Table at the end of this lab for the correct interface identifiers.

Note: Make sure that the routers and switches have been erased and have no startup configurations. If you are unsure, contact your instructor.

Required Resources

- 1 Router (Cisco 1941 with Cisco IOS Release 15.2(4)M3 universal image or comparable)
- 1 Switch (Cisco 2960 with Cisco IOS Release 15.0(2) lanbasek9 image or comparable)
- 1 PC (Windows 7, Vista, or XP with terminal emulation program, such as Tera Term, and a TFTP server)
- Console cables to configure the Cisco IOS devices via the console ports
- Ethernet cables as shown in the topology
- USB flash drive (Optional)

Part 1:   Build the Network and Configure Basic Device Settings

In Part 1, you will set up the network topology and configure basic settings, such as the interface IP addresses for router R1, switch S1 and PC-A.

Step 1:   Cable the network as shown in the topology.

Attach the devices as shown in the topology diagram, and cable as necessary.

Step 2:   Initialize and reload the router and switch.

Step 3:   Configure basic settings for each device.

a. Configure basic device parameters as shown in the Addressing Table.

b. To prevent the router and switch from attempting to translate incorrectly entered commands as though they were host names, disable DNS lookup.

c. Assign **class** as the privileged EXEC encrypted password.

d. Configure the passwords and allow login for console and vty lines using the **cisco** as the password.

e. Configure the default gateway for the switch.

f. Encrypt the clear text passwords.

g. Configure the IP address, subnet mask, and default gateway for PC-A.

Step 4:   Verify connectivity from PC-A.

a. Ping from PC-A to S1.

b. Ping from PC-A to R1.

If the pings are not successful, troubleshoot the basic device configurations before continuing.

Part 2:   (Optional) Download TFTP Server Software

A number of free TFTP servers are available on the Internet for download. The Tftpd32 server is used with this lab.

Note: Downloading a TFTP server from a website requires Internet access.

Step 1:   Verify availability of a TFTP server on PC-A.

a.   Click the **Start** menu and select **All Programs**.

b.   Search for a TFTP server on PC-A.

c.   If a TFTP server is not found, a TFTP server can be downloaded from the Internet.

Step 2:   Download a TFTP server.

a.   Tftpd32 is used in this lab. This server can be downloaded from the following link:

   http://tftpd32.jounin.net/tftpd32_download.html

b.   Choose the appropriate version for your system and install the server.

Part 3:   Use TFTP to Back Up and Restore the Switch Running Configuration

Step 1:   Verify connectivity to switch S1 from PC-A.

The TFTP application uses the UDP Layer 4 transport protocol, which is encapsulated in an IP packet. For TFTP file transfers to function, there must be Layer 1 and 2 (Ethernet, in this case) and Layer 3 (IP) connectivity between the TFTP client and the TFTP server. The LAN topology in this lab uses only Ethernet at Layers 1 and 2. However, TFTP transfers can also be accomplished over WAN links that use other Layer 1 physical links and Layer 2 protocols. As long as there is IP connectivity between the client and server, as demonstrated by ping, the TFTP transfer can take place. If the pings are not successful, troubleshoot the basic device configurations before continuing.

Note: A common misconception is that you can TFTP a file over the console connection. This is not the case because the console connection does not use IP. The TFTP transfer can be initiated from the client device (router or switch) using the console connection, but there must be IP connectivity between the client and server for the file transfer to take place.

Step 2:   Start the TFTP server.

a.   Click the **Start** menu and select **All Programs**.

b.   Find and select **Tftpd32** or **Tftpd64**. The following window displays that the TFTP server is ready.

c. Click **Browse** to choose a directory where you have write permission, such as C:\Users\User1, or the Desktop.

Step 3: Explore the copy command on a Cisco device.

a. Console into switch S1 and, from the privileged EXEC mode prompt, enter **copy ?** to display the options for source or "from" location and other available copy options. You can specify **flash:** or **flash0:** as the source, however, if you simply provide a filename as the source, **flash0:** is assumed and is the default. Note that **running-config** is also an option for the source location.

```
S1# copy ?
  /erase          Erase destination file system.
  /error          Allow to copy error file.
  /noverify       Don't verify image signature before reload.
  /verify         Verify image signature before reload.
  archive:        Copy from archive: file system
  cns:            Copy from cns: file system
  flash0:         Copy from flash0: file system
  flash1:         Copy from flash1: file system
  flash:          Copy from flash: file system
  ftp:            Copy from ftp: file system
  http:           Copy from http: file system
  https:          Copy from https: file system
  null:           Copy from null: file system
  nvram:          Copy from nvram: file system
  rcp:            Copy from rcp: file system
  running-config  Copy from current system configuration
  scp:            Copy from scp: file system
```

```
startup-config  Copy from startup configuration
system:         Copy from system: file system
tar:            Copy from tar: file system
tftp:           Copy from tftp: file system
tmpsys:         Copy from tmpsys: file system
xmodem:         Copy from xmodem: file system
ymodem:         Copy from ymodem: file system
```

b.   Use the **?** to display the destination options after a source file location is chosen. The **flash:** file system for S1 is the source file system in this example.

```
S1# copy flash: ?
  archive:        Copy to archive: file system
  flash0:         Copy to flash0: file system
  flash1:         Copy to flash1: file system
  flash:          Copy to flash: file system
  ftp:            Copy to ftp: file system
  http:           Copy to http: file system
  https:          Copy to https: file system
  idconf          Load an IDConf configuration file
  null:           Copy to null: file system
  nvram:          Copy to nvram: file system
  rcp:            Copy to rcp: file system
  running-config  Update (merge with) current system configuration
  scp:            Copy to scp: file system
  startup-config  Copy to startup configuration
  syslog:         Copy to syslog: file system
  system:         Copy to system: file system
  tftp:           Copy to tftp: file system
  tmpsys:         Copy to tmpsys: file system
  xmodem:         Copy to xmodem: file system
  ymodem:         Copy to ymodem: file system
```

Step 4:   Transfer the running-config file from switch S1 to TFTP server on PC-A.

a.   From the privileged EXEC mode on the switch, enter the **copy running-config tftp:** command. Provide the remote host address of the TFTP server (PC-A), 192.168.1.3. Press Enter to accept default destination filename (**s1-confg**) or provide your own filename. The exclamation marks (**!!**) indicate the transfer process is in progress and is successful.

```
S1# copy running-config tftp:
Address or name of remote host []? 192.168.1.3
Destination filename [s1-confg]?
!!
1465 bytes copied in 0.663 secs (2210 bytes/sec)
S1#
```

The TFTP server also displays the progress during the transfer.

Note: If you do not have permission to write to the current directory that is used by the TFTP server, the following error message displays:

```
S1# copy running-config tftp:

Address or name of remote host []? 192.168.1.3

Destination filename [s1-confg]?
%Error opening tftp://192.168.1.3/s1-confg (Permission denied)
```

You can change the current directory in TFTP server by clicking **Browse** and choosing a different folder.

Note: Other issues, such as a firewall blocking TFTP traffic, can prevent the TFTP transfer. Please check with your instructor for further assistance.

b. In the Tftpd32 server window, click **Show Dir** to verify that the **s1-confg** file has been transferred to your current directory. Click **Close** when finished.

Step 5:   Create a modified switch running configuration file.

The saved running configuration file, **s1-confg**, can also be restored to the switch by using the **copy** command from the switch. The original or a modified version of the file can be copied to the flash file system of the switch.

a. Navigate to the TFTP directory on PC-A by using the file system of PC-A, and then locate the **s1-confg** file. Open this file using a text editor program, such as WordPad.

b. With the file open, locate the **hostname S1** line. Replace **S1** with **Switch1**. Delete all the self-generated crypto keys, as necessary. A sample of the keys is displayed below. These keys are not exportable and can cause errors while updating the running configuration.

```
crypto pki trustpoint TP-self-signed-1566151040
 enrollment selfsigned
 subject-name cn=IOS-Self-Signed-Certificate-1566151040
 revocation-check none
 rsakeypair TP-self-signed-1566151040
!
!
crypto pki certificate chain TP-self-signed-1566151040
 certificate self-signed 01
  3082022B 30820194 A0030201 02020101 300D0609 2A864886 F70D0101 05050030
  31312F30 2D060355 04031326 494F532D 53656C66 2D536967 6E65642D 43657274
<output omitted>
  E99574A6 D945014F B6FE22F3 642EE29A 767EABF7 403930CA D2C59E23 102EC12E
  02F9C933 B3296D9E 095EBDAF 343D17F6 AF2831C7 6DA6DFE3 35B38D90 E6F07CD4
  40D96970 A0D12080 07A1C169 30B9D889 A6E2189C 75B988B9 0AF27EDC 6D6FA0E5
  CCFA6B29 729C1E0B 9DADACD0 3D7381
        quit
```

c. Save this file as a plain text file with a new filename, **Switch1-confg.txt**, in this example.

Note: When saving the file, an extension, such as **.txt**, may be added to the filename automatically.

d. In the Tftpd32 server window, click **Show Dir** to verify that the **Switch1-confg.txt** file is located in the current directory.

Step 6:   Upload running configuration file from TFTP server to switch S1.

a. From the privileged EXEC mode on the switch, enter the **copy tftp running-config** command. Provide the remote host address of the TFTP server, 192.168.1.3. Enter the new filename, **Switch1-confg.txt**. The exclamation mark (!) indicates the transfer process is in progress and is successful.

```
S1# copy tftp: running-config
Address or name of remote host []? 192.168.1.3
Source filename []? Switch1-confg.txt
Destination filename [running-config]?
Accessing tftp://192.168.1.3/Switch1-confg.txt...
```

```
Loading Switch1-confg.txt from 192.168.1.3 (via Vlan1): !

[OK - 1580 bytes]

[OK]

1580 bytes copied in 9.118 secs (173 bytes/sec)

*Mar  1 00:21:16.242: %PKI-4-NOAUTOSAVE: Configuration was modified.  Issue "write memo-
ry" to save new certificate

*Mar  1 00:21:16.251: %SYS-5-CONFIG_I: Configured from tftp://192.168.1.3/Switch1-con-
fg.txt by console

Switch1#
```

After the transfer has completed, the prompt has changed from S1 to Switch1, because the running configuration is updated with the **hostname Switch1** command in the modified running configuration.

b. Enter the **show running-config** command to examine running configuration file.

```
Switch1# show running-config

Building configuration...


Current configuration : 3062 bytes

!

! Last configuration change at 00:09:34 UTC Mon Mar 1 1993

!

version 15.0

no service pad

service timestamps debug datetime msec

service timestamps log datetime msec

no service password-encryption

!

hostname Switch1

!

boot-start-marker

boot-end-marker

<output omitted>
```

Note: This procedure merges the running-config from the TFTP server with the current running-config in the switch or router. If changes were made to the current running-config, the commands in the TFTP copy are added. Alternatively, if the same command is issued, it updates the corresponding command in the switch or router current running-config.

If you want to completely replace the current running-config with the one from the TFTP server, you must erase the switch startup-config and reload the device. You will then need to configure the VLAN 1 management address, so there is IP connectivity between the TFTP server and the switch.

Part 4: Use TFTP to Back Up and Restore the Router Running Configuration

The backup and restore procedure from Part 3 can also be performed with a router. In Part 4, the running configuration file will be backed up and restored using a TFTP server.

Step 1:   Verify connectivity to router R1 from PC-A.

If the pings are not successful, troubleshoot the basic device configurations before continuing.

Step 2:   Transfer the running configuration from router R1 to TFTP server on PC-A.

a.   From the privileged EXEC mode on R1, enter the **copy running-config tftp** command. Provide the remote host address of the TFTP server, 192.168.1.3, and accept the default filename.

b.   Verify that the file has been transferred to the TFTP server.

Step 3:   Restore the running configuration file to the router.

a.   Erase the startup-config file on the router.

b.   Reload the router.

c.   Configure the G0/1 interface on the router with an IP address 192.168.1.1.

d.   Verify connectivity between the router and PC-A.

e.   Use the **copy** command to transfer the running-config file from the TFTP server to the router. Use **running-config** as the destination.

f.   Verify the router has updated the running-config.

Part 5:   Back Up and Restore Configurations Using Router Flash Memory

For the 1941 and other newer Cisco routers, there is no internal flash memory. The flash memory for these routers uses CompactFlash (CF) memory. The use of CF memory allows for more available flash memory and easier upgrades without the need to open the router case. Besides storing the necessary files, such as IOS images, the CF memory can store other files, such as a copy of the running configuration. In Part 5, you will create a backup copy of the running configuration file and save it on the CF memory on the router.

Note: If the router does not use CF, the router may not have enough flash memory for storing the backup copy of running configuration file. You should still read through the instructions and become familiar with the commands.

Step 1:   Display the router file systems.

The **show file systems** command displays the available file systems on the router. The **flash0:** file system is the default file system on this router as indicated by the asterisk (*) symbol (at the beginning of the line). The hash (#) sign (at the end of the highlighted line) indicates that it is a bootable disk. The **flash0:** file system can also be referenced using the name **flash:**. The total size of the **flash0:** is 256 MB with 62 MB available. Currently the **flash1:** slot is empty as indicated by the — under the headings, Size (b) and Free (b). Currently **flash0:** and **nvram:** are the only available file systems.

```
R1# show file systems
File Systems:

      Size(b)        Free(b)      Type    Flags    Prefixes
          -              -        opaque    rw      archive:
          -              -        opaque    rw      system:
```

–	–	opaque	rw	tmpsys:
–	–	opaque	rw	null:
–	–	network	rw	tftp:
* 260153344	64499712	disk	rw	flash0: flash:#
–	–	disk	rw	flash1:
262136	242776	nvram	rw	nvram:
–	–	opaque	wo	syslog:
–	–	opaque	rw	xmodem:
–	–	opaque	rw	ymodem:
–	–	network	rw	rcp:
–	–	network	rw	http:
–	–	network	rw	ftp:
–	–	network	rw	scp:
–	–	opaque	ro	tar:
–	–	network	rw	https:
–	–	opaque	ro	cns:

Where is the startup-config file located?

_____

Note: Verify there is at least 1 MB (1,048,576 bytes) of free space. If there is not enough space in the flash memory, please contact your instructor for further instructions. You can determine the size of flash memory and space available using the **show flash** or **dir flash:** command at the privileged EXEC prompt.

Step 2: **Copy the router running configuration to flash.**

A file can be copied to flash by using the **copy** command at the privileged EXEC prompt. In this example, the file is copied into **flash0:**, because there is only one flash drive available as displayed in the previous step, and it is also the default file system. The **R1-running-config-backup** file is used as the filename for the backup running configuration file.

Note: Remember that filenames are case-sensitive in the IOS file system.

a. Copy the running configuration to flash memory.

```
R1# copy running-config flash:
Destination filename [running-config]? R1-running-config-backup
2169 bytes copied in 0.968 secs (2241 bytes/sec)
```

b. Use **dir** command to verify the running-config has been copied to flash.

```
R1# dir flash:
Directory of flash0:/

    1  drw-          0  Nov 15 2011 14:59:04 +00:00  ipsdir
<output omitted>
```

```
   20  -rw-    67998028   Aug 7 2012 17:39:16 +00:00   c1900-universalk9-mz.SPA.152-
4.M3.bin
   22  -rw-        2169   Feb 4 2013 23:57:54 +00:00   R1-running-config-backup
   24  -rw-        5865   Jul 10 2012 14:46:22 +00:00   lpnat
   25  -rw-        6458   Jul 17 2012 00:12:40 +00:00   lpIPSec


260153344 bytes total (64503808 bytes free)
```

c. Use the **more** command to view the running-config file in flash memory. Examine the file output and scroll to the Interface section. Notice the **no shutdown** command is not included with the GigabitEthernet0/1. The interface is shut down when this file is used to update the running configuration on the router.

```
R1# more flash:R1-running-config-backup

<output omitted>

interface GigabitEthernet0/1

 ip address 192.168.1.1 255.255.255.0

 duplex auto

 speed auto

<output omitted>
```

Step 3: Erase the startup configuration and reload the router.

Step 4: Restore the running configuration from flash.

a. Verify the router has the default initial configuration.

b. Copy the saved running-config file from flash to update the running-config.

```
Router# copy flash:R1-running-config-backup running-config
```

c. Use the **show ip interface brief** command to view the status of the interfaces. The interface GigabitEthernet0/1 was not enabled when the running configuration was updated, because it is administratively down.

```
R1# show ip interface brief
Interface                  IP-Address      OK? Method Status                Protocol
Embedded-Service-Engine0/0 unassigned      YES unset  administratively down down
GigabitEthernet0/0         unassigned      YES unset  administratively down down
GigabitEthernet0/1         192.168.1.1     YES TFTP   administratively down down
Serial0/0/0                unassigned      YES unset  administratively down down
Serial0/0/1                unassigned      YES unset  administratively down down
```

The interface can be enabled using the **no shutdown** command in the interface configuration mode on the router.

Another option is to add the **no shutdown** command for the GigabitEthernet0/1 interface to the saved file before updating the router running configuration file. This will be done in Part 6 using a saved file on a USB flash drive.

Note: Because the IP address was configured by using a file transfer, TFTP is listed under the Method heading in the **show ip interface brief** output.

Part 6: (Optional) Use a USB Drive to Back Up and Restore the Running Configuration

A USB flash drive can be used to backup and restore files on a router with an available USB port. Two USB ports are available on the 1941 routers.

Note: USB ports are not available on all routers, but you should still become familiar with the commands.

Note: Because some ISR G1 routers (1841, 2801, or 2811) use File Allocation Table (FAT) file systems, there is a maximum size limit for the USB flash drives that can be used in this part of the lab. The recommended maximum size for an ISR G1 is 4 GB. If you receive the following message, the file system on the USB flash drive may be incompatible with the router or the capacity of the USB flash drive may have exceed maximum size of the FAT file system on the router.

```
*Feb  8 13:51:34.831: %USBFLASH-4-FORMAT: usbflash0 contains unexpected values in par-
tition table or boot sector.  Device needs formatting before use!
```

Step 1: Insert a USB flash drive into a USB port on the router.

Notice the message on the terminal when inserting the USB flash drive.

```
R1#
* *Feb  5 20:38:04.678: %USBFLASH-5-CHANGE: usbflash0 has been inserted!
```

Step 2: Verify that the USB flash file system is available.

```
R1# show file systems
File Systems:
```

	Size(b)	Free(b)	Type	Flags	Prefixes
	–	–	opaque	rw	archive:
	–	–	opaque	rw	system:
	–	–	opaque	rw	tmpsys:
	–	–	opaque	rw	null:
	–	–	network	rw	tftp:
*	260153344	64512000	disk	rw	flash0: flash:#
	–	–	disk	rw	flash1:
	262136	244676	nvram	rw	nvram:
	–	–	opaque	wo	syslog:
	–	–	opaque	rw	xmodem:
	–	–	opaque	rw	ymodem:
	–	–	network	rw	rcp:
	–	–	network	rw	http:
	–	–	network	rw	ftp:
	–	–	network	rw	scp:
	–	–	opaque	ro	tar:
	–	–	network	rw	https:
	–	–	opaque	ro	cns:
	7728881664	7703973888	usbflash	rw	usbflash0:

Step 3:   Copy the running configuration file to the USB flash drive.

Use the **copy** command to copy the running configuration file to the USB flash drive.

```
R1# copy running-config usbflash0:
Destination filename [running-config]? R1-running-config-backup.txt
2198 bytes copied in 0.708 secs (3105 bytes/sec)
```

Step 4:   List the file on the USB flash drive.

Use the **dir** command (or **show** command) on the router to list the files on the USB flash drive. In this sample, a flash drive was inserted into USB port 0 on the router.

```
R1# dir usbflash0:
Directory of usbflash0:/

    1  -rw-       16216   Nov 15 2006 09:34:04 +00:00  ConditionsFR.txt
    2  -rw-        2462   May 26 2006 21:33:40 +00:00  Nlm.ico
    3  -rw-    24810439   Apr 16 2010 10:28:00 +00:00  Twice.exe
    4  -rw-          71   Jun 4 2010 11:23:06 +00:00   AUTORUN.INF
    5  -rw-       65327   Mar 11 2008 10:54:26 +00:00  ConditionsEN.txt
    6  -rw-        2198   Feb 5 2013 21:36:40 +00:00   R1-running-config-backup.txt


7728881664 bytes total (7703973888 bytes free)
```

Step 5:   Erase the startup-config and reload the router.

Step 6:   Modify the saved file.

a. Remove the USB drive from the router.

```
Router#
*Feb  5 21:41:51.134: %USBFLASH-5-CHANGE: usbflash0 has been removed!
```

b. Insert the USB drive into the USB port of a PC.

c. Modify the file using a text editor. The **no shutdown** command is added to the GigabitEthernet0/1 interface. Save the file as a plain text file on to the USB flash drive.

```
!
interface GigabitEthernet0/1
 ip address 192.168.1.1 255.255.255.0
 no shutdown
 duplex auto
 speed auto
!
```

d. Remove the USB flash drive from the PC safely.

Step 7:   **Restore the running configuration file to the router.**

a.   Insert the USB flash drive into a USB port on the router. Notice the port number where the USB drive has been inserted if there is more than one USB port available on the router.

```
*Feb  5 21:52:00.214: %USBFLASH-5-CHANGE: usbflash1 has been inserted!
```

b.   List the files on the USB flash drive.

```
Router# dir usbflash1:
Directory of usbflash1:/

    1  -rw-        16216  Nov 15 2006 09:34:04 +00:00  ConditionsFR.txt
    2  -rw-         2462  May 26 2006 21:33:40 +00:00  Nlm.ico
    3  -rw-     24810439  Apr 16 2010 10:28:00 +00:00  Twice.exe
    4  -rw-           71  Jun  4 2010 11:23:06 +00:00  AUTORUN.INF
    5  -rw-        65327  Mar 11 2008 10:54:26 +00:00  ConditionsEN.txt
    6  -rw-         2344  Feb  6 2013 14:42:30 +00:00  R1-running-config-backup.txt

7728881664 bytes total (7703965696 bytes free)
```

c.   Copy the running configuration file to the router.

```
Router# copy usbflash1:R1-running-config-backup.txt running-config
Destination filename [running-config]?
2344 bytes copied in 0.184 secs (12739 bytes/sec)
R1#
```

d.   Verify that the GigabitEthernet0/1 interface is enabled.

```
R1# show ip interface brief
Interface                  IP-Address      OK? Method Status                Protocol
Embedded-Service-Engine0/0 unassigned      YES unset  administratively down down
GigabitEthernet0/0         unassigned      YES unset  administratively down down
GigabitEthernet0/1         192.168.1.1     YES TFTP   up                    up
Serial0/0/0                unassigned      YES unset  administratively down down
Serial0/0/1                unassigned      YES unset  administratively down down
```

The G0/1 interface is enabled because the modified running configuration included the **no shutdown** command.

Reflection

1.   What command do you use to copy a file from the flash to a USB drive?

_____

2.   What command do you use to copy a file from the USB flash drive to a TFTP server?

_____

Router Interface Summary Table

Router Interface Summary				
Router Model	**Ethernet Interface #1**	**Ethernet Interface #2**	**Serial Interface #1**	**Serial Interface #2**
1800	Fast Ethernet 0/0 (F0/0)	Fast Ethernet 0/1 (F0/1)	Serial 0/0/0 (S0/0/0)	Serial 0/0/1 (S0/0/1)
1900	Gigabit Ethernet 0/0 (G0/0)	Gigabit Ethernet 0/1 (G0/1)	Serial 0/0/0 (S0/0/0)	Serial 0/0/1 (S0/0/1)
2801	Fast Ethernet 0/0 (F0/0)	Fast Ethernet 0/1 (F0/1)	Serial 0/1/0 (S0/1/0)	Serial 0/1/1 (S0/1/1)
2811	Fast Ethernet 0/0 (F0/0)	Fast Ethernet 0/1 (F0/1)	Serial 0/0/0 (S0/0/0)	Serial 0/0/1 (S0/0/1)
2900	Gigabit Ethernet 0/0 (G0/0)	Gigabit Ethernet 0/1 (G0/1)	Serial 0/0/0 (S0/0/0)	Serial 0/0/1 (S0/0/1)

Note: To find out how the router is configured, look at the interfaces to identify the type of router and how many interfaces the router has. There is no way to effectively list all the combinations of configurations for each router class. This table includes identifiers for the possible combinations of Ethernet and Serial interfaces in the device. The table does not include any other type of interface, even though a specific router may contain one. An example of this might be an ISDN BRI interface. The string in parenthesis is the legal abbreviation that can be used in Cisco IOS commands to represent the interface.

11.4.2.8 Lab — Researching Password Recovery Procedures

Objectives

Part 1: Research the Configuration Register

- Identify the purpose of the configuration register.

- Describe router behavior for different configuration register values.

Part 2: Document the Password Recovery Procedure for a Specific Cisco Router

- Research and record the process for password recovery on a specific Cisco router.

- Answer questions based on the researched procedure.

Background / Scenario

The purpose of this lab is to research the procedure for recovering or resetting the enable password on a specific Cisco router. The enable password protects access to privileged EXEC and configuration mode on Cisco devices. The enable password can be recovered, but the enable secret password is encrypted and would need to be replaced with a new password.

In order to bypass a password, a user must be familiar with the ROM monitor (ROMMON) mode, as well as the configuration register setting for Cisco routers. ROMMON is basic CLI software stored in ROM that can be used to troubleshoot boot errors and recover a router when an IOS is not found.

In this lab, you will begin by researching the purpose and settings of the configuration register for Cisco devices. You will then research and detail the exact procedure for password recovery for a specific Cisco router.

Required Resources
- Device with Internet access

Part 1:   Research the Configuration Register

To recover or reset an enable password, a user will utilize the ROMMON interface to instruct the router to ignore the startup configuration when booting. When booted, the user will access privilege EXEC mode, overwrite the running configuration with the saved startup configuration, recover or reset the password, and restore the router's boot process to include the startup configuration.

The router's configuration register plays a vital role in the process of password recovery. In the first part of this lab, you will research the purpose of a router's configuration register and the meaning of certain configuration register values.

Step 1:   Describe the purpose of the configuration register.

What is the purpose of the configuration register?

_____

_____

_____

_____

What command changes the configuration register in configuration mode?

_____

What command changes the configuration register in the ROMMON interface?

_____

Step 2:   **Determine configuration register values and their meanings.**

Research and list the router behavior for the following configuration register values.

0x2102 _____

_____

0x2142 _____

_____

What is the difference between these two configuration register values?

_____

_____

Part 2:   **Document the Password Recovery Procedure for a Specific Cisco Router**

For Part 2, you will describe the exact procedure for recovering or resetting a password from a specific Cisco router and answer questions based on your research. Your instructor will provide you with the exact router model to research.

Step 1: **Detail the process to recover a password on a specific Cisco router.**

Research and list the steps and commands that you need to recover or reset the enable or enable secret password from your Cisco router. Summarize the steps in your own words.

_____

_____

_____

_____

_____

_____

_____

_____

_____

_____

_____

_____

_____

_____

_____

_____

Step 2: **Answer questions about the password recovery procedure.**

Using the process for password recovery, answer the following questions.

Describe how to find the current setting for your configuration register.

_____

_____

Describe the process for entering ROMMON.

_____

_____

What commands do you need to enter the ROMMON interface?

_____

_____

What message would you expect to see when the router boots?

_____

_____

Why is it important to load the startup configuration into the running configuration?

_____

_____

Why is it important to change the configuration register back to the original value after recovering password?

_____

_____

Reflection

1. Why is it of critical importance that a router be physically secured to prevent unauthorized access?

_____

_____

_____

11.5.1.1 Class Activity — Design and Build a Small Business Network (Capstone Project)

Objectives

Explain how a small network of directly connected segments is created, configured, and verified.

In this activity, you will demonstrate that you know how to design, configure, verify, and secure a very small network. Documentation and presentation are also vital parts of this Capstone Project.

Background/Scenario

Note: This activity is best completed in groups of 2-3 students.

Design and build a network from scratch.

- Your design must include a minimum of one router, one switch, and one PC.

- Fully configure the network and use IPv4 or IPv6 (subnetting must be included as a part of your addressing scheme).

- Verify the network using at least five show commands.

- Secure the network using SSH, secure passwords, and console passwords (minimum).

Create a rubric to use for informal peer grading. Alternatively, your instructor may choose to use the rubric provided with this activity.

Present your Capstone Project to the class and be able to answer questions from your peers and Instructor.

Required Resources

- Packet Tracer
- Student/group-created rubric for assessment of the assignment

Reflection

1. What was the most difficult portion of this activity?

   _____

2. Why do you think network documentation is so important to this activity and in the real world?

   _____

Appendix A — Supplemental Labs

0.0.0.1 Lab — Initializing and Reloading a Router and Switch

Topology

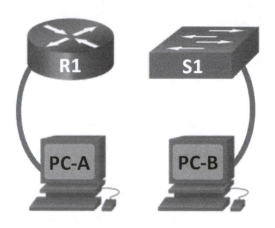

Objectives

Part 1: Set Up Devices in the Network as Shown in the Topology

Part 2: Initialize the Router and Reload

Part 3: Initialize the Switch and Reload

Background / Scenario

Before starting a CCNA hands-on lab that makes use of either a Cisco router or switch, ensure that the devices in use have been erased and have no startup configurations present. Otherwise, the results of your lab may be unpredictable. This lab provides a detail procedure for initializing and reloading a Cisco router and a Cisco switch.

Note: The routers used with CCNA hands-on labs are Cisco 1941 Integrated Services Routers (ISRs) with Cisco IOS Release 15.2(4)M3 (universalk9 image). The switches used are Cisco Catalyst 2960s with Cisco IOS Release 15.0(2) (lanbasek9 image). Other routers, switches, and Cisco IOS versions can be used. Depending on the model and Cisco IOS version, the commands available and output produced might vary from what is shown in the labs.

Required Resources

- 1 Router (Cisco 1941 with Cisco IOS software, Release 15.2(4)M3 universal image or comparable)
- 1 Switch (Cisco 2960 with Cisco IOS Release 15.0(2) lanbasek9 image or comparable)
- 2 PCs (Windows 7, Vista, or XP with terminal emulation program, such as Tera Term)
- Console cables to configure the Cisco IOS devices via the console ports

Part 1:   Set Up Devices in the Network as Shown in the Topology

Step 1:   Cable the network as shown in the topology.

Attach console cables to the devices shown in the topology diagram.

Step 2:   Power on all the devices in the topology.

Wait for all devices to finish the software load process before moving to Part 2.

Part 2:   Initialize the Router and Reload

Step 1:   Connect to the router.

Console into the router and enter privileged EXEC mode using the **enable** command.

```
Router> enable
Router#
```

Step 2:   Erase the startup configuration file from NVRAM.

Type the **erase startup-config** command to remove the startup configuration from nonvolatile random-access memory (NVRAM).

```
Router# erase startup-config
Erasing the nvram filesystem will remove all configuration files! Continue? [confirm]
[OK]
Erase of nvram: complete
Router#
```

Step 3:   Reload the router.

Issue the **reload** command to remove an old configuration from memory. When prompted to Proceed with reload, press Enter to confirm the reload. Pressing any other key will abort the reload.

```
Router# reload
Proceed with reload? [confirm]


*Nov 29 18:28:09.923: %SYS-5-RELOAD: Reload requested by console. Reload Reason: Re-
load Command.
```

Note: You may receive a prompt to save the running configuration prior to reloading the router. Respond by typing **no** and press Enter.

```
System configuration has been modified. Save? [yes/no]: no
```

Step 4:   Bypass the initial configuration dialog.

After the router reloads, you are prompted to enter the initial configuration dialog. Enter **no** and press Enter.

```
Would you like to enter the initial configuration dialog? [yes/no]: no
```

Step 5: **Terminate the autoinstall program.**

You will be prompted to terminate the autoinstall program. Respond **yes** and then press Enter.

```
Would you like to terminate autoinstall? [yes]: yes
Router>
```

Part 3: Initialize the Switch and Reload

Step 1: **Connect to the switch.**

Console into the switch and enter privileged EXEC mode.

```
Switch> enable
Switch#
```

Step 2: **Determine if there have been any virtual local-area networks (VLANs) created.**

Use the **show flash** command to determine if any VLANs have been created on the switch.

```
Switch# show flash


Directory of flash:/


    2  -rwx        1919   Mar 1 1993 00:06:33 +00:00  private-config.text
    3  -rwx        1632   Mar 1 1993 00:06:33 +00:00  config.text
    4  -rwx       13336   Mar 1 1993 00:06:33 +00:00  multiple-fs
    5  -rwx    11607161   Mar 1 1993 02:37:06 +00:00  c2960-lanbasek9-mz.150-2.SE.bin
    6  -rwx         616   Mar 1 1993 00:07:13 +00:00  vlan.dat


32514048 bytes total (20886528 bytes free)
Switch#
```

Step 3: **Delete the VLAN file.**

a. If the **vlan.dat** file was found in flash, then delete this file.

```
Switch# delete vlan.dat
Delete filename [vlan.dat]?
```

You will be prompted to verify the file name. At this point, you can change the file name or just press Enter if you have entered the name correctly.

b. When you are prompted to delete this file, press Enter to confirm the deletion. (Pressing any other key will abort the deletion.)

```
Delete flash:/vlan.dat? [confirm]
Switch#
```

Step 4:   **Erase the startup configuration file.**

Use the **erase startup-config** command to erase the startup configuration file from NVRAM. When you are prompted to remove the configuration file, press Enter to confirm the erase. (Pressing any other key will abort the operation.)

```
Switch# erase startup-config

Erasing the nvram filesystem will remove all configuration files! Continue? [confirm]

[OK]

Erase of nvram: complete

Switch#
```

Step 5:   **Reload the switch.**

Reload the switch to remove any old configuration information from memory. When you are prompted to re-load the switch, press Enter to proceed with the reload. (Pressing any other key will abort the reload.)

```
Switch# reload

Proceed with reload? [confirm]
```

Note: You may receive a prompt to save the running configuration prior to reloading the switch. Type **no** and press Enter.

```
System configuration has been modified. Save? [yes/no]: no
```

Step 6:   **Bypass the initial configuration dialog.**

After the switch reloads, you should see a prompt to enter the initial configuration dialog. Type **no** at the prompt and press Enter.

```
Would you like to enter the initial configuration dialog? [yes/no]: no

Switch>
```

Reflection

1.   Why is it necessary to erase the startup configuration before reloading the router?

_____

2.   You find a couple configurations issues after saving the running configuration to the startup configuration, so you make the necessary changes to fix those issues. If you were to reload the device now, what configuration would be restored to the device after the reload?

_____

0.0.0.2 Lab — Installing the IPv6 Protocol and Assigning Host Addresses with Windows XP

Objectives

Part 1: Install the IPv6 Protocol on a Windows XP PC

- Install the IPv6 protocol.
- Examine IPv6 address information.

Part 2: Use the Network Shell (netsh) Utility

- Work inside the **netsh** utility.
- Configure a static IPv6 address on the local-area network (LAN) interface.
- Exit the **netsh** utility.
- Display IPv6 address information using **netsh**.
- Issue **netsh** instructions from the command prompt.

Background / Scenario

The Internet Protocol Version 6 (IPv6) is not enabled by default in Windows XP. Windows XP includes IPv6 implementation, but the IPv6 protocol must be installed. XP does not provide a way to configure IPv6 static addresses from the Graphical User Interface (GUI), so all IPv6 static address assignments must be done using the Network Shell (**netsh**) utility.

In this lab, you will install the IPv6 protocol on a Windows XP PC. You will then assign a static IPv6 address to the LAN interface.

Required Resources

1 Windows XP PC

Part 1:   Install the IPv6 Protocol on a Windows XP PC

In Part 1, you will install the IPv6 protocol on a PC running Windows XP. You will also use two commands to view the IPv6 addresses assigned to the PC.

Step 1:   Install the IPv6 protocol.

From the command prompt window, type **ipv6 install** to install the IPv6 protocol.

Step 2:   **Examine IPv6 Address Information.**

Use the **ipconfig /all** command to view IPv6 address information.

```
C:\WINDOWS\system32\cmd.exe                                               _□×

Ethernet adapter Local Area Connection:

        Connection-specific DNS Suffix  . :
        Description . . . . . . . . . . . : VMware Accelerated AMD PCNet Adapter

        Physical Address. . . . . . . . . : 00-50-56-BE-25-87
        Dhcp Enabled. . . . . . . . . . . : Yes
        Autoconfiguration Enabled . . . . : Yes
        Autoconfiguration IP Address. . . : 169.254.39.128
        Subnet Mask . . . . . . . . . . . : 255.255.0.0
        IP Address. . . . . . . . . . . . : fe80::250:56ff:febe:2587%5
        Default Gateway . . . . . . . . . :
        DNS Servers . . . . . . . . . . . : fec0:0:0:ffff::1%1
                                            fec0:0:0:ffff::2%1
                                            fec0:0:0:ffff::3%1

Tunnel adapter Teredo Tunneling Pseudo-Interface:

        Connection-specific DNS Suffix  . :
        Description . . . . . . . . . . . : Teredo Tunneling Pseudo-Interface
        Physical Address. . . . . . . . . : FF-FF-FF-FF-FF-FF-FF-FF
        Dhcp Enabled. . . . . . . . . . . : No
        IP Address. . . . . . . . . . . . : fe80::ffff:ffff:fffd%4
        Default Gateway . . . . . . . . . :
        NetBIOS over Tcpip. . . . . . . . : Disabled

Tunnel adapter Automatic Tunneling Pseudo-Interface:

        Connection-specific DNS Suffix  . :
        Description . . . . . . . . . . . : Automatic Tunneling Pseudo-Interface

        Physical Address. . . . . . . . . : A9-FE-27-80
        Dhcp Enabled. . . . . . . . . . . : No
        IP Address. . . . . . . . . . . . : fe80::5efe:169.254.39.128%2
        Default Gateway . . . . . . . . . :
        DNS Servers . . . . . . . . . . . : fec0:0:0:ffff::1%1
                                            fec0:0:0:ffff::2%1
                                            fec0:0:0:ffff::3%1

        NetBIOS over Tcpip. . . . . . . . : Disabled

C:\>
```

Part 2:   Use the Network Shell (netsh) Utility

Network Shell (**netsh**) is a command-line utility included with Windows XP and newer Windows operating systems, such as Vista and Windows 7. It allows you to configure the IPv6 address information on your LAN. In Part 2, you will use the **netsh** utility to configure static IPv6 address information on a Windows XP PC LAN interface. You will also use the **netsh** utility to display the PC LAN interface IPv6 address information.

Step 1:   **Work inside the Network Shell utility.**

a.   From the command prompt window, type **netsh** and press Enter to start the **netsh** utility. The command prompt changes from **C:\>** to **netsh>**.

```
C:\WINDOWS\system32\cmd.exe - netsh                                       _□×

C:\>netsh
netsh>
```

b.   At the prompt, enter a question mark (**?**) and press Enter to provide the list of available parameters.

```
netsh>?

The following commands are available:

Commands in this context:
..              - Goes up one context level.
?               - Displays a list of commands.
abort           - Discards changes made while in offline mode.
add             - Adds a configuration entry to a list of entries.
alias           - Adds an alias.
bridge          - Changes to the `netsh bridge' context.
bye             - Exits the program.
commit          - Commits changes made while in offline mode.
delete          - Deletes a configuration entry from a list of entries.
diag            - Changes to the `netsh diag' context.
dump            - Displays a configuration script.
exec            - Runs a script file.
exit            - Exits the program.
firewall        - Changes to the `netsh firewall' context.
help            - Displays a list of commands.
interface       - Changes to the `netsh interface' context.
lan             - Changes to the `netsh lan' context.
nap             - Changes to the `netsh nap' context.
offline         - Sets the current mode to offline.
online          - Sets the current mode to online.
popd            - Pops a context from the stack.
pushd           - Pushes current context on stack.
quit            - Exits the program.
ras             - Changes to the `netsh ras' context.
routing         - Changes to the `netsh routing' context.
set             - Updates configuration settings.
show            - Displays information.
unalias         - Deletes an alias.
winsock         - Changes to the `netsh winsock' context.

The following sub-contexts are available:
 bridge diag firewall interface lan nap ras routing winsock

To view help for a command, type the command, followed by a space, and then
 type ?.

netsh>
```

c.   Type **interface ?** and press Enter to provide the list of interface commands.

```
netsh>interface ?

The following commands are available:

Commands in this context:
?               - Displays a list of commands.
add             - Adds a configuration entry to a table.
delete          - Deletes a configuration entry from a table.
dump            - Displays a configuration script.
help            - Displays a list of commands.
ip              - Changes to the `netsh interface ip' context.
ipv6            - Changes to the `netsh interface ipv6' context.
portproxy       - Changes to the `netsh interface portproxy' context.
reset           - Resets information.
set             - Sets configuration information.
show            - Displays information.

The following sub-contexts are available:
 ip ipv6 portproxy

To view help for a command, type the command, followed by a space, and then
 type ?.

netsh>_
```

Note: You can use the question mark (**?**) at any level in the **netsh** utility to list the available options. The up arrow can be used to scroll through previous **netsh** commands. The **netsh** utility also allows you to abbreviate commands, as long as the abbreviation is unique.

Step 2: **Configure a static IPv6 address on the LAN interface.**

To add a static IPv6 address to the LAN interface, issue the **interface ipv6 add address** command from inside the **netsh** utility.

```
netsh>interface ipv6 add address "Local Area Connection" 2001:db8:acad:a::3
Ok.

netsh>
```

Step 3: **Display IPv6 address information using the netsh utility.**

You can display IPv6 address information using the **interface ipv6 show address** command.

```
netsh>interface ipv6 show address
Querying active state...

Interface 5: Local Area Connection

Addr Type    DAD State    Valid Life    Pref. Life    Address
----------   -----------  ------------  ------------  -----------------------
Manual       Preferred        infinite      infinite  2001:db8:acad:a::3
Link         Preferred        infinite      infinite  fe80::250:56ff:febe:2587

Interface 4: Teredo Tunneling Pseudo-Interface

Addr Type    DAD State    Valid Life    Pref. Life    Address
----------   -----------  ------------  ------------  -----------------------
Link         Preferred        infinite      infinite  fe80::ffff:ffff:fffd

Interface 2: Automatic Tunneling Pseudo-Interface

Addr Type    DAD State    Valid Life    Pref. Life    Address
----------   -----------  ------------  ------------  -----------------------
Link         Preferred        infinite      infinite  fe80::5efe:169.254.39.128

Interface 1: Loopback Pseudo-Interface

Addr Type    DAD State    Valid Life    Pref. Life    Address
----------   -----------  ------------  ------------  -----------------------
Loopback     Preferred        infinite      infinite  ::1
Link         Preferred        infinite      infinite  fe80::1

netsh>
```

Step 4: **Exit the netsh utility.**

Use the **exit** command to exit from the **netsh** utility.

```
netsh>exit

C:\>
```

Step 5: **Issue netsh instructions from the command prompt.**

All **netsh** instructions can be entered from the command prompt, outside the **netsh** utility, by preceding the instruction with the **netsh** command.

```
C:\>netsh interface ipv6 show address
Querying active state...


Interface 5: Local Area Connection

Addr Type   DAD State   Valid Life   Pref. Life   Address
---------   ---------   ----------   ----------   -------
Manual      Preferred     infinite     infinite   2001:db8:acad:a::3
Link        Preferred     infinite     infinite   fe80::250:56ff:febe:2587

Interface 4: Teredo Tunneling Pseudo-Interface

Addr Type   DAD State   Valid Life   Pref. Life   Address
---------   ---------   ----------   ----------   -------
Link        Preferred     infinite     infinite   fe80::ffff:ffff:fffd

Interface 2: Automatic Tunneling Pseudo-Interface

Addr Type   DAD State   Valid Life   Pref. Life   Address
---------   ---------   ----------   ----------   -------
Link        Preferred     infinite     infinite   fe80::5efe:169.254.39.128

Interface 1: Loopback Pseudo-Interface

Addr Type   DAD State   Valid Life   Pref. Life   Address
---------   ---------   ----------   ----------   -------
Loopback    Preferred     infinite     infinite   ::1
Link        Preferred     infinite     infinite   fe80::1


C:\>
```

Reflection

1. How would you renew your LAN interface address information from the **netsh** utility?

    Hint: Use the question mark (**?**) for help in obtaining the parameter sequence.

    _____

    _____